Inside the Investor's Brain

Founded in 1807, John Wiley & Sons is the oldest independent publishing company in the United States. With offices in North America, Europe, Australia and Asia, Wiley is globally committed to developing and marketing print and electronic products and services for our customers' professional and personal knowledge and understanding.

The Wiley Trading series features books by traders who have survived the market's ever-changing temperament and have prospered—some by reinventing systems, others by getting back to basics. Whether a novice trader, professional, or somewhere in between, these books will provide the advice and strategies needed to prosper today and well into the future.

For a list of available titles, visit our Web site at www.WileyFinance.com.

Inside the Investor's Brain

The Power of Mind Over Money

RICHARD L. PETERSON

John Wiley & Sons, Inc.

Published by John Wiley & Sons, Inc., Hoboken, New Jersey
Published simultaneously in Canada.

Wiley Bicentennial Logo: Richard J. Pacifico

For general information on our other products and services or for technical support, please contact our Customer Care Department within the United States at (800) 762-2974, outside the United States at (317) 572-3993 or fax (317) 572-4002.

Wiley also publishes its books in a variety of electronic formats. Some content that appears in print may not be available in electronic formats. For more information about Wiley products, visit our Web site at www.wiley.com.

Library of Congress Cataloging-in-Publication Data

Peterson, Richard L., 1972-
   Inside the investor's brain : the power of mind over money / Richard L. Peterson.
      p. cm. – (Wiley trading series)
   Includes bibliographical references and index.
   ISBN-13: 978-0-470-06737-6 (cloth)
  1. Investments–Psychological aspects.   I. Title.
   HG4515.15.P48 2007
   332.601'9–dc22

                                               2006103091

Printed in the United States of America

10 9 8 7 6 5 4 3 2 1

To Sarah.

Your grace, warmth, and ease light up my world.
You made this book possible.

Contents

Preface

This book isn't written for you. At least, it's not intended for the rational, *thinking* you who was thrown off by that last sentence. This book is for the parts of you that were perturbed, the feelings that you can't quite access. Those feelings arise from deep in your brain, and they're largely subconscious. To get to them, I have to go through you—you the reader.

And there's the catch. If thinking could make everyone a great investor, then there wouldn't be market bubbles and panics, poverty, addiction, or criminal greed. But we do have those problems—in part because the thinking brain evolved about 100,000 years ago, while the feeling brain is one of our most primitive endowments (something we share with our pets), and the two brains don't always get along. How to manage them both in the wild world of the financial markets is the subject of this book.

In the financial industry, most investment decision making follows a rational process until, often at crucial times, that process breaks down. Whether you're an individual investor, portfolio manager, financial adviser, trader, analyst, or member of an investment committee, odds are you've experienced the powerful effects of the psychological forces that move the markets. This book answers two questions for investors: What are the deep "irrational" forces driving investment behavior, and what can be done to better manage them?

GOOD INVESTING IS MORE THAN BOOK SMARTS

Good investing requires a basic financial education. That's the straightforward part. However, to really *excel* in investing, you've got to learn the skills to manage *yourself*. Book smarts aren't enough. You've got to understand both the terrain of the markets *and* the topography of your mind.

This book is intended for educated investors (individuals, portfolio managers, venture capitalists, and bankers), financial analysts (security research, fundamental and technical analysts), and traders. Readers of this book will learn to identify subconscious mistakes (biases) in their financial decision making. Readers will develop an understanding of the brain origins of psychological biases, learn to recognize when they arise, and gain techniques for improving their financial judgment.

However, just because you *know* when you're likely to make a mistake doesn't mean you can stop yourself from doing it. Two methods are effective for learning to manage biases: personal experience and studying the examples of others. Gaining personal experience in the markets is costly. To enhance the study of others, this book contains examples of investors who have succumbed to biases, people who have overcome such mistakes, the decision-making tactics of great investors, and tips for creating an investment environment that supports effective decision making.

Much of the research on investor biases presented here is imported from the academic field of behavioral finance. Investigators in behavioral finance, in pioneering studies, have identified numerous systematic investing biases. Due to their origination in deep brain circuits, most biases influence investment decisions automatically and beneath awareness. When evidence from neuroscience, behavioral finance, and real-world practitioners is integrated, then a clearer picture of the fundamental issues and remedies is revealed.

ORGANIZATION OF THIS BOOK

Most chapters open with vignettes. Some are tragic, some uplifting, and some unusual. All are selected for the lessons they teach. The investors depicted in these stories are fabricated from my collective experiences with numerous individuals and through anecdotes I have heard from others. Any resemblance to real persons is completely coincidental.

In individual chapters, readers will learn to: (1) identify specific subconscious biases, (2) know when thinking and analysis will improve their investment process (and when it won't), (3) improve their emotional awareness, and (4) enhance the decision process.

One caveat: There is an emphasis on the neural origins of biases, yet few direct links between the brain and investment behavior have been proven. Nonetheless, this book attempts to simplify concepts and relationships as accurately as possible to make the discussion relevant to practitioners. In the introduction, the investment fallibility of Long-Term Capital Management, Sir Isaac Newton, and Samuel Clemens (Mark Twain) are used to illustrate some of the most basic and prevalent investor biases. Chapter 1 explains the challenges investors face in finding opportunities in a competitive marketplace, and it argues that the best remaining source of profits lies in understanding how other investors think. Chapter 2 educates the reader about basic brain structure and briefly reviews the research tools used in experiments. Chapter 3 describes the roles of belief and expectation in shaping one's experience. Chapter 4 is a discussion of neurochemistry including the common medications and substances that alter neurochemical balance and influence financial decision making.

Part II describes how various emotions impact judgment. Chapter 5 demonstrates the tremendous value of intuition and "gut feel" in investment decisions. Chapter 6 explains how overt emotions such as fear, excitement, anger, and sadness bias financial judgment. Chapter 7 looks at the brain origins and pathological investment effects of excessive greed and excitement. Chapter 8 examines the dangers presented by overconfidence and the hubris that results from a series of successes. Chapter 9 describes how anxiety and fear affect investor decision making, while Chapter 10 is specifically about stress and burnout. Chapter 11 describes pathological gambling, which affects some day traders and institutional "rogue traders." Chapter 12 investigates the personality traits that contribute to investing excellence.

Part III is a review of the cognitive (thinking and perception) biases. While these biases are influenced by emotion, research has primarily focused on the mental mechanisms that underlie them. Chapter 13 briefly explains modern decision-making theory, and illustrates how information about outcome size, probability, and ambiguity biases choice. Chapter 14 investigates how the framing of a decision biases judgment. Chapter 15 explains loss aversion – which results in "holding losers too long" – both in amateur and professional investors. Chapter 16 is a discussion of how time perception, such as time discounting, generates investment biases. Chapter 17 is about the process of social influence and herding, and how it impacts investment decision making and investment committees. Chapter 18 explains the perceptual pitfalls that arise during chart reading and data mining. Chapter 19 is a discussion of biases in attention and memory that affect investors. Chapter 20 looks at investment risk taking from the perspective of the differing biology of women versus men and the aged versus the young. It also examines the (very limited) cultural differences between Eastern and Western investors.

Part IV presents techniques for managing biases. Chapter 21 summarizes the book's major conclusions and offers self-help exercises for reducing biases. Chapter 22 provides a more in-depth approach to emotion management in the markets. Chapter 23 teaches the reader how to incorporate "neural" insights into their investing strategy and explains how to identify and take advantage of collective biases in market prices.

Acknowledgments

I wrote this book over several years. So many people influenced its production that I cannot possibly do justice to their contributions here. I am very appreciative of my family and friends, who provided their love and encouragement. Thanks especially to Sarah, my amazing wife, for her unflagging optimism and patience during the writing of the book. My gratitude is profound.

I am extremely indebted to the efforts of hundreds of researchers and research assistants whose experiments form the basis of this book's content. Without their dedication and passion, human knowledge would not advance.

Many scientists shared their ideas in countless hours of fascinating discussions, most of which made it into the book in spirit, if not explicitly. Brian Knutson has been an extraordinary mentor to me, and the completion of this book would never have been possible without the time I spent learning from him. I have many neuroscientists to thank. Ching-Hung Lin graciously provided his lab's fascinating data on the Soochow Gambling Task. Carrie Armel taught me the basics of facial EMG. I'd like to express my gratitude to Paul Zak for sharing his macro insights into the intersection of economic behavior and individual biology. Hilke Plassman, Scott Huettel, Paul Slovic, Greg Berns, Elke Weber, Ernest Barratt, and Jamil Bhanji were encouraging and generous with their time during our long discussions and interviews.

On the finance side of the aisle, special thanks to Richard Peterson (my father), who introduced me to the markets at an early age and with whom I've had hundreds of enjoyable financial discussions over the years. Camelia Kuhnen kindly shared insights into the limitations and strengths of behavioral finance and neurofinance. Hersh Shefrin, Mark Seasholes, David Leinweber, Zhaohui Zhang, Andrew Lo, and Hank Pruden helped me gain an (admittedly still feeble) grasp of the basics of modern behavioral finance and behavioral investment strategy. Bob Olsen has made an extraordinary contribution to this book through his editorship of the *Journal of Behavioral Finance*, whose articles provide numerous insights into the real-world effects of psychological biases.

Investing psychologists Frank Murtha, Doug Hirschhorn, Denise Shull, Flavia Cymbalista, Alden Cass, and Janice Dorn shared fascinating stories and insights from their practices. Performance psychologist and coach, Howard Fleischman, provided valuable advice during the preparation of the self-help chapters.

Michael Mauboussin illuminated some of the psychological realities of fund management through our fascinating discussions and his excellent books and articles. I am very grateful for insights from financial practitioners including David Strong, Martin Auster, Carlo Cannell, Patrick Acasio, Rafael Drouhy, Sean Phelan, Faris Hitti, Dan Beale, John Cammack, Bill Miller, Arnold Wood, Dan Case, and Emily Wong. They contributed an essential applied perspective to this book. Numerous financial advisers also provided insights, including Shirley Mueller, Ken Winans, Michael Lauren, Santosh Keni, Adil Yousufzai, Michael McDonough, Nitin Birla, and Andy Byer.

Tom Samuels has been an optimistic and enthusiastic friend, psychotherapy mentor, and supporter since I first overconfidently told him I could write this book in 40 hours. Richard Friesen has been inspiring, honest, and helped me remain grounded since the beginning. Without the kind prompting and patience of Emilie Herman at Wiley, this book would not have been. Pamela van Giessen and Bill Falloon gave me my "big break" in writing this book, and Christina Verigan at Wiley helped keep me on track.

And a final thank you to the investors who have shared their personal stories with me. They must remain nameless. Whether through their tragic disappointments or spectacular successes, they inspired my search for a road-map to the investor's mind. I hope that by sharing their stories, those who follow can avoid their dangerous financial wrong turns and model their high-performance secrets.

R.L.P.

About the Author

Richard L. Peterson is founder of Market Psychology Consulting, where he trains financial professionals for improved performance. Dr. Peterson has developed five psychological testing products including the "Money and Investing Personality Test." He is currently developing analytical market software and novel investment strategies for use in portfolio management.

Dr. Peterson received a BS in electrical engineering and a BA in Plan II Arts at the University of Texas in 1995. In 2000 he received a doctor of medicine degree from the University of Texas Medical Branch, with honors. He completed psychiatry residency training at San Mateo Medical Center in 2004, during which he was engaged in postdoctoral neuroscience research at Stanford University.

After completing his undergraduate studies, Dr. Peterson designed stock forecasting software and traded futures for an investment partnership. Thereafter, he investigated the role of emotions in financial decision making both during medical school and neuroimaging research at Stanford.

Dr. Peterson has published scientific papers in economics, finance, psychology, and neuroscience journals. He is an associate editor of the *Journal of Behavioral Finance* and is on the board of advisers of the Social Science Research Network (SSRN) in the experimental and behavioral finance area. He is a member of the Society for Neuroeconomics, the Institute of Psychology and Markets, and the American Psychiatric Association.

His primary professional interest is the role of emotion in investment decision making, and specifically, the arbitrage of neural-based anomalies in the financial markets. His long-term fascination with the markets grew out of his early investing (since age 12) and futures trading activities, and it continues with the application of psychological principles to investment strategy development. He plans to launch a quantitative psychology-based hedge fund in early 2008.

Dr. Peterson lives in the Los Angeles area with his wife and daughter.

Introduction

This introduction contains three vignettes about famous financial mishaps: the late 1990s hedge fund Long-Term Capital, Sir Isaac Newton and the South Seas bubble, and Samuel Clemens (a.k.a. Mark Twain) and the 1860s silver fever. There is a lot to be learned from such financial failures—both in the accounting facts and historical circumstances, but also in the psychology underlying the protagonists' faulty decision making. Reading the stories that follow, take note of the investment choices of the main players as their success, and confidence, grow.

BRAINS OF STEEL ... ARE NOT ENOUGH

In February 1994 the most esteemed hedge fund in history, up to that time, opened for business. Long-Term Capital Management (LTCM) was extremely secretive, though it was widely known that the fund's partners included brilliant academics and extraordinarily successful traders. LTCM's partners included Myron S. Scholes and Robert C. Merton, two Nobel Prize winning economists (one awarded in 1997) who were renowned both on Wall Street and in academia.

The founder of Long-Term Capital was John Meriwether. According to Michael Lewis, author of *Liar's Poker* and a colleague of Meriwether's on the bond desk at Salomon Brothers during the late 1980s, "[John] had, I think, a profound ability to control the two emotions that commonly destroy traders—fear and greed—and it made him as noble as a man who pursues his self-interest so fiercely can be."[1] Meriwether not only kept his emotions under wraps, but he was also roundly acknowledged as intellectually brilliant.

Furthermore, Meriwether had proven to have high confidence in his market opinions. If he believed that an opportunity in the markets would go in his direction, and instead it moved against him, he might increase the size of his bet. He used mathematics to determine fair values of securities and spreads. If his models identified a mispricing, he had confidence that it would return to fair value over time.

LTCM's launch was the largest in history at that time: $1.25 billion was raised. While LTCM's fees were above the industry average (taking 25 percent of net returns), the profits over the fund's first four years were large, seeming to justify the high fees. By April 1998, $1 invested in the fund at its inception in 1994 was worth $2.85 (after fees).

Unfortunately for LTCM, mathematical genius was insufficient to reap consistent profits. Other traders figured out many of LTCM's strategies, piggybacking on their trades, and LTCMs profitability began to erode. The mathematicians at LTCM looked for new markets in which to apply their basic models. They made assumptions that those new markets operated similarly to the old. Gradually, they grew greedier, took increasing risk, and spread their positions too widely. The founding partners bought out a large proportion of the original investors' capital so they could increase their own stakes in the fund.

After April 1998, LTCM's performance began an accelerating slide. Within a period of five months, from April 1998 to September 1998, LTCM lost 90 percent of its assets and could not meet its margin calls on the $1.3 trillion in outstanding positions it held. Many large Wall Street banks had loaned securities to LTCM on thin margin, and now some of those banks were threatened with catastrophic losses if they liquidated the fund's heavily in-the-red positions and triggered a "run on the bank."

Five months after the fund's peak, the original dollar invested in LTCM in 1994 was worth $0.23, and the fund's collapse had nearly caused the meltdown of the global financial system.[2] Financially, LTCM's collapse was caused by excessive leverage in illiquid positions. But how did these conditions come to be?

In the media reports about the fund, the root causes of its rapid demise were identified as psychological. After several years of success, greed, hubris, and arrogance infected the partners' decision making and impaired their communication. In investment management, mathematical genius may perform well in the short term, but it is no substitute for *emotional* intelligence.

CALCULATING THE MADNESS OF MEN

Sir Isaac Newton was one of the most influential scientists in history. He laid the groundwork for classical ("Newtonian") physics. He was the first to demonstrate that the motions of objects on Earth and the movements of the celestial bodies are governed by the same set of mathematical laws. His investigations into optics and sound formed the basis for centuries of research. Unfortunately, Newton's scientific acumen did not improve his investing decisions. On the contrary, he lost much of his wealth in the largest stock bubble of his age.

Like many members of the British aristocracy in the early 1700s, Newton owned shares of the South Seas Trading Company in 1720. The South Seas Company was organized with two missions: (1) as a monopoly over British trade with the Spanish colonies in America and (2) as a converter of British government annuities into long-term debt. The South Seas Company initially had a legitimate and profitable business monopoly courtesy of the British government. Furthermore, the Company was repeatedly successful in raising money on the British stock market for proposed expansions of its operations. As a result of their success, a series of corporate competitors arose and the Company's monopoly was placed in jeopardy.

Following the lead of the South Seas Company, joint-stock companies proposing a wide range of speculative ventures formed and began to raise money through share sales. Public enthusiasm for stock trading grew, and a price bubble formed among the traded shares. When the sometimes fraudulent promotions of new joint-stock companies became apparent to legislators, a law was passed by the British parliament in June 1720 (the "Bubble Act") to prevent non-royal-endorsed joint stock companies from issuing shares to the public. Even after the "Bubble Act" was passed, companies continued selling shares for absurd enterprises. One such offering advertised its business as follows: "For carrying on an undertaking of great advantage; but nobody to know what it is."[3]

In the midsummer of 1720, Newton foretold a coming stock market crash, and he sold his shares of the South Seas Company for a profit of 7,000 pounds. Subsequently, however, Newton watched the Company's stock price continue to rise, and he decided to reinvest at a higher price. Newton then remained invested as prices started a precipitous decline. Soon panic ensued, and the bubble collapsed. After the dust had settled from the stock market crash of August 1720, Newton had lost over 20,000 pounds of his fortune. As a result of these losses, he famously stated, "I can calculate the motions of heavenly bodies, but not the madness of people." Newton's fear of missing out on further gains drove him to buy shares as the price soared higher. His inertia during the panic led to the loss of most of his assets.

MARK TWAIN AND THE "SILVER FEVER"

The celebrated author and humorist Samuel Clemens (pen name Mark Twain) was the most widely recognized American in the last decade of the nineteenth century, both nationally and internationally.[4] Clemens's documentation of his experiences in the Nevada mining stock bubble are one of the earliest (and certainly the most humorous) firsthand accounts of involvement in a speculative mania.

After a brief stint as a Confederate militiaman during the beginning of the U.S. Civil War, Clemens purchased stagecoach passage west, to Nevada, where his brother had been appointed Secretary of the Territory. In Nevada, Clemens began working as a reporter in Virginia City, in one of Nevada's most productive silver- and gold-mining regions. He enviously watched prospecting parties departing into the wilderness, and he quickly became "smitten with the silver fever."[5]

Clemens and two friends soon went out in search of silver veins in the mountains. As Clemens tells it, they rapidly discovered and laid claim to a rich vein of silver called the "Wide West" mine. The night after they established their ownership, they were restless and unable to sleep, visited by fantasies of extravagant wealth: "No one can be so thoughtless as to suppose that we slept, that night. Higbie and I went to bed at midnight, but it was only to lie broad awake and think, dream, scheme."[6]

Clemens reported that in the excitement and confusion of the days following their discovery, he and his two partners failed to begin mining their claim. Under Nevada state law, a claim could be usurped if not worked within 10 days. Clemens lost his claim to the mine due to inattention, and his dreams of sudden wealth were momentarily set back.

But Clemens had a keen ear for rumors and new opportunities. Some prospectors who found rich ore veins were selling stock in New York City to raise capital for mining operations. In 1863, Clemens accumulated stocks in several such silver mines, sometimes as payment for working as a journalist. In order to lock in his anticipated gains from the stocks, he made a plan to sell his silver shares either when they reached $100,000 in total value or when Nevada voters approved a state constitution (which he thought would erode their long-term value).

In 1863, funded by his substantial (paper) stock wealth, Clemens retired from journalism. He traveled west to San Francisco to live the high life. He watched his silver mine stock price quotes in the newspaper, and he felt rich: "I lived at the best hotel, exhibited my clothes in the most conspicuous places, infested the opera. . . . I had longed to be a butterfly, and I was one at last."[7]

Yet after Nevada became a state, Clemens continued to hold on to his stocks, contrary to his plan. Suddenly, the gambling mania on silver stocks ended, and without warning, Clemens found himself virtually broke.

> *I, the cheerful idiot that had been squandering money like water, and thought myself beyond the reach of misfortune, had not now as much as fifty dollars when I gathered together my various debts and paid them.*[8]

Clemens was forced to return to journalism to pay his expenses. He lived on meager pay over the next several years. Even after his great literary and lecture-circuit success in the late nineteenth century, he continued to have difficulty investing wisely. In later life he had very public and large debts, and he was forced to work, often much harder than he wanted, to make ends meet for his family.

Clemens had made a plan to sell his silver stock shares when Nevada became a state. His rapid and large gains stoked a sense of invincibility. Soon he deviated from his stock sales plan, stopped paying attention to the market fundamentals, and found himself virtually broke.

Clemens was by no means the first or last American to succumb to mining stock excitement. *The World's Work*, an investment periodical published decades later, in the early 1900s, was beset by letters from investors asking for advice on mining stocks. The magazine's response to these letters was straightforward:

> *Emotion plays too large a part in the business of mining stocks. Enthusiasm, lust for gain, gullibility are the real bases of this trading. The sober common sense of the intelligent businessman has no part in such investment. [1907a, pp. 8383–8384]*[9]

While the focus of market manias changes, the psychology of speculators remains remarkably similar over the centuries.

Mathematical brilliance and Nobel Prizes (in the case of LTCM), scientific genius (in the case of Newton), and creativity (in the case of Clemens) do not insulate against investment failure. As we'll see in this book, accolades and success can actually impede investing success. In all three cases, as warning signs became apparent, the investors remained in an overconfident worldview, dismissing risks and turning their attention away from prudent money management. Then, as their wealth evaporated, they remained passive in the face of losses.

Regardless of their professional standing, the vast majority of investors underperform the markets, often for the same reasons as the three cases above. Emotions easily overwhelmed reasoning when money is at stake. When times are good, investors take them for granted and do not prepare for risks. When markets turn sour, they are not paying attention, often holding on to their positions too long while hoping for a comeback or denying that there is a problem.

WHAT'S THE USE OF NEUROFINANCE?

In neuroscience laboratories, revolutionary new tools are available for investigating investor behavior. These technologies enable researchers to watch changes in brain function in real time, allowing the precise characterization of the decision-making process. As researchers have come to better understand the brain, some fascinating and important findings have come to light regarding how people make good, and bad, decisions with money.

"Neurofinance" is the name for the interdisciplinary study and application of neuroscience to investment activity. Finance, psychology, economics, and neuroscience collaborators are exploring common questions, such as why and how people make nonoptimal financial decisions. Furthermore, with the contributions of clinical psychologists, psychiatrists, and neurologists to recent research, it has become apparent that some "neural" biases can be corrected by implementing therapeutic techniques.

PART I

Foundations

The Intersection of Mind
and Money

CHAPTER 1

Markets on the Mind

The Challenge of Finding an Edge

"I'd be a bum on the street with a tin cup if the markets were always efficient."

—Warren Buffett

E ven though trillions of dollars change hands in the financial markets every day, most active investors cannot find an edge over their competition. They are vulnerable to psychological biases that impair their investment decisions, and their profitability is eroded. Consider the fate of Internet-era day traders.

Day traders typically aim to earn money from small intraday price movements and trends. Most are not financial professionals by training or experience. Often, they enter day trading from other occupations, encouraged by the independence and high expected financial returns of trading.

A 1998 study sponsored by the North American Securities Administrators Association (NASAA) analyzed 26 randomly selected day-trading accounts. The year 1998 should have been an excellent year for day trading, with the S&P 500 up over 26 percent that year. However, the report's conclusions were pessimistic. "Eighteen (18) of the twenty-six accounts (70 percent) lost money. More importantly, all 18 accounts were traded in a manner that realized a Risk of Ruin of 100 percent." The "risk of ruin" is the statistical likelihood, based on swings in value, that the account will go bankrupt over the next year. The report noted that "Only three (3) of twenty-six (26) accounts (11.5 percent of the sample) evidenced the ability to conduct profitable short-term trading."[1] The report observed that most traders were limiting their profits and letting their losses ride, and "that's a surefire way of going broke."[2]

9

It wasn't only American day traders who lost money in the late 1990s. In an analysis of Taiwanese day traders on the Taipei Stock Exchange, most traders' profits were not sufficient to cover their transaction costs. "In the typical six month period, more than eight out of ten day traders lose money."

Short-term currency traders lose with similar consistency to day traders. One of the largest retail foreign exchange dealers in the United States is Foreign Exchange Capital Markets (FXCM). In 2005, Drew Niv, chief executive of FXCM, remarked to the *Wall Street Journal* "If 15 percent of [currency] day traders are profitable, I'd be surprised."[3]

While short-term trading looks like a losing proposition on average, in both the United States and Taiwan a small percentage of day traders were consistently profitable. Among the Taiwanese, "Traders with strong past performance continue to earn strong returns. The stocks they buy outperform those they sell by 62 basis points [0.62 percent] *per day*."[4] Most day traders aspire to be as successful as this small minority, but they find themselves held back by poor decision making.

What are the underlying reasons for the poor performance of most day traders? Researchers analyzed the daily trading records and monthly positions of investors at a large discount brokerage. They examined 10 years of trading records for 66,465 households, including over two million common stock trades. They divided the accounts into five groups based on the level of turnover in the stock portfolios. The 20 percent of investors who traded most actively earned an average net annual return 7.7 percent *lower* than the average household.[5] Based on this study, it appears that excessive stock turnover and the attendant transaction costs contribute to poor performance.

It is not simply overtrading, but choosing the wrong stocks to buy and sell, that reduces profitability. Individual investors underperform because psychological biases interfere with their investment decision making. In a different study, researchers analyzed the trading records of 10,000 brokerage accounts over six years, including 162,000 common stock trades.[6, 7] They compared the performance of losing stocks held to that of the winning stocks sold. One year after the sale, the losing stocks investors clung to had underperformed the winners they sold by an average of 3.2 percent.[8] Most investors sold winning stocks too early and held losing stocks too long.

In a broad study of mutual fund returns, Vanguard founder John Bogle calculated that while the stock market rose 13 percent annually from 1983 through 2003, the average mutual fund returned 10 percent and the average mutual fund investor gained only 6.3 percent.[9] Other researchers have found that the average mutual fund investor underperforms inflation.[10]

Mutual fund managers' decisions are impaired by psychological biases. In a study of mutual fund performance from 1975 to 1994, on a net-return level, the studied funds underperformed broad market indexes by one percent per year.[11] Mutual fund underperformance is due, in part, to fund manager overtrading.[12] Furthermore, the higher a mutual fund's management fee, the lower its performance. Mutual funds look like a lose-lose proposition. Even if you can control your own overtrading, your mutual fund manager may not be able to manage himself.

While the vast majority of mutual funds underperform their benchmarks over time, about 3 to 4 percent earn consistently high returns, year after year.[13] The persistent success of these star funds suggests that a small minority of portfolio managers have "the right stuff." Chapter 12 discusses the psychological characteristics of such star performers.

On average, both mutual fund managers and individual investors significantly underperform the markets due to psychological biases. Overtrading and its high associated transaction costs are one cause of poor performance. Other mistakes, such as holding losers too long and failing to stick to a prearranged risk management plan, are behind the "celebrity" mishaps of LTCM, Newton, and Clemens described in the introduction. Yet biases are not fated for most investors. With experience, bias severity declines (or the nonbiased preferentially survive) and as a result, returns increase.[14] Furthermore, biases are less prevalent if nothing of value is at stake in the decision. Some of the best-performing financial professionals are those who don't have to make actual trading decisions: stock analysts.

ANALYSTS AND DART BOARDS

While most mutual fund managers and individual investors struggle to keep up with the market, stock analysts' buy and sell recommendations are generally quite accurate. In 1967, Nobel Prize winning economist Paul Samuelson declared to a U.S. Senate committee: "A typical mutual fund is providing nothing for the mutual fund owner that they could not get by throwing a dart at a dartboard." Samuelson's assertion prompted a series of competitions between stocks selected randomly by throwing darts at the stock tables of a newspaper and stocks selected by professional stock analysts. Several major business news publications featured these contests, including a Swedish newspaper that trained a chimpanzee to throw the darts. The most highly regarded contest was that of the *Wall Street Journal* (WSJ), which ran from 1982 to 2002.

In the WSJ results from 142 six-month contests, professionals came out significantly ahead of the darts with a six-month average return of

10.2 percent. The darts averaged a 3.5 percent semiannual return, while the Dow Jones average climbed 5.6 percent.[15,16] It appeared that stock analysts' recommendations contained a great deal of value to investors. However, the pros' recommendations could *not* be acted on by individual investors to beat the markets. The stocks recommended by the analysts opened up an average of 4 percent from the prior day's close.[17] The advantage of analysts' expertise was eliminated by dissemination.

In general, professional stock analysts' strong buy recommendations outperform their strong sell recommendations by almost 9 percent annually.[18] However, because of frequent turnover and high transaction costs when investing based on analysts' advice, the excess return of such a strategy is not significantly above the market return. Analysts' forecasts are quickly priced into stocks, and the transaction costs accrued by following their frequent changes in opinion prevent excess returns for the general public.

Many funds employ analysts in-house so they can have instant access to their insights, and some hedge funds pay high trading commissions, which entitle them to "first-mover" insights from the best analysts at major brokerages. Due to much higher compensation, many excellent analysts work at hedge funds where their opinions are kept a closely guarded secret.

What does this mean for the individual investor? In the end, if you want an advantage, you've got to learn to be your own stock analyst. The first step toward that goal is to learn how analysts think.

DEVELOPING BETTER EXPECTATIONS

Analysts have better forecasts than others because they have superior expectations of likely stock price moves. Russ Fuller is a portfolio manager for the mutual fund group Fuller and Thaler Asset Management, based in San Mateo, California. Fuller has written that "having better expectations than the market is the mother of all alphas."[19] *Alpha* is the amount by which a portfolio manager outperforms his benchmark. The benchmark is usually a stock index of similar size, growth, or value characteristics to the stocks the fund is buying.

So how can investors develop better expectations to increase their alpha? According to Fuller, they can develop one of three advantages. First, they can have superior private information about company fundamentals or markets. Superior private information is often obtained through a better research process, such as through an in-depth examination of a company's growth prospects, earnings quality, product viability, or management team.

The second method for generating superior expectations, according to Fuller, is by processing information better. It is possible to find mathematically predictive relationships within fundamental and financial data based on quantitative, computerized information processing. Additionally, some expert human analysts can perceive predictive relationships in corporate data.

The third technique for developing better expectations is to understand investors' behavioral biases. Behavioral biases are caused both by (1) investors who are not wealth maximizing and (2) investors who make systematic mental mistakes.[20] Finding the impact of behavioral biases on stock prices requires psychological savvy, but it can be quite profitable. Fuller and Thaler's portfolios have returned average alphas of almost 4 percent since their inception,[21] a track record that has prompted the creation of many copycat "behavioral finance" funds.

This book will address each technique for developing superior expectations. In particular, it will help readers to identify and eliminate errors in analysis and modeling. The discussion of corporate management biases, particularly overconfidence in Chapter 8, should be useful for readers who are fundamental analysts. The description of data-interpretation errors (self-deception) in Chapter 20 is helpful for quantitative and technical analysts. The majority of the book is devoted to behavioral biases. To use behavioral biases in investment strategy, one should find where such biases affect the majority of investors and show up in characteristic market price patterns.

"THE WISDOM OF THE COLLECTIVE"

> "Markets can still be rational when investors are individually irrational. Sufficient diversity is the essential feature in efficient price formation. Provided the decision rules of investors are diverse—even if they are suboptimal—errors tend to cancel out and markets arrive at appropriate prices."
> —Michael Mauboussin, *More Than You Know*[22]

Michael Mauboussin is chief investment strategist at Legg-Mason Capital Management and a professor of finance at the Columbia Business School. He is also a polymath who has integrated elements of complex adaptive systems theory and behavioral finance into his investment philosophy. One aspect of his philosophy he calls "The Wisdom of the

Collective." Mauboussin has found abundant literature indicating that individuals (even experts) can estimate "correct" stock valuations no better than the consensus market price.

When people are asked to guess answers to problems as diverse as the number of jelly beans in a jar, the precise weight of an ox, or the location of a bomb, individual guesses (even guesses by experts) are relatively poor. Averaging the participants' guesses often produces a consensus average estimate that is the most reliable and accurate solution to the problem. In many ways, the stock market is a collective estimation about the future of the economy.

Mauboussin explains that humans are not rational agents in the markets, there is no steady-state market price equilibrium, and price changes are not normally distributed, thus the markets are a complex adaptive system. Using the assumption of complexity, one can account for real-world considerations: the markets are composed of boundedly rational agents (individuals driven somewhat by psychology), they have states of disequilibrium (prices are unstable even without new information), and they exhibit "fat-tailed" price change distributions (large price changes occur much more frequently than expected by chance).

As Mauboussin points out, the stock market has no defined outcome and no defined time horizon. Prices in the financial markets both *inform* and *influence* participants about the future. Diversity (or efficiency) is lost in the markets when investors imitate one another or when they rely on the same "information cascades." Information cascades induce market participants to make the same decisions based on the same signals from the environment, without consideration that others are doing likewise.

From Mauboussin's work one can draw several conclusions. In order to find advantages in the markets, one must search for "diversity breakdowns." Diversity breakdowns represent collective overreactions or underreactions to new information, often leading to mispricings that ultimately correct themselves. Investment profits can be made both as the mispricings form and as they break down.

When researchers find brain activation patterns leading to uniform buying or selling during market experiments, then they may have located a plausible brain mechanism for diversity breakdowns. As Mauboussin puts it, "So the issue is not whether individuals are irrational (they are) but whether they are irrational in *the same way at the same time*." He goes on, "While understanding individual behavioral pitfalls may improve your own decision making, appreciation of the dynamics of the collective is the key to outperforming the market."[23]

Diversity breakdowns may sound like a rare event, but in fact they occur every day in the financial markets. Because we are biological beings with common biological hardware, we are susceptible to common influences from the environment. Environmental factors that sway collective thinking can be overt (such as news releases) or beneath awareness. Natural cycles (such as variations in daylight) and meteorological events (such as cloud cover and geomagnetic storms) alter collective mood and behavior. These group-level shifts in emotion and thought have been shown to affect market price movements.

METEOROLOGICAL ANOMALIES AND OTHER ANIMAL SPIRITS

Calendar and meteorological effects are surprising both for the size of their impact on market prices and for the fact that they operate entirely beneath awareness. Short-term natural influences on investing behavior arise from six areas: Daily sunshine versus cloud cover, disruptions in sleep patterns, temperature extremes, lunar cycles, electromagnetic storms, and wind strength. A long-term biological influence on investor behavior is the gradual waxing and waning of daylight as seasons change.

Professor Hirshleifer at Ohio State University found that morning sunshine correlates with stock returns.[24] He examined 26 stock market indices around the globe for the period of 1982 to 1997. He looked at sunshine versus some cloud cover in the city of a nation's largest stock exchange. "In New York City, the annualized nominal market return on perfectly sunny days is approximately 24.8 percent per year versus 8.7 percent per year on perfectly cloudy days." He cites evidence that sunshine improves investors' moods. When their moods are elevated, investors are less risk averse and are more likely to buy.

Kamstra, Kramer, and Levi (2003) find that stock returns are significantly related to season. They examined stock market performance during the six months between the fall equinox (September 21) and the spring equinox (March 21) for the northern hemisphere and the opposite six-month period for the southern hemisphere. The authors found that overall, stock markets underperformed in the seasonal summer and outperformed in the winter. As an example, the authors cite the returns of a portfolio invested 50 percent in each of Sydney, Australia (the most southerly major market with the most daylight during the northern winter) and Stockholm, Sweden (the most northerly major market with the most daylight during the summer). From 1982 to 2001 this equal-weighted portfolio earned 13.1 percent annually. If the entire investment followed the darkness across hemispheres, investing in Stockholm from September to March and Sydney from March to September, the annual returns were 21.1 percent (versus 5.2 percent if doing the opposite strategy). The researchers hypothesized that emotional shifts, related to the biology underlying seasonal affective disorder (SAD), alter risk preferences and subsequent investment behavior on a collective level.[25]

Goetzmann and Zhu (2002) analyzed trading accounts of 79,995 investors from 1991 to 1996, and they found that *individual investors* do not trade differently on sunny days versus cloudy days. However, the authors found that *market-maker* behavior was significantly impacted by the degree of cloud cover: Wider bid/ask spreads on cloudy days were hypothesized to represent risk aversion among market makers. Other researchers discovered that morning cloud cover and wind speed in Chicago correlate with wider bid-ask spreads in the afternoon.[26] The weather in the exchange's home city affects market-maker behavior, but investors in other cities who place orders on the exchange are probably unaffected.

While it seems plausible that sunlight affects investor moods and trading behavior, some much more extraordinary correlations have been found. Researchers found that severe geomagnetic storms (a result of solar flares) caused world stock market underperformance over the six days following the event.[27] Interestingly, the psychology literature demonstrates a correlation between geomagnetic storms and signs of depression in the general population during the two weeks following. Depression is an emotional disorder characterized, in part, by risk aversion.

In addition to sunshine and geomagnetic storms, researchers found that poor sleep quality leads to subpar market returns. Daylight savings time serves as a proxy for sleep disruption (desynchronosis). Kamstra, Kramer, and Levi (2002) found that on the time-change weekends of daylight savings time there are below normal stock returns from the Friday market close to the Monday open (two to five times larger than normal). The authors hypothesize that this underperformance is due to impaired judgment secondary to sleep disruption. Expanding this hypothesis, the average weekend desynchronosis may explain the "Monday effect," where prices rise less on average on Mondays than on other days of the week.

Other environmental variables affect investors as well. Cao and Wei (2002) found that abnormal local temperatures affect stock prices in the city of a country's major stock exchange. The authors draw on psychology studies showing increased physical activity in unusually low-temperature environments and increased apathy and aggression during period of abnormally high temperatures.

Yuan, Zheng, and Zhu (2001) find a lunar effect on stock prices worldwide. The authors report that stock market returns in 48 countries are lower during the days surrounding a full moon than during the days around a new moon. The superior returns around the new moon amount to 6.6 percent annually.[28] In fact, the light of the full moon may contribute to more frequent nocturnal awakenings, sleep disruption, and subsequent next-day risk aversion.

These natural market anomalies tell a compelling story about the impact of the natural world on collective investor behavior and market prices. Seasonal and meteorological factors may contribute to market price anomalies via collective changes in emotional states (and thus risk preferences). These findings indicate that investors' mood states are the basis of some of the predictable volatility in the markets. Importantly, such market patterns are predictable and significant, and result from unconscious changes in collective behavior.

SENTIMENT

If investors' emotional states can predict market price movements, is there a way of measuring investors' average emotion in advance to predict market prices? Of course, the above authors measured environmental stimuli such as sunlight and magnetism, which are known to influence mood and behavior. In the finance literature, surveys that ask investors how "bullish" or "bearish" they feel are available.

Researchers found that both newsletter writers[29] and individual investors[30] show increased optimism about future stock market gains (bullishness) following high recent returns. Additionally, as the S&P 500 declined over a 12-month period, investor optimism about the stock market's future declined in tandem with prices.[31] Investors' projections of future market action reflect their feelings about recent price trends.

Perhaps paradoxically, Fisher and Statman (2000) noted that the percentage of investors who believed the market was overvalued was correlated with expectations of future returns from 1998 to 2001.[32] That is, even though investors knew that the market was "overvalued," their expectations of future gains actually increased the more they thought it was overpriced. Based on this surprising finding, it appears that investors' intellectual assessment ("overvalued") is decoupled from their underlying feeling of optimism ("it's going up!"). In general, sentiment levels do appear to be negatively correlated with (and somewhat predictive of) future market price changes.[33]

Across individuals, biological commonalities in information processing, such as those generated by emotion, lead to diversity breakdowns in market prices. The large and repeating effects of meteorological and calendar events on market prices indicates that subtle biological forces influence group investment activity. The dissociation between intellectual assessments of market value and sentiment suggests that different brain systems are mediating decision making. Understanding both the neural origins and provocateurs of diversity breakdowns may lead to novel investment strategy development and training programs to eliminate those biases.

The next chapter introduces the brain circuits responsible for biased investment behavior.

CHAPTER 2

Brain Basics

The Building Blocks

"In terms of biological design for the basic neural circuitry of emotion, what we are born with is what worked best for the last 50,000 human generations. ... The slow, deliberate forces of evolution that have shaped our emotions have done their work over the course of a million years; the last 10,000 years have ... left little imprint on our biological templates for emotional life."

—Daniel Goleman, Emotional Intelligence[1]

Investors' emotions and motivations are often unconscious, but they are nevertheless powerfully influential over decision making. Fortunately, new tools in psychology and technologies in neuroscience are revealing the deep neural origins of investors' emotional biases and suggesting techniques to ameliorate their effects on judgment. The next two chapters describe the neural and mental foundations of financial decision making, beginning here with the brain origins.

Some psychiatric disorders manifest through repeatedly poor financial decision making. Compulsive stealing, hoarding unneeded items, shopping out of control, and making wildly speculative gambles are all characteristics of different types of mental illness. When I was training as a psychiatrist, we occasionally evaluated patients who had no known neurological, addictive, or mental disorder but who nonetheless demonstrated chronically poor financial judgment.

At San Francisco General Hospital, the psychiatry consultation team was called to assess the decision-making capacity of a patient named Lee.

One year earlier, after months of increasing headaches, visual abnormalities, and difficulty concentrating, a tumor had been detected in Lee's brain. Lee was 53 years old and a partner in an accounting firm at the time. He was suffering from a rare, benign tumor of the brain called a meningioma. These tumors arise in the meninges, the thin but dense membrane that separates the brain from the skull. In Lee's case, the tumor had swelled upward from the base of his skull, displacing the brain tissue along the midline of his frontal lobes. It was the size of a lemon by the time it was discovered.

Neurosurgery was performed and successfully led to the tumor's removal. As in many cases like this, some normal brain tissue had been starved of oxygen by the tumor, and the dead tissue was also removed from the brain. As a result, Lee lost part of his brain's orbitofrontal cortex (OFC).

A few weeks after surgery, Lee returned home from the hospital and tried to go back to life as usual. Even though he had lost part of his brain, Lee was still an intelligent man. His IQ remained superior, and his neuropsychological testing showed no significant motor, perceptual, visuospatial, or calculation deficits.

However, according to his wife, he demonstrated some unusual behavior during his first two months at home. He made a few large, unnecessary purchases on his credit card, including two new cars and a boat. His wife asked him to stop making such purchases, as they already had what they needed. He was agreeable to this request, and returned one of the cars and the boat. Yet he continued to make large purchases at an alarming rate, quickly maxing out his credit card limits and further distressing his wife.

His performance at work was characterized by an inability to multitask. He often became totally involved in doing one activity all day even though many others urgently needed his attention. His performance dropped off, and over six months it became clear that he couldn't continue to manage his current projects. He left his workplace, taking early retirement.

After retirement, he continued to make bad investment decisions. He bought several vacation time-shares with little money down, encouraged by slick sales pitches. He bought penny stocks based on fax and e-mail promotions. He lost large sums of money in most of these investments. After several months, he could no longer afford his mortgage payments. He and his wife were on the brink of bankruptcy and divorce.

We were seeing Lee one year after his surgery. As psychiatrists, it was our job to determine if Lee was still competent to manage his own medical, legal, and financial decisions. If not competent, some of these decisions could be taken over by his wife.

Lee was intellectually aware that he had been making very risky investments with his limited resources. He acknowledged that this was completely new behavior for him. Previously, he had been a conservative investor, and he didn't like to gamble. Now he knew how he *should* feel about the financial risks he was taking, but he didn't feel afraid. In fact, he didn't feel much of anything about risk. He didn't restrain himself from taking large speculative risks because the investments didn't *feel* risky to him.

Our team determined that Lee was normal in every way except in his assessment of risk. He was not inhibited by fear, and he was easily enticed by potential opportunity. Lee's situation illustrates that risky decision making is rooted in somewhat fragile neurological processes. Most people are occasionally tempted to invest in speculative ventures or to purchase prohibitively expensive luxury goods, but they exercise self-restraint due to the potentially negative consequences of excessive debt. Because they are afraid of the consequences, they refrain from indulgence. During background research we realized that Lee was experiencing similar impairments to a group of patients studied extensively by neurologist Antonio Damasio at the University of Iowa.

DAMASIO AND THE IOWA GAMBLING TASK

Lee had a lesion in the OFC of his brain. Damage in other areas of Lee's brain could have led to similar problems as he was experiencing if it had affected the broad brain circuit, part of which was removed from Lee's OFC, called the "loss avoidance system." When a brain tumor or other event leads to damage in part of the loss avoidance system (such as the OFC, depicted in Figure 2.2 on page 24), how individuals perceive and process risky situations is altered.

In the early 1990s, then at the University of Iowa, the neurologist Antonio Damasio took an interest in several patients with OFC lesions in his neurology clinics. His patient group had lesions of the ventromedial prefrontal cortex (the midline aspect of the OFC). Like Lee at my hospital, these patients retained their basic intelligence, memory, and capabilities for analytical reasoning and for logical thought,[2] but they made poor decisions in risky situations.

Many of these patients reported that they knew when they *should* feel afraid, but they had difficulty both (1) experiencing emotions and (2) associating their feelings with anticipated consequences. Essentially, they had a deficit in their ability to integrate emotions and thinking.

It turns out that the part of the brain these patients were missing, the OFC, evaluates the relevance of emotional input to one's decision making.[3] Damasio's patients could not understand what emotional

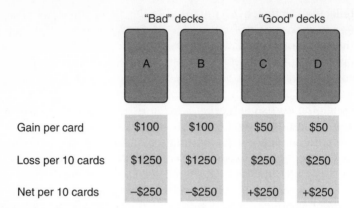

FIGURE 2.1 The Iowa Gambling Task. Notice that the net return per deck is negative for decks A and B and positive for decks C and D. Additionally, the range of gains and losses is much smaller in decks C and D.

information was important. Just like Lee, they knew when they should be afraid, but they could not use fear to help them avoid taking a dangerous financial risk.

Damasio wanted an instrument to detect his patients' problem with risk processing. He designed a card-playing game, called the Iowa Gambling Task, to measure physiological and behavioral responses to risk in these patients. The participants were connected to electrophysiological arousal monitoring devices (as in lie-detector tests) such as a skin conductance response (SCR) monitor. In the task, four decks of cards were laid out in front of brain-lesioned patients and normal controls.[4] The subjects then selected cards from any of the four decks with the overall goal of maximizing their financial gain. See Figure 2.1 for a depiction of the card decks, outcomes, and odds for each deck.

Subjects were not told the overall odds or payoffs of the card decks. They were simply told to play the game and to try to make as much money as possible. The two decks on the left, "A" and "B," yielded either cards valued at $100 or −$1,250. The two decks on the right yielded cards valued either $50 or −$250. The expected value of each card in decks A and B was −$250 while for decks C and D it was $250.

Damasio found that the patient group was more likely to choose cards from decks A and B (the "bad" decks). The patients did not generate anticipatory SCRs to the risky decks (A and B), and they played deficiently overall. "Even after several of them realized which decks were bad, they still made the wrong choices."[5] Without the ability to integrate emotion and reason in the OFC, the patients' danger assessment of the "bad" decks was intellectually intact, but it did not alter their decision making, and they continued to choose cards from the losing decks.[6]

Unlike the brain-damaged patients, normal subjects learned to avoid the losing decks. After flipping the first 10 cards, normals began to show physiological "stress" reactions on the SCR measurements when hovering over decks A or B. Patients never showed such responses. Furthermore, even though the normal subjects experienced a physiological stress reaction after 10 card flips, they could not consciously identify that decks A and B were the money-losing decks until over 40 card flips later. Normals began to flip more cards from the "good" decks C and D before they were consciously aware that these decks were "good." That is, normal people had "gut" stress reactions to the losing decks after 10 flips, and changed their behavior to prefer decks C and D. Yet they only articulated a "hunch" which were the losing decks after 50 card flips. They could explain their hunch with certainty only after 80 flips.

Damasio's research implies that people *need* feelings to signal when to avoid losses in risky environments. When making risky decisions, there is a gap between what the emotional brain (the limbic system) knows about risk and one's conscious awareness of the actual danger. Intuitive decisions, where "gut feel" drives judgment, arise from such limbic knowledge and are discussed in Chapter 5. In the brain-damaged gamblers, a brain region that integrates risk-related feelings with reasoned decision making had been taken off-line.

THE BRAIN: STRUCTURE AND FUNCTION

In order to gain insight into the brain-lesioned patients' deficiency in risk processing, it's useful to pause for a basic tutorial on how the brain operates. The human brain is the product of millions of years of evolution, and it is designed to efficiently and effectively interpret information, compete in a social hierarchy, and direct activity toward achieving goals while avoiding danger. However, our brains evolved in a stone-age world where dangers and opportunities were largely immediate, and social interactions were limited to other members of the clan. Now, as the modern world becomes more interconnected and fast paced, it is apparent that the stone-age brain is not optimized for managing the complexities of modern life.

In a generalization that will be repeated throughout this book, the brain can be conceptualized as having three anatomical divisions. Each division is like the layer of an onion, with complex processes such as analytical decision making in the outer layer, motivations and drives arising from the middle layer, and life-sustaining physiological processes originating in the innermost core. This conceptual schema is termed the "Triune" brain.[7]

The cortex is the brain's logistical center. It is the director of executive function and motor control. The part of the cortex called the prefrontal cortex is of most interest to this discussion. The prefrontal cortex is involved in abstract thinking, planning, calculation, learning, and strategic decision making.[8] Another part of the cortex, called the insular cortex, is evolutionarily distinct from the neocortex. In this book, when using the word *cortex*, I am broadly referring to the neocortex and the prefrontal cortex, but excluding the insular cortex.

The brain's limbic system is the emotional driver of the brain. The limbic system is the source of primitive motivations and emotions including fear and excitement. Both the cortex and the limbic system are displayed in Figure 2.2. The third division of the brain is called the midbrain (a.k.a. "the reptilian brain"). The midbrain manages the body's basic physiological

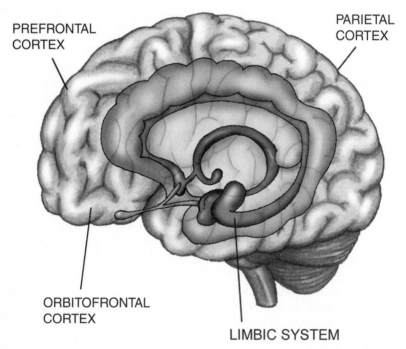

PREFRONTAL
CORTEX

PARIETAL
CORTEX

ORBITOFRONTAL
CORTEX

LIMBIC SYSTEM

FIGURE 2.2 A depiction of the whole brain. The limbic system is seen situated underneath the cortex. The prefrontal cortex lies behind the forehead. The orbitofrontal cortex (OFC) is located behind the eyes and above the sinuses. The parietal cortex is situated at the posterior of the brain.

processes, including respiration and heart rate, and it will not be discussed further in this book.

Running across the three brain divisions are neural circuits that operate two types of goal-directed behavior: (1) reward pursuit and (2) loss avoidance.[9] The existence of reward approach and loss avoidance systems has been hypothesized since the time of Aristotle in ancient Greece.[10] Prior to the late twentieth century, both the reward and the loss systems were thought to drive organisms toward pleasure and away from pain. Currently, scientists believe that these systems encompass complex brain processes involving emotions, cognitions (thoughts), and actions. While the reward and loss systems are largely independent, when one system is highly activated, it may trigger a reciprocal deactivation of the other.

First, I will describe the reward system. Objectives we want to achieve and items we want to possess are called "rewards," and the pursuit of such rewards is headquartered in the brain's "reward system." The reward system is involved in scanning the environment for, evaluating, and attempting to procure desired gains (rewards).

The reward system is comprised of neurons that predominantly communicate via the neurotransmitter dopamine. Dopamine has been called the "pleasure" chemical of the brain, because people who are electrically stimulated in the reward system report intense feelings of well-being.[11] Illicit drug use causes dopamine release in the nucleus accumbens (part of the reward system), which is why street drugs are colloquially called "dope." The reward system coordinates the search for, evaluation of, and motivated pursuit of potential rewards. See Figure 2.3 for a depiction of the reward system.

The motivational systems allow us to quickly assess and value potential opportunities and threats in the environment. When we perceive something valuable, our reward system is activated, and we desire it. Many items and goals are valuable to us. We value pleasant tastes (especially fatty, sweet, and salty foods).[12] We value sex appeal[13] and generosity[14] in others. We value status symbols (such as luxury goods and sports cars[15]). We value laughing[16] and loved ones, and we value revenge and the punishment of deviants.[17] These valued events all activate the brain's reward system.

A second motivational circuit governs "loss avoidance." The "loss avoidance system" is activated when we become aware of threats or dangers in our environment. Anxiety, fear, and panic are emotions that arise from the loss avoidance system, and pessimistic and worried thoughts are the cognitive sequelae of loss system activation.

The anatomy of the brain's loss system is less well defined than that of the reward system. The loss system is thought to consist of the anterior insula (pain and disgust), the amygdala (emotional processing), the

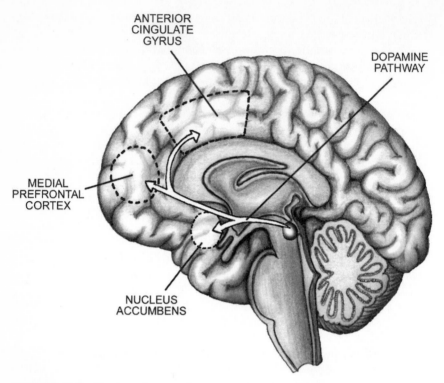

FIGURE 2.3 The brain's reward system. A bundle of dopamine neurons in the midbrain sends projections throughout the prefrontal cortex.

hippocampus (memory center), and the hypothalamus (hormone secreting center). See Figure 2.4.

Loss system activation affects the entire body through bloodstream hormone and neurotransmitter release. The perception of a threat activates the hypothalamus-pituitary-adrenal axis (HPA axis), which results in stress hormone and epinephrine ("adrenaline") secretion into the bloodstream. The body's sympathetic nervous system (SNS) prepares the whole body for the "fight-or-flight" response to danger with nerve signals transmitted to every major organ system. When under threat and experiencing fear, signs of SNS activation include trembling, perspiration, rapid heart rate, shallow breathing, and pupillary dilation. The SNS is also responsible for the physical signs and symptoms of panic.

Because the reward and loss systems influence thought and lie beneath awareness, they often direct behavior automatically through subtle emotional influences on judgment, thinking, and behavior. In Damasio's patients, the interface between fearful feelings generated by the loss

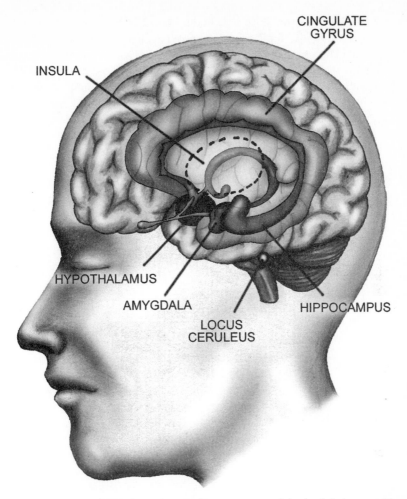

FIGURE 2.4 An illustration of several components of the brain's loss avoidance system.

avoidance system and reasonable thought generated by the prefrontal cortex was interrupted. Fortunately, investigators have a number of tools for assessing the health of the brain's reward and loss avoidance systems.

THE BRAIN-DAMAGED INVESTOR

According to a 2005 *Wall Street Journal* article, "Lessons from the Brain-Damaged Investor," brain-damaged traders may have an advantage in the markets.[18] Study participants who had a brain lesion that eliminated their ability to emotionally "feel" were compared against "normals" in an investment game. The chief researcher, Professor Baba Shiv (now at Stanford University), used a mixed sample of patients with damage in emotional centers including either the orbitofrontal cortex, the amygdala, or the insula.

In Shiv's experiment, each participant was given $20 to start. Participants were told that they would be making 20 rounds of investment decisions. In each round, they could decide to "invest" or "not invest." If they chose *not* to invest, then they kept their $1 dollar and proceeded to the next round. If they chose to invest, then the experimenter would first take the dollar bill from their hand and then flip a coin in plain view. If the coin landed heads, then the subject lost the dollar, but if it were tails, then $2.50 was awarded. On each round, participants had to decide first whether to invest. The expected gain of each $1 "investment" was $1.25 (average of $0 and +$2.50), while each "not invest" decision led to a guaranteed $1. The expected value of the gamble being higher ($1.25), it was always the most rational choice. Thus, one might assume that subjects always "invested" in order to make more money.

In fact, the results are not uniform. Normals (without brain damage) invested in 57.6 percent of the total rounds, while brain-damaged subjects invested 83.7 percent of the time. Many normal subjects (42.4 percent) were "irrationally" avoiding the investment option. Following an investment loss in the prior round, 40.7 percent of the normals and 85.2 percent of the patients invested in the subsequent round (see Figure 2.5). After recent losses, normals invested 27 percent less often. They became even more "irrationally risk avoidant" after a loss.

Of the patients with different brain lesions, the insula-lesion patients showed the least sensitivity to risk, investing in 91.3 percent of all the rounds and in 96.8 percent of the rounds following a loss. As a result, it appears that the insula is one of the most important drivers of risk aversion. Without an insula, brain-damaged patients were more likely to "invest."

On the lighter side, neurologist Antoine Bechara ventured that investors must be like "functional psychopaths" to avoid emotional influences in the markets. These individuals are either much better at controlling their emotions or perhaps don't experience emotions with the same intensity as others. According to Professor Shiv, many CEOs and top lawyers might also share this trait: "Being less emotional can help you in certain situations."[19]

Now you still might be wondering, "Is there a brain area that sabotages my investing?" The answer is not clear. It turns out that the lesion patients can have pretty miserable financial lives—accumulating credit card debt, not showing up to work on time, falling for Internet scams, and ultimately declaring bankruptcy. Even though they score normally on IQ tests, there

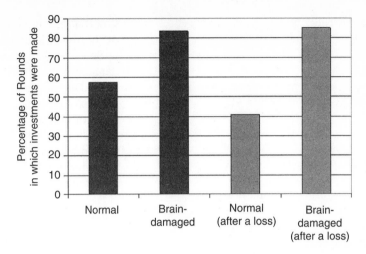

FIGURE 2.5 Investment choices of brain-damaged and normal subjects in Shiv's experimental task, on average, and following a loss.

is clearly something wrong with their judgment about financial risks. They can't seem to recognize the downside of risk or the possibility of catastrophic loss. So while they make the more "rational" decisions in Professor Shiv's tasks, they cannot adequately avoid catastrophic risks in other situations (such as the Iowa Gambling Task).

Most investors avoid financial risk after a recent loss, to their financial detriment. Risk avoidance is pretty smart after most types of losses—that's how we learn from mistakes. For example, if the executives of a company you are invested in are caught "cooking the books," leading to a nasty price decline, then you might be more wary and do more due diligence before investing in a similar company. That caution is a good thing, because that's how people learn to avoid unhealthy risk.

In the markets, most investors take away lessons where none exist. They learned to avoid technology stocks after the losses of 2001, even though the bear market losses should have had little impact on non-Internet stock performance going forward. After suffering bear market losses, most investors wait for price "confirmation" before jumping back into stocks. They may even sit out the market until new highs are reached. Of course, waiting for confirmation means missing much of the price move, but that's the price many people are willing to pay for enhanced confidence.

So far you've seen how researchers used a card game (Iowa Gambling Task) and a coin-flipping gamble (Shiv's task) to assess financial decision-making behavior in brain-damaged people. Many other techniques have been used in decision-making research. As you'll see below, the technologies available to researchers have exploded in complexity over the past decade.

RESEARCH METHODS

There are many levels of function in the brain, from the actions of individual molecules to broad communications between lobes. At a molecular level, neural activity is driven by neurochemicals, small electrical currents, and genetic transcription. On the anatomical level, there are neural circuits that cross brain regions and give rise to complex thoughts and behaviors. These are building blocks of a neurological understanding of the brain.

Researchers utilize a variety of sophisticated tools to understand how the brain works. Neuroimaging is the most widely used technology for understanding decision making. Most of the neuroimaging studies cited in this book use functional magnetic resonance imaging (fMRI). fMRI allows researchers to visualize changes in oxygenated blood flow, which serves as a proxy for brain metabolism. fMRI can yield resolution of brain voxels as small as $2 \times 2 \times 2$ millimeters over time intervals of two seconds. Positron emission tomography (PET), which is an alternative neuroimaging technique to fMRI, has a larger spatial resolution of approximately $3 \times 3 \times 3$ millimeters and can detect changes in glucose metabolism and blood flow only when a radioactive tracer has been injected into the subject.

Other investigative technologies include behavioral measures, subjective reports, psychological tests, and electrophysiology. Electrophysiology involves measurements of heart rate, blood pressure, galvanic skin response (sweating), and other physical variables, many of which are indicators of reactive brain activation in limbic and midbrain regions. Pupillary eye measurements allow researchers to directly monitor the activity of the SNS. As previously mentioned, the SNS is involved in the "fight-or-flight" response.

Electromyograghs (EMGs) measure electrical activity during muscle contraction. When EMGs are used on facial muscles, very subtle states of happiness and concern can be measured. For example, analysts who are excited about an investment idea have greater activation of their *zygomatic* facial muscles when they talk about that investment. The zygomatic muscles control smiling. The frontalis muscle on the forehead is activated by concern, revealed in a furrowed brow, and is more active in traders during stressful market volatility.

Historically, many researchers used electroencephalograms (EEGs) for experimentation. An EEG is a test used to detect fluctuations in the electrical activity of the surface of the brain's cortex. EEGs are often used clinically to diagnose seizures. Some psychotherapists use EEGs for emotional biofeedback (so called "neurofeedback"). For example, a family therapist may use EEGs to monitor when the limbic system of one member of a family is triggered by another. The triggered member is likely to respond automatically and emotionally to provocations. Self-monitoring EEG activations allows the triggered family member to learn to interrupt and prevent automatic emotional responses that might be hurtful to another.

Single-neuron recording techniques are very invasive and are performed primarily on monkeys and rats. Such techniques have allowed researchers to model the activity of tiny neuronal bundles, including those used while computing the expected value of various decision options. Genetic sequencing technologies such as the polymerase chain reaction (PCR) have revealed that genes correlate with prominent personality and behavioral traits. Assays of blood and cerebrospinal fluid allow researchers to measure hormones (such as those mediating trust and the stress response) and neurotransmitters (including those involved in impulsiveness).

A research technique most often used by neurologists is the study of patients with specific brain lesions. Lee is an excellent example of this type of patient. Small brain lesions secondary to focused strokes or tumors can cause isolated impairments. These impairments can teach us a great deal about the function of specific brain regions.

The human brain contains approximately 100 billion neurons with 100 trillion connections between them. The neuron count inside our heads is comparable to the number of stars in our galaxy, the Milky Way. With this extraordinary complexity, it is unlikely that we will ever have a "model" of what it is to be human. No amount of brain research can adequately portray a feeling, a memory, or an experience.

Describing the mind in terms of brain circuits, personality traits, and genetic influences is deceptive. Individuals are not pieces thrown together into one predictable whole. Each person is different, unique, and incomprehensibly complex. They each nurture their own authentic interests, hopes, and aspirations. The human brain is the complex organ that gives rise to who we are, and its mysteries remain largely uncharted.

NEUROSCIENCE PREVIEW

The following is a very quick and general description of many of the brain regions discussed in this book. It is intended as a resource that you can refer back to from future chapters. It is quite dense with information, and you don't need to internalize this all at once. Feel free to skim ahead to the next chapter.

The functions of the prefrontal cortex, reward system, and loss system in financial decision making are discussed in this book. Much of optimal financial psychology lies in the self-awareness and self-control of limbic (emotional) impulses. By exercising "emotional intelligence," one can maintain flexibility in the face of opportunity and danger. Emotional intelligence is derived from the prefrontal cortex and the strength of its connections to the limbic system.

The prefrontal cortex has several regions that assist with different aspects of emotion management. The prefrontal cortex assists with planning for the future, following rules, directing focus and attention, executive decision making, and exerting self-control. More specifically, the orbitofrontal cortex (OFC) integrates reason and emotion, while the anterior cingulate cortex (ACC) resolves decision conflicts and prioritizes emotional information as either relevant or unimportant.

The limbic system has two major divisions of relevance to investing—the reward pursuit and loss avoidance circuits. Reward pursuit involves everything from how people value various prospects to how positive and motivated they feel toward obtaining desired goals, to their search for novelty. The loss avoidance system underlies fear and hesitation and drives the avoidance of perceived threats.

The reward system is the origin of several important financial biases. Increased reward system activation can generate optimism, overconfidence, and excessive risk-taking. The major regions of relevance in the reward system are the nucleus accumbens (NAcc) and the medial prefrontal cortex (MPFC).

The NAcc is the brain's center of lust and desire. The NAcc is activated by the anticipation of earning money, and it drives pursuit of the items or investments that one wants. High NAcc activation drives excessive financial risk taking. The MPFC, which is one terminus of the dopamine neurons of the reward system, is activated by trust and certainty, satisfaction when rewards are received, learning how to obtain rewards, and learning from successes and mistakes.

Hypoactivation or desensitization of the reward system results in a propensity to feel apathetic, have low energy, and engage in compensatory excitement and novelty-seeking behaviors such as pathological gambling and compulsive shopping. Short-term gains energize dopamine flow in the reward circuit.

Activation of the brain's loss system results in stress, anxiety, disgust, pain, and even panic. The behavioral bias of loss aversion is fueled by fears of disappointment and regret, and arises from amygdala activation. The anterior insula is an area of primitive cortex that governs the experiences of disgust, pain, and loss. Anterior insula activation precedes excessive risk aversion in one investment experiment. The physical and mental effects of stress are generated by hormonal and chemical pathways in the loss system.

The next chapter will discuss the links between brain and mind. In particular, the mental origins of emotions, expectations, beliefs, and self-deception are described.

CHAPTER 3

Origins of Mind

*Expectations, Beliefs,
and Meaning*

> *"What gets us into trouble is not what we don't
> know. It's what we know for sure that just ain't so."*
> —Mark Twain

I did some of my psychiatry training at the San Mateo Medical Center psychiatric emergency room (ER). In the ER we provided urgent mental health services for the northern part of Silicon Valley. I had the privilege of working with interesting and diverse clients in crisis, including engineers, venture capitalists, and executives.

Doug was wheeled into the ER on a gurney one evening in August 2001. He had been working late, and he was found by a security guard slouched over his desk, crying uncontrollably. He told the officer he felt like dying, so the officer called 911.

During my evaluation of him in the ER, he told me the following story: In 1999, while working as an accountant for Oracle, he became a paper millionaire. His Oracle stock options had rocketed in value. For him, this wasn't a big deal; it seemed like everyone he knew at the time was worth more than $1 million.

He bought two nice cars and a large home. More importantly, he felt like a *somebody*, "like I had finally arrived." He was in the center of action at an unparalleled time in world business history. He was young (30 years old), financially secure, valued at his workplace, and enjoyed life. Though he was born, raised, and educated in the U.S. Midwest, there was an instant intimacy and rapport among the in-crowd in the Valley.

As the stock market began to slide in late 2000 and early 2001, and his options' value declined, he tried not to pay attention. "It'll come back," he told himself, "we're changing the world." By mid-2001 he grew concerned, and he decided to check what his options were currently worth. He was shocked by what he discovered. He told me, "Doc, the options were a tenth of what they had been. They had been worth $2.6 million, and now I was almost broke!" For two weeks he felt vacant and in utter despair. At work he checked Oracle's stock price often, refreshing his Web browser every few minutes to get the latest quotes. He felt buoyed by up days, but increasingly depressed by the more frequent down days. Within weeks his options were trading under water, worth nothing.

Doug was obsessed with his sudden loss in wealth and the continuing slide in Oracle's share price. Over and over he asked himself, "How could this happen?" He couldn't sleep at night. He lost his appetite. Doug said that out of the blue he began to feel intense periods of dread at work. He didn't want to go in anymore. No matter how hard he tried to stay positive, he began to have unexpected and unwelcome thoughts of suicide.

He was so overwhelmed by options losses that he was considering suicide. Yet his losses had all been on *paper*. Nothing substantial had changed in his life when he lost that paper wealth. His actual salary remained the same. He could still easily afford his house and car payments, and he remarked that his net worth was positive.

So if nothing "real" had changed in Doug's life, why was he feeling suicidal? I asked him this question, and he earnestly responded, "Because I can't retire now."

I asked, "Retire now, at 30?"

"Yeah, now I've got to work the rest of my life. Who am I without that money? I was a millionaire, and now I'm just another guy."

Doug's identity was tied up in his money, and now he had lost it. A future that had seemed wide open with possibility now appeared dreary, lonely, meaningless, and dull. He had few real friends or outside interests in California. He had no other way to measure his worth other than his financial status. And his wealth, which he had thought was a reflection of his goodness as a person, was erased. So here he was, a complete failure in terms of his value system, now paralyzed by fear that he could never recover what he once had. He saw no reason to go on living.

We discussed how his wealth and the culture of Silicon Valley had altered his values. We talked about meaningful connections from his childhood and college years, and his belief in a universe that is greater than himself. He talked excitedly about the passion for numbers that had driven him to study accounting in the first place.

When Doug's visit to the psychiatric emergency room was concluded, and I was walking him to the exit with a sheaf of papers listing our treatment recommendations, he turned to me with a smirk and said, "The CFO told me we're going to beat our numbers next week, so maybe I'll be all right after all."

Doug hadn't needed the millions he had accumulated in stock options. But having that money in the bank changed how he saw himself. When it was gone, the conflict between his previous "Internet millionaire" status and his new self-identity as "an accountant in a dead-end job" was overwhelming. Yet nothing had fundamentally changed for Doug. All the wealth he had "lost" was on paper. The only tangible change was one of *perception*.

EMOTIONS AND PERCEPTIONS

How each person deals with changes in wealth depends on how they create personal meaning out of losses and gains. Whether a person is overwhelmed or resilient is more contingent on his beliefs and expectations than on his physical reality. One's life conditioning, innate personality traits, recent events, culture, and environment all influence how events are interpreted. And it is a person's interpretations of events that give rise to strong emotions, such as the depression that afflicted Doug.

Because emotions underlie so much of thought, behavior, and perception, and they are largely unconscious, they are discussed in detail in this book. Emotions are subjective feelings that serve as easy shortcuts (or *heuristics)* for the brain. In particular, emotions tell us how one is doing related to specific goals and threats. On the one hand, the emotion of excitement indicates that one has identified an opportunity. Excitement propels increased risk seeking and exploratory behavior. On the other hand, the emotion of fear notifies one of potential danger. Fear gives rise to behaviors of risk aversion and withdrawal.

Simplistically speaking, emotions are like a traffic light for the brain. When considering an opportunity or threat, emotions indicate whether one should go forward with risk-taking (excitement), proceed with caution (concern), or stop and withdraw (fear). Such emotions are *anticipatory*. They help people broadly prepare for threats or opportunities, and they are fundamental to the coordination of thought and action away from danger (loss avoidance) or towards opportunity (reward seeking).

When a threat becomes reality, resulting in immediate danger, then one may make a panicked effort to flee (flight), freeze in terror, or become combative (fight), giving rise to the colloquial expression "the fight or flight response." This response is a *reaction* to danger. If one is anticipating danger, fear is experienced, but if one is reacting to danger, then the "fight-or-flight" response is provoked.

This distinction between anticipatory and reactive emotions is important. Amateur investors often buy stocks based on their expectation of a price change in their favor. Anticipatory positive emotions are likely to bias this investor's expectations and inappropriately diminish their risk perceptions. Investors often sell stocks in reaction to events, whether a bigger than expected profit or a piece of unexpected negative news. Such reactive selling is typically not in response to a rational plan, but rather emotionally driven.

Emotions influence thoughts and perceptions, driving pessimistic or optimistic thinking styles. As an example of emotions biasing cognition, recall that Doug's powerful experience of financial disappointment drove him to have unwanted thoughts of suicide. As a further example, among many investors fear leads to knee-jerk expectations of an impending recession or price decline, and it often drives premature selling of risky holdings. Yet if you ask a fearful investor why they are selling, they usually won't say, "Because I'm afraid"; rather, they might cite negative economic events. Emotional investors are unaware that it is not facts that are driving their outlook, but perceptual distortions caused by feelings.

Affect is a word that broadly refers to emotional experience. Feelings, moods, and attitudes are all affects. Shortcuts in the thinking process due to feelings are functions of "the affect heuristic." A *heuristic* is a type of mental "short-cut," where rather than objectively reasoning through a decision, individuals choose based on a "hunch." The term *affect heuristic* was coined by Professor Paul Slovic.

Emotionally, the affect heuristic refers to the feeling "tags" that people place on complex judgments. For example, when asked about Google and IBM, an investor may feel (and subsequently think): "Google is good and exciting" or "IBM is old and boring." Their thoughts arise from internal emotional tags that are attached to each concept. These tags serve as simple and rapidly accessible judgments. The affect heuristic allows for quick decision-making under conditions of time-pressure and uncertainty. The affect heuristic refers to chronic, low-intensity emotional tags.

Strong anticipatory and reactive emotions alter judgment and guide decision making through a brain system that generates and monitors goal pursuit. A diffuse brain system called the *comparator* assesses whether one is making expected progress toward one's goals. When expectations of goal progress are exceeded, happiness arises. When expectations are not met, disappointment occurs. The comparator underlies most human motivation and behavior.

EXPECTATIONS AND THE COMPARATOR

The brain's comparator assesses one's actual goal progress against one's *expected* progress. When self-monitoring, it is where one stands *relative to expectations* that determines which emotions arise and how one will consider a strategy for closing the gap going forward. The comparator is a feedback system that maintains motivation.

The intensity of the feelings that arise in response to comparisons differ based on three characteristics: (1) the size of the discrepancy between expectations and reality, (2) one's conditioning (experience) with similar situations, and (3) any significant associations or memories. A little discrepancy between expectations and reality produces a small signal, while a larger difference gives rise to a stronger emotion, and thus a more powerful motivation. The comparator (see Figure 3.1) receives input from both the reward system (goal approach) and the loss avoidance system (goal avoidance).

Goal approach refers to the motivational actions of the reward system, driving individuals toward achieving desired and expected goals. Feelings related to elation, such as happiness, joy, euphoria, and contentment are generated when goal approach progress exceeds one's expectations. When goal approach is inadequate relative to one's expectations, feelings related to disappointment such as sadness, upset, discomfort, and depression arise.

	Goal Approach	Goal Avoidance
Positive Progress	ELATION	RELIEF
Negative Progress	DISAPPOINTMENT	ANXIETY

FIGURE 3.1 The brain's comparator generates emotional experience based on the difference between one's expectations and actual goal progress.
Source: Derived from Carver, C. S., and M. F. Scheier. 2001. "On the Structure of Behavioral Self-Regulation." In M. Boekaerts, P. Pintrich, and M. Zeidner (eds.), *Handbook of Self-Regulation*. New York: Academic Press, pp. 42–80.

Goal avoidance refers to the function of the loss system, which motivates individuals to avoid or escape dangerous circumstances. When loss avoidance is successful, feelings of relief occur. Feelings of anxiety, worry, concern, and nervousness arise when one is not avoiding dangers as well as anticipated.

Supporting the model of the comparator, neuroimaging shows that expected financial rewards activate the reward system less when they are received. When goal progress is equal to expectations, then no emotional reaction occurs.[1] However, both unexpected rewards and unexpected news that one is going to receive a reward are highly activating, because they both exceed expectations of goal progress.[2]

Interestingly, when news of an impending reward is received, but the expected reward never comes, then the brain will show inhibited activity. Specifically, there is decreased dopaminergic neuronal firing in the reward circuits at the precise time when the expected reward should have occurred.[3] Perhaps this is a neural representation of disappointment.

COUNTERFACTUAL COMPARISONS

Emotions often arise when one compares his or her life circumstances to those of others. Psychologists set up an experiment in which they clipped out the photos of Olympic medal winners' faces during the award ceremony at the Olympic Games. Strangers were then asked to rate the level of positive or negative emotion on the faces of the medal winners, without knowing which medal they had won. The researchers found that, as expected, gold medal winners expressed the highest level of positive feeling. Surprisingly, bronze medal winners had the second-highest level of positive emotion, while silver medalists came in third.[4] Why are silver medalists less happy than bronze medalists?

The Olympians were experiencing counterfactual comparisons. Bronze medalists make a downward comparison, due to a "cutoff effect," and they felt happy that they had earned a place on the winners' podium. Silver medalists made an upward comparison, and they felt slightly disappointed by what they saw—someone who performed better.

Counterfactual comparisons also affect how people feel about profits and losses. Professor Barbara Mellers at the University of California at Berkeley designed a gambling experiment to assess emotional reactions to losses (gains) if a larger loss (gain) had been avoided. Subjects were asked to play a 50–50 gamble. In one version, subjects would either win $8 or win $32 (each with 50 percent probability). In another gamble, subjects would either lose $8 or lose $32 dollars, again with 50 percent probability. The subjects had no choices to make, but they were asked to rate their feelings after seeing the results of the gamble.

Subjects reported feeling slightly positive when they lost $8 if they had avoided losing $32. When the subjects won $8, they reported slight dissatisfaction because the other outcome was to win $32. The subjects felt good about losing $8 if the gamble was in the "loss frame," and they felt bad about winning $8 in the "gain frame." Their comparison of the actual outcome to the gamble's expected value (in this experiment the expected values were $20 in the gain frame and –$20 in the loss frame) determined how they felt about the outcome.

This comparison phenomenon occurs throughout the business world, where measures of self-esteem and accomplishment are often made tangible. Silicon Valley billionaires may feel jealous of the size of each others' yachts, leading to a boom in the construction of ultra-luxury vessels as each tries to outdo the others. A nonbillionaire sailor may feel happy simply to be in the same marina as such beautiful boats.

Portfolio managers can also suffer from the comparison effect. When managers miss out on a market rally, then they can become disappointed that they are not achieving their expected performance and anxious about underperforming their benchmark (and their colleagues).

Sometimes the best-performing money managers are lauded with praise. Yet too often this praise is followed by underperformance. Why? Perhaps they lose the motivation that was driving them in the first place when they achieve their goals. When one measures success by comparing oneself to another (like the hare in Aesop's fable of the tortoise and the hare), then winning the comparison makes one feel happy, but also deprives one of the motivation to continue working hard. If one is outperforming expectations, then why continue to work so hard? Success can thus be a performance trap if it is measured by comparison to others or other external benchmarks.

Alternatively, when success is measured according to an internal benchmark, such as an improved decision process or clearer judgment, then it remains an enduring motivation and leads to long-term excellence. Portfolio managers who focus on refining their decision process, stoking their curiosity, and developing a sound investment philosophy are more likely to be long-term outperformers. Chapter 22 discusses this issue in more detail.

Via the comparator, emotions arise when feedback about one's expectations is received. The level of attachment to one's expectations (ego involvement) determines the strength of his or her emotional responses to goal-related feedback. This explains the popularity of Zen- and Buddhist-themed books for traders and investors. Teaching detachment from the outcome, not the process, is the goal of these books.

Outcome comparisons arouse emotions. Detaching oneself from outcomes reduces one's emotional arousal and emotion-driven judgment biases. People who practice Buddhist meditation may more easily perceive the quiet murmurs of intuition while calming the loud voices of excessive emotion. Unfortunately, because most investors *are* attached to the outcomes of their trading (e.g., because their bonuses depend on those outcomes), they are vulnerable to the influence of reactive emotions.

BELIEFS AND EXPECTATIONS: THE PLACEBO EFFECT

Sometimes expectations of successful goal progress create a self-fulfilling prophecy. A belief in one's ability to achieve a goal activates inner resources to support goal pursuit. Such success beliefs prompt supportive neurochemical shifts, which enhance mental and physical endurance. The placebo effect is an important example of how one's beliefs, desires, and expectations can align to change his or her state of being. When a physician gives a patient a medicine, it represents a belief that the patient will get better, which reinforces the patient's internal motivation to regain health.

Irving Kirsch, a psychologist at the University of Connecticut, analyzed 19 clinical trials of antidepressants and concluded that the expectation of improvement, not adjustments in brain chemistry, accounted for 75 percent of the drugs' effectiveness.[5] "The critical factor," says Kirsch, "is our beliefs about what's going to happen to us. You don't have to rely on drugs to see profound transformation." Between 35 and 75 percent of patients benefit from taking an inactive sugar pill in studies of new drugs. For centuries, Western medicine consisted of almost nothing but the placebo effect.[6]

While the placebo effect can improve health based on a belief in a positive outcome, a nocebo effect is an ill effect caused by the *suggestion* or *belief* that something is harmful. In both the placebo and nocebo effects, the expectation of an outcome creates a self-fulfilling prophecy.

In the markets, participants' expectations are rapidly priced in. Much of the art of investing is the ability to understand one's own expectations, the market's expectations, and the economic fundamentals. When the market's expectations deviate from underlying fundamentals, an expectation-related emotional shock is more likely going forward. For example, when Internet stocks with high price-to-earnings (P/E) ratios climbed far beyond reasonable expectations for growth, pricing in the market's overoptimistic expectations, it became clear that the differential between expectations and reality would eventually be narrowed as these stocks failed to keep up with investors' lofty goals.

A stock's P/E ratio generally reflects investors' growth expectations. Ironically, stocks with low ratios (and low expectations of growth) often outperform those with high ratios over time. This is one tenet of value investing (see Chapter 23). One reason why value strategies work well is that investors' low expectations are more frequently positively surprised, leading to increased positive emotion being associated with the low P/E stock, while high P/E stocks more often disappoint because the "good news" is already priced-in.

MAKING SENSE OF THE NEWS

Every day after the markets close, journalists interview traders looking for the *reasons* behind the day's market action. The proffered explanations are typically concrete and logical. Market moods are often explained in a cause-and-effect relationship with recent events. For example, following the October 19, 1987, crash in world stock markets, the BBC attributed the market plunge to rational news-driven panic: "Trading activity was driven down by growing fears of rising interest rates and a falling dollar. These were exacerbated by the news that the US had retaliated against Iranian attacks in the Gulf by bombarding an offshore oil rig."[7]

The BBC's logic is faulty because it attributes the panic entirely to recent price action and world events. News and price changes do influence investors' emotions, and there is a positive feedback effect from such events on how investors feel. Yet the depth of the panic did not reflect the intensity of the mildly negative news. Investors were already predisposed to panic on that October day.

In a post-note to the BBC article, the editors admit that, "The debate over the cause of the crash continued for many years after the event but economists have never been able to name a single factor that ushered in Black Monday."[8] In hindsight, the news-driven explanation for the crash was dismissed, and uncertainty was given its due.

Why does the BBC seek a single-factor explanation for the panic? Maybe because its readers are uncomfortable with uncertainty and the lack of control it implies. If you hear that investors panicked, you immediately want to know *why* they panicked. "Because they were afraid" isn't a satisfying explanation. "Because they were overconfident" is also inadequate. "Because interest rates rose" fits into a neat mental model.

One deficiency of causal reasoning in market commentary lies in the direct attribution of investor emotion (such as fear and greed) to recent news events. Yet sometimes bad news doesn't provoke fear or move the market, while other times it does. Why does some news cause fear at one time, but similar news provokes no reaction a few months later? How investors interpret news and events depends on their underlying emotional outlook. Optimistic investors see a sharp price plunge as an opportunity to "bargain shop" for cheap shares, while pessimists view it as evidence that the global financial system is collapsing.

Interestingly, there are periods of time when strongly negative news doesn't impact an optimistic market, and times when positive news cannot revive a bear market. During these periods, investors are succumbing, on a group level, to emotional defense mechanisms. Emotional defense mechanisms are a form of self-deception that distort investors' interpretations of news that contradicts their strongly held beliefs.

SELF-DECEPTION

While the media "rationalize" market events in hindsight, individual investors have their own emotional defenses and contortions of logic to contend with. Especially when under stress or when confronted with negative personal information, the brain has a tendency to cope by means of self-deception.

Emotional defense mechanisms are the process by which the mind minimizes the negative emotions that arise from an unfavorable comparison. Negative emotion can be attenuated through distorted logic (rationalization), avoidance (denial), believing an internal feeling is also being felt by another (projection), or blaming circumstances out of one's control (externalization). In an example of projection, when investors feel uncertain about the market's future direction, they often believe their own disorientation is a result of "market uncertainty." More often than not, the source of the uncertainty is in the investors themselves. One example of externalization is retail traders blaming their market losses on "manipulators" rather than taking responsibility for them. Defense mechanisms operate unconsciously, yet they have a profound effect on the ability to perceive reality and develop accurate expectations.

A few biases discussed in this book result from emotional defense mechanisms. The hindsight bias, rooted in memory, involves excessively optimistic assessments of one's past accomplishments, often fueling further misguided endeavors. The confirmation bias drives an active search for facts that support one's opinions and beliefs, while contradictory information is ignored. The projection bias involves misjudgments about one's future needs and desires, arising from one's belief that one's current emotional state is similar to what one will feel in the future.

EMOTIONAL DEFENSE MECHANISMS AND MOTIVATED REASONING

One defense mechanism, which is a type of rationalization, is called *motivated reasoning*. Motivated reasoning is thinking biased to produce preferred conclusions and support strongly held opinions.[9] Like other defense mechanisms, motivated reasoning can be viewed as a form of emotion regulation, in which the brain moves one toward minimizing negative and maximizing positive emotional states. Motivated reasoning as a strategy for emotion regulation was first described by the Viennese neurologist and father of psychoanalytic psychiatry, Sigmund Freud, who observed that people can adjust their thought processes to avoid negative feelings such as anxiety and guilt.

Professor Ditto at the University of California at Irvine set up an experiment to investigate motivated reasoning. He videotaped participants as they self-administered a bogus medical test. The subjects were coached that one result color on the test strip was favorable, while the other was an unfavorable (but unnoticeable) diagnosis. Subjects who received the unfavorable diagnosis required more time to accept the validity of the test result, were more likely to spontaneously recheck it, and believed that the test had lower accuracy than those with the favorable results.[10] Not only do people underestimate the likelihood of negative feedback about themselves, but even after they are presented with it, they tend not to believe it (and actively argue against it)!

Researchers at Emory University studied motivated reasoning in politically active individuals before the 2004 U.S. presidential election. They presented contradictory statements from each candidate, George W. Bush and John Kerry, to subjects while they were observed in an fMRI scanner. After a short delay, the contradictory statements were then excused by an exculpatory statement provided by the experimenters.

Initially, when subjects were presented with their favored candidate's contradictory statements, they demonstrated greater nucleus accumbens activation (an area associated with positive emotion and motivation in the reward system). The authors speculate that this activation occurred because "when confronted with information about their candidate that would logically lead them to an emotionally aversive conclusion, partisans arrived at an alternative [positive] conclusion." The nucleus accumbens activation represented the emotion of relief as the threatening information was reconciled with their positive opinion of the candidate. The subjects were experiencing a positive emotional reaction to the resolution of tension. According to the authors, the nucleus accumbens activation may represent the subjects' motivation to find excuses for obvious contradictions.[11] It's pleasurable for them to resolve the contradiction, so they are motivated to do it.

Interestingly, in the Emory study, "Motivated reasoning was not associated with increased neural activity in regions previously linked to 'cold' reasoning."[12] When using motivated reasoning, partisans are rewarded (with nucleus accumbens activation) by resolving the contradictory statements in their favor, and the brain regions associated with negative emotion (the insula and lateral orbital-frontal cortex) are quieted.[13] These results suggest that emotional defense mechanisms may be a neural process in which individuals are driven to find information or adopt beliefs that increase reward system activation (and reduce negative emotions).

People who engage in motivated reasoning perform more poorly on decision-making tasks than those who are less defensive about negative information. Researchers designed a card-sorting task where the fastest solutions were achieved by considering threatening information. "Participants who considered a Wason task rule that implied their own early death (Study 1) or the validity of a threatening stereotype (Study 2) vastly outperformed participants who considered nonthreatening or agreeable rules." In conclusion, "A skeptical mindset may help people avoid confirmation bias ... in everyday reasoning."[14] Actively confronting uncomfortable information led to superior decision making.

Courage is essential when facing uncomfortable negative emotions. During a bear market it is easy to think about the economy pessimistically—everyone is doing it. The goal in such a situation is to look for the positive aspects of the economy—the ones that are being overlooked. This requires balanced thinking, courage, and a willingness to look at all available information with equanimity. George Soros indicated that one of the keys to his acumen is the ability to nonjudgmentally think about why his investment reasoning process may be wrong (his theory of fallibility).

Understanding the effects of expectations, counterfactual comparisons, and emotional defenses on decision making is the first step toward improving performance. The next chapter will move back to a micro-level focus on the neurochemical origins of financial decision making.

CHAPTER 4

Neurochemistry

This Is Your Brain on Drugs

"Depressives have Prozac, worrywarts have Valium, gym rats have steroids, and overachievers have Adderall."

—Joshua Foer, Slate.com[1]

The chemical components of foods, herbs, medicines, and illicit drugs can profoundly alter financial decision making. Some substances, such as alcohol, are well understood in their effects on financial judgment—so much so that casinos offer alcohol free of charge to weaken gamblers' self-control. However, the behavioral effects of some foods and herbs are little known outside obscure medical journals.

Many pathological mood states (such as depression, mania, anxiety, and obsession), neurological conditions (such as Parkinson's disease and Alzheimer's disease), and impulse-control disorders (such as kleptomania, compulsive shopping, and pathological gambling) are known to affect financial decision making: depression is associated with risk aversion, mania with investing overconfidence, anxiety with "analysis paralysis," and compulsions with overtrading. Interestingly, the financial symptoms of these illnesses can be reduced by medications.

In this chapter, we examine how such chemicals change the perception, processing, and judgment of risk-related information. For investors, the financial effects of ingested chemicals is not an academic issue. With trillions of dollars exchanged daily on global markets, optimal judgment is crucial. A minor improvement in decision-making accuracy can reap millions of additional dollars in profit.

The chemicals discussed in this chapter alter neurotransmission. *Neurotransmission* refers to how signals travel between neurons. For most people, healthy levels of neurotransmitters such as dopamine, serotonin, norepinephrine, and stress hormones can be maintained using a balanced diet, a supportive social community, spontaneous play, regular exercise, and prayer or meditation. In some people, substance abuse, medications, overwhelming stress, or innate genetic propensities lead to chemical imbalances. It is for those states of imbalance that a fine-tuning of brain chemistry can have its most beneficial effects.

INTRODUCING THE NEUROTRANSMITTERS

What is the use of learning about neurotransmitters in a book about investing? Each individual is uniquely affected by financial ups and downs. They have different expectations and widely varying needs for stimulation, excitement, and security, and their differences are largely a product of their unique biology, including their neurochemistry.

Neurotransmitters are the molecules that carry communication signals between neurons in the brain. One's personal neurotransmitter endowment is based on (1) genetics and (2) past experiences. In this section, we'll look at correlations between neurotransmitters and those behaviors and emotions that are relevant to investors.

Some neurotransmitters are active in the cerebrospinal fluid, which bathes the brain's cells. Small fluctuations in their overall levels lead to profound alterations in the frequency and intensity of neural signaling.

Other neurochemicals are secreted from the ends of neurons, transmitting signals directly to downstream neurons. They act on specific receptors (see Figure 4.1). They fit into these receptors like a key fitting into a lock. These transmitters stimulate a fast electrical or slow genetic response in the second neuron (see Figure 4.2). Neurotransmitters are recycled from the synapse by the neurons that released them.

Very rarely is one neurotransmitter responsible for creating a particular emotion or behavior. Instead, there is vast network of neurons releasing many neurotransmitters, most stimulating or inhibiting the activities of each other. Furthermore, many neurotransmitters act on multiple receptor subtypes (there are currently at least 12 known serotonin[2] and five known dopamine receptor subtypes[3]), and there are currently 108 identified neurotransmitters. Five of those neurotransmitters act throughout most of the brain: Histamine, serotonin, dopamine, gamma-aminobutyric acid (GABA), and acetylcholine. Of those five, we'll be discussing serotonin

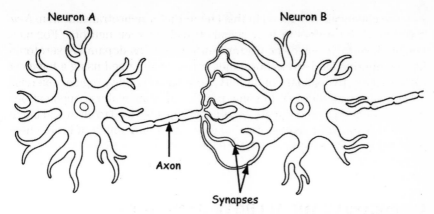

FIGURE 4.1 The principles of neurotransmission. Neuron A sends signals to Neuron B via its axon.

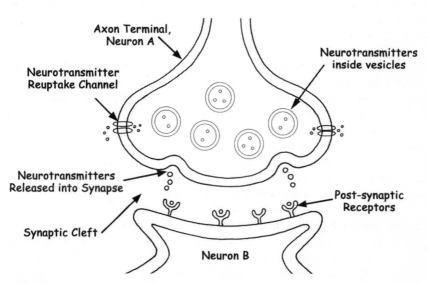

FIGURE 4.2 A synapse. Neuron A releases neurotransmitters into the synaptic cleft. When they fit into receptors on Neuron B, they activate ion channels and genetic processes, which represent the intended signal.

and dopamine in depth, and histamine, GABA, and acetylcholine in brief. Additionally, local actions of opioids, norepinephrine, stress hormones, and omega-3 fatty acids affect behavior and decision making. And if that weren't enough, common medications, street drugs, and foods also should be considered for their neural effects on judgment.

Serotonin

Since the introduction of the antidepressant Prozac, serotonin has become a household word. In 2005 in the United States, over 150 million prescriptions were filled for serotonin-increasing antidepressant medications.[4] Brain levels of serotonin are blamed for everyday maladies from premenstrual syndrome (PMS) to severe depression and suicide. Serotonin is a neurotransmitter, and when its concentration or receptor sensitivity changes, judgment is altered.

In the 1970s, researchers discovered that people who committed violent suicide appeared to have lower levels of brain serotonin than people who died by other means. Scientists then developed chemicals that blocked the presynaptic neurons' natural recycling of serotonin molecules. These serotonin reuptake inhibitor medications (SSRIs) delay the natural clearance of serotonin after it has been released into the synapse. SSRI medications are used for the treatment of several emotional and behavioral disorders. Fluoxetine (Prozac) is the prototype of these compounds.

Since the introduction of Prozac, several other SSRIs have been discovered and marketed by pharmaceutical companies, including brand-name drugs Paxil, Zoloft, Celexa, and Lexapro. SSRI medicines were found to decrease the severity of the symptoms of several disorders: Depression, anxiety, obsessive-compulsive disorder, post-traumatic stress disorder, and premenstrual dysphoric disorder, among others. Fortunately, the SSRIs have been a phenomenal success in reducing the symptoms of depression and anxiety worldwide. Antidepressants are the third largest selling class of drugs in the United States—$11 billion dollars per year. As of 2003, antidepressant use had been increasing at the rate of 17 percent per year. Other classes of antidepressants exist, but I'll focus only on SSRIs for simplicity's sake.

There are weak, but significant, genetic links between serotonin transporter genes and self-reported negative emotion. People who have two copies of the short-form (S allele) of the 5-HTT (serotonin transporter gene) are slightly more emotionally reactive and prone to depression than people with two of the long form (L alleles) of the gene.[5] Furthermore, individuals with two S alleles show greater amygdala activation (a proxy for negative emotion) on negative emotion-inducing functional magnetic resonance imaging (fMRI) tasks than those with two L alleles.[6]

Experimentally, brain serotonin levels can be decreased by removing an essential amino acid, a precursor building block of serotonin, from the diet. The amino acid tryptophan (Trp) is converted into serotonin in neurons. In order to manufacture serotonin, people must consume Trp in their diets, as their bodies have no way of synthesizing it *de novo*. When Trp is restricted from one's diet, brain levels of serotonin should fall (as should levels of melatonin—leading to an impaired sleep cycle). Trp is found as a component of dietary protein, and is particularly plentiful in chocolate, oats, bananas, dried dates, milk, yogurt, cottage cheese, fish, turkey, chicken, sesame, chickpeas, and peanuts. Genetic research shows that mutations in serotonin and tryptophan genes each lead to decreased serotonin effectiveness and increased emotional sensitivity.[7]

Dopamine

Dopamine was originally thought to be the "pleasure" chemical of the brain. A more accurate, modern view is that dopamine is involved in numerous cognitive and motor functions, including being the substrate of desire, motivation, attention, and learning. Illegal drug use is perhaps the most common public association with dopamine. All known addictive drugs act, in part, through dopamine release in the brain. In fact, the word *dope*, used to describe illegal psychotropic drugs, was derived from the word dopamine.

In a famous experiment in 1954, researchers placed electrodes into the "pleasure center" of rats' brains. When the rats were given the opportunity to press a lever to electrically stimulate this center (a dopamine way station) they did so compulsively. In fact, many of the rats died from exhaustion. The rats avoided food, water, and sex, preferring to self-stimulate with the electrode. Initially, dopamine received all the credit for the rats' addictive, pleasure-seeking behavior. Later research revealed that the electrodes were stimulating more than just the brain's dopamine supply. They were also triggering opiate and endorphin release in the brain.

Nevertheless, dopamine became known as a "pleasure chemical." Currently, the role of dopamine in the reward system is known to be threefold: (1) to motivate reward pursuit, (2) to enhance learning, and (3) to concentrate attention. Psychological effects of dopamine release in the reward system include improved mood and increased arousal. Dopamine makes people feel good, pay attention, and feel motivated. Dopamine is released in five large neural pathways, but we'll focus solely on one in this book—the reward system (see Figure 4.3).

Some illicit drugs have direct effects on dopamine release and reuptake. Cocaine and amphetamines are dopamine reuptake inhibitors. These substances prolong the release of dopamine and increase its

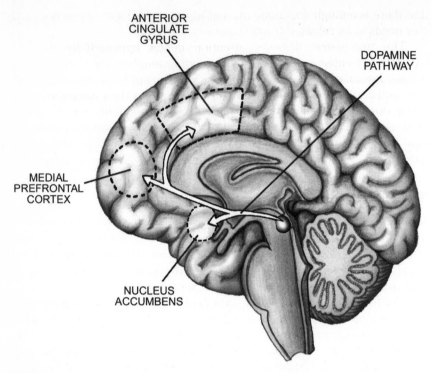

ANTERIOR
CINGULATE
GYRUS

DOPAMINE
PATHWAY

MEDIAL
PREFRONTAL
CORTEX

NUCLEUS
ACCUMBENS

FIGURE 4.3   The reward system begins as a nucleus of dopamine neurons in the midbrain and its axons travel throughout the limbic system and prefrontal cortex.

concentration in the synapses. Following long-term amphetamine or cocaine use, dopamine receptors are desensitized and one's capacity for pleasure and excitement are diminished (often leading to increased depression vulnerability).

Medications that affect dopamine receptors are typically either receptor blockers that prevent the transmission of dopamine signals (as in antipsychotic medications) or receptor activators. Dopamine receptor activators are used to stimulate movement and cognition in Parkinson's disease sufferers. Dopamine-activating medications can improve mood and, in high doses, trigger hypomania (a state of heightened confidence and risk taking), and even pathological gambling. In fact, pathological gambling is a frequently recognized side effect of a dopamine receptor (type 3)–stimulating medication called pramipexole (Mirapex). Other dopamine-stimulating medications such as bupropion (Zyban, Wellbutrin), are used as antidepressants and assist in smoking cessation. It is speculated that bupropion decreases nicotine craving by fooling the brain into believing that there is enough dopamine present in the reward system, so none further needs to be released through smoking a cigarette.

The psychiatric disorder attention deficit hyperactivity disorder (ADHD) is treated with dopamine-activating amphetamines (in a slow-release formulation). By increasing the brain's supply of dopamine, children and adults with ADHD are better able to focus their attention. Long-acting dopamine agents, such as time-release amphetamines and chewed or steeped coca leaves (cocaine releasing), increase stamina, focus, and confidence without as much danger of addiction as immediate-action varieties.

Norepinephrine

Norepinephrine was historically called *noradrenaline*. Norepinephrine is released during sudden stress. Norepinephrine itself stimulates the release of the stress hormone cortisol, described below. Norepinephrine causes the rush of tension that people feel when precipitously surprised, and it prepares the body for the "fight-or-flight" response.

During acute stress, people experience psychological symptoms of decreased attention span, hypervigilance, all-or-none (black-and-white) thinking, and increased focus. Physical signs of sudden stress include increased heart rate, sweating, flushed skin, and rapid breathing. Many of these symptoms are the direct result of norepinephrine release in the body.

Panic is a result of sudden norepinephrine release from a deep midbrain region called the locus ceruleus. It takes great cognitive control to prevent panicky feelings from escalating into catastrophic thinking and impulsive "fight-or-flight" behavior.

One physiologic change resulting from repeated norepinephrine release is high blood pressure. High blood pressure is common on Wall Street, and it may be a sign that investors are under excessive chronic stress. Common medications used to treat high blood pressure include beta-receptor blockers, such as propranolol. Beta-blockers act on a subtype of norepinephrine receptor. These medications can manage both the physical effects of chronic stress (high blood pressure) and the brain basis of acute anxiety.

According to researchers, propranolol alters risk/return perceptions in financial experiments: "Propranolol [a beta blocker] produced a selective change in volunteers' decision-making; namely, it significantly reduced the discrimination between large and small possible losses when the probability of winning was relatively low and the probability of losing was high."[8] That is, people who took propranolol saw less risk, but their perceptions of potential rewards were not affected. Propranolol is commonly prescribed to reduce "stage fright" during public speaking, and it is occasionally used in the treatment of other types of anxiety. Propranolol helps people take risk by decreasing their fear of large potential losses.

An investor I know commented that his beta-blocker medications, which he takes for high blood pressure, help him feel more clear-minded when judging risky investments. "Beta blockers help me be more rational and not get so afraid of risk..." He uses this effect to his advantage by changing his focus. While most investors are preoccupied with potential risks, he can objectively watch other investors: "I can see whether people are buying risky assets." He uses these observations to inform a contrarian investment strategy. On days he forgets to take his beta blockers, he feels more anxious and reactive to risk-related news.

Opiates

Opiates are also known as *endorphins*. Opiates induce positive feelings and reduce pain. Opiates are small proteins that act on several subtypes of receptors on the downstream neurons. When they act on the mu opiate receptor, they trigger the release of dopamine. For this reason, scientists believe that opiate-based street drugs, such as heroin and opium, are addictive via their stimulation of the mu receptor (and thus their ability to cause spikes in dopamine levels and increase endorphins).

For some investors the excitement of quick gains can become addictive. Pathological gamblers, whose disease is an addiction to the "thrill" of risk and opportunity, secrete a large surge of opiates in their limbic systems just before they gamble. Pathological gamblers are most likely to gamble if they are home alone, in the evening, thinking about their finances. These can be depressing circumstances, and endorphin release provides a quick "pick-me-up."

Stress Hormones

Most investors are familiar with financial stress. Stress hormones flood the body after sudden losses, leading to a number of effects on one's mind and brain. Stress hormones, such as cortisol, are designed to help us respond to sudden threats, and are longer-acting than other stress chemicals such as noprepinephrine, which was described above. See Chapter 10 for more details about the stress response.

After experiencing chronic stress, prolonged elevations of cortisol can cause depression, fatigue, weight gain, and short-term memory loss. Brain scans show that an area of the brain called the hippocampus (where short-term memories are stored) shrinks in size in people undergoing chronic stress. People who are high in the personality trait of neuroticism have decreased cortical volume (gray matter). This brain shrinkage may be caused by the chemical effects of chronic nervousness—oxidative neuronal damage from chronic elevations in stress hormones.

Caffeine

Caffeine is unusual in its diversity of neurological effects. Caffeine itself promotes vigilance in some people, but a sizable minority of caffeine users experience nervousness and irritability. Caffeine is consumed in coffee, black tea, green tea, energy drinks, sodas, and other beverages. While caffeine increases alertness, improves mood, and facilitates faster task performance in the short term, its role in financial decision making appears unstudied. Two notable findings have emerged regarding both high-dose caffeine use and green tea consumption.

Caffeine causes an increase in stress hormone levels. Lovallo (1996) found a 30 percent increase in cortisol levels one hour following a caffeine dose equivalent to three cups of coffee.[9] It is not clear whether other chemical compounds in coffee, besides caffeine, also have physiological or psychological effects. Many studies have demonstrated that there are no known adverse long-term effects of caffeine use. Caffeine's exacerbation of anxiety could feasibly increase financial risk perception, but no studies have documented that effect.

In a study of over 1,000 elderly Japanese, frequency of green tea intake was correlated with a more than 50 percent reduction in age-related cognitive impairment.[10] Coffee, black tea, and oolong tea consumption did not demonstrate such an effect. Research into the cognitive effects of caffeine consumption has yielded few notable results.

GABA, Acetylcholine, and Omega-3 Fatty Acids

GABA is found virtually everywhere in the brain. The GABA chemical is a small protein fragment (an amino acid derivative). GABA slows down electrical activity globally in the brain. Most anticonvulsant medications, used in epileptics for preventing seizures, increase the brain's saturation with GABA to reduce neural excitability (and thus prevent seizures). Additionally, many anticonvulsants are used as mood stabilizers, because they decrease the excitability and mood swings of bipolar disorder (historically called *manic-depressive illness*).

Some medications (such as benzodiazepines and alcohol) increase brain levels of GABA. Common benzodiazepine medications include Valium, Restoril, Klonopin, Ativan, and Xanax (at one time the most widely abused prescription medication). Alcohol is known as a central nervous system depressant due to its effect on GABA receptors. Alcohol may disinhibit some people's behavior because it relaxes frontal cortex control over impulses arising in the limbic system.

Of course, nothing is simple in neuroscience. There are two types (and further subtypes) of GABA receptors, and both benzodiazepines and alcohol have effects on one subtype that has been linked to their addictive properties. Medications that act on the other subtype exclusively are being marketed as nonaddictive sleeping medications.

Acetylcholine helps the brain to encode short-term memories. Drugs that *decrease* acetylcholine levels, including over-the-counter antihistamines such as diphenhydramine (Benadryl) and many common pesticides, impair short-term memory encoding and learning. Alzheimer's disease is characterized by memory loss and behavioral disinhibition. Most medications designed to treat Alzheimer's work by *increasing* brain acetylcholine levels, and thus strengthening one's recall.

Research has showed that people who eat more omega-3 fatty acids in their diets are happier, less impulsive, and healthier than others. Omega-3 fatty acids comprise 8 percent of the brain's fat content. Omega-3 fatty acids are most concentrated in cold-water fish oil (anchovies, herring, mackerel, sardines, salmon), seeds (flaxseed, pumpkin, and sunflower), nuts (almonds, Brazil nuts, peanuts, pine nuts, walnuts), and sea vegetables (arame, nori). Omega-3 fats improve neuron cell wall flexibility and enhance regeneration after damage.

Omega-3 fats compete with omega-6 fatty acids in a biochemical pathway called the *arachidonic acid pathway*. Corn oil has become the number one source of fatty acids in the Western diet. The high omega-6 content of corn oil outcompetes omega-3 fats in the arachidonic acid pathway and may lead to proinflammatory changes in the body that exacerbate atherosclerosis (heart disease) and autoimmune diseases. In one study with British prisoners, those given omega-3 and vitamin supplements had a 20 percent reduction in disciplinary infractions, presumably related to improved impulse control.[11] Omega-3s are inadequate in the modern Western diet, and fish-oil supplements have been found useful in various studies for improving mood, impulse control, immune function, and emotional stability. In general, investors may benefit from eating more fish or omega-3 supplements.

THE CHEMISTRY OF (FINANCIAL) MENTAL DISORDERS

The neurochemical origins of financial risk taking can be partially understood by an analysis of *disordered* financial behavior. Some mental illnesses, as defined by the diagnostic manual for mental health professionals, the *Diagnostic and Statistical Manual of Mental Disorders IV-TR* (2000), result in abnormal financial decision making. For example, acute mania is a pathological mood state typically characterized by euphoric mood and excessive risk taking (including with money). Some manic patients who have access to brokerage accounts will rapidly trade stocks, often until the account is drained. One Web site notes that some manic patients "go on shopping sprees, spend food money to buy lotto tickets, or try to make a killing in the stock market."[12] Ronald Fieve is a psychiatrist who has collected stories of manic and overconfident investors in his book *Moodswing*.[13]

Mania is caused by overactive dopamine and norepinephrine circuits in the brain, including in the reward system. Treatments for mania include antipsychotic medications that directly block or limit the neural stimulation caused by dopamine release. These treatments are often rejected by patients because they also dampen the euphoric high and peak confidence that accompany an acute manic episode.

The lifetime prevalence of pathological gambling disorder in the United States is less than 3.5 percent.[14] Recent neuroimaging studies demonstrate a hypoactivity of the reward circuitry in these individuals. Pathological gamblers are gambling to feel excitement, which they achieve by activating their uncommonly desensitized reward circuits.

While behavioral therapy is one of the best treatments for pathological gambling, some medications can significantly decrease the frequency of gambling. The most effective medication treatment for pathological gamblers is naltrexone (ReVia),[15] which is a mu opiate receptor *blocker*. In the reward system, mu opiate receptors stimulate dopamine release.[16] Blocking opiate receptors with naltrexone decreases dopamine release in the nucleus accumbens, which results in decreased subjective feelings of pleasure.[17] Gamblers taking naltrexone are not compelled to seek reward system stimulation through further gambling, possibly because they feel reduced pleasure from gambling.

Some subtypes of depression, such as "melancholic" depression, are characterized by decreased dopamine activity in the reward pathway. This reward system hypoactivity leads to several depression symptoms, including difficulty experiencing pleasure, excessive sleepiness, and (importantly for investors) chronic risk aversion. Bupropion (a weak dopamine stimulant) and amphetamines (a stronger stimulant) are often used to treat melancholic depression.

Anxiety also biases financial decisions. When pathological, anxiety is characterized by exaggerated risk perception and hypervigilance. When mild, anxiety may slightly increase individual risk taking (be aware that moderate levels of stress prompt dopamine secretion), and it is often noted in the media that the markets climb a "wall of worry" when investors are nervous. At high levels, anxiety gives way to panic selling as investors run for safety. For an individual investor, a number of factors influence whether panic is triggered, including one's anxiety-coping strategies, past losses, personality style, and general risk sensitivity.

Two mental disorders on the obsessive-compulsive spectrum merit discussion. Compulsive shopping disorder (CSD) is currently assumed to be a subtype of the obsessive-compulsive disorders. Moderately successful treatment of compulsive shopping can be achieved with the use of an SSRI antidepressant (citalopram).[18] The disorder of hoarding, wherein sufferers accumulate excessive quantities of one type of good or asset, is also considered a subtype of obsessive-compulsive disorder. Currently, only behavioral and psychotherapy approaches have shown success in the treatment of hoarding.[19] While CSD sufferers report tension relief as a result of purchasing, hoarders have a different problem. Hoarders are unable to get rid of items they have already collected.

THE NEUROCHEMISTRY OF FINANCIAL PERFORMANCE

The use of chemicals to enhance performance is controversial. Professional athletes, such as the baseball player Barry Bonds, have been castigated by the media for using steroid precursors to improve their baseball statistics. Lance Armstrong's teammate Floyd Landis yielded his 2006 Tour de France title following artificial testosterone use. The list of athletes discredited for using performance-enhancing chemicals is long.

As opposed to physical performance, decision making cannot be easily improved with chemicals. Nevertheless, caffeine and alcohol are two of the most widely used mind-altering substances in the world, largely due to their cognitive effects. This section of the chapter suggests that cognitive performance can be improved with certain medications, foods, and illicit substances, but there are no "easy" fixes.

It is currently considered unethical to use medications to enhance mental performance. Such practice has been dubbed "cosmetic psychopharmacology." I have not done this in my psychiatry practice. Yet the use of substances to improve cognitive performance is already occurring.

The U.S. Air Force gives its pilots "go pills" (time-release amphetamines) to improve their stamina during long flights. However, amphetamines have many potential side effects (including paranoia and anxiety) and are of unknown benefit in dynamic thinking exercises. "Go pills" were investigated as the possible cause of a friendly fire incident in Afghanistan, in which Canadian soldiers were bombed by an American pilot returning from a 10-hour mission. The pilot believed he was under attack from the ground, and he became impatient while awaiting target clearance from his operations base.

As many as 20 percent of college students report having used amphetamines to help them study.[20] The consequences of this type of abuse can be tragic. My psychiatrist colleagues have treated Stanford undergraduates in the psychiatric emergency room who became psychotic after inadvertently overdosing on Ritalin and Adderall (amphetamine derivatives used to treat ADHD), which they had been using to improve their stamina during final exams.

One nationally known poker player claims that a time-release amphetamine-derived medication (Adderall) helped him win millions of dollars in tournaments. "With Adderall in my system, I am like an information sponge, able to process data from several players at once while considering my next action."[21] The author speculates that it is the increased concentration, wakefulness, and stamina promoted by amphetamines that aids poker playing, especially at the end of a long tournament day. In his case, where the goal is short term and the benefits are clear, amphetamines may improve financial performance.

A new stimulant medication called modafinil has less serious side effects than amphetamines and is nonaddictive. I have known traders who took a low dose of modafinil (Provigil) for ensuring alertness during the trading day, but the results were unclear.

One psychiatrist I met believes that modulation of medications may help some traders perform better. He mentioned that a trader patient of his takes a lower-than-therapeutic dose of lithium for his bipolar disorder. This patient is a currency trader, and both he and his boss want him alert overnight to watch world markets and incoming news. When taking too much lithium, he was merely "average" in his speed and ability, and he slept eight hours per night. When not taking lithium, he quickly became hypomanic—he took too much risk and traded too often. So he, his boss, and the psychiatrist had worked out a system for preventing emotional extremes by taking a low dose of lithium. A low level of adaptive traits remained—a decreased need for sleep, high energy, self-confidence, and risk seeking. These symptoms were present for the 16- to 20-hour workday of this currency trader, and he appreciated the benefits to his trading performance.

SEROTONIN AND MARKET BUBBLES

An article written by psychiatrist Randolph Nesse in February 2000 was headlined "Is This Market on Prozac?" The article noted that prescriptions for psychoactive drugs increased from 131 million in 1988 to 233 million in 1998. The author went on to speculate, "I would not be surprised to learn that one in four large investors has used some kind of mood-altering drug."[22] Nesse remarked that some of his patients on SSRI medications "report that they become far less cautious than they were before, worrying too little about real dangers." He wondered whether the clear disregard for risk among many investors of the time could in part be attributed to the common use of antidepressant medications.

Some executives refer to Prozac as the "Teflon medicine" because it allows them to look past perceived threats, decide quickly without ruminating, and remain more optimistic during stress. In the best-selling book *Listening to Prozac*, psychiatrist Peter Kramer frets about the potential use of SSRI antidepressants as "steroids for the business Olympics."[23]

Professor Brian Knutson at Stanford University gave normal subjects therapeutic doses of the antidepressant paroxetine (an SSRI). Knutson's subjects experienced a reduction in threat perception and an increase in affiliative behaviors.[24] In another study, subjects who were administered the SSRI medication citalopram showed decreased amygdala (fear-related) activations on fMRI.[25] These characteristics—decreased threat perception and increased social affiliation—mirror the blind optimism and herding of excessively bullish investors. It is as if bubble investors have partial deactivation of their brains' loss-avoidance systems.

Robert Rogers at Oxford University has performed several studies using Trp depletion to decrease brain serotonin levels. Rogers found that Trp depletion led to an inability to attend to the size of a potential gain—Trp-depleted subjects poorly differentiated between large or small gain sizes. For investors, Trp depletion (and low serotonin levels) might impair the distinguishing of large from small potential payoffs, leading to overtrading for smaller stakes.

Other researchers have found that Trp depletion causes the time discounting curve to become steeper, so investors prefer small immediate rewards over larger, later rewards when their serotonin levels are low. This suggests that low serotonin levels (due to Trp depletion) may, in fact, prompt impulsive reward pursuit and overtrading.

From an evolutionary perspective, the relationship between low serotonin and overtrading makes sense. Investors who have suffered a series of losses want to change their circumstances, if only to get out of the hole they've found themselves in. They are willing to accept any possible investment to get out of their deficit, impulsively pursuing small possible gains.

One patient in treatment for depression kept all of her assets in cash. Because of her fears of taking financial risk, she was reluctant to invest even in U.S. government bonds. She was concerned that the

U.S. government might default on payments to bondholders. While a U.S. government default is a risk, it is a very small risk. She was paralyzed by her exaggerated risk perception, unable to realistically perceive the risks and rewards of various investment options open to her. Her thought distortions were directly related to her depressive illness and its neurochemical basis—low serotonin. Successful treatment with SSRI antidepressant medications was followed by improved mood and small, tentative purchases of bonds and mutual funds.

RECREATIONAL DRUGS AND ALCOHOL

Numerous drugs of abuse alter financial decision making. In general, drugs such as THC (tetrahydrocannabinol), alcohol, and benzodiazepines have similar effects on risk taking. THC, the active ingredient in marijuana, biases financial decisions. When given a choice between a certain but low-value positive expected value option ($0.01) or a zero expected value option with high return variability, THC-intoxicated subjects preferred the risky option significantly more than control subjects who had been administered a placebo. If they lost money after selecting the risky option, THC-intoxicated subjects were significantly more likely to persist with the risky selection, while controls were more likely to move to the positive expected value option.[26]

Alcohol similarly promotes needless risk-taking behavior. Alcohol-intoxicated subjects, in the same experimental task described immediately above, were more likely to choose the risky option than controls.[27] Researchers have found that alcohol use correlates with decreased loss discrimination. That is, people don't attend to the difference between large and small losses when intoxicated with alcohol. This is the same effect observed with propranolol and is likely a result of alcohol's action on the benzodiazepine receptors, which reduces risk perception.[28]

Benzodiazepines increase preference for high potential rewards, especially when odds are low, and they increase overall risk taking. In one experiment, a dose of the benzodiazepine Valium increased the number of points wagered in a risk-taking task only in those trials with the lowest odds of winning but the highest potential payoff.[29] In the risk-taking task used for both THC and alcohol experiments above, administration of the benzodiazepine alprazolam produced increased selection of the zero-expected value risky option. Importantly, there is evidence that whether an individual is vulnerable to the behavioral effects of drugs of abuse depends on their personality style: "Risk-seeking personality traits may be predictive of acute drug effects on risk-taking behavior."[30]

Alcohol

Alcohol, in small doses, is disinhibiting. It decreases anxiety and makes drinkers feel more sociable and confident. Many investors drink at the end of the workday to "shake off" the tension. The social contact involved in drinking is positive, and drinking after work helps investors chemically drown out the nervous feedback from their overstimulated fear circuits. Unfortunately, alcohol use can easily lead to unexpected longer-term decision-making problems.

The problems with alcohol use by investors may be threefold. Alcohol can be addictive and tolerance promoting, and can lead to subtle long-term performance decrements. Alcohol allows investors to avoid dealing with one of the core problems in their investing, which is often anxiety about financial uncertainty. The short-term withdrawal effect (the next-day hangover) of alcohol is characterized by fatigue, mental dullness, and a lack of creativity and productivity. Investors with a hangover have endured a night of impaired sleep and as a result they have impaired learning and impulse control, and are delayed in their response times compared to the usual.

Cocaine

Cocaine and amphetamines have been used historically as energy boosters. South American indigenous people in the Andes often chew coca leaves or drink coca-leaf tea for extra energy and stamina when doing high-altitude physical labor. Yet in rapid-acting forms (such as powder or rock), cocaine causes a rapid spike in dopamine levels and is very addictive.

Cocaine addiction appears to be more likely among those of lower social status. Monkeys who are higher in the social dominance hierarchy have higher levels of brain dopamine and do not become addicted to cocaine as easily as those who are lower in the hierarchy.[31] Presumably, higher-status monkeys do not need external boosting of dopamine to feel good—they already produce enough dopamine internally to feel confident and strong.[32] Investors with low self-esteem, and those who perceive themselves as being less successful than their colleagues, are more likely to abuse cocaine. Cocaine abuse was rumored to be widespread on the floors of major American stock exchanges, especially in the 1980s and 1990s. Cocaine was probably used by floor traders to replenish or boost dopamine in their exhausted reward systems, effectively boosting their confidence and motivation during the workday.

The above studies illustrate that common chemical compounds, both medications and drugs of abuse, can have profound effects on an individual's risky choice. In particular, frequently prescribed antidepressants and anxiolytics (SSRIs) appear to decrease threat perception and increase social affiliation. Time-release amphetamines increase alertness and smooth the reward system's reactivity to potential financial gains. Common blood pressure medications (beta blockers) decreased aversion to potential financial losses.

The point of all this information on neurochemistry is that many commonly ingested substances alter neurotransmission and financial judgment. Investors should be aware of how their chemical intake may be affecting their financial decision making.

In Part II of this book, the effects of emotions on financial judgment will be described in detail.

Feelings and Finances

CHAPTER 5

Intuition

The Power of Listening to Your Gut

"Buy to the sound of cannons, sell to the sound of trumpets."
—Attributed to British banker Nathan Mayer
Rothschild, during the Napoleonic wars[1]

An investment banker friend of mine is no stranger to high stakes. He frequently negotiates deals worth hundreds of millions of dollars with multiple competing parties.

In early 2006, he was negotiating to purchase a small mining company for a client. A deal had been hashed out at terms that were very favorable for his team, and the consensus was to close the deal the following day. For $220 million his client would take control of significant land holdings with mineral rights, an operating metals mine, and a small prospecting division.

The night before the deal was to close, my friend couldn't sleep—not even a wink. Initially, he didn't know why, but by 3 A.M. he had an inkling. Early in the morning, he called the other party and canceled the deal.

Initially, his colleagues were incredulous. The deal had been agreed. How could he renege without consulting them?

He asked them to keep their cool. He had a hunch. He requested that they make no phone calls and discuss nothing with their counterparties. "Zip it," he told them.

Twenty-four hours later, the seller's broker called back offering a 10 percent discount. The new papers were drawn up (with a new price of $198 million). He got a good night's sleep the night before the signing, and the deal was closed the next day.

How did he know that they hadn't been getting the best possible terms? "I can't say," he told me. "When these things happen, I don't think about it; I just go with it." He explained, "I knew that if I wasn't sleeping the night before the deal, then I had to call it off. I wanted us to keep our heads down for a few days until we heard from the other side. And the other side gave in . . . like I suppose I figured they would."

He had a hunch he wasn't getting the best deal for his clients. His body told him something was wrong before he was consciously aware of what it was. By listening to his physical sensations (and his inability to sleep), he was able to infer an optimal strategy as events developed. He made an intuitive decision—one that he couldn't rationally explain—that turned out to be extremely profitable.

ANALYSIS AND INTUITION

Nobel Prize winner Daniel Kahneman postulates that there are two broad neural systems underlying decision making: the analytical and the intuitive. Analytical judgment is primarily logic based, while the intuitive system is rapid and feeling based.

This chapter describes the process of optimal intuitive decision making in market-like conditions—risky, uncertain, and with performance expectations and time pressure. If the mind is well managed, these conditions are optimal for the flourishing of intuitive decision making.

Intuitive decisions rely on "gut" knowledge. This chapter demonstrates how listening to one's "gut" has tremendous advantages (and potential dangers) for market participants.

Ancient Greek conceptualizations of emotion assumed that feelings should be tightly controlled, lest they disturb rational thought and deliberation. Even today, it's tempting to speculate that if everyone were fully rational and analytical, the world would be better off. This idea conjures Mr. Spock, the character in the *Star Trek* television series who was half Vulcan. The creator of *Star Trek*, Gene Roddenberry, designed Vulcans as an advanced humanoid race who struggled mightily to make decisions based solely on logic.

In the *Star Trek* series, Vulcans suppressed emotional influences by living lives of rigid self-control. Vulcans relied on meditative techniques and mental discipline to keep feelings from influencing their judgment. But like humans, Vulcans could not entirely escape emotions in order to live by logic, so they established elaborate rituals to channel and safely release emotional and sexual energies. Vulcans periodically returned to their home planet for a well-guarded annual rite in which they yielded to an all-consuming catharsis of emotion. Additionally, episodes of *Star Trek* routinely ended with a conciliatory vindication of human emotion as opposed to cold Vulcan logic.[2]

So how do humans integrate "messy" emotions and "soft" intuitions into a rational decision-making process?

INVESTMENT PRACTICE

Traditional investment theory assumes that people use reasoning and objective analysis during decision making. According to traditional theory, investors slowly and mechanically judge potential outcomes, weighing their probabilities and their potential gains or losses, to arrive at a *rational* analytical decision. They arrive at a choice after a series of calculations—a "risk-reward analysis." Yet, in a world where ultimate outcomes are uncertain and volatility can arise unexpectedly, investment practice is not as rational as theory suggests. Currently, however, there is no single coherent psychological theory to counter the assumption of investor rationality.

What I see in my coaching practice is professional investors following primarily reason-based judgment—with an important dose of intuition (gut feel) injected just before the actual choice. Many of the best portfolio managers initially perform a rational analysis of known facts and figures. They gather information from corporate management, customers, suppliers, employees, and stock analysts. But in order to consolidate all this complex information into a single decision, they use an intuitive process. They sum up all this information by asking themselves, "Does the investment 'feel' right?" More often than not, intuitive "gut feelings" guide some aspects of the research and determine the ultimate buy or sell decision.

Fortunately, the first part of the investment decision-making process can be controlled. Many investors define the indicators they are looking for in advance (called their "investment philosophy"). Once they collect the quantitative information, they perform a disciplined and objective analysis of the facts at hand. Most beginning investors fix their attention on one or two positive or negative factors and make their decision. But often the best investors go one step further. The best pay attention to and are guided by their feelings about certain aspects of an investment. They may be uncomfortable with cash flow volatility or off–balance-sheet transactions, so they ask their analysts to dig deeper. They may have a positive "aha" feeling about the potential of a company's products. Perhaps they feel that most analysts' forecasts are too cautious, and they use that information to weigh in favor of buy decision. However intuition comes into play, it is far more widespread in investment practice than most theorists concede.

WHAT DOES YOUR "GUT" TELL YOU?

The human senses relay about 10 million times more pieces of information per second to the brain than can be consciously perceived.[3] How can the brain possibly process all this data? The brain uses simplifications and shortcuts to facilitate information processing.

The vast majority of our daily decisions are *intuitive* decisions—decisions made rapidly, automatically, and beneath conscious awareness. Intuition and "gut feel" often underlie some of our most consequential decisions. Intuitive decision making is honed unconsciously, through experience, and it is the foundation of more than 90 percent of all decisions.

Too often, deliberately keeping track of intuition doesn't work. Part of its grace and simplicity is that it operates subconsciously, not accepting input from higher cognitive levels. Thinking about a decision brings the process into conscious awareness, and such conscious deliberation drowns out important aspects of the fragile intuitive process. Without practice, if one consciously *tries* to tap intuition when making a decision, he or she usually fails.

In business, deciding from "the gut," especially for experts, is a common way of handling decisions with uncertain outcomes. "The gut" refers to an experienced and intuitive consideration of the current situation. This intuitive "hunch" comes to attention as a feeling, as in, "I've got a good feeling about this." This feeling represents a subconscious emotional process that is manifested in physical sensations.

Some business leaders credit their style of intuitive "gut" decisions with their success. Former General Electric CEO Jack Welch even entitled his autobiography *Jack: Straight from the Gut*. Outcomes in the business world are high stakes and inherently uncertain, an ideal environment for integrating intuition and expert judgment.

Some experienced investors, such as George Soros, are intuitively tuned into subtle physical cues. George Soros is a Wall Street icon for his outstanding long-term performance. Anyone who had invested $1,000 in his Quantum Fund when it opened in 1969 would have realized a cumulative 30-plus-percent annual return (about $4 million) by the turn of the century.

Soros occasionally uses the physical cues of intuitive hunches to inform his strategy. George Soros's son remarked that "the reason he changes his position on the market or whatever is because his back starts killing him. It has nothing to do with reason. He literally goes into a spasm, and it's this early warning sign."[4] Soros can observe his physical sensations to aid his decision making, much as other experts use "gut feeling" or "hunches."

Soros generates investment plans by integrating both his intellectual theory of market action and his somatic (bodily) sensations. "According to Soros, his theory informs his decisions, and his body gives him the signals.

The making of a self-reinforcing trend brings water to his mouth. The need for a portfolio shift makes his back hurt. His body 'knows' he needs to take action, or to take careful note of a situation before his intellect can grasp it."[5] Soros is tuned in to subtle somatic sensations reflecting potential risk and opportunity. Importantly, he does not operate solely based on intuition; rather, he utilizes his physical sensations to complement an analytical assessment of market price action.

Trading coach Doug Hirschhorn administered the Myers-Briggs, a common personality test, to a large group of portfolio managers. The personality trait Intuition (N) was present in 80 percent of portfolio managers and 25 percent of analysts. This differential suggests a separate skill set. Portfolio managers were more likely than analysts to follow an intuitive decision process rather than relying on explicit data.[6]

Intuition isn't always easy to follow. Sometimes strong emotions drown out gut feelings. Several factors generate emotions that overwhelm intuition. Feelings that result from remembering, experiencing, or anticipating large gains or losses will negatively bias intuitive judgment. Any environments in which one is under significant time, social, or performance pressure (such as within contentious investment committees or when considering one's performance at the end of the fiscal year), can easily bias intuitive judgment. Fortunately, quiet reflection can open one up to the intuitive consideration of complex information.

LISTENING WITHOUT THINKING

As you'll see in the example below, detachment from memories, expectations, and current pressures facilitates the unfolding of the intuitive process. Here's how one top hedge fund manager described his investment decision process. The following are my notes from our talk.

Peterson: How do you know what to invest in?

Investor: I just feel a lot of information. I gather it all up and then I sit on it. Like an information sponge most of the time—really, like a sponge. I'm not trying to do anything with it [the information]. I'm not looking for answers, I just sit on it, and when the time is right, it comes to me. I'll feel a little tickle that tells me to pay attention to something, like a tiny 'look at that' kind of feeling. I don't know what I'm looking at exactly, but I just pay some more attention to it.

Peterson: And how does that translate into action?

Investor: Often without knowing why, I start planning deals. It may be to buy shares in an Indian refrigerator manufacturer, or a pipeline, or mineral rights in Peru. Who knows what the inkling will lead to? But that's how it works. It's like I step out of the way. I can't have distractions, I can't think too much about it, or explain how I do it. I just get into the zone and I don't get out of it until I do what the feeling is compelling me to do.

Peterson: Those are pretty diverse examples. Where do you get your "intelligence" about so many different industries?

Investor: The information I take in is workplace stuff—strategic and financial information that my traders and analysts bring me or that I see over the terminals. Nothing more than what everyone else is seeing, except that I'll go, or send someone to go, to get deeper information when I feel the need for it.

This investor is acting like an information filter, allowing his intuition and experience to identify patterns and setups that other investors have overlooked or not yet identified. If he were to consciously think about the information he is looking for in detail, then he would lose the ability to be "in the zone." Notice that he's maintaining mental equanimity during this process. He's not recalling past deals or thinking about how much money he might make or lose. Rather, he pursues his inkling with open curiosity, which leads to a general idea, which directs him to an opportunity.

INTUITION AND EMOTION IN INVESTING

> *"I had no business to think because my business is to trade—that is, to stick to the facts before me and not to what I think other people ought to do."*
> —Edwin LeFevre[7]

In simple decision-making situations, conscious thought usually leads to better decisions, but after a certain level of informational complexity is reached, the quality of conscious choices falls below that of affective choice. Feelings provide mental shortcuts, allowing people to quickly and easily judge the "rightness" and "wrongness" of complex scenarios.[8] According to Professor Paul Slovic's theory of the "affect heuristic," briefly introduced in Chapter 3, decision makers usually rely on affective (emotional) meaning to guide judgments and decisions in everyday life. All of the images in a person's mind are tagged to varying degrees with affect. The "affect pool" contains all tags that are consciously or unconsciously associated with the images. Since affective information remains readily available in a pool of tags, it can generate quick and easy reactions to a host of familiar stimuli.

Emotion, via the affect heuristic, can act as information to help form judgments. It can serve as a generalization shortcut, allowing people to rapidly sort through and integrate multiple pieces of related information. Affect can also help people focus on salient or relevant aspects of a decision. Finally, affect is motivating, leading to faster and more determined decisions.[9, 10]

Affect is thus an essential aspect of daily decision making, where it supports the subtle processes of intuition. Unfortunately, when affect is biased by "special interests" (strong emotions generated by the brain's comparator), its effects on financial decisions can be problematic. When emotions are powerful, especially when produced in anticipation of, recall of, or reaction to external events, they can overwhelm intuition and negatively bias judgment and decision making. In order to distinguish which affects (emotions) are helpful and which are potentially biasing, it's useful to turn to the insights of psychologists who study emotional intelligence.

EMOTIONAL INTELLIGENCE

In order to harness the power of gut feel while avoiding indulgence of emotional "special interests," an aptitude called "emotional intelligence" can be developed. The study of "emotional intelligence," pioneered by business psychologist Daniel Goleman, arises out of evidence that emotional competencies are more conducive to business success than purely intellectual IQ.

According to Goleman, emotional intelligence refers to "the capacity for recognizing our own feelings and those of others, for motivating ourselves, and for managing emotions well in ourselves and in our relationships."[11] There are five basic emotional competencies that together comprise one's emotional intelligence: (1) self-awareness, (2) self-regulation, (3) motivation, (4) empathy, and (5) social skills. In a study of executives at 40 companies, strength in emotional intelligence was more prevalent among "stars" on the job (53 percent) than intellectual intelligence (IQ) or subject expertise (27 percent).[12] It is possible that high emotional intelligence correlates with investing success as well, but I am not aware of any scientific studies on that issue.

SUBLIMINAL EMOTION

One of the skills essential to emotional intelligence is self-awareness. If people are not aware of what they are feeling, then they cannot distinguish helpful gut feel from biasing emotions. Such subconscious emotions can be dangerous because they alter how people think about financial opportunities and risks. Furthermore, self-awareness of such emotions requires a high level of expertise.

Researchers have found that emotions induced by one event will color how we think about other, unrelated situations. Emotions induced by watching movies, enjoying sunny weather, or experiencing stressful exams have been shown to influence judgments of unrelated topics and objects.[13] For example, in one experiment, participants who read happy newspaper articles subsequently made more optimistic judgments about risk than those who had just read sad articles.[14]

Perhaps frighteningly, there is solid scientific evidence that people are often not consciously aware of what they are feeling or its likely effect on their judgment. Professors Winkielman and Berridge, at the University of California–San Diego and the University of Michigan, respectively, performed a series of experiments in which participants were subliminally presented with a happy face or an angry face and then asked to pour, consume, and value a beverage. "Subliminal smiles caused thirsty participants to pour and consume more beverage (Study 1) and increased their willingness to pay and their wanting more beverage (Study 2). Subliminal frowns had the opposite effect." Participants reported no change in their subjective feelings resulting from the subliminal smiling or frowning faces.[15] Yet even though they felt no different after seeing the faces, their financial behavior changed.

STIRRING THE UNCONSCIOUS

In a study of subliminal emotion during financially risky decisions, Professors Trujillo and Knutson at Stanford University designed a study in which subjects decided among risky options after viewing a photo of an emotional face.[16] The faces were expressing prominent emotions such as fear, anger, or happiness. Participants were asked to name the gender of the face before proceeding on to the gamble, to ensure that they had been paying attention, though they were not warned that the facial expression might affect their decision making.

The researchers ran three experiments in which subjects chose between different risky financial options. Interestingly, but unsurprisingly, participants were most likely to select the riskiest option after viewing happy faces. However, after an angry or fearful face was viewed, participants were more likely to choose the safe option. There were no differences between effects of anger versus fear. However, viewing an angry face decreased the likelihood of investing on the subsequent trial.

Importantly, the faces' emotional expressions influenced participants' decisions regardless of their performance feedback (how much money they made or lost). In general, positive expressions (happiness) increased risk taking, while negative expressions (anger and fear) decreased it. Furthermore, happy faces increased risk taking (when measured in terms of payoff variability), even when there was no advantage to be gained by taking more risk. In conclusion, the researchers speculated that transient subconscious activations of the brain's fear (amygdala), anger, and happiness (nucleus accumbens) processing centers biased the ability of the cortex to correctly value risky gambles.

Investors are probably affected by other sources of unconscious emotions, besides faces. The workplace mood, the tone of business news broadcasts, the content of the morning newspaper, and one's home emotional environment may all be factors that unconsciously bias how one approaches risky decisions. Even if the influence of these factors is small, a 1 percent alteration in risky choice can lead to a large cumulative gain or loss over years.

This chapter has emphasized the value of intuition in expert investment decision making. Yet the pitfalls of overthinking, strong emotional biases, and subliminal emotions render intuitive judgment excessively biased for most investors. Experience (gained through honest appraisals and rapid feedback) and emotional intelligence (specifically self-awareness) are the remedies that excellent investors use to fortify the intuitive process. The emotions that bias intuition lead to characteristic financial mistakes. The next chapter will describe in detail the specific effects of emotions on financial judgment.

CHAPTER 6

Money Emotions

Clouded Judgment

Sometimes at social events, if I mention my occupation as "investment psychologist," people are curious. Often, their questions are market related ("Where do you see the market in 12 months?"), and sometimes they are personal ("Why is my spouse so hopeless with a budget?").

In early 2006, when Jodie heard my profession at a dinner, she asked me defensively, "Did someone send you to talk to me?"

"Uh, no," I answered.

"Are you sure?" She said, eyeing me sideways.

"Er, yeah." I was perplexed.

"Come over here. I need to talk to you." She motioned me to a quiet corner of the room.

"Um, okay," I said.

After some pleasant conversation, Jodie opened up. She told me that she'd been having nightmares about poor old people living under bridges. In many dreams she herself was destitute. When she saw commercials on TV about happy older couples in retirement, tears would come to her eyes. This had been happening for about a year, and she didn't really understand it, but she thought she might have a clue.

"What clue is that?" I asked.

"Well, I used to work at a major investment bank as a broker in the late 1990s. We were responsible for getting retirees to buy recommended investments in their private accounts. When I started in mid-1998, everyone wanted to buy Internet stocks. We'd call clients, offer a few shares in an IPO [initial public offering], and recommend some other stocks as well. They'd usually follow our advice without questioning, and they'd be much better off for it. In late 1999, we started offering these Internet mutual funds, and we would charge two points on the buy, in addition to our regular commissions."

"Wow, that's huge," I muttered.

"Yeah, my boss told us that we'd be fired if we couldn't sell the fund to 80 percent of our client accounts. It was my job to persuade dozens of mostly older retirees to buy shares in the Internet fund. Some of them wanted to put all their money in it, and I let them."

"What happened?"

"I left in early 2001, when clients were calling me wondering why their accounts were shrinking. I told them to hold on, that things would recover. . . ." She paused. "I feel so rotten now. People really trusted me." Jodie took a sip of her drink and her eyes inspected the faces in the room, as if looking for someone else to talk to.

It didn't seem like a fitting end for her story. "Then what?" I persisted.

"I got my real estate license, and now I'm a real estate agent."

"No, I mean what happened with the clients and the funds?"

"I don't know, I imagine the department was shut down. I think some of the clients lost most of their retirement savings. Right before I left, one of the clients told me that he was going to have to postpone retirement 10 years based on what I'd sold him." She studied her shoes.

"Have you talked about this before?"

"No, not really—why would I?"

"It seems like the whole episode scarred you pretty deeply."

She thought for a moment and then said matter-of-factly, "Yeah, I just feel so terrible about the whole thing."

Jodie was wracked by guilt. Some of her clients, whom she had meant to help, had to postpone retirement. She was harboring deep regrets about her actions, and they were starting to surface in unlikely situations—she was crying when watching retirees on television and seeing them in her dreams.

She told me she hadn't invested in the markets at all since 2000. All of her own retirement savings was in cash, almost as if she were paying penance for what she had done. The worst part of the episode, for her, was that she had thought the bubble would burst all along—she never bought the "new economy" hype, and she regretted blithely selling Internet funds to retirees when deep inside she knew the funds weren't in their best interest.

Regrets and feelings of guilt can stay with people for years. The attempt to avoid them leads people to wall off associated memories. But sometimes regrets won't be ignored, springing to the surface at inconvenient times or in unexpected ways. Jodie had never accepted and worked through her experiences, so the strong associated emotions sprang up whenever she had related experiences.

EMOTIONAL BIASES

The content of this book is treading on psychologically sensitive ground. Not only is there a social taboo around money, but there is also discomfort when emotion is openly discussed. Most people feel vulnerable during such conversations because the thing being addressed, emotion, lies protected underneath awareness.

Traditionally, emotions have been considered "messy," and they are assumed to be more damaging than constructive for judgment. Yet research has proven that emotion is central to both good and bad decision making. In the previous chapter you saw that excellent intuitive decision making is often based on gut "feel." However, at moderate to high levels, emotions overwhelm intuition rather than support it. This chapter describes the specific biases that arise from specific emotions.

Emotions can be short-term (lasting minutes to hours) or longer-term, such as *moods* (lasting hours to weeks). When emotions are chronic, they are called *attitudes*, and when they represent permanent ways of dealing with the world, they are *personality traits*.

The research literature has identified many ways in which emotions alter the brain's information processing and decision-making capacities.[1] Emotional decision makers often become attached to information that supports their emotional state while ignoring contradictory evidence.[2] Short-term emotions and moods (all called *emotion* henceforth) arouse an inclination to take action. If an action is not taken, then the emotion will linger. Subconscious emotions will bias judgment and decision making very subtly until they are appropriately discharged.[3] (Jodie is an excellent example of the lingering and inadvertent expression of unprocessed emotions).

It's human nature to react emotionally when events do (or do not) go one's way. Furthermore, nothing has to *happen* for someone to experience emotional reactions. The simple act of imagining possible outcomes, such as great successes or terrible losses, stimulates emotion. Virtually every investor has emotional reactions to market price action, especially when starting out. Most investors have felt nervousness during sideways markets, elation during bull markets, and intense doubt and fear during sharp market downturns. Each emotion uniquely alters how investors think and what they subsequently do with their capital.

What are some of the specific pitfalls of emotional biases in decision making? Table 6.1 summarizes the broad effects of emotion on processing and judgment.

TABLE 6.1 How Emotions Influence Decision Making

How Emotions Influence Decision Making[4]	Example
Current emotional state changes processing style.	Happy people are more confident in the accuracy of their decisions. Depressed investors are more detail oriented and indecisive.
Underlying disposition or personality biases perception.	Extraverted and optimistic individuals are predisposed to seeing less risk than neurotic (chronically anxious) people.
Gut feelings—when one asks himself, "How do I feel about it?"	Jack Welch decides "straight from the gut." George Soros's trades are influenced by somatic sensations.
Considering possible consequences induces an emotional reaction.	Worrying about the potential of a corporate bankruptcy filing provokes avoidance.
How one expects to feel after he or she receives a payoff.	Anticipating the joy of receiving a large royalty payment prompts anticipatory buying.
How one expects to feel after he or she experiences a loss.	Fearing the disappointment one will feel if an investment goes sour provokes deeper, more detailed analysis.
Emotions linger, affecting judgment, until they are discharged ("worked through").	Consider Jodie's case. Her regret drove her to avoid the stock market, cry when watching commercials about retirees, and eventual nightmares.
Projection bias—people estimate that they will feel the same in the future as they feel today.	Not saving for retirement because "I'm financially comfortable now." Fearful investors think the stock market will always be weak.
Motivated reasoning—people justify their current beliefs with illogical arguments in order to minimize negative emotion.	Pundits repeatedly advised investors to "dollar-cost average" into Internet stocks as the NASDAQ fell during 2000–2001.

THE DIFFERENCE BETWEEN POSITIVE AND NEGATIVE FEELINGS

Positive emotions signal that life is going well, goals are being met, and resources are adequate. In these circumstances, people are ideally situated to "broaden and build.[5] " Negative emotions, such as fear and sadness, are characteristic of a self-protective stance in which the primary aim is to guard existing resources and avoid harm. Each stance, optimism and pessimism, has characteristic effects on financial judgment.

Positive emotions prepare the individual to seek out and undertake new goals.[6] Positive emotions, such as happiness, contentment, satisfaction, and joy, are characterized by confidence, optimism, and self-efficacy. Happy people interpret their own negative moods and damaging life events with more optimism and respond to them in more positive, affirming ways than more pessimistic people.[7] There is a positive feedback effect of good mood on well-being. Chronically positive people have better immunity and physical health than others.

Researchers have found numerous effects of positive mood on judgment. Subjects in a positive emotional state tend to reduce the complexity of decisions by adopting a simpler process of information retrieval. Happiness is associated with the greater use of cognitive heuristics ("shortcuts") such as stereotypes.[8] Positive people disregard irrelevant information, consider fewer dimensions, recheck less information, and take significantly less time to make a choice than people who are feeling negative.[9, 10]

During financial gambles, positive people choose differently than negative ones. When stakes are high, people in positive emotional states try to maintain their positive state and avoid substantial losses.[11] In contrast, if stakes are low, joyful decision makers become risk seeking in order to benefit from the gain (though without wagering so much as to risk their happiness). In terms of *behavior*, happy people act to avoid the possibility of a large loss in order to protect their positive emotional state.[12] So while happy people make more optimistic judgments, in situations where they foresee a reasonable likelihood of large losses, they avoid taking risk.

While positive emotions broaden one's focus, negative emotions narrow it.[13] Negative moods are associated with a more ruminative and vigilant (hyperalert) thought process.[14] Negative emotions predispose to excessive risk perception and overreaction to losses.

Professor Paul Slovic and colleagues at the Center for Decision Research measured subjects' personality propensities, either as "negatively reactive" or "positively reactive." They then asked these subjects to play a modified Iowa Gambling Task (IGT; see Chapter 2 for description). Slovic found that participants high in negative reactivity learned to choose fewer high-loss options (perhaps because they are more sensitive to loss), while those high in positive reactivity learned to choose more high-gain options. These characteristic choice behaviors led to less overall profit for positive people playing the IGT.

Table 6.2 provides a summary and comparison of positive and negative emotions on decision making, judgment, and behavior.

TABLE 6.2   Positive and Negative Emotion's Effects on Thought

People in a Positive Mood	People in a Negative Mood
Reduce the complexity of the decisions.	Detail-oriented.
Adopt a simpler process of information retrieval.	Vigilant and broad analysis.
Disregard irrelevant information.	Often excessively focused on minutiae.
Consider fewer dimensions.	Broad observations.
Recheck less information.	Repeat and double-check.
Take significantly less time to make a choice.	Slow and thoughtful, occasional "analysis paralysis."
Take more risk in low-stakes gambles.	Avoid small risks when possible.
Take less risk in high-stakes gambles.	More likely to spend excessive amounts of money on large purchases or risky bets.
Less reflective after a failure; more resilient after losses.	Ruminate about setbacks and have more trouble getting back on their feet.

REGRET AS A SELF-FULFILLING PROPHECY

Regret is an uncomfortable but intrinsic part of investing. Inevitably, some decisions are bound to go wrong, leading to losses. Those who can't "take a loss" objectively will experience regret. It is very experienced investors who can be detached from the emotional impacts of large losses. It is regret's discomfort that drives two of the most common behavioral biases.

In behavioral finance research, one of the most prevalent biases is the tendency to hold losing stocks longer than winning stocks. That is, most investors too frequently "let their losers run and cut their winners short." This is called the *disposition effect* (discussed in detail in Chapters 14 and 15). Many academics believe that the disposition effect is due to the "fear of regret."

Selling a losing stock is tantamount to admitting that one was wrong. Feeling wrong inspires painful regret. To avoid regret, investors hold on to losing stocks while hoping for a comeback that will vindicate their initial buy decision.

They sell winning stocks too soon because they fear that the stock will drop, giving back their gains, and they will regret not having taken their paper profits off the table while they had the chance. So whether one's stocks are up or down, investors often make biased decisions in order to avoid experiencing regret.

Professor Barbara Mellers at the University of California at Berkeley designed gambling experiments in which she found that the fear of regret leads to lower returns. After choosing a gamble and being hit with an unexpected loss, many subjects avoided subsequent higher-expected-value gambles that were offered. Regret about a recent loss, even a loss as a result of a random event (such as the flip of a coin), drove people to irrationally reduce their risk taking.[15]

The fear of regret also affects how investors make initial buy and sell decisions. Researchers conducted surveys and experiments with a large group of individual investors and undergraduate students in the U.S. Midwest. In the survey, investors were asked, "Thinking back to investment decisions you now regret, do you feel more regret for: (1) selling a 'winning' stock too soon or (2) not selling a 'losing' stock soon enough?"[16] Fifty-nine percent reported more regret for not selling a loser soon enough, and 41 percent for selling a winner too soon. Each side of the disposition equation (winners and losers) was provoked. Regret was more aroused by not selling a losing stock soon enough.

The same experimenters asked subjects to participate in a game where they made their own investment decisions (buy, sell, or hold) over several periods of a simulated market. During the experiment, they were intermittently given the option of following the recommendation of a hypothetical broker they met at a party.[17] After they purchased a stock, they watched its price performance over a period, and then had the option of making another decision. As the experiment progressed, participants were asked their level of satisfaction with their prior decisions.

Interestingly, subjects reported more overall satisfaction simply from owning a stock, regardless of the outcome. When the broker had given accurate advice, and the subjects had followed the good advice, they reported less overall satisfaction with the investment outcome than if they had made the buy decision independently. Making one's own investment decisions is more emotionally gratifying than following a broker's advice. However, if they lost money on a stock, they felt more regret if the initial decision to buy had been theirs alone. Following a broker's recommendation reduced the emotional impact of losses. Brokers' recommendations were emotional shock absorbers, attenuating reactions to both profits and losses.

This finding may explain why most investors are willing to pay a premium for actively managed funds and personal investment advisers. These professionals function as intermediaries between oneself and the outcomes of one's investment decisions. Investors feel less emotional when deferring some responsibility for financial outcomes onto another.

AN AMICABLE DIVORCE

Of every marriage performed this year in the United States, just over 40 percent will end in divorce.[18] Even when consensual, divorce has profound emotional effects on the couple. To comfort themselves during divorce, women often seek the solace of other friendships. Men generally have fewer intimate relationships than women, and they may be more socially and emotionally isolated during the transition into single life.

Doug came to my office seeking help with his investing. He explained that he had been unsuccessfully trading volatile biotech and mining stocks. He had done such trading in the past with modest profitability, but now he couldn't handle the downside swings. He felt compelled to sell out on declines and frenetically chase fast-moving stocks higher during rallies. He had never traded so rapidly or poorly in the past, and he wondered what was happening. Overall, he was losing money quickly. In fact, by the time he came to see me, Doug had lost *50 percent* of his retirement savings.

During our first interview, Doug casually mentioned that he was going through a divorce that had been initiated two months previously. According to Doug, the breakup was mutual and final, and he didn't think it was causing his investing problems. Yet during out conversation, it became apparent that Doug was deeply attached to his ex-wife and her family. Without her family and her circle of friends, he had few close relationships. He had no one to talk to about his emotional pain following the divorce. Now his deep hurt was impairing his judgment.

Without realizing it, Doug's sadness and grief were increasing his risk taking. Fortunately, recent studies have shed light on the role of sadness in risk taking. Psychologists think sadness creates the desire to change one's circumstances. Sadness-driven stock transactions are fueled by hopes of quick gains and offer a distraction from psychological pain.

SADNESS AND DISGUST

> *"The most common cause of low prices is pessimism—sometimes pervasive, sometimes specific to a company or industry. We want to do business in such an environment, not because we like pessimism but because we like the prices it produces. It's optimism that is the enemy of the rational buyer."*
>
> —Warren Buffett, 1990 Chairman's Letter to Shareholders

All negative emotions, while of the same *valence*, do not affect decision making similarly. Researchers have performed studies to tease out the effects of specific negative emotions. Professor Jennifer Lerner at Carnegie-Mellon University induced states of sadness and disgust in subjects using short movie clips. She then studied how they priced their bids and offers in a simulated marketplace. For example, she asked participants to fill out a questionnaire in which they chose a price they would accept in exchange for an item they had been given (such as a pen highlighter set). In another condition, subjects without the item indicated how much they would pay for it.

Lerner found that participants in a disgusted emotional state were emotionally driven "to expel." That is, disgusted people want to "get rid" of items they own, and they do not want to accumulate new ones. As a result of the experimental subjects' disgust, they reduced both their bid and offer prices for the consumer items.

The "endowment effect" is a common cognitive bias in which people overvalue items they already own. The endowment effect causes the average seller to demand a higher price for an item than the average buyer thinks is reasonable. Inducing disgust led to the elimination of the endowment effect among both buyers (disgusted buyers lowered their average bids) and sellers (disgusted sellers lowered the average offer price).

In the case of sadness, Lerner noted that "sadness triggers the goal of changing one's circumstances, increasing buying prices [bids] but reducing selling prices [asks]." When the researchers provoked sadness in the subjects, the endowment effect was *reversed*.[19] That is, compared to people in neutral emotional states, people who had viewed sad movie clips subsequently valued items they owned less and items they did not possess more. Recall that disgusted people valued all items less, whether they owned them or not.

Based on the inversion of the endowment effect, sad people should be more likely to buy and sell items. Lerner speculated that this inversion is responsible for "shopping therapy" (in which people go shopping to lift their depressed spirits), and it may drive compulsive shopping, which is a type of psychiatric disorder. In fact, the best medication treatments for compulsive shopping are antidepressants. Lerner notes that compulsive shoppers tend to experience depression, that shopping tends to elevate the depressed moods of compulsive shoppers, and that antidepressant medication tends to reduce compulsive shopping.[20]

In the story of Doug, I speculated that the unacknowledged sadness around his divorce was driving excess transactions and risk taking in the stock market. In fact, Doug did well after he stopped trading and entered psychotherapy treatment. When he resumed investing nine months later, he was able to maintain a disciplined plan and he continues to trade successfully up to this writing.

FEAR AND ANGER

In another series of experiments, Professor Lerner examined the roles of anger and fear in driving financial risk taking. In advance of the experiment, she measured participants' dispositional levels of fear, anger, and "optimism about the future" using standard surveys. Interestingly, she found that as levels of both anger and happiness increase in people, they report increasing optimism about the future. For angry people this optimism is presumably because they feel in control. Fearful people report increasing pessimism as their level of anxiety increases. Again, two emotions of negative valence (fear and anger) have different effects on future expectations.[21]

According to Lerner, emotions characterized by a sense of certainty (such as happiness and anger) lead decision makers to rely on mental shortcuts, while emotions characterized by uncertainty (such as anxiety and sadness) lead decision makers to scrutinize information carefully.[22,23] Anger and fear, while negative, differ in their dimensions of control, certainty, and responsibility that accompany them. Angry people feel more certain about the nature of an infraction, they feel that they have more control over outcomes, and they feel that others are responsible for the provocation. Fearful people are uncertain where the source of danger lies, lack a sense of control over stopping it, and are unclear who or what is responsible for the threat.[24] In order to identify the danger, they investigate their surroundings and new information more thoroughly.

Fearful people are averse to risk, while angry people are as comfortable with risk as happy people. The decisive factor in risk taking is perception of control. Fearful investors feel insecure and out of control. As a result, during market declines, the fearful are more likely to sell out. Angry investors have identified the enemy and feel in control of the situation. They hold on to declining stocks because they are more certain of their position.

It is possible that the effects of fear and anger were seen in investor behavior after the September 11, 2001, terrorist attacks in New York City. For the first two weeks after the attacks, sad and fearful investors sold stock. Then, as no further threats materialized and the identities of the Al-Qaeda perpetrators became known, fear transformed into goal-directed anger, and the U.S. stock market rallied strongly for several months as the initial war against the Taliban was prepared, initiated, and successfully executed.

PROJECTION BIAS

Emotional individuals often have trouble predicting how they will feel in the future. They incorrectly assume that their future emotional state will resemble their current one. As a result, they imagine that their current preferences will remain constant into the future. Because they cannot accurately project themselves into the future and subsequently empathize with their condition, they have a bias of "projection" when planning for their future selves.

For example, someone who receives a financial windfall may have trouble setting aside part of it in retirement savings. He is feeling that he will always have enough money, and when the idea of retirement savings is broached, he feels, "Why worry about squirreling money away when I'm so flush?" Studies have found the projection bias in people in emotional states including anxiety,[25] pain,[26] and embarrassment.[27]

As a result of projection, most people underappreciate their powers of adaptation to unforeseen events.[28] For example, if investors anticipate that an international crisis might drive the U.S. dollar to all-time lows, they may extrapolate excessive damage to the American economy while underestimating the power of U.S. businesses to adapt.[29,30] They may invest less in equities, even if they are earning lower expected returns in bonds.

Another error caused by projection is the exaggeration of the impact of attention-grabbing events.[31] People generally assign a level of importance to events that is proportional to the frequency they are mentioned. For example, investors are likely to overestimate the importance of widely publicized world events (such as Middle East conflict) to their investment portfolio. Meanwhile, they overlook other, much more profoundly world-changing events such as the emergence of China as an economic and political power. Chapter 19 examines the nuances of this "attention effect" in detail.

One remedy for the projection bias lies in maintaining a healthy skepticism when attributing "moods" to the market. Another solution is to better appreciate how one's current and future emotional states alter one's perceptions of financial risk.

MANAGING FEELINGS

Most investors confuse emotion *management* with emotion *control*. Control often refers to repression, which is dangerous. As noted in Table 6.1, when an emotion is not discharged, its pressures on judgment linger until it is worked through. Unfortunately, efforts to control emotional experience meet with little success, and they often have the unintended effect of increasing sympathetic nervous system activity[32] (e.g., by raising blood pressure). High blood pressure can literally be a result of "bottling up" emotion.

Researchers have found that encouraging subjects to attribute their feelings to situational factors and neutral facts reduces the impact of current emotional state on judgment. For example, reading a sad story lowers most peoples' estimates of life satisfaction. However, when people focus on the cause of their sad feelings before rating life satisfaction, this effect is reduced.[33] People who understand why they are feeling sad (due to their reading of the sad story) are more satisfied with life.

Unfortunately, if one's emotional state matches his or her personality style, then it may be more difficult to manage. Neurotic people (with prominent anxious personality traits) will continue to rely on clues from their anxiety to direct future decisions, even after they have identified their anxiety as emanating from a neutral cause.[34]

When people first become aware of the emotional influences on their decision making, they often have difficulty with over- or undercompensation. Increased vigilance and self-awareness can be effective for reducing the effect of weak to moderate emotions on decision making. It is helpful if one sets up techniques for emotion management in advance for self-awareness interventions to be effective.[35] When in a particular emotional state, one cannot clearly see how their thinking patterns have changed.

Since emotions alter one's susceptibility to financial decision biases, an ability to forecast future feelings could be used for personal benefit. For example, the rare clients who tell their financial planners, "Don't let me sell if the market drops X percent," are requesting that an external enforcer help them plan in advance for periods when their financial anxiety is high.

SUMMARY

As seen in Chapter 5, low-level emotions underlie decision-making heuristics, such as the affect heuristic. Heuristics make possible a rapid, unconscious consolidation of complex information. The affect heuristic relies on subtle emotional "tags" that indicate the relative "goodness" or "badness" of a decision option. The affect heuristic is a process by which complex information is simplified and given meaning. When information that has been simplified using the affect heuristic is weighed and combined with other emotional cues, through a filter of experience, a "gut feeling" results.

A "gut feeling" refers to the subtle, unconscious emotional judgment that forms in response to an uncertain decision situation. If one has experience with such situations, then gut feelings can be quite accurate judgments. Optimal "gut feel" is the experienced interpretation of emotional cues.

Intuition relies on the rapid judgments that gut feel provides. Analytical decision making can often be improved with intuitive input.

While gut feel can contribute to more accurate analytical decisions, moderate or strong emotions often lead to biased decision making. Fortunately for those who want to improve their decision-making process, emotion can be detected and managed with the right psychological tools, primarily through the internal honing of emotional intelligence skills.

A lot of technical information about moderate to strong emotions was communicated in this chapter, and I'll quickly summarize the effects of specific emotions here. Regret, such as Jodie was feeling in the introductory story, prompts conservatism with existing assets and increased risk taking with money-losing ones (holding onto losers). Anger gives rise to mild optimism, a sense of control, and certainty about one's financial choices. Overall, angry investors have less stock turnover. Sadness (perhaps unusually) leads to increased investment risk taking and increased trading. When afraid, investors usually overestimate danger and are more likely to believe threat-related information. When happy, they underestimate risks and trust positive prognostications from similarly optimistic experts.

Chapters 7 through 10 detail the emotional states that most impair objective investing: fear, stress, greed, and hubris.

CHAPTER 7

Excitement and Greed

Hooked on a Feeling

"If investing is entertaining, if you're having fun, you're probably not making any money. Good investing is boring."

—George Soros

Jonathan Lebed was 14 years old the first time he was subpoenaed by the Securities and Exchange Commission (SEC). Then at the age of 15, Lebed was again subpoenaed, this time for "pump-and-dump" schemes. Such schemes entail buying the shares of illiquid or infrequently traded stocks, advertising the benefits of the stock widely, and then selling one's shares as other eager buyers snap them up at a higher price. In a press release, the SEC accused Lebed of touting stocks so that he could make a quick profit on their price jumps:

> On eleven separate occasions between August 23, 1999 (when Lebed was 14 years old) and February 4, 2000, Lebed, of Cedar Grove, New Jersey, engaged in a scheme on the Internet in which he purchased, through brokerage accounts, a large block of a thinly-traded microcap stock. Within hours of making the purchase, Lebed sent numerous false and/or misleading unsolicited e-mail messages, or "spam," primarily to various Yahoo! Finance message boards, touting the stock he had just purchased. Lebed then sold all of these shares, usually within 24 hours, profiting from the increase in price his messages had caused.[1]

The SEC explained that Lebed was criminally liable because the stock forecasts that he posted on web sites and through e-mail "included baseless price predictions and other false and/or misleading statements."

Yet Lebed was a marketing genius. According to Michael Lewis, author of the best-selling books *Liar's Poker* and *Moneyball*, Lebed learned to gradually hone the appeal of his promotional messages. It should have been apparent to investors buying his recommendations that they were on the wrong side of the trade. Through a trial-and-error process, Lebed learned which aspects of his stock appeals drove investors to buy in spite of any conscious misgivings.

According to Michael Lewis, two days before the SEC's subpoenas arrived, Lebed had logged on to the Internet and posted 200 separate times the following plug for a company called Firetector (ticker symbol FTEC):

> *Subj: THE MOST UNDERVALUED STOCK EVER*
>
> *Date: 2/03/00 3:43* PM *Pacific Standard Time*
>
> *From: LebedTG1*
>
> *FTEC is starting to break out! Next week, this thing will EXPLODE. ...*
>
> *Currently FTEC is trading for just $2 1/2! I am expecting to see FTEC at $20 VERY SOON.*
>
> *Let me explain why. ...*
>
> *Revenues for the year should very conservatively be around $20 million. The average company in the industry trades with a price/sales ratio of 3.45. With 1.57 million shares outstanding, this will value FTEC at ... $44.*
>
> *It is very possible that FTEC will see $44, but since I would like to remain very conservative ... my short-term target price on FTEC is still $20!*
>
> *The FTEC offices are extremely busy. ... I am hearing that a number of HUGE deals are being worked on. Once we get some news from FTEC and the word gets out about the company ... it will take off to MUCH HIGHER LEVELS!*
>
> *I see little risk when purchasing FTEC at these DIRT-CHEAP PRICES. FTEC is making TREMENDOUS PROFITS and is trading UNDER BOOK VALUE!!!*[2]

Lebed found that he could hide his identity on the Internet. He could send compelling messages, with a veneer of expertise, while none of the readers knew the author was only 15 years old.

Arthur Levitt, chairman of the SEC during the Lebed indictment, described Lebed's scheme in a pithy remark on a *60 Minutes* special: "A pump-and-dump is really buy, lie, and sell high."[3]

The SEC's case against Lebed was settled out of court. Lebed repaid $285,000 (including interest) to the SEC on behalf of investors who had been duped by his pump-and-dump schemes. The settlement allowed Lebed to keep more than $500,000 earned during his stock promotion activities.

As of 2006, at age 22, Lebed continued to do small company research promotions through both his web site (www.lebed.biz) and promotional e-mails.

The SEC indicted Lebed because they claimed he was seeking to manipulate the market. Yet pump-and-dump hyping happens with some frequency. Why do people fall for this scam over and over when it directly and unmistakably leads to financial loss?

Stacie Zoe Berg, writing in TheStreet.com, identifies the lure of the pump-and-dump as playing into investors' "belief that it's easy to find winners." Berg suggests that pump-and-dump scams primarily recruit naive investors: "Others fall for scams because they were late entering the market and want to catch up with the winnings it seems everyone else is reaping. This greed and desperation make investors putty in the hands of those willing to take advantage of them."[4] Yet the question remains: what predisposes investors to "greed and desperation," and how is a speculative frenzy ignited?

This chapter examines the origins and the anatomy of investors' excitement, hope, and greed. Recent studies into the financially destructive consequences of excessive excitement during decision making are discussed. Finally, it delves into the anatomy of the promotional language that excites investors.

BROKERS KINDLE IRRATIONAL EXUBERANCE

It wasn't only Lebed who was preying on excited and gullible investors during the Internet bubble. In the late 1990s online brokerage advertisements refined their appeal for day traders' unconscious triggers. Television commercials for online stockbrokers emphasized both the ease and profitability of such trading and were rich in positive emotional imagery.

Professor Brad Barber at the University of California at Davis performed a content analysis of 500 television commercials from 13 brokerages. He found that 28 percent of all commercials between 1990 and 2000 depicted images and messages likely to induce good or positive moods in viewers, and the percentage of such commercials more than doubled from 12.39 percent in 1990–1995 to 32.98 percent in 1996–2000. Barber speculates that because people in moderately positive moods tend to be less thorough and less vigilant decision makers, are more subject to cognitive biases, and rely more on heuristics (than people in moderately negative moods), the brokers were trying to induce such moods in their viewers.[5]

One Discover Brokerage Direct television commercial depicted a conversation between a passenger and a stock-trading tow-truck driver who owned an island-nation all his own.[6] Other television commercials included a stock-trading teenager who owned his own helicopter.[7] A series of Schwab commercials featured such celebrities as teenage Russian tennis star Anna Kournikova. An E*TRADE advertisement claimed that "on-line investing is 'A cinch. A snap. A piece of cake.' "[8]

Former SEC chairman Arthur Levitt said, "Quite frankly, some advertisements more closely resemble commercials for the lottery than anything else. When firms, again and again, tell investors that on-line investing can make them rich, it creates unrealistic expectations. . . . [M]any investors are susceptible to quixotic euphoria. . ."[9] New York Attorney General Eliot Spitzer observed that online brokerage advertisements "convey a message of convenience, speed, easy wealth, and the risk of 'being left behind' in the on-line era."[10] In a January 26, 2001, report about online trading, the SEC expressed concerns that certain types of aggressive online brokerage ads may cause investors to possess unrealistic expectations over the risks and rewards of investing.[11]

THE ANATOMY OF STOCK HYPE

Lebed's promotional messages primed readers to buy dubious investments by circumventing their reason and appealing directly to their neural reward systems. He was successful because he included the following reward system activators in his messages. Reward system provocateurs such as those listed below will be discussed further in this and subsequent chapters:

1. **Novelty.** Lebed suggested stocks in new or overlooked areas of the market, which was sure to stimulate curiosity (another function of the reward system).

2. **Anticipation of a Large Gain.** Anticipation of monetary gains activates a deep, automatic area of the reward system called the *nucleus*

accumbens. Lebed suggested that investors could expect a *"HUGE"* pay-off. Size matters to the reward system, where extremely large possible gains override a rational ability to incorporate probability information.

3. **Information Overload.** Lebed's sales pitches were loaded with a plethora of corporate statistics such as projected revenues, earnings, and potential market size. For most people, a long list of detailed statistical information will shut down their critical faculties. Many readers of Lebed's messages threw up their hands in exasperation, asked "What's in it for me?," and skipped ahead to the conclusion. Confused investors were given a simple answer by Lebed: "Buy now, sell at $20."

4. **Bargain Buying.** He appealed to investors' search for a bargain. He used phrases like "under book value" and "dirt cheap." Buying something at such a bargain implies that one can't lose. On a neural level, good deals have been found to activate the brain's reward system.

5. **Author as Expert.** Lebed sounded like an authority on each stock. He clearly had done some homework, and he delivered verifiable financial data. Investors were apt to *trust* his projections based on his depth of knowledge and the thoroughness of his research. Lebed's use of difficult-to-find data heightened his aura of authority.

6. **Time Pressure.** He appealed to readers' time-discounting functions. If they didn't act "VERY SOON," then they were going to miss out. Time pressure hinders critical analysis and causes limbic system activity to bypass the cognitive considerations of the prefrontal cortex.

In Lebed's promotions, gullible investors were coached to anticipate large gains, as revealed to them by an "expert." The hyped stock was new and interesting, and the investment required immediate action. Little downside risk was apparent, according to the "expert." By the time interested potential investors looked at the latest price quote, odds were that other eager investors (including Lebed himself) had already started buying, and their pressure pushed the price upwards. For an investor considering an opportunity, the idea of missing out overcomes the last remnants of resistance. They jumped in, and Lebed was waiting to sell to them.

GREED: THE BASICS

"An excessive desire to acquire or possess more than what one needs or deserves, especially with respect to material wealth."
—The American Heritage Dictionary of the
English Language, Fourth Edition, 2000,
Houghton Mifflin Company

*"An eager desire or longing; greediness; as, a greed
of gain."*
—Webster's Revised Unabridged Dictionary,
1998, MICRA, Inc.

*"Reprehensible acquisitiveness; insatiable desire
for wealth (personified as one of the deadly sins)."*
—WordNet 2.0, 2003, Princeton University

For millennia, greed has been identified as a source of financial folly.
In the Bible, as one of the seven deadly sins, greed is called *avarice.*
The Buddha referred to greed as *desire* and called it the source of all
human disappointment and suffering. Charity (the antithesis of greed)
is one of the five pillars of Islam. In Victorian England, Charles Dickens
parodied the greed of his character Ebenezer Scrooge, who today serves
as a stark reminder of the loss of human connection that can accompany
an excessive desire for financial gain.

Greed has been popularly portrayed in the media as a negative attribute. Michael Douglas, playing the fictional corporate raider Gordon
Gekko in the 1987 movie *Wall Street*, waxed philosophical about the
true nature and necessity of greed before the shareholders of a corporation he intended to buy, Teldar Paper. Perhaps the most memorable
scene in the movie is a speech by Gekko to a Teldar Paper shareholders'
meeting:

> *The point is, ladies and gentleman, greed is good. Greed works, greed
> is right. Greed clarifies, cuts through, and captures the essence of the
> evolutionary spirit. Greed in all its forms, greed for life, money, love,
> knowledge has marked the upward surge in mankind—and greed,
> mark my words—will save not only Teldar Paper but the other mal-
> functioning corporation called the U.S.A.*

Gekko's self-serving desire to lay-off Teldar workers and auction off its
separate divisions for profit ominously lurked beneath his claimed altruistic motives. Gekko's speech was reportedly based on Ivan Boesky's 1985
commencement address to the graduates of the University of California at
Berkeley, in which Boesky declared: "Greed is all right, by the way. I want
you to know that. I think greed is healthy. You can be greedy and still feel
good about yourself." Boesky was a Wall Street arbitrageur who was later
convicted of federal crimes. He paid a $100 million penalty to the SEC to
settle insider-trading charges in 1986.

Economists from Adam Smith to Milton Friedman have seen greed
as an inevitable and, in some ways, desirable feature of capitalism. In a

well-regulated and well-balanced economy, greed helps to keep the system expanding. But it also ought to be kept in check, lest it undermine public faith in the entire enterprise.[12]

As economist Paul Krugman noted in the *New York Times*, the theory that "greed is good" for society may contain a fatal flaw: "A system that lavishly rewards executives for success tempts those executives, who control much of the information available to outsiders, to fabricate the appearance of success. Aggressive accounting, fictitious transactions that inflate sales, whatever it takes."[13]

Among investors, greed leads to financial losses through overtrading, entering investments too late, and inadequate due diligence. It shares a biological foundation with psychological biases such as overconfidence, the illusion of control, and the house money effect. Greed that follows a series of profits is fuel for hubris. Broadly speaking, greed is a result of a convergence of factors: the desire for gain, the motivation to pursue opportunities, the disregard of risks, and a penchant for excess.

On an individual level, greed has deleterious effects on performance, yet greed is a common facet of human behavior. Can learning about greed improve one's profits in the markets (to be sure, a greedy motivation)? For many investors, locating stocks with large profit potential and anticipating their high returns is one of the exciting (and occasionally addictive) aspects of investing. Managing the greed that accompanies a normal investment process is an enduring challenge.

In order to understand the type of greed that drives investors to fall for pump-and-dump scams, chase fast-moving stocks, and otherwise take excessive risk, it's revealing to look inside the brain. Neuroimaging shows how greed arouses the neural circuitry, what types of information intensify greed, and which interventions appear to rein it in.

THE BIAS TASK

Studies by researchers at Stanford University have revealed some of the brain origins and expensive consequences of greed. The researchers have identified a part of the brain that generates excitement about potential gains, occasionally leading to excessive financial risk seeking. Additionally, they found that a different area of the brain is activated when investors fear loss, and that area powers excessive financial risk aversion. Such neuroimaging studies greatly simplify the investment decision-making process due to experimental constraints. Nonetheless, they have provided deep insight into how investors assess and choose investment options.

Since 1999, professor Brian Knutson has performed brain imaging experiments that illuminate the characteristics of an emotional state called *positive activation*. Positive activation refers to the excited anticipation of a good outcome. Some positive emotions, such as comfort and satisfaction, are not associated with arousal. Other positive emotions, such as excitement and elation, consist of both positive emotion and physiological arousal (activation). Experimentally, an excellent way to induce positive activation is to offer subjects money.

In his first experiments, Knutson found that different regions of the brain's reward system were activated at different times during financial gambles. In particular, he found that anticipating financial gains activated different reward system centers than when those gains were received. A deep brain area called the nucleus accumbens (NAcc) (see Figure 7.2 on page 101) was primarily activated by reward anticipation. An area of the medial prefrontal cortex (MPFC) (see Figure 8.1a and b on page 113), just behind the eyes in the midline, was activated when monetary rewards were received.

In subsequent experiments, Knutson localized areas of the reward system that are activated during anticipation of different-sized gains. As the size of a potential reward increases, the NAcc is increasingly activated. He also identified the brain area where the probability of receiving a reward is encoded. As the probability of getting a reward increases, the MPFC is increasingly activated. Through 2004, Knutson's studies revealed how people anticipate and learn about financial rewards when the magnitudes, probabilities, and expected values of those rewards change.

In 2005, Stanford finance graduate student Camelia Kuhnen (now assistant professor at Northwestern University–Kellogg School of Management) designed a study with Knutson to discern how individuals decide to take investment risk. She hypothesized that areas of the reward system might drive excessive risk taking and risk avoidance. Kuhnen and Knutson refined an investment experiment in which they could visualize the moment of decision making. Their study was the first using functional magnetic resonance imaging (fMRI) to visualize brain activity during investment decisions.[14]

In their experimental task, called the Behavioral Investment Allocation Strategy (BIAS) task, Kuhnen and Knutson asked subjects to make an investment choice among three alternatives. Two of the alternatives were risky "stocks" (either "Stock A" or "Stock B"), and one was a "bond." After the subjects selected one of the three choices, the results of each option were revealed to the subjects. If the subjects had made money, it was added to their account, but if they lost money, it was subtracted.

One of the two stocks had a net positive payoff over the 10 trials, and the other had a net negative payoff. At the beginning of each block of 10 trials, subjects did not know which stock was profitable or which was money losing, so they learned via trial and error. The "good" stock had a random payoff distribution of +$10 (50 percent likelihood), $0 (25 percent), and –$10 (25 percent), for an expected value per trial of $2.50. The "bad" stock had payoffs of +$10 (25 percent), $0 (25 percent), and –$10 (50 percent), for an expected value per trial of –$2.50. The only difference between the two stocks was a 25 percent shift in the likelihood of the highest value (+$10) and lowest value (–$10) outcomes. The third choice, the bond, yielded a constant return of $1 per trial.

Potential Choice Payoffs of the BIAS Task

Bond   = $1 per trial
Stock A = Averaged either +$2.50 or –$2.50 per trial
Stock B = Averaged either +$2.50 or –$2.50 per trial

While subjects' goal in the BIAS task was to make as much money as possible (they kept their earnings), they did not know which stock was the high-paying one when they first begin playing the game. After watching the payoff of each stock over several trials, subjects would develop a greater sense of certainty about which was the "good" one. To prevent the subjects from always knowing which stock was best, after 10 trials the stocks were randomized and a new block of 10 trials initiated.

Dear Reader: If you're feeling mathematically inclined, decide how you would choose in this experiment. Would you start out choosing a stock? If not, how would you proceed? After how many trials would you know with some certainty which was the high-payoff stock? (Do this quickly before reading on.)

As the first few trials pass, subjects can generate a probabilistic sense of which stock is high paying and which is not. One should optimally begin to choose the "good" stock when 70 percent certain of its identity, in order to maximize expected value. After each trial, you can calculate the odds that a stock is the "good" stock using Bayes's theorem. Subjects made decision "mistakes" when they did not follow Bayes's theorem as they attempted to maximize their profits. Of course, it was impossible for the subjects to mentally calculate Bayesian probabilities in the limited time provided, so they had to rely on general impressions, and they made many mistakes.

In "risk-aversion" mistakes, subjects would choose the bond even though they had enough information to know which stock was the "good" stock with at least 70 percent probability. Activation in an area of the brain called the anterior insula *predicted* risk-aversion errors (see Figure 7.1) in this experiment.

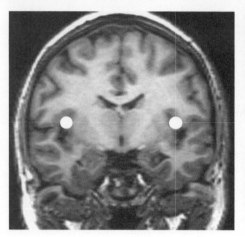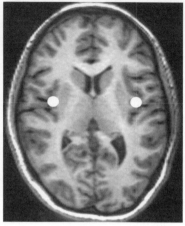

FIGURE 7.1 These images demonstrate the location of the insula. Note that the anterior insula is the forward portion. The insula is an evolutionarily older type of cortex. Newer cortex (neocortex) tissue in the temporal and parietal lobes folds in over the outside of the insula. Activity of the anterior insula is associated with the experience of pain and predicts risk-aversion mistakes in the BIAS task.

In fMRI experiments by other researchers, the anterior insula was activated by pain, loss, and disgust. Kuhnen and Knutson noticed that subjects' anterior insulas were activated when they learned they hadn't chosen the most lucrative option. When such a "counterfactual loss" occurred, they were more likely to jump to the bond (thus making a risk-aversion mistake). It should have been apparent to the subjects that, given the odds, the "good" stock would occasionally pay less than the "bad" stock. Nonetheless, subjects had difficulty sticking with the "good" stock after a counterfactual loss.

Some subjects who had performed well in the first portion of an experimental block became more conservative toward the end, apparently fearful that they might "give back" some of their winnings. This is a type of risk-aversion mistake (called "cutting winners short") that is discussed in Chapters 14 and 15. Experiencing a counterfactual loss (in the first example) or accumulating large profits (in the second) predicted subjects would choose the safety of the bond, thus making a *risk-aversion mistake*. The subjects' anterior insulas became activated just before they made the switch to a more conservative, risk-averse strategy.

Investors who sell their long-term investments after a brief period of underperformance are demonstrating risk aversion. Additionally, investors who sell a rising stock, effectively "cutting a winner short," may similarly be displaying insula-driven risk aversion.

THE NUCLEUS ACCUMBENS

In the BIAS task, when subjects invested in one of the stocks before they were 70 percent sure that it was the "good" stock, they committed what is called a *risk-seeking mistake*. Kuhnen and Knutson found that the NAcc of the reward system was activated before subjects made risk-seeking mistakes, thus predicting the mistake that subjects were about to make (see Figure 7.2).

The nucleus accumbens is well known among neuroscientists due to several interesting characteristics:

1. **The Pleasure Center**. Neurosurgeons found that people undergoing surgery reported intense sensations of well-being (and some had orgasms) when electrically stimulated in the NAcc.[16] More recently, scientists demonstrated that NAcc activation is correlated with subjective reports of positive emotionality.[17] While pleasure is undoubtedly one function of the NAcc, there are other functions such as motivation and learning that are also of interest to neuroscientists.

2. **Drug Abuse**. All drugs of abuse activate dopamine neurons in the reward system, which has terminals in the NAcc. Thus, the NAcc is thought to be the brain center responsible for drug craving.

3. **Reward Anticipation**. The NAcc is activated on fMRI scans when people are anticipating or expecting to make money.[18] Other rewards can

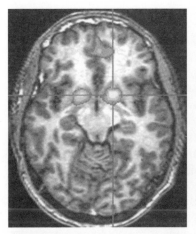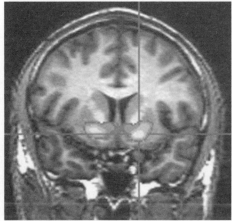

FIGURE 7.2 These are images of nucleus accumbens (NAcc) activation. Activity of the NAcc is associated with the experience of positive excitement and predicts risk-seeking mistakes in the BIAS task.

activate the NAcc, such as chocolate, luxury items, and pornographic pictures.

Activation of the NAcc does not in itself predict risk-taking mistakes. Rather, it is excessive activation, as compared to baseline, that correlates with investment decision errors. "On average, the participants in the study made rational choices 75 percent of the time and made mistakes 25 percent of the time," according to Knutson in the article's accompanying press release, "and the brain areas lit up even when rational choices were being made, just not as much."

Some businesses use cues or triggers in order to activate customers' risk-taking brain regions to induce them to take more financial risk. Per Knutson in the press release, his findings "may also explain why casinos employ 'reward cues' such as free drinks and surprise gifts as anticipation of other rewards that may activate the NAcc and lead to changes in behavior. . . . Insurance companies might employ the opposite strategy, using strategies that would activate the anterior insula." From the previous discussion of brokerage advertising during the late 1990s, it is clear that such cues have been used widely in the financial industry to encourage investment risk taking.

Investors are experiencing NAcc activation when they feel excited about "hot" stock investment opportunities. Stocks in new or high-growth industries and those with lucrative-sounding stories trigger NAcc activation and the experience of greed for gain.

EXCITED ABOUT A GOOD DEAL

The BIAS task demonstrated how "irrational" risk-taking decisions could be predicted by watching changes in brain activation. Researchers then turned their attention to the mechanics of the "buy" decision in a retail environment. Professor Knutson, Professor George Loewenstein (at Carnegie Mellon University), and others designed an experiment to measure whether there is a "buy signal" in the brain. Specifically, are there brain areas that drive purchases of consumer items?

In the experimental task, the researchers displayed a number of routine consumer products (such as a box of Godiva chocolates, an MP3 player, or a *Dodgeball* DVD). Alongside the items they posted the prices at which subjects could buy them from the researchers. Interestingly, the prices of the items had been discounted approximately 70 percent from their retail prices. The discount was necessary because subjects had been unwilling to buy the items near the full retail price.

Knutson found that activity in three brain regions predicted purchasing decisions. Activity in the NAcc was associated with a preference for a product (a desire to possess it), and predicted that the participant would buy the item. The participants' MPFC was activated when prices were very cheap, and its activation also predicted that the subjects would buy. Decreased activity in the brain's pain center, the insula, occurred during this experiment, and this decreased activity also predicted buying. In conclusion, it appears there are three neural predictors of buying consumer items—desire for the product (increased NAcc), a cheap price for the product (increased MPFC), and little perceived risk (decreased anterior insula).[15]

There are several speculative applications of these findings to investment practitioners. The satisfaction value investors feel as a result of hunting for bargain-priced stocks may be due to MPFC activation. It's possible that value investors such as Warren Buffett, David Dreman, and Bill Miller are tuned in to "bargain" signals from their MPFCs.

Stock investors who look for an exciting or desirable story may be buying stocks based on NAcc activation. These are the investors who buy stock in a "good company" that they like, forgetting that a good company does not equal a good stock.

Investors who see little risk in an investment are driven to buy by the absence of a perceived "downside" (decreased anterior insula activation). Because they don't see how they could lose, they are more willing to take a risk and buy. The MPFC, NAcc, and insula are all part of the neural circuitry with which investments are evaluated. Interestingly, patterns in their activation also predict purchase decisions.

IMPROVING BIASED DECISION MAKING

Emotions are part of *both* rational and irrational choice behavior. It's the *extremes* of emotion that lead to excess. Intense emotions, such as greed and fear, are indicators that one is susceptible to the risk-aversion and risk-seeking mistakes seen in the Kuhnen and Knutson study.

People can use the physical signs of emotion (feelings) as signals for when they are likely to make errors in their investment decision making. Using feelings as predictive signals requires a high degree of self-awareness. Self-awareness of feelings and consciously monitoring recent decisions for emotional influences can significantly improve decision making. Deliberate action to interrupt emotional decision making, even something as simple as taking a deep breath, may be the most efficient means for reducing excessively emotional decision making. The real message may be a common-sense one: Whenever you're facing a big decision, and you feel excited, step back a moment and think it over.

For example, if an investor has experienced a recent loss and notes that he is either feeling nervous or exhibiting signs of irrational risk avoidance behavior such as (1) hesitating in entering new positions, (2) deliberating about further potential losses, or (3) seeing more financial threats than usual, then he is experiencing excess anxiety. He should identify that anxiety is the origin of his decision problems and take action to either reduce the anxiety or bolster his self-discipline.

Conversely, if an investor has recently made large gains and is feeling (1) celebratory, (2) infallible, and (3) like taking more risk, then he ought to take a step back. Is he focusing solely on potential returns while ignoring prudent risk control? If so, then steps should be taken to reinforce investment discipline.

GREED IN THE MARKETS

> *"I will tell you how to become rich. Close the doors. Be fearful when others are greedy. Be greedy when others are fearful."*
> —Warren Buffett, lecturing to a group of students at Columbia University (he was 21 years old)

One proxy for excessive emotionality is the language that investors use to describe their investments and the current market conditions—their verbal *framing* of the investment climate. If investors express themselves in a negative emotional tone, then they are likely to be feeling risk averse. However, when investors use positive words to express their market sentiments, they are more likely to be taking excessive risk. A simple way to test this hypothesis is to count the number of negative and positive words in the media.

In May 2005, I counted such words using the online transcripts of the television business news programs *Nightly Business Report* with Paul Kangas and CNN's *Moneyline* with Lou Dobbs. *Moneyline*'s transcripts ran from January 3, 2000, to June 12, 2003, while NBR's are available from January 3, 2000, up until this writing. When the number of positively and negatively toned words are summed, one can get a pretty consistent idea of the amount of negativity and positivity in the business news during any given broadcast.

I ran a simple linear regression to see if there is a correlation between the number of positive or negative words and the future market direction.

It turns out that when there is a high frequency of positive words, the stock market (S&P 500) is more likely to decline over the following week. The reverse pattern is true using negative words—a high frequency of negative words precedes market advances. While interesting, these patterns do not lead to investment profits due to transaction costs.

Based on this informal language study, the "sentiment" of the media appears to reflect the risk perceptions of the average investor. During highly negativistic business news broadcasts, the average investor will feel the emotional inclination to be risk averse, but in fact would have greater long-run profitability if she were *buying* stocks during those times. The opposite pattern is true during excessively positive newscasts.

These findings seem to support advice Warren Buffett wrote to a hypothetical market timer in the 2004 Berkshire Hathaway annual newsletter: "And if they insist on trying to time their participation in equities, they should try to be fearful when others are greedy and greedy when others are fearful."

The next chapter looks at the effects of overconfidence and hubris on investor decision quality.

CHAPTER 8

Overconfidence and Hubris

Too Much of a Good Thing

"The line separating investment and speculation, which is never bright and clear, becomes blurred still further when most market participants have recently enjoyed triumphs. Nothing sedates rationality like large doses of effortless money. After a heady experience of that kind, normally sensible people drift into behavior akin to that of Cinderella at the ball. They know that overstaying the festivities—that is, continuing to speculate in companies that have gigantic valuations relative to the cash they are likely to generate in the future—will eventually bring on pumpkins and mice. But they nevertheless hate to miss a single minute of what is one helluva party. Therefore, the giddy participants all plan to leave just seconds before midnight. There's a problem, though: They are dancing in a room in which the clocks have no hands."
　　　　　　　—Berkshire Hathaway 2000 Annual Report,
　　　　　　　　　　　　　　　February 28, 2001

Victory disease refers to the tendency for military commanders, after a series of triumphs in the field, to subsequently demonstrate poor judgment. The fortunes of victors reverse due to arrogance, complacency, reliance on stereotypes of enemies, and an ignorance of or inability to develop new tactics. Famous examples of victory disease include the failure of the imperial Japanese navy to set up a defensive perimeter following their initial string of victories in World War II and Napoleon's ill-fated invasion of Russia.

Nobel Prize disease is a notable form of intellectual decay among Nobel Prize winners. Economist Paul Samuelson described the symptoms of the "disease" among afflicted Nobel laureates: "After winners receive the award and adulation, they wither away into vainglorious sterility. More than that, they become pontificating windbags, preaching to the world on ethics and futurology, politics and philosophy. At circular tables, where they sit they believe to be the head of the table."[1]

Directly related to investors' concerns, the business press has coined the term *CEO disease* to refer to the tendency of CEOs to underperform after achieving the top position in their organization.[2] All three afflictions (victory disease, Nobel Prize disease, and CEO disease) follow a similar psychological pattern. The remainder of this chapter will discuss the psychology and neuroscience underlying the investor biases of overconfidence and hubris.

THE PSYCHOLOGY OF HUBRIS

> *"Meriwether and his sidekicks had a bad case of hubris. As Kaufman puts it: "There are two kinds of people who lose money: those who know nothing and those who know everything." With two Nobel Prize winners in the house, Long-Term Capital clearly fits the second case."*
>
> —R. Lenzner[3]

My medical school senior project involved researching the psychological origins of financial risk taking and asset bubbles. This was timely research, begun in January 2000, and inspired by my amazement with the Internet stock bubble. At the time, I read a book by David Dreman entitled *Psychology and the Stock Market*, which was first published in 1977. Dreman describes a speculative mania in "-onics" stocks in the early 1960s during which short-term traders called *gunslingers* made and lost fortunes: "The more esoteric the concept, the better the public liked it. Any company ending in '-onics' was almost guaranteed an enthusiastic reception."[4] I felt like I was reading the script for the Internet bubble, with *.com* and *day traders* substituting for *-onics* and *gunslingers*.

I became intensely interested in the fact that Internet stocks were clearly experiencing a bubble, yet investors continued to recklessly pour money in—as if they were confidently counting on a bigger fool to buy their shares at a higher price sometime in the future. In my mind, there seemed no better example of hubris.

The English word *hubris* is derived from the Greek word *hybris*. It refers to the excessive pride that usually precedes the downfall of the tragic hero in Greek drama. Hubris is found among successful individuals who see external goals as their primary metric of success. Anywhere acclaim is awarded according to some extrinsic metric, such as wealth, beauty, or athletic prowess, achievers are vulnerable. Hubris is one of the most dangerous emotional states that investors can experience, as it often precedes the greatest losses.

The first stage of hubris is to have a series of gains or acclaim. If those gains are attributed to one's unique talents, skills, or intelligence, then they can contribute to a persistent pattern of overconfidence. For overconfident investors, risks are ignored and their belief in themselves is hypertrophied.

OVERCONFIDENCE

> *"According to a ... Washington Post poll, ... 94 percent of Americans said they are "above average" in honesty, 89 percent "above average" in common sense, 86 percent "above average" in intelligence, and 79 percent "above average" in looks."*
> —Chuck Shepherd, *News of the Weird*, 2006

In the United States, the cultivation of self-confidence is widespread. Confidence is thought to be so important that schools design curricula to support children's self-esteem. And for the most part, confidence is a good thing. Without self-confidence, people wouldn't undertake challenging or risky endeavors.

The problem with confidence is so-called overconfidence. As seen in the quote that opens this section, a majority of people are overconfident. In many domains, belief in one's capabilities creates a self-fulfilling prophecy of success. Yet in the financial markets, overconfidence seriously impairs performance. High levels of overconfidence and the illusion of control have been correlated with subpar performance among subjects in trading experiments.[5,6]

When queried, a majority of people report that they are above average drivers, lovers, athletes, and investors. Yet how can such a large majority of people be above average? Clearly, somebody is overestimating his or her talents.

Some people are biologically predisposed to be overconfident (especially, for example, young men). Others learn to be overconfident.

There are several varieties of what is generally referred to as *overconfidence*. One type of overconfidence is the "better-than-average" effect. Researchers who ask subjects to rate their abilities, such as skill in driving, athletic ability, or running a business, find that most people consider themselves better than average.[7] All humans overestimate their abilities—depending on the study, between 65 and 80 percent believe they are above-average drivers. In fact, 9 out of 10 males report the belief that their penises are longer than average.

Another type of overconfidence is called *miscalibration*. Some individuals overestimate the precision of their knowledge and tend to use confidence intervals that are too narrow.[8] If a CEO is asked to provide an estimated range for his company's annual earnings, the 90 percent confidence interval is the range into which the actual value should fall 9 out of 10 times. The typical miscalibrated CEO would give too narrow an earnings range, with the actual earnings number frequently falling outside his 90 percent confidence interval.

In one multiyear survey, chief financial officers (CFOs) were asked to give their 80 percent confidence intervals for the stock market close over the next year. When over 4,300 forecasts were measured against the actual stock market performance, only 30.5 percent were accurate within the CFOs' 80 percent confidence intervals.[9] One might hope that CFOs would have a better sense of their limitations in financial forecasting.

A third type of overconfidence involves one's belief of control over random, independent events—called the *illusion of control*. Many people erroneously believe that they can control, predict, or somehow influence random events. The following experiment elicited the illusion of control.

In a (rigged) coin-tossing experiment subjects were asked to predict the outcome of a coin toss. The experimenters ensured that each participant would successfully "predict" exactly 15 of the 30 coin tosses (50 percent total accuracy).[10] The experiment was further rigged so that one-third of the subjects were correct on their first four predictions, one-third were incorrect on four of the first five coin flips, and one-third had a random pattern of success.

After all the subjects had completed the experiment, they were asked to retrospectively estimate their accuracy. The one-third of participants who began with four of five wins rated their overall accuracy significantly better than the other participants. When asked how they would do in predicting 100 further coin flips, those who started with a series of wins expected to make significantly better predictions in subsequent games. Altogether, 40 percent of the players believed that their performance would improve with practice (even though they intellectually knew that the coin tosses were random).[11] The authors concluded that "An early, fairly consistent pattern of successes leads to skill attribution, which in turn leads subjects to expect future successes."[12]

One's confidence in his or her ability to predict the outcome of a gamble is stoked by a series of early wins. In a bull market, almost everyone wins. Amateurs who start investing during a bull market quickly come to believe that they have a special talent or skill at stock picking. An old Wall Street adage notes, "Everyone's a genius in a bull market." Early winners are more likely to continue buying stocks as the market turns sour, since early on they learned to believe in their investing genius.

Overconfidence actually changes how people remember. Individuals' memories of prior events are biased to support their current overconfidence. There is a hardwired tendency for individuals to preferentially remember their wins over their losses. What's more, most people "misremember their own predictions so as to exaggerate in hindsight what they knew in foresight."[13]

There is also a tendency to blame negative outcomes on uncontrollable circumstances and to take credit for positive outcomes as a result of one's foresight and expertise. Too often, people attribute success to their own judgment (and expert predictive ability) and loss to external forces beyond anyone's capacity to forecast.[14]

Experts are particularly susceptible to overconfidence. Possibly due to pressure from the social consensus that they have more knowledge and skill than others, experts trust their own judgment more highly than they should. Overconfident decision making has been found to be a consistent pattern among financial experts and professionals, including entrepreneurs,[15] investment bankers,[16] executives, and managers.[17, 18]

There are conditions in which overconfidence is rapidly extinguished, such as during decision-making tasks where (1) predictability is high, (2) swift and precise feedback about the accuracy of the judgments is provided, and (3) tasks are highly repetitive.[19] "Correspondingly, expert bridge players, race-track bettors, and meteorologists were found to be well-calibrated in their predictions."[20]

The financial markets are characterized by unstable payoffs (predictability is low) and often require a dynamic frequency of transactions (sometimes high activity, sometimes quiet). For traders, swift and precise feedback is provided, yet this feedback is unstable and depends on market conditions. Investors receive much less frequent feedback. As such, overconfidence is a particularly acute problem among investors. In general, investors who are overconfident believe they can obtain large returns; thus, they trade often and they underestimate the associated risks.

ILLUSION OF CONTROL

What conditions provoke investor overconfidence? In the above study, it was clear that an early series of wins leads to overconfidence. In the study that follows, subjects were found to be overconfident if they had more control over the decision-making process. Subjects were either given a lottery ticket with random numbers or allowed to choose their own numbers. After receiving their ticket, they were then offered a trade for a lottery ticket with better odds. People who had chosen their own numbers preferred to keep their tickets more often than those who had been given a random ticket. Those who chose their own numbers wanted an average $9 to give the ticket up. Those who were randomly assigned a lottery ticket wanted only $2. Based on this result, the experimenters argued that familiarity and choice lead to an illusion of control.[21]

Other researchers found that the illusion of control is actually an overconfidence in one's predictive abilities, not a belief that one can control the outcome. People are more attached to, and value more highly, their personal prognostications and stock picks. In general, researchers have found that the illusion of control is more likely when:

- Many choices are available.
- One has early success at a task.
- The task one is undertaking is familiar.
- The amount of information available is high.
- One has personal stake in the outcome of the choice.
- One has more control over the decision process.[22]

WINNING CHANGES THE BRAIN

Overconfidence may arise as a result of learning that one is performing well. In functional magnetic resonance imaging (fMRI) studies, Brian Knutson found that winning money activates the MPFC. The MPFC is at the terminus of the dopamine pathways of the reward system, and it is associated with both positive feelings and reward learning. In particular, activation of the MPFC signals that a reward pursuit action was successfully completed.

When the MPFC is activated, it represents a signal that one is on track toward desired goals. When an action has yielded large rewards consistently, to the point of satiation, then one can shift his or her cognitive resources elsewhere. Soon, the risky activity will be undertaken with little attention paid to potential dangers.

The MPFC is activated by many types of reward besides money. For example, seeing a favorite product (such as a favored brand of coffee, beer,

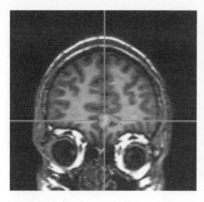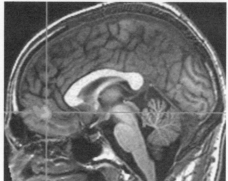

FIGURE 8.1 Coronal and axial views of the medial prefrontal cortex (MPFC) after subjects received a monetary reward.

or soda) activates the MPFC. This brand-based activation indicates satisfaction with the product. Trusted others also activate the MPFC to some extent. Injections with cocaine and amphetamines activate the MPFC, suggesting a mechanism for the positive feelings associated with these drugs. The MPFC may be where drug addicts have learned to associate drug use with pleasure. This same brain region is associated with reward learning, such that financial success may lead to less motivation in reward pursuit and a stronger attachment to the status quo. Figure 8.1 depicts the MPFC just after subjects received monetary rewards.

For many people, there is an internal success thermostat. That is, when investors achieve their financial goals, then their motivation drops off. People need challenge to prosper, and when victorious at one activity repeatedly, the novelty wears off and complacency sets in. As a result of this complacency, risks are disregarded, and losses may suddenly ensue.

A very successful trader I met mentioned that he has a "profit ceiling" that inhibits his success beyond his internal set point. He said that he has all the money he will ever need, he gives lavishly to charities, and the only reason he continues to trade is to achieve his personal expected annual return. Beyond that internal benchmark, he is unmotivated.

This lack of motivation caused some stress in his life. If he didn't trade after he achieved his goal in June, then what was he to do for the rest of the year? Often, he would trade poorly, churning his account until the new year. When trading out of obligation and boredom, he reported occasionally forcing trades that he didn't have his heart in—too often with negative outcomes. To combat the boredom, he appealed to his competitive nature, setting personal benchmarks and challenging himself to meet them after his primary goal had been achieved.

THE NEUROCHEMISTRY OF EXPLORATION

How people approach challenges depends on their personal neurochemistry. Individuals either (1) set about exploring their environment or (2) pause to take advantage of an opportunity. Whether they do (1) or (2) depends on their neurochemical balance.

As seen in the examples above, when a reward is found, dopamine neurons reinforce the reward-producing behavior. Dopamine neurons modify the strength of the signals that led to the reward-obtaining behavior (usually by increasing signaling to the MPFC). This is a process of reward learning via the dopamine pathway.

If a behavior is no longer rewarding, then norepinephrine levels increase in the brain. Norepinephrine stimulates scanning for new opportunities.[23] Norepinephrine, a chief neurotransmitter responsible for vigilance and attention, induces people to explore their environment and shift their attention frequently. Higher (but not excessive) norepinephrine activity causes increased vigilance and improved focus.[24] Some of the newest medications to treat attention deficit–hyperactivity disorder (ADHD) act exclusively on norepinephrine receptors (e.g., atomoxetine, a norepinephrine reuptake inhibitor).

When investors are extraordinarily profitable for a year or two, they begin to feel confident that they can continue to perform highly. Their dopamine-based reward learning process encodes a profitable pattern of behavior. Subsequently, however, highly profitable traders may have difficulty maintaining the same level of attention to risk management because of a chemical shift in their brains. They become slightly bored and push the limits of their abilities (and risk exposure in order to continue to feel challenged. The combination of low relative dopamine levels during trading (because they have already learned profitable techniques) and elevated norepinephrine levels provokes increased boredom, distractibility, and scanning for new opportunities.

ONE WHO KNOWS: CHRISTIAN SIVA-JOTHY

Christian Siva-Jothy was formerly one of the biggest proprietary traders on Wall Street. While head of proprietary trading at Goldman Sachs, "his trades, the size of his bets, the consistency of his annual profits for the bank, and his grace under pressure had become the stuff of legend among traders."[25]

In 1994, while at Goldman Sachs, Siva-Jothy was under pressure to beat his performance from 1993, during which he had earned $100 million for the firm through currency and derivative trading; 1992 had also been an excellent year, and as a result, "I'd been on a bit of a roll and got carried away with it." As Siva-Jothy explains, "I was a bit full of myself...." Going into 1994, Siva-Jothy had built up a large long yen position. By early February, his position was up $40 million. As his profits grew, "People were starting to say, 'Christian is going to do it again.' "[26]

During the first weekend in February 1994, Bill Clinton verbally assaulted Japanese trade policy. As a result, the yen sold off and Siva-Jothy's positions began to unwind. "I was selling out of the position as fast as I could, but I was selling just to stand still because I was short these puts. It was a disaster. Markets have a way of taking it out of you."[27]

Goldman lost between $100 and $200 million as a result of the trade. But Siva-Jothy didn't emotionally collapse, "On day eight of this episode, when the biggest move happened and I lost about $40 million in one day, I remember this overwhelming desire to get up and walk out, to pretend it wasn't happening. It was such a powerful emotion. Instead of walking out, though, I took a deep breath and liquidated everything."[28]

Instead of yielding to a powerful denial urge, Siva-Jothy executed the necessary trades. In strongly emotional situations, our cognitive "defenses" can be our worst enemies. Honing the courage to face one's powerful emotions requires practice and inner strength.

When hedge fund consultant Steven Drobny asked Siva-Jothy what he learned from his 1994 loss, he replied, "Confidence is a very, very dangerous thing. Simply because you've had a good run doesn't mean it will continue. In fact, once you've had a good run you're at your most dangerous. Overconfidence is an absolute killer.... It doesn't matter how well things are going, you should always kind of pinch yourself, take a step back, and ask, 'what can go wrong?' In fact, the better things are going, the more you should look at where your risks are and what the downside is."[29]

CONFIDENCE—THE "GOOD" KIND

> "I always knew I was going to be rich. I don't think I ever doubted it for a minute."
>
> —Warren Buffett

> "One of the most strikingly evident traits of all the market wizards is their high level of confidence.... But the more interviews I do with market wizard types, the more convinced I become that confidence is an inherent trait shared by these

> *traders, as much as a contributing factor to their*
> *success as a consequence of it. ... An honest self-*
> *appraisal in respect to confidence may be one of the*
> *best predictors of a trader's prospects for success in*
> *the markets."*
>
> —Jack Schwager[30]

Jack Schwager, author of the Market Wizards series, explains that any trader who does not have "absolute confidence in their ultimate success should be cautious about entering the business." Yet that confidence must be grounded in reality. Great traders are confident they can manage volatility and unexpected events because they are flexible. Information that contradicts their positions is eagerly investigated. Great traders are realistic, adaptable, and prudent—they use good money management techniques and recognize that they can lose.

Confidence is largely learned through experience, as one becomes comfortable with one's ability to cope with, and even take advantage of, market volatility. In great investors, confidence underlies resilience following losses, and it allows one to change strategy on a whim. Confidence lies atop an intrinsic sense of certainty and self-esteem, usually learned by successfully overcoming challenges, and confidence itself perpetuates success in many businesses.

Confidence is imperiled in traders who invest without a plan. Market volatility and unpredictability will quickly erode their self-esteem and unnerve them. Self-discipline and preparedness are necessary to maintaining healthy confidence.

Dr. Van K. Tharp, a psychologist who works with traders and investors, suggests that one of the most basic traits of winning traders is that they believe "they've won the game before the start." A European researcher who mailed a survey to hundreds of currency traders discovered that a "tackling attitude" is deemed necessary by traders for success in their line of work.[31] Other investigators report that decisiveness is essential for traders, regardless of the stressors they are facing on or off the trading floors.[32]

All of these traits—supreme self-assuredness, a tackling attitude, and decisiveness—are developed through competence and experience. Feeling humility in the face of the markets and yet "comfortable in my own skin" are important for traders. Given that healthy confidence can easily grow into unhealthy overconfidence, how can one maintain perspective?

The appropriately self-confident are humble and realistic, but also prepared and assured. The overconfident are self-centered and narcissistic. They blame external circumstances for their mistakes and take credit for chance successes. The best word to describe the difference between overconfidence and self-confidence is *ego*. Overconfident people put their ego in the game. It's all about them.

SOLUTIONS

Overall, overconfidence leads to a number of mistakes in decision making. The overconfident attribute bad outcomes to uncontrollable circumstances and good outcomes to their own excellence. Furthermore, they have trouble learning from feedback that is not immediate because they have a hindsight bias—they are less likely to try to learn from their mistakes because they think "I knew it all along... I'll prepare better next time." They then distort feedback so it feels better and makes them appear in a favorable light.

In one study, educational seminars reduce the effects of one behavioral effect of overconfidence (not saving enough). Education may attenuate overconfidence in other arenas as well. A technique for minimizing overconfidence among individual investors involves alerting people to the nature and negative consequences of overconfidence.[33] Among venture capitalists, studies have shown that improved knowledge may improve their decision quality and minimize the effects of overconfidence.[34, 35]

Besides education, journaling can be an effective (if time-consuming) way of self-correction. Journaling involves keeping written records of one's thought process (logic), subsequent decisions (actions), and outcomes (results). If one reviews his journal entries periodically, he may see patterns of thinking that underlie bad decision making. The journaling process is described in detail in Chapter 21.

Siva-Jothy reports, "I impose discipline on myself by keeping a trading diary. Every morning I go through the same process: If I have my positions on, I ask why do I have the positions? What has changed?"

Siva-Jothy describes the primary qualities he looks for when hiring traders as "passion and humility." Passion is a product of a strong reward system (particularly the NAcc), and humility is an antidote to overconfidence. Furthermore, conscientiousness is crucial if one is to learn from mistakes and keep one's passion well directed: "Integrity is the single most important thing to me in hiring." Regarding his own trading success, Siva-Jothy comments, "A lot of this is luck, but humility is probably the most important thing.... You also have to enjoy it. Too many people come into this business for the money, and that's not going to work out over time."[36]

The next chapter will report on the emotional flip side of overconfidence—fear.

CHAPTER 9

Anxiety, Fear, and Nervousness

How Not to Panic

"If you spend more than 14 minutes a year worrying about the market, you've wasted 12 minutes."
—Peter Lynch

Fear is uncomfortable, and it can drive investors to make rash, often poor, financial decisions. Fear can be so overwhelming that it overrides reason, patience, and good judgment. When less intense, fear is experienced as a gnawing sense of worry. In either form, fear has distinctive effects on financial decision making.

Among investors, intense fear often leads to panicked selling. Many novice investors first experience panic when the price of a stock they have overweighted in their portfolio begins a rapid and unexpected plunge. Watching one's wealth evaporate like this is a terrifying experience. Surprisingly, it's not only inexperienced investors who experience intense fear during the trading day.

Jim Cramer, former hedge fund manager, founder of TheStreet.com, and currently star of CNBC's television show *Mad Money*, is intimately familiar with investing emotions. In one of the columns he wrote for financial web site TheStreet.com, he described the feeling of being caught in a rapidly losing position. In the following excerpt from that column, he is dramatizing the experience of being caught on the wrong side of a short squeeze in the fictional stock "National Gift." Traders who are short shares of a rapidly climbing stock experience a pressured "squeezing" feeling as they quickly lose money, hence the phrase "short squeeze":

Now the world is collapsing around you. Your breath, it isn't happening, it is forced. Your forehead is flushed. You are sweating profusely and you are scared. You can't even panic. You can't even react. You can't do a thing.

"Buy 200,000 National Gift at the market!" you shout out as the hammer that's been slamming your head instantly goes away. "Just &*$&##@ buy the &*(%$&\$ thing.". . .

It has to do with fear. Fear is the real driver of stocks. . . . Head traders like Todd Harrison can smell fear from symbols and prices. And you can never hide the smell of your own fear.[1]

Jim Cramer's lucid account of panicked selling highlights two of the chief emotional obstacles for investors—fear and panic. Yet fear doesn't always sabotage investors; by summoning courage, it can be used to one's advantage. Panic, however, is always a bad thing. While fear can crescendo into panic, they are quite disparate experiences. In this chapter I will primarily describe fear and its financial effects.

There are five principles essential to understanding fear and panic:

1. Fear leads to physiological changes in the body (forced breathing, sweating, head pressure). Thus, it can personally be identified.

2. Fear causes changes in how people think about and react to bad news (indecision, paralysis, building pressure, and panic). Thus, it often leads to bad decisions.

3. Fear is different from panic. Fear is an anticipatory emotional state. Fearful people see many risks. Panic is reactive, and it is characterized by an urgent pressure to act immediately.

4. It takes tremendous effort and fortitude to "keep one's cool" when frightened.

5. Other investors' fear can be detected in the markets, often via an experienced reading of price dynamics.

People's natural reaction to perceived threats is to get away from them. Yet most experts can coolly stand back, take a deep breath, and analyze the dangerous situation logically. The courage required to push back against fear and the panic reflex is honed through experience, practice, and mental exercise. The inner strength needed to look at all sides of an investment objectively, including one's own emotional reactions, is one of the key traits of successful investors.

While it isn't difficult to be conscious of one's anxiety, it is tremendously challenging to objectively question the merits of it when experiencing it. Anxiety orients one's cognitive resources toward preparation for the perceived threat, making deviations from such a train of thought extremely uncomfortable and effortful. There is also a socially infectious element to fear. In the markets, part of the reason it's hard to fade (trade against) fear relates to the collective changes in thinking and behavior that accompany it, which are often reflected in the media and among colleagues. If one can objectively observe investor anxiety, such as by using mental training exercises, learning the signs of fear in market prices, and employing sentiment indicators, then it can be used to improve investment returns.

CLIMBING A WALL OF WORRY

It's an old adage that the stock market "climbs a wall of worry." Often, stock prices seem to rise while investors and the business media are fretting about one or another potential danger. However paradoxical, worry actually provides opportunity. The following *Wall Street Journal* quote, from June 1997, illustrates: "Market watchers and investors alike expressed a measure of awe—and a dose of trepidation—as the market scaled what looked to them like a sheer cliff."[2] While investors were nervous that the market rally would falter, a growing sense of confidence in the economy drove them to buy.

Intense fear is different from the worry that accompanies rallies. Strong anxiety cannot last long, though it feels interminable to shortsighted investors. Investors are biologically induced into short-term thinking by the stress hormones released during episodes of acute fear. Fear has the effect of inducing concrete short-term thinking with poor flexibility in judgment. Following a fearful event, as stress hormone release abates, and the intensity of the fear subsides, investors start seeing bargains where they previously saw only danger. In the short term, periods of high market fear usually present excellent buying opportunities (such as the fear that preceded the 2003 invasion of Iraq).

Figure 9.1 is a chart of the S&P 500 (the SPY index) from June 2001 to February 2002. Two sentiment indicators are superimposed on the index prices. The first indicator is the amount of fear expressed in the business news (the *Nightly Business Report*), while the second is the amount of joy expressed in that broadcast. Notice how the stock market appears to rise when the level of fear is greater than the level of joy. The market appears to fall when joy is more prevalent than fear.

This is a "cherry-picked" example of a period in history where joy and fear levels correlated with market price trends. Usually, such correlations, while significant in a statistical sense, do not provide for excess trading returns.

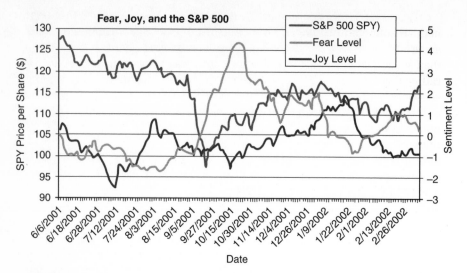

FIGURE 9.1 The levels of fear and joy in the *Nightly Business Report* around the September 11, 2001, New York City terrorist attacks. The values are superimposed on the S&P 500 (SPY). Notice that when fear is dominant over joy, the market tends to rally, and when joy is more prevalent, the market declines. This technique works only in emotion-driven markets.

DREAD IN THE MRI

> *"The key to making money in stocks is not to get scared out of them."*
>
> —Peter Lynch

It makes sense, evolutionarily, that anxiety is such a powerful driver of thinking and behavior. For our ancestors on the Serengetti, not heeding signs of danger could lead to sudden death by crocodile or lion. People without rapid panic reactions couldn't last long. In fact, agoraphobia (fear of open spaces) runs in families. It is thought that this gene was preserved by those of our ancestors who experienced hair-trigger anxiety when walking across an open plain (where they could be targeted by predators or enemies). Because of their hypervigilance, they presumably would be the first to escape the danger zone and continue their genetic lineage.

Anxiety is such an uncomfortable feeling that people will often accept greater short-term pain just to end an anxious waiting period quickly. There is a psychic cost to anticipating a negative event, which is a result of the attention and energy our minds devote to "dread."

Professor Gregory Berns at Emory University used functional magnetic resonance imaging (fMRI) to measure neural activity as subjects awaited electric shocks. Some individuals dreaded the shocks so much that, when given a choice, they preferred to receive more voltage sooner rather than waiting for a less painful shock later. These "high dreaders" showed greater activation in their brain's pain circuits during *anticipation* of the shock. Even during an experimental condition in which they had no opportunity to hasten the delivery of the shock, the "high dreaders" continued to display greater neural pain system activation. Such neural pain circuit activation implies that the "high dreaders" were mentally replicating the anticipated "pain" of the shock as they were waiting for it.[3] They accepted greater pain in the short term just to end their ongoing (mental) suffering. The anticipatory pain truly was "all in their heads," but to them, the experience of it was real.

As an event approaches in time, anticipatory fear intensifies. Even when an event's expected probability and severity remain constant, anticipatory dread escalates as it approaches in time.[4] When research subjects are told that they will receive an electric shock at a specific point in time, their heart rate, galvanic skin response, and reported anxiety all increase as that time approaches.[5]

"Chickening out" is one result of increasing anticipatory anxiety. In one study, students were asked if they would perform mime routines in front of their class the following week for a payment of $5. Sixty-seven percent (six of nine) of the students who had agreed to mime chickened out when the designated time arrived. Yet the students reported the same probability and severity estimates of possible negative consequences in both weeks. Their objective observations of risk remained constant, but their decisions changed.

In a modified version of the above experiment, students who had recently watched a fear-inducing film clip were significantly less likely to initially volunteer to tell a joke in front of the class the following week than those who had not seen the movie clip.[6] Experiencing fear from an extraneous source prevented risk-taking in other areas.

NATURE VERSUS NURTURE

Fear arises from several brain regions that together form the loss avoidance system. Long-term fear-based memories are recorded in the brain's amygdala (fear processing) and hippocampus (memory center). During periods of high (but not extreme) stress, fearful memories are recorded in greater detail in these structures.

There are two fear-related pathways that travel through the amygdala. The fast pathway drives automatic, reflexive responses to threats—activation of this circuit occurs below conscious awareness and is not affected by prefrontal cortex inputs. Being exposed to passive threats, or witnessing fear in one's colleagues, can be enough to activate unconscious fear.

Amygdala sensitivity is both related to past experiences and one's genetics. The short form (polymorphism) of the promoter region of the serotonin transporter gene (5-HTT) has been associated with susceptibility to fear conditioning (after traumatic experiences) as well as increased anxiety and emotional illness. This gene may be associated with greater vulnerability to life stress, such that individuals with this gene are less resilient and more likely to develop anxiety disorders when exposed to intense threats.

Another way to measure the role of genetics versus environment in shaping emotional responsivity is to look at the prevalence of psychiatric disorders in relatives. Anxiety disorders, even in people with identical DNA (identical twins), have less than one in three odds of simultaneous occurrence. "Nurture" (life experience and environmental events) has the dominant role over "nature" (genes) in determining who ends up with anxiety disorders. This dominance of "nurture" over "nature" is true for most types of anxiety: panic disorder, generalized anxiety disorder, and social phobia, among others.

While anxiety does have genetic contributions, one's life experiences and environmental events are most influential in determining whether someone will develop a full-blown anxiety disorder. For example, after a large stock loss, one may become afraid of the markets for a brief period. This type of fear is "conditioned." After one has been conditioned to be afraid of an event or circumstance, without concerted intervention, it can take decades for that fear to be extinguished. For example, many adults learned to fear bank savings accounts during the Great Depression, and some Depression survivors put their money "in the mattress" for decades after the economy had recovered. Habits borne out of self-protection die hard. There is likely a lifelong interaction between biological factors (e.g., genetic) and environment in the establishment and remodeling of networks involving fear and fear memory.[7] Regardless of one's personal sensitivity to fear, we can all use similar techniques to learn to manage it.

IT'S ALL IN YOUR HEAD

Neuroimaging data shows that cognitive techniques help manage fear. In several fMRI studies, amygdala and limbic system activation are reduced after individuals are trained to use cognitive fear-reduction techniques.

When they are confronted with feared items (such as spiders) or events (such as public speaking), their fear circuits are less active than prior to the training.

The placebo effect is a fascinating example of the prefrontal cortex's power—demonstrating how beliefs and expectations alter how we experience the world. Most people's level of anxiety is reduced by placebos,[8] implying that there is a significant element of cognitive control that underlies fear. In one study, researchers placed a cream on the arms of experimental subjects before they received a series of painful electric shocks. In the first condition, participants were told that the cream was a highly effective new topical anesthetic that would reduce the pain of the impending shock. In another condition, subjects were told that the cream was electrode paste, intended to improve the conduction of the shock to their skin. In fact, the cream was inert and identical in both conditions.[9]

About one-third of subjects experienced decreased pain when given the alleged anesthetic. For subjects who expressed less pain when given the purported "anesthetic," researchers noticed a significant reduction in activation of their brain's insula (pain processing) and increased activation in their prefrontal cortex (cognitive attentuation of emotional intensity). Increased activation in the prefrontal cortex predicted pain relief. Furthermore, researchers found that prefrontal cortex activation reduced their insula activity in response to the shock (after it was delivered).

The researchers concluded that expectations of pain relief, working through the prefrontal cortex, could control "even the most primitive and conserved of evaluative mechanisms: the visceral response to pain."[10] These results demonstrate that how we think about danger, whether electric shocks or an impending bankruptcy, significantly alters one's emotional experience of it. It is possible to profoundly alter physical and emotional experience by altering one's beliefs.

EMPATHY GAPS

Jim Cramer, the celebrity investor cited in the opening vignette, illustrates the challenge of managing intense feelings while losing money in an investment. Most investors have had experiences like Cramer describes, on some level, multiple times. If fear is so painful, why do investors leave themselves vulnerable to it by trading "too big," and not using protective stops or price alerts?

There is a "projection bias" that unites how people feel today and how they expect to feel in the future. That is, they project their current feelings into the future and expect to feel the same then as they do now.

In one study of people working out at a campus gym, everyone entering and leaving the gym was asked to read a short vignette and answer a question in exchange for a bottle of water. The vignette described three hikers who had become lost in the dry Colorado mountains without food or water. One follow-up question asked whether hunger or thirst would be more unpleasant for the hikers. Another question asked whether, if the subject were in the hikers' position, they would find hunger or thirst more unpleasant. Of people entering the gym, 61 percent thought the hikers (and themselves) would find thirst more unpleasant. Of those leaving the gym after their workout, 92 percent thought the hikers would find thirst more unpleasant. Those leaving the gym were projecting their own feelings of thirst onto others.[11] It is difficult to imagine a future outside one's window of recent experience.

These findings suggest that if the markets are calm, investors will tend to project the tranquility into the future. Similar projections probably hold true for established bull markets, bear markets, and long periods of price volatility. Fearful investors often cannot take the pain, in part, because they project that it will continue indefinitely. They sell in order to escape the pressure of declining positions—pain for which they can see no end.

During calm markets most investors don't prepare adequately for volatility. They cannot accurately forecast how they will feel and what they might do in such conditions. They project their current sense of security onto their future self. Some naïve investors take on excessive credit risk because they see no threats on the horizon and they project an excellent borrowing climate into the foreseeable future. Investors caught with excessive risk exposure during a credit contraction are the origin of the Wall Street adage, "It's only when the tide goes out that you learn who's been swimming naked." When credit dries up, those who took excessive risk, whatever their justifications, are exposed.

Many people intellectually understand that they will feel differently about risk in the future, but they still do not prepare adequately for those conditions because they cannot *feel* now how they will feel then. Recall the college students who intellectually estimated the social risks of performing a mime routine in front of their class. They then agreed to perform the routine. Yet when the time arrived to perform, two-thirds of the students anxiously backed out even though their intellectual risk assessments remained constant. There are several techniques that can be used to reduce the projection bias.

PAIN RELIEF

Much of the battle in debiasing from fear lies in education, self-awareness, and courage, all functions of the prefrontal cortex. One's ability to rationally evaluate and respond to threats, rather than reacting to internal tension or feelings, hinges on his or her ability to plan, control impulses, and make reasoned decisions. While the amygdala generates panicked reactions, its activation can be modulated by activity in the prefrontal cortex.

It is extremely difficult to challenge fear, so courage is necessary. Courage underlies one's attempts to find counterexamples for every nervous assumption and inclination. As seen with the placebo effect, fear generates a self-fulfilling prophecy of loss and financial pain. Fortunately, everyone has the power to change their point of view and maintain an objective perspective by consciously manipulating their thoughts, beliefs, and expectations.

Exercises such as cognitive reframing and "thinking through" alter how one thinks about potential threats. Psychotherapies such as cognitive-behavioral therapy (CBT) use conscious thought manipulation (including "thought replacement") to decrease anxiety. Further descriptions of these techniques appear in Chapter 22.

In the markets, many investors use sentiment scales, which measure levels of market fear. Interestingly, by measuring others' fear, they themselves often don't feel it as intensely, and they can be more objective while others are suffering. On sentiment scales, extreme fear readings serve as an indication that the market is likely to rebound. Investors who sell during fearful market periods are likely to miss large subsequent rallies as the fear subsides and confidence returns.

INVESTMENT LESSONS

When investors anticipate further short-term losses before a stock recovers, and this is especially true for those with vivid imaginations and "high dreaders," they will be compelled to sell out immediately in order to avoid expending further (painful) attention on the bleeding position. On the flip side, it is emotionally difficult to buy a declining stock whose current shareholders are panicky.

When considering entering a risky investment, anxiety gives rise to risk-averse behaviors such as "hesitation pulling the trigger," "second guessing," "analysis paralysis," "reflecting," "delaying," and "fear of entry." In fact, many investors want to see price "confirmation" before feeling confident enough to buy. This may be a result of the projection bias in which declining stocks are seen as likely losers and rising stocks are extrapolated into the future as winners.

On one hand, the stock market climbs a "wall of worry." Most investors avoid investing when anxious, preferring to wait until their uncertainty has cleared. As a result, they wait too long to invest and buy into rallies. Their delayed entry leads to subpar long-term performance. As with many things in life, doing the hard thing—exercising emotional courage and buying during periods of high anxiety—leads to better long-term outcomes.

One does not hear about the stock market climbing a "wall of panic." During periods of extreme fear, the market falls sharply. The most apt advice for these times is, "Don't catch a falling knife." For most investors, watching their portfolio values declining is extremely painful. As investors' pain collectively rises, many start "jumping ship," selling out just to relieve the tension. Taking the pain now feels better than holding tight through a market downturn.

During market panics, out-of-the-money put option premiums rise far beyond rational levels, indicating that panicky investors, trying to hedge their portfolios, are buying puts in droves. The actual likelihood of a crash is overestimated by panicky investors, who are driven more by stress hormones than reasoned thought. Individuals with the temerity to sell puts to panicked traders can earn large returns.

OF HURRICANES, RISK PERCEPTIONS, AND OPPORTUNITY

Hurricane Katrina struck the Gulf Coast of the U.S. in 2005, and it was followed by another powerful hurricane several weeks later—Hurricane Rita. Katrina flooded New Orleans. Vivid images of people stranded on their rooftops begging for help, and bodies floating in the brown water that submerged residential neighborhoods, saturated the media. Katrina was the most expensive natural disaster in U.S. history. Insurers were liable for billions of dollars in damage claims and they raised their premiums over 50 percent each of the following two years.

There was an increasing perception that category 5 hurricanes would devastate this area of the U.S. more frequently. An excellent scientific study was published in 2005 that indicated a strong increasing trend in the rate of powerful hurricanes in the Atlantic, and Al Gore's movie, *An Inconvenient Truth*, about the catastrophic environmental risks of global warming, was released after the hurricanes struck. Because of representativeness, the recency effect, and the attention bias (see Chapter 19), many Americans were afraid that such global catastrophes would occur with vastly increased frequency.

Savvy investors, especially reinsurers, smelled opportunity in the astronomically high risk perceptions. Both Warren Buffett's Berkshire Hathaway and billionaire investor Wilbur Ross have poured money into Gulf

Coast reinsurance enterprises. Reinsurance firms sell insurance to insurance companies themselves, assuming the responsibility for massive claims that would bankrupt small insurance companies. In a *Wall Street Journal* interview, Ross explained such investments by stating, "What we are betting on is that the perceived risk exceeds the actual risk. That's fundamental to the theory of everything we do." Fear irrationally drives up risk perceptions, and savvy investors locate such opportunities and exploit them.

SUMMARY

In summary, fear prevents most investors from taking an optimal level of market risk. People are especially afraid of anticipated negative events, and they sell in increasing force as the event approaches. Anticipating a negative event is so psychically painful that many people will sell for a loss simply to avoid having to "take the pain."

Personal susceptibility to fear is primarily a function of environmental influences, life experiences, and genetic background. Many investors are conditioned to fear stock market volatility after they lose money in shares. Because of their fear, many will be unable to stomach buying bargain-priced stocks during a declining or bear market. Unfortunately for them, it is during periods of high fear that the best short-term stock bargains are found.

Many people cannot predict what they will do during stock routs or bear markets because they cannot empathize with their future selves. Rather, they project their current feelings onto themselves in those circumstances, and they think, "I'm fine with risk."

Fortunately, automatic fearful responses to risk can be changed by consciously modifying one's beliefs. Many psychotherapy techniques now exist to decrease financial risk aversion.

The next chapter explores the physiological reactions to fear and stress that power such cognitive distortions.

CHAPTER 10

Stress and Burnout

Traders Age in Dog Years

"I can put my hand on my heart and say I don't get stressed out by the markets. ... I've seen people get very stressed, and if you're stressed, you can't do this job effectively."

—Christian Siva-Jothy[1]

Successful portfolio manager Jon Brorson was profiled in the *Wall Street Journal* in the summer of 2006.[2] He had made a good call for his investors at Neuberger Berman in May 2006, shifting toward "defensive" stocks before the market took an 8 percent plunge that month. As the *Wall Street Journal* put it, "When the market cracked in mid-May, he was exultant, as his move to caution had put him ahead of the more bullish competition." Yet Brorson remained defensive, missing the market rebound in late summer and early fall of 2006.

Brorson was growing worried as the market climbed. The market's price action contradicted his expectations, and he felt that he was missing out. As the Dow hit new all-time highs, Brorson became increasingly distressed—immersing himself in information via his two trading terminals, CNBC, and his analysts. Throughout September he worked long hours and slept poorly. As CNBC floor commentators called the market's mood "optimistic," Brorson muttered disagreement, "Time to sell. Time to sell."[3] Brorson and his associates believed that third-quarter earnings could disappoint, so they decided not to chase winners in the weeks before earnings, choosing instead to wait until late October to jump back in.

Brorson was experiencing escalating stress. Unaccustomed to falling behind, he now found himself in a market that contradicted his expectations and beliefs. He decided to allow an external criterion (earnings) make his timing decision for him. But he found himself psychologically trapped—he needed his fund to at least stay even with the market, inclining him to chase securities upward, while simultaneously trying to wait for the anticipated negative earnings reports, after which he could pick up bargains. Because of his dilemma—being caught between his own expectations and the contradictory behavior of the market—he was unable to relax until either (1) the market sectors he disliked dropped or (2) he capitulated and bought rallying stocks.

STRESS

> *"Stress is the condition that results when person-environment transactions lead the individual to perceive a discrepancy—whether real or not—between the demands of a situation and the resources of the person's biological, psychological or social systems."*
>
> —Edward P. Sarafino[4]

Stress arises out of the discrepancy between where one is and where one imagines they should be – a conflict between their expectations and reality. If that difference is too large, for too long, chronic stress will physically wear them down, leading to burnout. Anxiety, antagonism, exhaustion, frustration, distress, despair, overwork, and fear are all types of stress.

There is an important distinction between different intensities of short-term (acute) stress. At low levels acute stress can be motivating: it stimulates activity, sharpens attention, and enhances goal focus. Additionally, brief episodes of high or moderate stress, such as experienced during an amusement park roller-coaster ride, can be exhilarating. However, at extreme levels, acute stress often induces an overwhelming "fight-or-flight" urge (panic).

Prolonged high stress leads to a number of negative physical and mental consequences. Such chronic stress impairs short-term memory and concentration and promotes hypervigilance—too often leading to interrupted sleep, high blood pressure, and adverse metabolic effects. Chronic stress contributes to accelerated aging, decreased immune function, depressed mood, apathy, and diminished energy. Eventually, chronic stress results in "burnout."

Many traders experience chronic stress at work. A common saying relating traders' stress to its physical consequences is that, "Traders age in dog years." As if for each year of trading, that trader ages seven years. The rest of this chapter will examine investment stress, its neuroscience, consequences, and strategies for reducing its adverse effects.

CRAMER ON STRESS

On March 11, 2000, days from the all-time high of the NASDAQ, Jim Cramer published a rewrite of his wife's 10 trading commandments on TheStreet.com. Her fourth trading commandment addressed the paralysis accompanying extreme stress—a consequence of unbearable losses:

> *If you feel like a position of yours is going to drown you in your own pool of losses, please the trading gods and throw a maiden in the volcano. ... (**I can't tell you how important it is to have your head clear. The only way to clear it when you are having the &(&*%*% knocked out of you is to take a small loss. It loosens the vise and allows you to think again. You need to be clear-headed to make money. If there is a position that is dogging you, take some of it off, throw the maiden in the volcano and please the gods. This is not as silly as it sounds. You will breathe regularly and you will be able to make a better decision. Also you will have your eyes open for the next big chance.)* [original bold]*[5]*

CHOKING FOR RUPEES

Dan Ariely is a psychology professor at Harvard where he frustrates (with brain puzzles), shocks (electrically), freezes (in cold water), and otherwise stresses out his student volunteers. None of his experiments threatens permanent damage, but they do have interesting effects on participants' state of mind. Ariely induces and Cramer describes market-style stress.

In high-pressure environments, where a lot of money is at stake, why do many people "choke"—underperforming their actual abilities? Ariely was curious about the effect of financial incentives, such as end-of-year bonuses, trying to close a large deal, and stock market gains and losses, on individual performance. The conventional assumption was that higher pay leads to better performance in such incentive-based decisions, but Ariely suspected that such an assumption is inaccurate.

When designing an experiment to investigate choking, Ariely quickly realized that he couldn't afford to run the study in the developed world.

He thought salaries in the United States and Europe were too high for his meager research budget to make an impact on subject decision making. Having already developed a network of university students in India, Ariely traveled there to run his experiment in one of his students' home villages (where average salaries were incredibly modest). Workers in the chosen village spent, on average, $10 per month.

Ariely designed his experiment so that subjects would play one of several different types of games. Some required superior cognitive skills, and others demanded physical performance in the effort to earn a large jackpot. The highest-paid players could earn several weeks' expenses based on one outstanding performance. They could earn a total of six months' expenses if they executed the tasks perfectly. To his subjects, Ariely's financial rewards seemed enormous.

Ariely divided the subjects into three groups. In each task, the first group received 0 Indian rupees (Rs) if they performed poorly, 2Rs if they did "good," and 4Rs if they had "very good" results. The second group played for 0Rs, 20Rs, or 40Rs depending upon their performance, while the third group could win 0Rs, 200Rs, or 400Rs. The third group was playing for, relatively speaking, very high stakes. (Approximately 45Rs equal US$1).

Subjects played several different tasks, including the classic memory game Simon, the concentration game Labyrinth, and the motor skills game Dart Ball, among others. Subjects played each game 10 times. They achieved "very good" performance if they accomplished a predetermined success criterion. Eighty-seven subjects participated, with one-third selected randomly for each payoff group.

Ariely found that participants in groups 1 and 2 had a statistically similar rate of achieving "very good" results, approximately 30 percent of the time. However, participants in group 3, who were playing for several weeks' expenses in each game (the equivalent of over $2,000 for the average American), performed worse than the other groups, achieving "very good" performance only 10 percent of the time. Playing for high stakes sabotaged their performance.[6]

In many experiments where subjects make large amounts of money, they often relax their attention as their wealth accumulates, decreasing the rate of their earnings. Interestingly, Ariely found no such "wealth effect." Subjects in Ariely's experiment who initially earned large gains did not experience performance reversals during the later tasks.

Outsiders who were asked how they thought people would do in Ariely's experiment predicted that performance would improve as the amount of money at stake increased. In general, most people are unaware that stress over high stakes will adversely affect their performance. If they had such insight, they could take preemptive action against excess stress—performing relaxation exercises or using cognitive reframing techniques.

Among some financial market professionals—investment bankers closing large deals and negotiators for single high-stakes outcomes—choking is more likely. In many ways, "choking" stress is purely perceptual: we think that stakes are high, but as in Ariely's Indian experiment, "high" stakes are relative to one's context and experience.

WHICH GOES WRONG—THE BRAINS OR THE BRAWN?

Ariely had found that performance stress caused "choking" among the most highly rewarded subjects. Yet it wasn't clear to Ariely whether stress was impairing the subjects' cognitive or physical performance. For example, it was possible that stress did not impact their thinking, but rather it impaired their dexterity and motor coordination. In order to verify his results in the developed world and clarify whether the decreased performance was primarily due to the motor or cognitive effects of stress, Ariely designed a new experiment for Massachusetts Institute of Technology (MIT) student volunteers.

In the motor task, subjects were asked to type a series of letters on a keyboard as rapidly as possible. On the cognitive task, subjects were asked to find two three-digit numbers (e.g., in the format 1.23) whose sum was 10. These numbers were hidden within a 3×3 matrix of like numbers. Students with "very good" performance on either the motor or the cognitive task could earn $300.

Ariely found that as task payoffs increased, motor skills increased, but cognitive skills decreased. Importantly, subjects performed worse at the mathematics task when more money was at stake.[7] According to Ariely, this cognitive decline when under stress is due to a shift in decision-making strategy. Under stress, the brain shifts its processing and decision functions from "automatic" to "manual" control. "Manual" control implies that the participants are overthinking their task strategy. The brain's realignment to a "manual" strategy is unconscious and very difficult to reverse once play has begun. Recall that a similar effect—the distortion of intuition by conscious analysis—was discussed in Chapter 5.

As stakes increase, investors have trouble using smooth intuitive decision making. When they realize that the amount of money at stake in their investments is larger than ever before, they can easily lose their focus and concentration. They inadvertently shift from automatic to manual cognitive control, and this shift ruins their ability to fluidly respond to market events.

In a third experiment at MIT, Ariely examined the role of social observation on performance. Participants were asked to solve anagrams (mixed-up collections of letters that spell a word when decoded) either at private cubicles or on a blackboard in front of three people. Performance was rewarded financially. Subjects who solved the puzzles in private solved 1.16 anagrams per minute, while subjects who solved publicly figured out only 0.67 per minute. Being observed had a strong detrimental effect on cognitive performance.[8]

Many financial planners, advisers, brokers, and portfolio managers experience the stressful effects of observation on their performance. When clients are closely watching a manger's gains and losses, the manager's investment skills are likely to be constrained. Besides the disproportionate time they require, this may explain why nervous and controlling clients are so irritating to many financial planners.

Hedge fund managers who utilize a two-year lock-up of client funds may feel less social pressure, though quarterly reporting requirements prevent true independence from client observation.

STRESS AND TREND PERCEPTION

The following study demonstrates that stress intensity is not only proportional to how bad things actually are. In fact, much of the stress response is generated by perceptions of a worsening in conditions. A "really bad" situation that appears to be improving to "pretty poor" status provokes relief, while a "neutral" situation that is worsening toward "poor" can be quite stressful.

Researchers examined the stress responses of two groups of rats after they were subjected to painful electric shocks. Group 1 received painful electric shocks 10 times per hour, while Group 2 was shocked 50 times per hour. The second day, all rats were shocked 25 times per hour. At the end of the second day, rats from Group 1 (who experienced an increase in shock rate) had elevated blood pressure (a physical sign of stress). Rats from the second group (who experienced a decrease in shock rate) had normal blood pressure.[9] Why the difference?

The rats were responding to the perception of a worsening or improving situation. The Group 1 rats were in a worsening situation. On day two, the rats in Group 1 were stressed to experience 25 shocks per hour, while the Group 2 rats were relieved to be subjected to the very same event.

In the markets, if investors believe that the economy is going from bad to poor, they may feel relieved and subsequently buy stocks. On the other hand, if they believe that the economy is going from neutral to poor, then they will feel stressed and will prepare for increased economic risk by selling stocks. Perceptions of future stress are felt now.

NEUROCHEMISTRY OF STRESS

When people worry or get stressed out, their bodies secrete chemicals that prime them to fight, flee, or perform other quick evasive actions. Animals under stress relieve their discomfort by *acting*, but humans are usually left to simmer in their stress hormones, often never acting out in a way that relaxes the stress response.

The psychological effects of acute stress response are often adaptive: "If you're in dangerous conditions it helps to be distractible, to hear every little sound in the woods and react rapidly, instinctually. . . . It's like getting cut off on the highway. You don't want to be a slow, thoughtful creature. . . . You want to react and hit brakes."[10]

Chronic stress results from a series of acutely stressful events that chemically "prime" the body for adverse circumstances. Over time, the bodies and minds of the chronically stressed adapt to the chemical priming agents, resulting in the negative physical and mental effects described below.

The chemistry of the human stress response is understood as resulting from two primary brain pathways. The immediate stress response prepares the body for urgent struggle. Within seconds the sympathetic nervous system (SNS) is activated. A small nerve bundle in the brain stem called the locus ceruleus (see Figure 10.1) releases norepinephrine, triggering a cascade of physical preparations for struggle. The SNS is a network of nerve fibers running to large skeletal muscles, the heart, the skin, the diaphragm, and the sphincters (among other areas). When SNS nerves fire in alarm, physical signs such as trembling, perspiration, rapid heart rate, shallow breathing, and pupillary dilation occur. The SNS is responsible for the physical reactions to acute stress and panic.

The second neural pathway manages the stress response over minutes to hours. During acute stress, a signaling hormone is secreted from the hypothalamus, which travels via the bloodstream to the pituitary gland where it triggers the release of a second hormone, adrenocorticotropic hormone (ACTH). Via the bloodstream, ACTH travels to the adrenal glands, where it triggers the release of cortisol and epinephrine (adrenaline). The hypothalamic-pituitary-adrenal (HPA) axis is the control structure of the

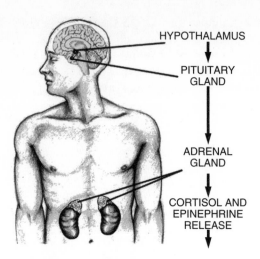

FIGURE 10.1 Hypothalamic-pituitary-adrenal (HPA) axis. The stress hormones travel through the bloodstream and trigger a cascade of physical and hormonal reactions.

chronic stress response, involving the interactions of the hypothalamus, the pituitary gland and the adrenal glands.

The interactions between the rapid and slow stress responses are variable, depending on the nature, intensity, and duration of the stressor. One of the most straightforward ways to measure short-term and chronic stress is via levels of the hormone cortisol, which can be sampled in saliva (cheek swabs) or blood (vein draws). Cortisol levels naturally vary throughout the day, rising in the morning from 4 A.M. to a daily peak 30 to 45 minutes after awakening. One's cortisol level then slowly declines until a smaller late afternoon peak, and later begins a precipitous drop at 10 P.M. until the 4 A.M. trough.

Beyond daily variations, cortisol levels are also raised by threat perceptions. There are anatomical connections among the amygdala (the brain's urgent fear center), the hippocampus (the memory center), and the hypothalamus (the HPA axis control center), which facilitate cortisol release when a threat is recognized.

BIOLOGICAL EFFECTS OF STRESS

The biological effects of stress are many. Atrophy of the hippocampus, due to severe stress, results in poor concentration, short-term memory loss, increasing impulsivity, and difficulty delaying rewards (time discounting).

Chronic stress impairs immune system functioning and increases susceptibility to viral and bacterial infections.[11, 12] Weight gain and high blood pressure can result from chronically elevated stress hormones.

Behaviorally, passivity follows from stressful experiences. High
cortisol levels in monkeys undergoing stress are correlated with conflict
avoidance and decreased aggression.[13] There are also indications that
lower social rank leads to chronic stress and flattened cortisol levels.

Stress, especially uncontrollable stress, elevates levels of a brain
enzyme called protein kinase C (PKC). PKC affects parts of the brain
involved in abstract reasoning, concentration, and short-term memory.
High PKC levels impair short-term memory, concentration, focus, and
judgment. Additionally, high levels of PKC increase impulsivity and
susceptibility to thought disorders (such as delusions).[14]

According to one stress expert, stress is most damaging when one feels
a loss of control: "It doesn't have to be traumatic, as long as you feel out of
control," she said. "Control is the essential factor. . . . If you are confident,
you don't have these problems."[15] Unfortunately for investors, control is
exactly the thing they lack over the markets. Therefore, to manage investment stress, control must be exerted where it will have an effect, such as
in designing bulletproof money management systems, performing superior
research, establishing a solid investment philosophy, and communication
with clients.

ADRENALINE JUNKIES

If only it were so simple as "stress = bad" and "cortisol = bad." Yet
"adrenaline junkies" and "roller-coaster riders" enjoy recreational stress.
There is a paradox here. For most people, moderate stress, over a short
period, feels good. Successfully coping with moderate stress can have beneficial physical and emotional effects.

In the brain, moderate amounts of cortisol facilitate dopamine release
in the reward pathways. The essence of enjoyable stress is the knowledge
that it is taking place in a safe and benign environment, is under control
(someone can stop the ride if a malfunction occurs), is somewhat unpredictable, contains surprises, and occurs over short periods—seconds in the
case of slot machines, and minutes in the case of a roller coaster.

Most investors enjoy the rush of trading. They like taking risk and
savoring the thrills of the market roller coaster. A number of financial
planners recommend setting aside a small percentage of one's total capital
for recreational trading. This allows retail investors to get a thrill using
a small portion of their total assets without jeopardizing their long-term
financial security.

MANAGING INVESTMENT STRESS

In general, if a stressful event is predictable, then it evokes a decreased stress response. The markets are anything but predictable, leading to greater stress among investors who are trying to forecast future price movements. If one becomes acclimated to a stress trigger (such as the fear of heights for an experienced parachutist), then the stress response diminishes to almost nil. Experienced traders do in fact have decreased stress responses to market volatility, but not improved performance.[16]

Some financial information predisposes investors to stress. The way that price and order information is displayed taxes cognitive resources. Traders who watch price quotes, tick by tick, are particularly susceptible to chronic stress and burnout. The more one checks stock quotes, the more likely they are to see volatility. When the brain weighs every downtick twice as heavily as every uptick (as described in Chapter 14), the brain undergoes a slow stress erosion. To prevent stress when observing market prices, avoid watching current positions unless they hit a predetermined alarm level (most brokers offer such alarms). Additionally, it can be very helpful to reduce ambient noise. Pressures to multitask during the workday, unless you find those distractions useful for macro pattern recognition, should be minimized.

Many traders can tell a woeful story about the time they shifted their attention during the trading day, maybe to an urgent phone call from a family member, and when they returned to the markets they had lost a huge sum. It's crucial to minimize distractions during the workday.

Stress is increased by such a lack of control and a perception of conditions worsening. Researchers found that dogs who were given electric shocks that they could terminate by making body motions got fewer ulcers than "yoked" dogs who were given identical but uncontrollable sequences of shocks.[17] Our perceived ability to exert some control over a noxious event reduces the amount of anxiety and distress we experience.

Many investors operate in isolation from others, acquiring information via impersonal computer monitors or telephone calls with strangers. Social support diminishes the stress response, but many investors have little intimate contact with their families, friends, and even colleagues. Attendance at professional social groups, such as the Technical Security Analysts Association, can be very helpful for finding social support from others dealing with the same challenges in the markets.

Many great investors report that constant information monitoring, while isolating them from their family, helps them to identify developing opportunities before others. Yet, in order to spend more quality time with family or friends, it's helpful to set strict boundaries on the information that one will monitor after hours.

Investors need to be prepared for every contingency. As positions deteriorate and stress levels rise, the brain becomes cognitively inflexible and unable to think of solutions. Suddenly, panicking out of bleeding positions may appear the only viable option.

SUMMARY

Stress affects every market participant, often in very different ways. Financial advisers working with difficult clients and proprietary traders in volatile markets have very different stressors, but their bodies' responses are the same.

Investors making high-stakes transactions are susceptible to "choking." As seen in Ariely's Indian study in this chapter, choking caused two-thirds fewer subjects to exhibit "very good" performance when they were playing for the highest payoffs. The choking was caused by a performance-deteriorating shift from "automatic" to "manual" control of decision making and behavior. The effects of stress were entirely cognitive, as motor accuracy and speed actually increased in stressed subjects.

Short-term stress triggers hypervigilance, physical preparedness for action, and attention shifting. Acute stress leaves an "action-potential" residue that lingers until it is discharged. Many people develop stress-related disorders because they chronically do not discharge their stress-primed action tendencies. This may be one reason why exercise is so beneficial for health—it discharges the physical action potential.

Chronic stress shrinks the hippocampus and impairs memory, learning, mood, and sleep cycles. Additionally, the chronically stressed have lowered immunity and increased susceptibility to chronic illnesses.

Moderate stress triggers dopamine release in the reward system and promotes learning and development. However, stressors that are unpredictable, uncontrollable, or of worsening severity provoke a more negative stress reaction.

Professionals who experience overwhelming stress may "throw a maiden in the volcano" (sell part of a stressful position) to relieve some of the stress intensity and regain their automatic, intuitive decision-making capacity. Social networks, exercise, and self-discipline in money management are essential to stress reduction.

The next chapter is a cautionary tale of the tragic consequences of gambling in the financial markets.

CHAPTER 11

Love of Risk

Are You Trading or Gambling?

*"We should know that too much of anything, even a
good thing, may prove to be our undoing ... [We]
need ... to set definite boundaries on our appetites."*
—William J. Bennett[1]

During the lunch break at a mutual fund industry conference, I
mentioned to my neighbor at the lunch table that I'm an investment psychologist. I was overheard by someone a few seats
away.

Andrew was seated across the table, and it was apparent that he
was interested in my profession. He got my attention and said, "Let's
talk."

"Sure," I responded. He stayed seated and didn't say anything else until
the end of lunch.

After about 20 minutes, the chair to my left emptied. Andrew moved
into the vacant seat. He was about 60 years old, short and portly, with a
mischievious shine in his eyes. He had physical presence and charisma.

Andrew said he was a broker-dealer in Fairfield, Connecticut, a
wealthy exurb of New York City. He wasted little time getting to his point.
"Richard, I need to talk to you."

"Okay," I responded.

"I want to talk about trading." His tone was matter-of-fact, but there
was a tremor in his voice.

"All right. Do you want to talk about it here, now?" I asked.

"What is you opinion of Netflix stock?" He asked abruptly. (Netflix is
an online movie rental company.)

I began to explain my limited thoughts on Netflix.

"What do you think about Baidu?" (Baidu is a Chinese Internet search engine and was a recent initial public offering [IPO] on the U.S. stock market.)

I reoriented myself. As I started to ask why he was interested, he again cut me off. He didn't care to hear my stock opinions. Something else was eating at him. He fixed a long stare on me, and he then he began the real story.

"I have hunches, and I follow my hunches," he said. "Over the last few years, my hunches have been very good to me."

He looked at me thoughtfully. "Can I tell you something that's very personal?" I nodded.

"I have lost $7 million dollars since January." He paused for effect.

"What happened?" I asked.

Andrew explained that he had made, and subsequently lost, multimillion-dollar sums three times over the past two years in his personal account. A year previously he took out a home equity loan for $500,000 to play one of his hunches in the markets. His hunch was that Netflix stock would soar over the next three months. He bought calls, using almost the entire $500,000 on one undiversified bet.

Fortunately for Andrew, he was initially right—Netflix rallied all through the spring of 2005, and he made $4 million. Then he got a hunch about eBay stock. He again bought calls—$3.75 million worth. eBay's price stayed flat, with brief terrifying downturns and short-lived, but hope-inspiring, rallies. By the Monday of options expiration week, his calls were worth only $650,000. By Friday, they had expired worthless. He had only $250,000 left in his account from his original $500,000 home equity loan. He let that money sit in his account for three months until his next big idea emerged.

In October 2005, he got another "hunch" about Netflix stock. He bought as many calls as he could. As Netflix climbed over the next three months, he rolled them over into the front month each month through December. As their value increased, his account ballooned to $7 million. He took a trip to Kansas to see his extended family over the winter holidays, and he let his positions ride into the new year.

Andrew told me, "Maybe I never should have left those positions open, but I couldn't think straight anymore." On the flight from JFK to Kansas City, he recalls, "I couldn't get it out of my head—I could have bought the ticket of everyone flying to Kansas that day. I was intoxicated with the money, and I didn't know what to do."

"So what did you do?" I asked.

"Nothing," he said.

"What do you mean 'nothing'?" I was stunned that he (1) didn't have some type of strategy and (2) lost $7 million he couldn't afford while he was on vacation for three weeks.

"When I got back they were worth a lot less—maybe $700,000. Then I rolled them over for the next two months and they eventually expired worthless. Today, I have $81,000 left—that's all, and it's all in out-of-the money Baidu calls that expire in three weeks." His speech became pressured. "And you know what's the worst thing?" he asked me. "I owe millions of dollars in capital gains taxes. I didn't sell any of my positions to raise money for taxes. Now I don't have the money. I don't even know how I'm going to pay for my kids to go to college anymore. I have to pay the home loan back."

His short-term trading profits had led to a massive IRS bill at the turn of the year while he was in Kansas. And then he had lost everything, including the money to pay the taxes. He was in debt $2.7 million to the IRS.

After the conference's afternoon workshop, Andrew invited me to look at his brokerage account figures on his laptop. He showed me the highs and lows of his statements over the past year, month by month. He had been taking on so much risk that he was virtually guaranteed to go broke. His "risk of ruin" was 100 percent.

As we were looking at his account statements, Andrew repeatedly told me, "I should have sold when I had $7 million. If only I'd sold when I was up."

After we examined his trading records, Andrew asked me point blank, "Do you think I'm a gambler?" He was a broker who certainly had seen a few wild speculators at some time in his career, yet he couldn't identify his own behavior.

He thought the problem with his boom-and-bust trading profits lay in the markets. He had a series of "what if" questions tailored to avoid taking responsibility for his terrible performance: "What if I hadn't gone to Kansas City?," "What if I hadn't bought more calls in January?," "What if I had paid more attention to the markets?"

Yet, just like him, I couldn't help but wonder, "Andrew made a 10-fold return three times over the past two years. While his risk management is suicidal, what about his hunches? Could he be doing something right?" It is easy to be seduced by short-term, but unsustainable, profits.

Investors who make a big win early in their careers are more likely to develop a gambling problem in their investing style. Perhaps because they attribute their success to an innate skill or talent, and not to random luck, they spend many years trying to revisit their initial performance peak.

Before we parted from the weekend, Andrew agreed to take the free "Gambling or Trading?" screen on the marketpsych.com web site. He called me a few days after the conference to ask: "Baidu is still trading sideways; do you think it's going to go up?"

"Did you take the gambling screen on the web site?" I asked.

Andrew said he had taken the screen, and he was classified as "High Risk for a Gambling Problem." He acknowledged that his trading was just like gambling. But he still wanted to know what to do with his large long position in Baidu.

I tried to give him some perspective. "You just indicated you've got a gambling problem, and then you asked me to comment on your betting strategy."

Andrew replied, "But I need to pay my taxes, and I have a hunch about Baidu."

"Well, what you just said sounds like trouble. You're trading to get back your money. You must know that never works," I said.

"I don't know what to do," he replied.

"I can't tell you what to do. Everything you've told me indicates you're gambling, and you need to cut your losses."

"I know, but I have a hunch about Baidu."

The conversation went along like this for a few minutes.

Baidu never rallied enough to put his calls in the money. I suspect he lost everything on that position. I wish I could relate a happy ending, how he paid off his home loan and packed his kids away to college with confidence, but I haven't heard from him since.

The story of Andrew illustrates one of the ugly sides of trading. While some traders achieve tremendous success, others take excessive and unsustainable risk. The thought traps that gamblers fall into are exaggerated versions of the cognitive biases that afflict many investors.

KNOWING WHEN TO FOLD 'EM

Gambling in the markets is more dangerous than casino gambling due to the high leverage available. The widespread use of futures and options and the anonymity and sense of personal control allowed by online trading accounts incite investors' risk-seeking urges. Some traders take excessive risk because they are unable to weigh probabilities of gain and loss accurately. That is, they do not understand sustainable risk management. That was certainly the case with Andrew, whose story I told at the beginning of this chapter.

Researchers have found that most individual investors buy stocks with "lottery" characteristics (high volatility, good stories, low probability of large gains). Similar to lottery ticket sales, the demand for lottery-type stocks increases during bad economic times. Even more, there is a correlation between states that have legalized gambling and the tendency of investors in those states to purchase lottery-type stocks.[2]

Some investors turn into gamblers during bull markets. They start making money easily. They increase their position sizes. They do well and feel invincible. Money comes to them effortlessly. They don't realize how much risk exposure they have taken on. Then one day they find themselves rapidly losing, and they don't understand what is happening. Because their "illusion of control" (see Chapter 8) has been reinforced by early gains, they continue with the same old strategy, and they lose more and more, until they've lost not only their paper profits, but also their principal.

Not all high-stakes risk taking is problematic. In some areas of business, such as in start-up companies, the margin between spectacular success and dismal failure can be very narrow. Successful entrepreneurs have often taken risks that others deemed unwise. If those entrepreneurs had failed, they may have been pathologized as "gamblers" or "rogue traders." Furthermore, many investors trade risky or speculative stocks for recreation, and they rationally understand and accept the risk of total loss. In the markets, when does investment risk taking become outright gambling?

There are a few key differences between people who invest recreationally and those who have a gambling problem. Most recreational investors trade with money that they can afford to lose. They don't lie about or misrepresent their wins and losses when describing them to others. Their statistical "risk of ruin" is very low. The "risk of ruin" represents the mathematical odds that all one's assets could be lost in the markets, given the average size of one's positions and their price volatility.

It's possible to diagnose gambling characteristics in one's trading by asking a series of tough personal questions. The following questions are modified versions of the DSM-IV criteria for diagnosing pathological gambling. If you answer "yes" to two or more of the questions in Table 11.1, then you are at risk of having a gambling problem in your trading.

PATHOLOGICAL GAMBLING

> "The gamester seeks the gambling-house, and wonders, his body all afire, 'Will I be lucky?'"
> —The Rig Veda, Hymn 10.34

Studies of gambling have focused on two measurable aspects of the gambling experience. Psychological surveys often gather information on

TABLE 11.1	The "Trading or Gambling?" Screen (also available at www .marketpsych.com)

If you are a trader who suspects you may have a gambling problem, please answer the following questions.	**Yes or No Response**
Are you preoccupied with trading (e.g., preoccupied with reliving past trading experiences, planning the next venture, or thinking of ways to get money with which to trade)?	
Do you need to trade with increasing amounts of money or leverage in order to achieve the desired excitement?	
Have you had repeated unsuccessful efforts to control, cut back, or stop trading?	
Are you restless or irritable when attempting to cut down or stop trading?	
Do you sometimes trade as a way of escaping from problems or of relieving a negative mood (e.g., feelings of helplessness, guilt, anxiety, or depression)?	
After losing money on a trade, do you often return to the markets to get even ("chasing" your losses)?	
Do you ever lie to family members, colleagues, or others to conceal or minimize the extent of your involvement with trading?	
Have you committed illegal acts such as forgery, fraud, theft, or embezzlement to finance your trading?	
Have you jeopardized or lost a significant relationship, job, or educational or career opportunity because of trading?	
Have you relied on others to provide money to relieve a desperate financial situation caused by trading?	

Note: These questions were adapted from the *Diagnostic and Statistical Manual of Mental Disorders,* 4th edition (DSM-IV) diagnostic criteria for pathological gambling.

the cues (triggers) and cognitions (thoughts) that accompany or activate gambling behavior. Neuroscience studies attempt to understand how the brains of pathological gamblers operate differently than normal brains.

Pathological gambling is the oldest documented financial disorder, having been described in both ancient Greek texts and in the Rig Veda of the Upanishads. Problem gambling, which is less severe than pathological, afflicts 3.6 percent of women and 6.9 percent of men in the United States. While the current incidence of pathological gambling is between 0.5 and 1.0 percent of the population, the lifetime prevalence of compulsive or pathological gambling disorder in the United States is between 3.5 percent and 6.3 percent.[3]

Pathological gambling is psychiatrically classified as an impulse-control disorder, and it is characterized by a psychological insensitivity to risk, increased impulsivity, a lack of self-control, a loss of appropriate social value priorities, and the pursuit of pleasure through risk taking. Pathological gamblers have higher rates of emotional afflictions such as depression, anxiety, and substance abuse (particularly alcohol) than others.

Some specific emotions and cognitions fuel pathological gambling. Studies have shown that gamblers are triggered to bet by feelings of distress and irrational hopes. Other triggers include being alone in the evening and thinking about one's finances.

When asked to describe their gambling, those who use positive, hopeful terms, rather than realistic concerns, are more likely to continue gambling. Gamblers who mentally compartmentalize losses versus gains are unable to recognize that their net return from gambling is negative, and they tend to persist in gambling even after large losses.

THE GAMBLER'S BRAIN

Risk and potential return have a powerful allure for gamblers. According to Hans Breiter, MD, co-director of the Motivation and Emotion Neuroscience Centre at the Massachusetts General Hospital, "Monetary reward in a gambling-like experiment produces brain activation very similar to that observed in a cocaine addict receiving an infusion of cocaine."[4]

Each of the primary motivational systems, the reward-pursuit and loss-avoidance systems, has a distinctive character in pathological gamblers. On the one hand, gamblers appear to be less reward responsive. They have decreased concentrations of dopamine receptors, making them less sensitive to everyday novelties and interests. This finding is borne out in studies of gambler physiology during gambling experiments. Gamblers showed both (1) less anticipatory heart rate increase when facing likely losses and (2) less heart rate increase following wins. Gamblers are not as afraid of loss, and they are less excited after winning, than nongamblers.[5]

In further support for the contention that gamblers are underaroused, neuroimaging research shows that gamblers have decreased activity in their neural reward systems on functional magnetic resonance imaging (fMRI) scans. In fact, the severity of their gambling illness correlates with the lack of activity in the reward system.[6]

Desensitized dopamine systems drive gamblers to self-stimulate with games of chance, temporarily increasing their dopamine levels when rewards are anticipated and received. Paradoxically, Parkinson's disease patients, who have chronically low dopamine levels in their brains, can become pathological gamblers (up to 40 percent) when given a dopamine receptor activating medication (pramipexole) in their treatment course.[7]

As explained previously, the prefrontal cortex is essential for planning, reasoning, and impulse control. Gamblers have decreased performance on tasks requiring prefrontal skills such as inhibition, time estimation, cognitive flexibility, and planning.[8] During gambling experiments, the best performers (those who learn to avoid high-risk/low-reward options) have the highest prefrontal cortex activity on fMRI scans.[9] However, gamblers have neural activations associated with poor impulse control during decision-making experiments.[10] The origins of problem gambling lie in poor impulse-control and hypoactivity of all three major brain systems: prefrontal cortex, reward system, and loss system during risky decision making.

OUGHT TO KNOW BETTER

Many celebrities enjoy casino gambling. Among some celebrities and politicians, a common justification for excessive gambling is, "I can afford it, so what's the problem?"

The former United States drug czar (under President George H. W. Bush) Bill Bennett had made dozens of trips to casinos in Atlantic City and Las Vegas in the 1990s and early 2000s. He was a "preferred customer" at several casinos, and sources put his total losses at more than $8 million.[11] When *Washington Monthly* and *Newsweek* reporters interviewed Bennett about his gambling habit, he responded: "I play fairly high stakes. I adhere to the law. I don't play the 'milk money.' I don't put my family at risk, and I don't owe anyone anything."[12] Bennett himself claimed to have been nearly breakeven in his gains and losses: "Over 10 years, I'd say I've come out pretty close to even."

Bennett is also the author of the best-selling *Book of Virtues*, which intends to instruct children and adults in living a principled life. In the book he writes, "There is much unhappiness and personal distress in the world because of failures to control tempers, appetites, passions and impulses."[13]

Bennett may not have a gambling problem in a strict sense. He is a wealthy man, and he has no debt or family disruption due to his gambling. However, his preference for high-stakes slot machines, late at night (midnight to 6 A.M.), mirrors the behavior of many problem gamblers. He is likely suffering from a gambler's cognitive distortions when he asserts that he is nearly break-even. Most likely, he is unable to accurately assess the magnitude of his actual losses; otherwise, he would probably quit (as he stated an intention to do after the *Washington Monthly* article was published).

Celebrities who report large gambling losses include basketball legend Charles Barkley (having lost at least $10 million) and professional golfer

John Daly (who claims to have lost $50 to $60 million). Basketball great Michael Jordan enjoys gambling, and there are published accounts of his large financial swings in casinos. Some experts speculate that people with a competitive nature, such as athletes, are susceptible to developing gambling problems. They want to win against the gods, even though the gods of the odds play by different (mathematical) rules.

REDUCING GAMBLING

Medications, psychotherapy, and educational interventions have all been studied as treatments for pathological gambling. Medication treatments use one of three neural strategies: (1) improving impulse control in the prefrontal cortex, (2) increasing fear of loss in the amygdala, or (3) decreasing gambling cravings by bolstering the reward system. Psychological treatments, such as psychotherapy, target cognitive distortions that minimize losses and the social costs of gambling.

Education about mathematical probabilities did not change gambling behavior in one study, indicating that the decision to gamble tends to be an emotional, not an intellectual, process.[14] Warnings that describe irrational gambling beliefs do decrease gambling behavior,[15] which implies that irrational beliefs and expectations can be changed when they are directly contradicted (as can happen in psychotherapy).

The most widely used medication treatment for pathological gambling is naltrexone.[16] Both naltrexone and nalmefene are medicines that block mu opiate receptors, and they have both been found useful in reducing gambling among gambling addicts.[17] In the reward system, mu opiate receptors stimulate dopamine release.[18] Blocking opiate receptors with naltrexone decreases dopamine release in the nucleus accumbens, which results in decreased subjective feelings of pleasure.[19] Gamblers taking opiate blockers are not compelled to seek reward-system stimulation through further gambling, possibly because they feel reduced pleasure from the financial ups and downs.

The medication bupropion (which is popularly known as Wellbutrin or Zyban) modulates dopamine pathways in the reward system. This medication also appears to reduce gambling behavior somewhat, with fewer side effects than the opiate receptor blockers.[20]

SUMMARY

Pathological gambling is not a lifelong illness. It often waxes and wanes over one's lifetime. It can arise unexpectedly in previously disciplined investors, or it can suddenly disappear after years of struggle. Many celebrities have experienced problem gambling. Among traders with annual incentives, excessive risk taking can be rational (from a self-interest perspective) but lead to pathological losses for their clients. For investors who find themselves succumbing to excessive, and dangerous, risk taking in the markets, a gambling screen for traders is available at the marketpsych.com web site to help them assess their vulnerability.

Gambling feels good to people who have desensitized reward circuits. The rush of dopamine release that accompanies wins is a deeply satisfying, and addictive, pleasure. Problem gamblers see losses as less threatening than nongamblers. Furthermore, they have less impulse-control originating from the prefrontal cortex. As a result, pathological gamblers use wins to feel good, experience little pain due to losses, and have trouble controlling their urges to engage in gambling.

Treatment for pathological gambling involves psychotherapy to correct cognitive distortions, behavioral therapy to reinforce impulse control, and medication treatment to block the rush of excitement gamblers feel from dopamine release in the reward system. Pathological gambling can be successfully treated, but it requires motivation on the part of the afflicted to make it work, and that is often the primary obstacle to successful treatment.

CHAPTER 12

Personality Factors

What Are Great Investors Like?

"Investment philosophy is really about temperament, not raw intelligence. In fact, a proper temperament will beat high IQ all day."
—Michael Mauboussin[1]

In the 1983 movie *Trading Places*, Eddie Murphy (a wily street con artist) and Dan Aykroyd (an Ivy League heir and investor) had their identities reversed by two wagering millionaires. Could Eddie Murphy, with no prior experience, succeed in the trading pits? Could Dan Aykroyd pull himself out of poverty and homelessness with nothing but his own smarts? The comedic pair ultimately outwitted their interlopers and made a killing in "frozen orange juice" futures, bankrupting the millionaires in the process. Yet the question those two devious gentlemen gambled on remains unsolved: is it innate skill or life experience that makes a trader great?

The truth is—as with most psychological issues—there is no easy answer. The first stage of successful investing is having an edge. The second step involves conditioning one's mind for peak performance. This chapter is about the personality roots of personal excellence in the markets—those characteristics and traits that differentiate the great mind from the good.

Some characteristics of great investors are popularly known. For example, Warren Buffett has a keen intuitive sense of probabilities.[2] George Soros enjoys examining his investment thinking process for flaws, taking pleasure when he finds one. Most great investors are extremely

153

confident in their ability to succeed.[3] Yet these characteristics are not common to all great investors. Some investors have strength in one or another of these traits. One of the keys to investing success is to heavily exploit one's strengths while strictly avoiding areas of weakness.

While many success factors are intrinsic, some are learned through experience. Success is derived from strength in four psychological realms: (1) personality style (reviewed in this chapter), (2) cognitive faculties (mental acuity, critical thinking, speed, and intelligence), (3) emotional intelligence (motivation and passion, courage, emotional coping skills, and self-awareness), and (4) conditioning (training that improves personal weaknesses and enhances strengths). First, one should have a personality (internal disposition) that supports one's chosen investing style. Second, one should have excellent critical thinking skills including the ability to formulate prospects in terms of probabilities and expected values. Third, emotional intelligence and psychological traits such as confidence, decisiveness, and resilience after losses (which significantly overlap with personality traits) are important. Fourth, one should engage in training, develop resilience skills, and gain experience successfully navigating various crises and contingencies in markets.

A terrific challenge lies in studying diverse investor characteristics within a systematic framework. Anecdotes abound about what makes investors successful, but without systematic scientific study, it is impossible to develop a reliable sense of the ideal investor "profile." Another problem presents itself in the diversity of markets and personal characteristics necessary for investing success. Different people succeed in different markets at different times. Are there any broad traits that all great investors share? Personality research provides the best scientific technique for answering such a question.

This chapter is devoted to exciting developments in personality research. Personality is a collective pattern of character, behavioral, temperamental, emotional, and mental traits.[4] Recent academic research has shown that personality can be broken down into five general characteristics. These five traits (the "Big Five") are related to how people describe themselves using language. The "Big Five" traits are by no means complete. Among researchers there continues to be controversy over how many traits should be included in a taxonomy of personality (16 traits is another possibility[5]), but five is the best estimate so far. Remarkably, personality traits remain generally stable, within individuals, over the adult life span (exceptions are noted where applicable).[6] This chapter is primarily devoted to "Big Five" personality traits, while other psychological traits of great investors are mentioned toward the conclusion.

THE "BIG FIVE"

In 1936, two American psychologists, Gordon Allport and H. S. Odbert, hypothesized that: "Those individual differences that are most salient and socially relevant in people's lives will eventually become encoded into their language; the more important such a difference, the more likely is it to become expressed as a single word."[7]

In the 1970s, Lewis Goldberg, a professor of psychology at the University of Oregon, adopted a list of 1,250 phrases describing personality characteristics. He and his students went door to door, asking 750 homeowners in Eugene and Springfield, Oregon, to rate how well each of the 1,250 phrases described them. The phrases were statements such as "Like parties," "Follow rules," or "Fear for the worst." Subjects rated how well that phrase described themselves on a 1-to-5 scale. They circled either: "Strongly disagree," "Disagree," "Neither agree nor disagree," "Agree," or "Strongly agree."

Responses from 300 of the original 1,250 phrases statistically grouped into five different clusters. For example, people who agreed with "Like parties" also tended to agree with the statement "Radiate joy," implying that social and optimistic people have one type of personality trait (subsequently called "extraversion"). The five phrase clusters were named the "Big Five" personality traits: (1) neuroticism, (2) extraversion, (3) openness, (4) agreeableness, and (5) conscientiousness[8] (see Table 12.1). Many of the trait descriptions and item examples below are adapted from

TABLE 12.1 The "Big Five" Personality Traits

Personality	High Scores	Low Scores
Neuroticism	Scattered, indecisive, or pessimistic. Nervous.	Emotionally stable. Relaxed and mellow.
Openness	Open to experimenting with new ideas and experiences.	Traditional and conventional. Prefers continuity over change.
Extraversion	Gregarious, optimistic and social.	Introverted. Often enjoys being alone.
Conscientiousness	Self-disciplined, delays gratification, organized, rule-following, punctual.	Impulsive and disorganized. Difficulty following set methods or rules.
Agreeableness	Values cooperation and getting along with others, generous.	Self-interested and often mildly suspicious of others' intentions.

Professor John Johnson's free online NEO personality inventory which grew out of his work with Goldberg.

Statistically, test takers' responses distribute in a normal curve, with 40 percent of people scoring in the "average" range. Each test taker scores on a range from "very low" to "very high" on each trait. One who scores low on the extraversion scale is called an introvert, and one who scores high is called an extravert. "High" and "low" scores are more than one standard deviation from the average. Each personality trait has a primary pole and an opposite pole (which describes those who score low on the primary measure). Thus, a low scorer on extraversion is, by definition, high on introversion.

Taken together, all five personality traits balance each other in one's personality *style*. Some people have multiple strong personality traits. People who score highly on both conscientiousness and neuroticism are "perfectionists." An example of a celebrity high in multiple traits is the film director Woody Allen. Allen often makes light of his strong tendency to neuroticism. He is also quite extraverted, gregarious, and open, as apparent in his public persona. Being both extraverted and neurotic, he enjoys putting his nervousness on display, to humorous effect, in his movies. One's personality style is not determined by one predominant trait, but rather by how one copes with one's unique strengths and vulnerabilities and how all the traits work together.

Having some traits but not others does not make one a better or worse person. Each trait represents a way of seeing the world that is useful in some, but not all, situations. As we'll see later in the chapter, some traits do correlate with financial success, but the usefulness of traits depends on context. The same traits that facilitate success in a venture capitalist may impede the performance of a short-term trader.

Personality traits are somewhat heritable, which indicates that they have a genetic basis (although it is multifactored and complex). Personality traits are mild variants on a spectrum of experience and behavior that includes clinical psychiatric disorders at its extremes.

When reading the descriptions below, remember that these personaliy traits represent extremes of people's responses on several similar questions on the NEO test. Forty percent of respondents are "average" on each cluster. That means they share a balanced mix of each pole of the trait.

Extraversion versus Introversion

On the extraversion scale, high scorers are called "extraverts" and low scorers are called "introverts." Extraverts enjoy being with people, are full of energy, and often experience positive emotions. Extraversion is characterized by a desire to socialize, gregariousness, and a tendency toward optimism. Extraverts are more likely to strongly agree with phrases such as

"Love life." They tend to be enthusiastic and action oriented and engage in opportunities for excitement. In groups they like to talk, be assertive, and draw attention to themselves. Interestingly, functional magnetic resonance imaging (fMRI) studies show that extraverts have more reward-system activation to financial gains than do introverts.[9] That is, extraverts are more excited and motivated by opportunities for financial gain.

Introverts are typically quiet, low-key, deliberate, and less engaged with the social world. Introverts are comfortable without much social involvement, and this is neither due to shyness nor depression; they simply need less stimulation than an extravert and are more likely to prefer being alone. Introverts agree with statements such as "Avoid crowds." Introverts are motivated from an internal drive rather than from outside stimulation. That is, they generate motivation and excitement internally rather than seeking for external triggers.

Neuroticism versus Emotional Stability

Neuroticism is on the opposite pole from emotional stability. Those who score high on neuroticism experience more negative feelings such as anxiety, anger, or depression and are more emotionally reactive than others. They are more likely to identify with the phrase "Panic easily." Their difficulty in emotion regulation when under stress can impair their ability to think clearly, make decisions, and cope. In one fMRI experiment, the degree of participants' insula activation when threatened was correlated with their level of neuroticism.[10] This finding implies that neurotic people are more sensitive and reactive to signs of danger than emotionally stable people. This hypervigilance to threat can be exhausting, but it also ensures that they are prepared when real calamity strikes.

Low neuroticism scorers are "emotionally stable" and tend to be calm and free from persistent negative feelings. They are more likely to find the phrase "Remain calm under pressure" descriptive of themselves. Freedom from negative feelings does not necessarily mean they experience more positive feelings. In general, they are secure, hardy, and relaxed even under stressful conditions. The super-relaxed attitude of the emotionally stable can be a problem when real dangers loom. Neurotic people may sound the false alarm more often, but they also are sure to be attentive to potential risks.

Conscientiousness versus Impulsiveness

Conscientiousness concerns the way in which people control, regulate, and direct their impulses. Conscientiousness describes a tendency to plan and organize towards achieving goals, to follow rules while pursuing those goals, and to control one's impulses along the way. Conscientious people typically agree with the statement: "Know how to get things done."

Impulsiveness is on the other end of the conscientiousness pole. Impulsive people are likely to identify with the statement "Often make last-minute plans." In times of play rather than work, their spontaneity and impulsivity can be fun. A problem with impulsive acts is that they may produce immediate rewards but undesirable long-term consequences. Their accomplishments may sometimes appear small, scattered, and inconsistent.

Openness to New Experiences versus Traditionalism

Openness to new experiences describes a willingness to experiment with tradition, to seek out new experiences, and to think broadly and abstractly. Open people are intellectually curious, appreciative of art, and sensitive to beauty, and they are more likely to identify with the phrase "Like to solve complex problems." Open people often think and act in individualistic and nonconforming ways.

Traditionalists prefer the plain, straightforward, and obvious over the complex, ambiguous, and subtle. Traditionalists agree with the statement "Am attached to conventional ways." Compared to traditionalists, open people are often more aware of their feelings. Open and traditional styles of thinking are useful in different environments. An open intellectual style may serve one well as a psychologist or professor, but research has shown that traditional thinking is related to superior job performance in police work, sales, and a number of service occupations.

Agreeableness versus Self-interest

Agreeable people believe others are basically honest, decent, and trustworthy. Agreeableness reflects concern with cooperation and social harmony. Self-interested people place their own concerns above getting along with others. They are generally less interested in others' well-being, and therefore are unlikely to extend themselves for other people.[11] Agreeableness was not measured in the marketpsych.com Investor Personality Test, described below, due to space constraints. Yet it is of interest as one of the "Big Five" traits.

THE GENETICS OF PERSONALITY

One's unique life experiences have a large role in shaping who they are. During development, people learn how to respond to adversity and

TABLE 12.2	The Genes Weakly Associated with Risk Taking and Risk Attitude

Genes	Abnormal Variant
Serotonin transporter 5-HTT	Anxiety and depression sensitivity
Dopamine D4 receptor	Novelty and sensation seeking

opportunity from their caregivers and role models. Beyond such developmental conditioning, individuals are all endowed with inborn psychological differences rooted in genetics and biology. These hardwired differences are the basis of personality and are seen in infants. Exuberant infants tend to remain emotionally positive, social, and novelty seeking, while negatively reactive and inhibited infants are more likely to remain shy throughout their childhood (but not necessarily into adulthood).[12]

There are two genes that correlate (weakly) with scores on neuroticism and extraversion in individuals (see Table 12.2).

In the past four years, DNA analysis has revealed two personality findings related to genetics. The serotonin transporter (5-HTT) gene can have a polymorphism (producing a short version of the 5-HTT protein) that is present in a significant proportion of the population. The 5-HTT protein is a reuptake channel, similar in structure to that pictured in Figure 4.2 on page 49. The shortened transporter removes serotonin from the synaptic cleft more slowly. When serotonin molecules linger in the synaptic cleft, downregulation of the postsynaptic serotonin receptors occurs, causing serotonin desensitization and an experience of lower serotonin levels at baseline.[13] Neuroticism scores are correlated with the presence of the short serotonin transporter gene in individuals,[14] but the variance is high. It is an interesting finding, but it is by no means deterministic. The odds that one who carries this gene will become neurotic are only slightly greater than among noncarriers. Overall, the expression of neuroticism is multifactorial, depending on the interrelationship of multiple genes and life experiences.

Another gene-personality link involves the dopamine 4 (D4) receptor. The D4 receptor regulates sensation seeking (an aspect of personality similar to "novelty seeking"). Sensation seeking is one facet of extraversion. People who have the D4 polymorphism have more difficulty staying in monogamous relationships, and they report significantly more extramarital affairs in one study.

A high score on the personality trait of "sensation seeking" is indicative of risk-taking propensities in many domains (financial, recreational, social, and health). Sensation seeking is a highly consistent predictor of various kinds of risk taking, including compulsive gambling and participation in high risk activities.[15, 16] In fact, a Finnish study found that the sensation-seeking personality trait is correlated with overtrading stocks.[17]

Substantial heritability of sensation seeking may be inferred from evidence linking individual D4 concentrations and venturesome personality.[18] A recent study indicates that a combination of the D4 polymorphism with a polymorphism of the catechol-O-methyltransferase (COMT) gene predisposes individuals toward hypomania and extraversion.[19] Further research is needed to substantiate these links.

As seen from the evidence above, the gene-personality link is significant, but tenuous. Many genes are not expressed (turned on) unless a particular environmental event triggers them. Furthermore, single genes do not determine one's personality, rather it is a multifactorial (many gene) construct. For now, these findings indicate that we have only slightly greater odds than chance of knowing who will become neurotic or sensation-seeking. Simple pencil-and-paper tests, such as that described below, still do a better job of classifying people's personality styles than genetic studies.

INVESTING PERSONALITY

> *"Success in investing doesn't correlate with I.Q. once you're above the level of 25. Once you have ordinary intelligence, what you need is the temperament to control the urges that get other people into trouble in investing."*
>
> —Warren Buffett[20]

Do investors' scores on the "Big Five" correlate with performance? To investigate the performance/personality link, I set up a 70-item online personality test. The test uses 60 of the most significant personality phrases created by Goldberg and Johnson, and it has 10 research questions at the end. In designing this test I was looking for correlations between personality traits and financial decision making. The test measures four of the "Big Five" personality traits: neuroticism, extraversion, openness, and conscientiousness. First I'll explain the methodology underlying the study, and then the results follow.

By the time of this writing, 1,000 people had taken the test on marketpsych.com. Each test taker registered as a "businessperson," "trader," or "investor." In order to ensure data quality, I deleted all test reports that had clear response patterns (all "Strongly agree" answers, for example). I also deleted responses from people aged under 25 or over 80, from those originating in nondeveloped countries, and from people who had less than 5 years' experience. The personality items were numbers 1 through 60.

The experimental questions, listed below, followed the personality questions. The experimental questions were prefaced by a statement requesting honest self-report. Experimental Questions 62 and 63 asked about caffeine and alcohol use, and did not yield significant results. The provided responses used the "Strongly disagree" to "Strongly agree" format or, in Questions 69 and 70, used five numeric ranges from low to high values. The experimental questions follow:

61. (Dream) I think or dream about the markets or my positions while I am in bed, trying to sleep.

64. (Exit plans in place) I have exit plans in place, considering all the possible contingencies, before I enter my trading or investment positions.

65. (Hold losers too long) I hold my losing positions too long (often longer than I had planned).

66. (Cut winners short) Sometimes after my positions go up a lot, I take my profits even though I had not originally planned to.

67. (Double-or-nothing) Sometimes after taking losses, I find myself taking more risk in order to make the money back (to get back what I lost).

68. (Win left open) Often after I've had a big paper win in trading or investing, I leave my position(s) open, and my profits disappear.

69. (Total returns) The total returns of my trading or investing from January 2000 through December 2004 was approximately:

70. (Largest loss) The largest loss I have ever personally taken from a single trade or investment position, between 2000 and 2004, as a percentage of my total asset value, was approximately. . .

One major weakness of asking people to describe their behavior is called self-report bias. For example, people answer according to their innate biases. Those who are neurotic may be more likely to agree with negative self-descriptions. Extraverted people might be overconfident and excessively optimistic about their investment performance. Fortunately, other studies have looked at individual's actual investing behavior and compared it to their personality traits, so these findings can be compared to others'.

First, I'll report the results of my online study in technical terms and then layman's language. Comments about other NEO-based investor personality studies follow this section. Below are the results of correlations between each of the four measured personality traits and the responses on the experimental questions. The following correlations were performed

	Linear Correlations between Personality Trait Scores and Research
TABLE 12.3	Questions (up arrows indicate a positive correlation and down arrows an inverse one). Please read on for further explanation

Personality Test Results	Extraversion	Neuroticism	Conscientiousness	Openness
Q61. Dream	—	↑	↓	↑
Q64. Exit plans in place	↑	↓	↑	↑
Q65. Hold losers too long	↓	↑	↓	↓
Q66. Cut winners short	↑	—	—	↑
Q67. Double-or-nothing	—	↑	↓	—
Q68. Win left open	↓	↑	↓	↓
Q69. Total returns	↑	—	—	↑

using linear regression and are reported if they meet a 95 percent confidence interval. In fact, all correlations but one met a 99 percent confidence criteria ($p < 0.01$). The full results are shown in Table 12.3. There were no significant correlations for Question 70 (largest loss), as if no single personality trait predisposed investors to poor risk management. Because the table is a bit dense, the results are explained verbally in the following pages.

Up arrows indicate a positive linear correlation between a personality trait and the bias noted in the left-hand column. For example, referring to Table 12.3, if someone scored highly on the personality trait extraversion, they were significantly more likely to have agreed with Question 64, "I have exit plans in place..." Down arrows are inverse correlations; that is, the opposite pole of the personality trait is positively correlated. For example, people who scored highly on neuroticism were significantly less likely to have agreed with Question 64.

And if that's not confusing enough, consider the opposite pole of each personality trait. Because "emotional stability" is the opposite pole of neuroticism, high emotional stability scorers were significantly more likely to have agreed with the statement in Question 64. Also consider that extraversion is correlated with higher investment returns (Question 69), while its inverse (introversion) has a negative relationship with returns.

Neurotic Investors

In terms of investment biases, neuroticism appears to be the single most dangerous trait for investors. Interestingly, neuroticism does not lead to lower investment returns (Question 69). Neurotic people are typically more hypervigilant to danger and self-critical. As such, they may be able to use these tendencies to their advantage. They are more aware that they have biases, and they use this personal insight to prevent mistakes.

In general, neurotic people report dreaming about positions at night (Question 61), holding losing positions too long (Question 65), taking more risk to earn back losses (doubling down) (Question 67), and leaving positions open and losing paper profits (Question 68). Neuroticism is *inversely* correlated with Question 64; neurotic investors are *less likely* to have exit plans in place than emotionally stable investors.

In psychology studies, the trait of neuroticism was found to correlate with episodes of clinical depression and anxiety disorders, both of which can impair sleeping patterns (as in Question 61) and lead to indecision when under stress (as in Questions 64 and 65).

The inverse of neuroticism is "emotional stability," which is therefore one of the traits least correlated with investment biases. However, emotionally stable people don't have higher returns than neurotics, and the reason for this may be in their lack of critical self-awareness. They may suffer from biases without realizing it.

Test takers who described themselves as "traders" were significantly less neurotic than "investors" or "businesspeople." This makes sense. People dealing with short-term fluctuations in market prices can't be overly nervous or stress sensitive; if so, they would quickly burn out.

As we'll see later in this chapter, successful investors must match their personality to their trading style. In the case of neurotic people, most appear to avoid short-term trading and compensate for their biases. Thus, they have equivalent returns to emotionally stable investors.

Extraverted, Open, and Conscientious Investors

Extraverts report that they tend to have exit plans in place for all market contingencies, they sell when their positions appreciate a lot, and they reported higher total returns than introverts. Extraversion was inversely correlated with the results of Questions 65 (hold too long) and 68 (leave open). Keep in mind that this means introversion was positively correlated with those biases.

Extraverts deny that they hold their losing positions too long, and they deny leaving winning positions open and losing their paper profits. Overall, extraverts report greater returns than introverts. This could be due to confirmation bias, where extraverts are representing their skills and returns according to what they think the researchers want to see. However, they do acknowledge cutting their winners short as their one weaknesses, so they are not painting a perfectly rosy picture of themselves.

Openness yields results identical to extraversion, with one added correlation. Openness is positively correlated with Question 61 (dreaming):

Open people report more thinking about their investment positions at night. Overall, openness and extraversion are the personality traits most correlated with overall investment returns.

Jim Rogers is probably the most famous open and extraverted investor. He actively seeks out new experiences and is in the *Guinness Book of World Records* for his long motorcycle and automobile journeys crisscrossing the continents. He has written two books: *Adventure Capitalist* and *Investment Biker*. He created a commodity index in the late 1990s, when few investors were paying attention to that sector, and he has recommended investing in markets as diverse as Botswana, Nicaragua, and Bolivia. More recently, he announced that he and his family are relocating from New York City to a Chinese-speaking hub in Asia so he can be closer to the business epicenters of the new millennium. Rogers was an early partner of George Soros in the Quantum Fund. Rogers's openness and extraversion have served him well both in the markets and in creating a rich quality of life.

The personality trait of conscientiousness correlated with responses to Question 64 (exit plans). Conscientious investors are more likely to have exit plans in place. Inverse correlations appeared with Questions 61 (dream), 65 (holding too long), 67 (doubling down), and 68 (leaving positions open). That is, as compared to more impulsive individuals, conscientious people report more discipline in their trading decisions: cutting losses sooner, not taking more risk when down, and taking profits off the table before they disappear. They deny that investing thoughts intrude on their sleep. Given the number of good decisions conscientious people report making, one might expect higher returns from them, but that's not evident in the data.

In occupational research, conscientiousness is correlated with career success in most types of work. One might then expect conscientious investors to perform better in the markets, but they don't report higher returns. The discrepancy between occupational and market performance is puzzling. However, investing is not like a regular 9-to-5 job with known rules and regulations. The markets are complex and dynamic. Perhaps a rigid, rule-based approach to market analysis sabotages an investor's adaptability.

OTHER PERSONALITY RESEARCH

Using the NEO, other researchers have found significant performance correlations with personality traits. When consolidated, the results of the following studies suggest that investors and traders may benefit from different personality traits. Partial support for my personality findings comes from a small study in Australia. Durand, Mewby, and Sanghani tracked the brokerage account performance of 18 Australian investors. The authors mailed surveys to gather psychological, personality, and financial performance data. After one year, they found that extraverts held more stocks, traded less, and made more money than introverts.

The authors also found that investors who scored higher on openness and neuroticism took greater portfolio risk. Neurotics traded more frequently than the emotionally stable. Conscientious investors took on less risk than the impulsive. Agreeable people took on more risk.[21] Perhaps their finding that conscientious investors take on less risk explains why they do not have greater returns than impulsive investors.

The paragraphs that follow describe psychological test results from short-term traders. Trading requires a different skill-set than longer-term investing or portfolio management. Therefore, some of these researchers' findings contradict my results. However, keep in mind that my results covered a mixed group of 1000 traders, investors, and businesspeople, with traders less than 25 percent of the overall sample.

In line with my finding that traders are generally not neurotic, but going against some of my other findings, Fenton-O'Creevy and colleagues concluded from a study of 118 professional traders at investment banks that successful traders tend to be emotionally stable (low on neuroticism scale), introverted (low on extraversion scale), and open to new experiences.[22] While openness correlates with success in both our studies, the researchers' finding that introversion is correlated with success may be specific to their short-term trader clientele and not applicable to business owners and investors (who were the primary sample in my experiment).

Trading coach Brett Steenbarger performed personality tests on 64 traders at one of Linda Bradford Raschke's LBR trading seminars. He found that high conscientiousness scores were the most reliable predictor of trading success—again, a finding I did not get with a mixed audience of investors and businesspeople. Conversely, Steenbarger found that high openness and high neuroticism are correlated with trading problems.[23] Steenbarger's finding relating to high openness and poor trading results are difficult to explain, except perhaps that short-term traders must remain focused and undistracted. He summates these findings as, "One important lesson: success in trading is related to the ability to stay consistent and plan-driven."

Trading coach Doug Hirschhorn performed a NEO personality study of traders for his psychology PhD dissertation. Having played division one baseball himself, Hirschhorn suspected that playing athletics at a high level teaches one a mental discipline that is beneficial for short-term trading. Interestingly, Hirschhorn found that having a sports background did not contribute to trading success in his sample. The only NEO trait that he found correlated with trading success was low scores on openness.[24] Short-term traders may need to be focused and conservative in their trading analyses, and that may be why both Steenbarger and Hirschhorn found a correlation with low openness. Long-term investors may benefit from awareness of diverse economic trends and abstract financial concepts, which may explain why both Durand and I found that high openness scores were correlated with investor performance.

Lo, Repin, and Steenbarger examined the trading patterns, personality characteristics, and daily emotional reactions of 80 traders over 25 trading days. In part due to a market decline of 20 percent during the study period, only 33 traders of the original 80 completed the study. While this sample was probably too small to find statistically significant correlations, Lo and his co-authors concluded that personality traits are themselves not related to trading success.[25]

Thomas Oberlechner from Webster University in Vienna mailed a survey form to 600 professional foreign exchange traders in Europe and the United Kingdom.[26] Fifty-four percent of the survey forms were returned. Each survey form asked traders to rank the most important characteristics of successful traders out of a list of 23. Of the individual items, the most highly ranked were (1) quick reaction time, (2) discipline, (3) experience, (4) concentration, and (5) stress resistance. Out of eight "factors" he derived from subgroupings of the 23 characteristics, "disciplined cooperation" was ranked most highly. Subjects who scored high on a measure of impulsivity (the opposite of self-discipline) placed more trades, without improving performance.[27]

In summary, it appears that for investors, extraversion and openness are correlated with higher risk taking and higher overall returns. For traders, emotional stability (low neuroticism) and conscientiousness support higher trading returns. Conscientiousness drives plan-driven trading, which is especially important for short-term traders who need the patience to wait for high risk-reward opportunities.

It is not only measurable personality traits that influence decision making. Many other investor characteristics are important as well. Such factors cannot always be measured directly; rather, they are often revealed through observation of patterns of decision making, critical thinking, problem solving, and behavior. Some of the important cognitive and emotional traits of excellent investors are discussed below.

TRADING PSYCHOLOGY

The use of psychological and emotional tools to improve executive and investor performance has been increasing rapidly.[28] An excellent example of this trend is one of the world's most successful hedge fund managers, billionaire investor Steve A. Cohen. According to Jack Schwager, author of *Stock Market Wizards*, Steve Cohen is "unquestionably one of the world's greatest traders."[29] Cohen is the principal of SAC Capital, where a former Olympic psychiatrist, Ari Kiev, MD, is "a permanent fixture." Cohen's employment of a performance psychiatrist suggests that psychological management has a beneficial effect for financial risk takers, including those already functioning in the top tier.

While observing Cohen trade, Schwager is "struck by his casualness." Schwager notes: "He also seemed to maintain a constant sense of humor while trading." Cohen's sense of humor and ease demonstrate that he isn't taking his trading gains and losses "to heart." He is not affected emotionally (at least not outwardly). How can the average financial decision maker maintain emotional balance and a healthy perspective on his or her trading outcomes?

It is crucial for investors to cultivate opinions without value judgment, to detach ego, and to maintain flexible expectations. In particular, practitioners should not focus on the outcome of their decisions, but rather on developing an excellent decision-making process. Investors who pressure themselves to achieve specific outcomes are at risk of "choking" if pressure is too high (see Chapter 10). Furthermore, it is crucial to remain "present" with what is happening in the markets. Rumination or deliberation about past events is self-defeating. Recalibrate yourself to each day, so that every position appears fresh, as if it was just opened.

George Soros, one of history's greatest traders and philanthropists, provides an excellent example of nonattachment with his well-publicized "Belief in Fallibility." "To others, being wrong is a source of shame. To me, recognizing my mistakes is a source of pride. Once we realize that imperfect understanding is the human condition, there's no shame in being wrong, only in failing to correct our mistakes."[30] Soros's belief structure prevents a crisis of confidence during downturns. While others might be wracked by fear and self-doubt, thus worsening their judgment, Soros maintains emotional equanimity and intellectual curiosity.

Mental flexibility is a key to success in the markets. A trader, Jean-Manuel Rozan, "once spent an entire afternoon arguing about the stock market with [George] Soros. Soros was vehemently bearish, and he had an elaborate theory to explain why, which turned out to be entirely wrong. The stock market boomed. Two years later, Rozan ran into Soros at a tennis tournament. 'Do you remember our conversation?' Rozan asked. 'I recall it very well,' Soros replied. 'I changed my mind, and made an absolute fortune.' He changed his mind!"[31]

For most people, the possibility of being wrong is threatening. It gives rise to anxiety, especially if one has internal or external performance pressures or benchmarks that will not be met. "The difference between Soros and most other traders is that he accepts fallibility, so he starts out by assuming his hypothesis is wrong, rather than right like almost everyone else."[32] By maintaining a belief in fallibility, Soros remains open-minded about his positions. His emotional reactions, such as denial, disappointment, and anger, are minimal when his decisions do not go in his favor. In fact, his emotional reactions may seem somewhat paradoxical. Soros wrote of his logical process, "I derived actual pleasure from discovering a mistake."[33] Soros's mental flexibility and personal courage are contributors to his success.

In the next section of this book, the primarily cognitive decision biases are outlined. The fundamental components of analytic decision making, such as an understanding of probabilities and trust, are explained. Further chapters examine systematic cognitive and self-control distortions.

PART III

Thinking about Money

CHAPTER 13

Making Decisions

The Effects of Probability, Ambiguity, and Trust

"Take the probability of loss times the amount of possible loss from the probability of gain times the amount of possible gain. That is what we're trying to do. It's imperfect, but that's what it's all about."
—Warren Buffett, speech given at the Berkshire Hathaway Annual Meeting in 1989[1]

In 2000, during the run-up to the June Mexican presidential elections, an outsider was poised to overturn the PRI political legacy that had ruled Mexico for more than 80 years. Vicente Fox, candidate of the PAN party, was polling ahead of the candidate of the incumbent PRI political party, Francisco Ochoa. The PRI had retained power through a corrupt system of vote buying, ballot-box stuffing, nationalist rhetoric, and intimidation. The PRI party bosses were angered by the possibility of their candidate's defeat. Two weeks before the presidential election, Ochoa expressed his hope that there would be no "riots" or "blood on the street" if the PRI lost the election.

Ochoa's words were interpreted as a veiled threat, though he denied any ill intent. The Mexican stock market (Bolsa) and the Mexican peso dropped 20 percent over the next week. Political violence, which had seemed unlikely, suddenly was in the realm of possibility, even probability.

Two weeks after Ochoa's comment, the Sunday of the elections passed uneventfully, with Fox declared the victor by a 6 percent margin in the popular vote. Immediately after the official results were announced, Fox held a press conference. In his victory speech, he expressed faith in Mexico's market economy and vowed to continue economic and political reforms.

No violence came to pass. Within two days the Bolsa and the peso surged through their levels of two weeks prior.

Investors in Mexico were frightened by the possibility of political violence. As we'll see in the following pages, investors' risk probability assessments are distorted by their feelings—in this case, fear. Risk perceptions are often excessively low (especially after recent gains) or too high (such as following losses), creating opportunities for astute investors.

Risk perceptions are formed from three characteristics of a decision situation: (1) the perceived timeline of the outcome (prolonged outcomes appear less risky), (2) the associations the scenario induces (e.g., fears of bankruptcy), and (3) one's evolutionary preparedness for certain emotional reactions (e.g., is one constitutionally nervous or optimistic?).[2] Each of these factors can lead to distortions in probability assessment.

In this section, we look at how investors *ought* to assess probabilities of potential outcomes and how they *actually* do it. In particular, we'll examine how investors misjudge expected values and overreact to ambiguity.

EXPECTED VALUE AND EXPECTED UTILITY

> *"Every day, investors must translate investment opportunities into probabilities—indeed, this is an essential skill. So we need to think carefully about how we come up with probabilities for various situations and where the potential pitfalls lie."*
> —Michael Mauboussin[3]

According to traditional economic theory, it makes no sense for someone to buy a lottery ticket. It's not *rational*. The "expected value" of a lottery ticket is about $0.40 for every dollar spent, meaning that the average lottery ticket buyer is losing $0.60 on their $1.00 investment.

Yet people do play the lottery, and they go to casinos, and they daytrade stocks and currencies—even when they consistently lose. As seen in this book, over the past 30 years behavioral economists have begun investigating *why* people decide to pursue negative–expected-value gambles.

Most decisions in which potential outcome sizes and probabilities are known are made according to the guidance of expected-value calculations. These calculations are functions of the brain's analytical (not the intuitive) decision-making system. Analytical decisions consider mathematical outcome characteristics like the exact sizes, probabilities, and time delays for potential gains and losses.

In an expected-value calculation, each decision option is examined separately to determine which has the highest average return. For every choice, the probability of each possible outcome is multiplied by its likely magnitude. Then the various products are summed into an overall expected return. Given that most investment decisions produce uncertain outcomes of unknown size, such formulas must be used cautiously.

Many people gamble and trade stocks because they like the markets, they enjoy discussing strategy with their colleagues, and they enjoy the emotional thrill. Liking something, regardless of mathematical outcomes, is called *utility*. Decisions made using "expected utility" rely on considerations of what people value *qualitatively*. Because the market future is fundamentally uncertain, most investors make decisions based on expected utility rather than expected value calculations.

Utility is a largely subjective phenomenon. Decision theorists say that a sense of utility comes from: (1) current feelings (moment utility), (2) the feelings one expects to have after receiving an outcome (outcome utility), (3) the process of making the decision itself (decision utility), and (4) one's recall of past similar experiences (experienced utility). The theme that runs through these various types of utility is *feelings*—utility is boiled down to how one *feels* about a decision and the expected outcomes. In the end, investors often pursue the decision that they expect to make them *feel* the best.

In a challenging decision environment such as the stock market, most people make systematic errors in their outcome probability and size estimations. These errors are often due to the biasing influences of feelings on the analysis of uncertain or ambiguous information. Perhaps surprisingly, even in perfect circumstances where all outcome information is known, investors still demonstrate biased decision making. This chapter will first address the biases of finite expected value calculations (such as are possible at casinos), with biases related to ambiguous outcome information following.

THE JACKPOT TRAP

In casinos the game with the lowest expected value is keno. In keno, players select six numbers between 0 and 50. If any of their selected numbers is a match with six randomly generated numbers, then they win a jackpot. Casinos take approximately $0.29 for every $1.00 invested in keno, giving players the *lowest* expected return per dollar of any casino game. It's the keno jackpot, displayed in large numbers over the keno seats, that is so appealing to gamblers.

Brain imaging studies show a disproportionate effect of outcome size versus probability on decision making. As the size of a potential monetary gain increases, so too does reward system activation (specifically the nucleus accumbens).[4,5] Potential reward size is more emotionally arousing than proportional changes in probability.[6,7]

When I worked in Professor Knutson's lab at Stanford in 2003, we designed an experiment to measure the neural effects of changes in a reward's expected value. Equivalent expected rewards caused radically different brain responses depending on how the potential reward characteristics (size and probability) were displayed.

We designed an experiment to sort out the different effects of reward size (magnitude) and probability on the brain. In our preliminary results, the reward system's response when anticipating a $5 gain was much more intense than when anticipating a $1 gain. However, when we controlled for (eliminated) the effects of reward size from the brain's activation map, the results were much different.

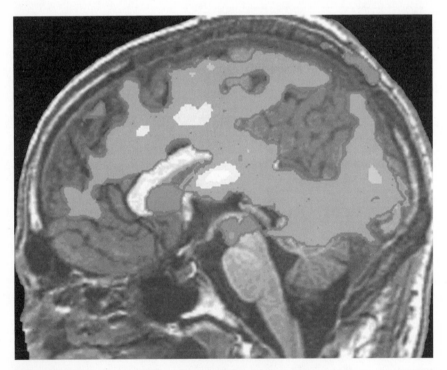

FIGURE 13.1 The brain's activation when playing for a $5 gain, contrasted against the anticipation of a $1 gain.

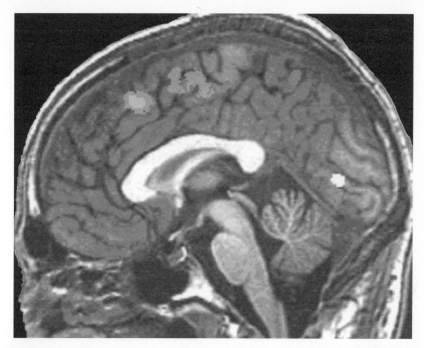

FIGURE 13.2 The brain's activation pattern when playing for an 80 percent chance of winning $5 ($4 equivalent) versus a 20 percent chance of gaining $5 ($1 equivalent). These images were recorded at the same significance threshold, and they show the brain's preferential activation to size.

If we looked at people's brains while they were anticipating rewards of different expected values, with the magnitude of reward held constant at $5 but the probability of receiving it varied, the brain did not activate much differently. For example, an 80 percent chance of winning $5 (expected value $4) was only slightly more activating than a 20 percent chance of winning $5 (expected value $1). The largest absolute reward ($5) was extraordinarily more exciting than the absolute $1 reward. That is, subjects were watching primarily the *size* of the potential reward, not the *probability*, even when they had equivalent expected values.

In Figures 13.1 and 13.2, equal statistical thresholds were used to generate the images. That is, these activations were recorded as if with a camera whose shutter speed and aperture were held constant. In the top image, one can see the profound, and widely distributed, effect of gain size ($5 versus $1) on brain activation. In the lower image, the highest probability of gain (80 percent) is compared against the lowest probability (20 percent) with the reward size of $5 held constant. The greater absolute magnitude is much more activating.

Please understand the above results as illustrative but not watertight. This study was never published due to problems with the "high" and "low" probabilities—some subjects' "low" probabilities were actually 50 percent due to their better skill than others. After a redesign that ensured constant reward probabilities regardless of skill, a similar subsequent study was published in the *Journal of Neuroscience*. However, Figures 13.1 and 13.2 are derived from the first study, and the probability confound may account for some (but not all) of the dramatic activation difference between the two brain images.

Does this increased activation to size lead to psychological effects? In fact, in previous studies subjects report more "happiness" (positive activation) when awaiting larger rewards.[8]

In some laboratory experiments, participants trade money in simulated stock markets. Many times, bubbles and crashes appear in the prices of the stocks traded during these experiments. Researchers investigated this phenomenon by testing for the presence of probability judgment errors in traders during the life cycle of an experimental market. They found that bubbles are correlated with traders' preference for high-value, low-probability gains in their investments. This finding makes intuitive sense. Bubble investors are making probability errors by seeking high rewards at low probabilities (overweighting low probabilities). They are overweighting the possibility of large gains.[9]

Professor Paul Slovic has found that emotion plays a leading role in distorting probability judgments. According to the "affect heuristic," when the outcome of a gamble has a strong emotional meaning, people mentally overweight the size of the potential reward (or loss) versus its actual probability in their decision making.[10] Slovic's finding may explain why, in my experiment with Knutson, I saw so much reward system activation for college students (presumably poor) playing a game for a series of potential $5 payouts (outcomes that are very exciting for them).

PROBABILITY MISJUDGMENTS

> *"It is principally at games of chance that a multitude of illusions support hope and sustain it against unfavourable chances."*
> —Simon Laplace, 1796

Misjudgments of probabilities are systematic and universal. Recent experimental evidence shows precisely how people misestimate probabilities when facing simple gambles.

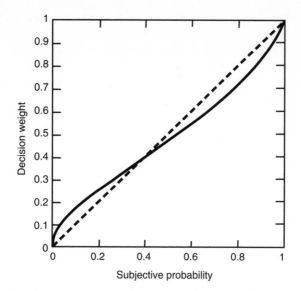

FIGURE 13.3 The probability weighting curves for most assessed risks. The different curves represent probability functions for gambles framed as gains, losses, and other permutations. The straight line represents the actual probability.
Source: Prelec, D. 1998. "The Probability Weighting Function." *Econometrica* 60: 497–528.

When an outcome is possible but not probable, people tend to overestimate its chance of occurring. This is called the *possibility effect.*

When an outcome is likely, people tend to underestimate its odds. This bias has been named the *certainty effect.*[11]

Events of probability less than 40 percent are susceptible to the possibility effect. Outcomes with greater than 40 percent probability are in the realm of the certainty effect[12] (see Figure 13.3).

For example, long shots in pari-mutuel wagering (horse and dog racing) tend to be preferred bets of amateurs. Due to amateurs excessively betting on long shots, their expected payoffs are lower than their actual odds of winning suggest they should be (based on how tracks figure odds). The more people who bet on the long shots, the weaker their odds and thus the lower the payout if they win.

Because bettors mentally underweight the probability of high likelihood winners actually winning, they avoid these bets. As a result, highlikelihood winners are often a good bet, having a better chance of winning than predicted by most bettors.[13]

For the most part, there is a dissociation between intellectual judgments of risk and emotional feelings about risk. Emotions in uncertain or risky situations are more sensitive to the possibility rather than the probability of strong consequences, contributing to the overweighting of very small probabilities.[14] In general, naïve investors think that very low probability but emotionally loaded events (such as potential market crashes) are much more likely than they actually are.[15] High-likelihood, emotionally weighted outcomes, such as bull markets, are assumed to be less likely than they actually are The probability weighting curve shows exaggerated misestimations of probability when the potential outcomes are emotionally weighted (see Figure 13.4).

Probability assessments are biased not only by the emotions associated with the event outcome, but also by one's internal emotional state. People who are generally happy are more optimistic, judging higher probabilities for positive events and lower probabilities for negative events.[16] The inverse pattern was found for subjects in a negative emotional state.[17]

The misjudgment of probabilities described above occurs for choices that are not repeated over time (except in the case of pari-mutuel wagering). The tendency to overweight small probabilities is true for single choices. This pattern does not hold true, however, for choices based on experience. Investors with experience can often identify when amateurs as a group are over or under-weighting probabilities.

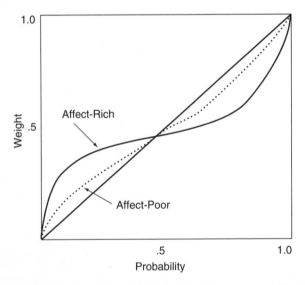

FIGURE 13.4 The probability weighting curve when emotion (affect) is aroused by the potential outcomes. People further overestimate low probabilities and underestimate high probabilities when an emotional outcome is involved.
Source: Hsee, C. K., and Y. Rottenstreich. 2001. "Money, Kisses, and Electric Shocks: On the Affective Psychology of Risk." *Psychological Science* 12: 185–190.

VIVIDNESS, IMAGINATION, AND DESIRE

> *"Our probability assessments shift based on how others present information to us."*
> —Michael Mauboussin[18]

Emotionally, investors have stronger reactions if possible outcomes are more vivid or imaginable. Before the Mexican elections, anticipation of rioting in Mexico City brought to mind images of violence, chaos, destruction, and bloodshed. Likewise, a vividly imagined possibility of bankruptcy, personal poverty, job loss, or market panic will generate the desire to sell any assets that carry such risks. The possibility of wealth and material success in an impulsive and inexperienced investor will lead to a strong drive to buy securities that appear promising.

Feelings of fear or worry in the face of decisions under risk or uncertainty have an all-or-none characteristic: they are more sensitive to the possibility rather than the probability of negative consequences. For example, the thought of receiving a painful electric shock is enough to spark intense fear in experimental subjects. Changes in the precise likelihood of being shocked have little impact on the degree of fearfulness. The increasing vividness of a potential reward or catastrophe exaggerates the possibility effect.[19]

People who have more control over their imaginative faculties are more physiologically responsive to images. For example, researchers found that these people salivate more when thinking of their favorite food, become more sexually aroused in fantasy exercises, and have a greater ability to increase their heart rate using visual imagery. In all likelihood, the possibility and certainty effects are exaggerated in these individuals. It's tempting to speculate that imaginative people are thus more motivated by fantasies of imminent financial wealth or ruin.

AMBIGUITY AND UNCERTAINTY

> *"The fundamental law of investing is the uncertainty of the future."*
> —Peter L. Bernstein

Most people are averse to uncertainty and ambiguity. A classic experiment into ambiguity aversion studied subjects' choices between two urns of red and black balls. Participants were asked if they would rather bet on the drawing of a black ball from the urn in which the proportion of red and black balls was unspecified, or one in which the ratio was 50:50. Most subjects avoided ambiguity, preferring to bet on the urn with the known ratio of red to black balls.[20]

People shy away from decisions about which they have insufficient information, especially when an alternative decision with more information is available or the decision maker has less information about a choice than others. People prefer to make decisions where they know the odds and the possible outcomes, and they avoid investing where the odds are unknown. With experience, they learn to infer the approximate odds in a situation.

AMBIGUITY IN THE MARKETS

"The future is never clear, and you pay a very high price in the stock market for a cheery consensus. Uncertainty is the friend of the buyer of long-term values."

—Warren Buffett

Ambiguity aversion is reflected in the returns of stocks of companies with ambiguous information on their balance sheets (e.g., research and development spending) that cannot traditionally be correlated with future valuations. Stocks with poorer earnings quality (having more ambiguous information) have greater long-term returns than those with better (more transparent) accounting.[21] As a result of aversion to ambiguous items on accounting statements, investors mistakenly avoid such stocks and miss out on greater long-term returns.

The effect of accounting ambiguity may be to bias how investors feel about the stock in question. Investors with limited information about a stock are more likely to rely on their feelings when judging whether to buy or sell shares. In the case of poor earnings quality, those feelings are likely to be excessively negative. However, there are some interesting exceptions.

Typically, investors prefer to avoid stocks with ambiguous accounting, but when optimism is high, investors may project an unfounded positive spin onto the uncertain data. In the late 1990s, initial public offerings (IPOs) of Internet companies with *negative* cash flows had relatively higher initial trading prices. According to researchers, "The role of earnings in valuation of these firms . . . completely disappeared in 1999."[22] Presumably, investors considered negative cash flows to be an investment in the future. The lack of concrete earnings information led to an exaggerated projection of investors' optimism. In such cases of "irrational exuberance," investors are ambiguity loving. In summary, investors are usually ambiguity averse, especially when they are pessimistic, but during periods of optimism, they become ambiguity loving.

Investors' sentiment influences both their purchasing behavior and stock price performance. To investigate how market sentiment affects the returns of stocks with ambiguous or subjective information on their balance sheets, researchers compared a composite measure of investor sentiment with their subsequent performance. Highly subjective stocks were considered to be small stocks, young stocks, high volatility stocks, unprofitable stocks, non-dividend-paying stocks, extreme growth stocks, and distressed stocks. The researchers discovered that when investors are optimistic, stocks with ambiguous, uncertain and generally subjective information underperform over the subsequent period (one year). When investors are pessimistic, the opposite occurs. A contrarian approach to sentiment improves returns in more ambiguous and uncertain stocks.[23]

Emotion also plays a role in how investors feel about the "idea" or story behind a stock. Researchers found that emotion and imagery, aroused by the concept of a stock, bias predictions of stock performance. According to researchers, emotion and imagery may be the only judgmental bases on which individuals are able to rely when information about a financial offering is vague.[24] Stocks with exciting stories cause people to forecast higher stock returns.

Interestingly, during times of greater uncertainty in the markets, when prices are volatile and trading volume high, investors tilt their portfolios toward familiar local stocks.[25] Investors prefer the familiar and the known when market price action indicates potential danger. Perhaps this preference is driven by a need for certainty and comfort, which are more likely to be found closer to home.

Additionally, investors' behavioral biases are increased by uncertainty. When stocks are more difficult to value using objective accounting data, investors exhibit a stronger disposition effect. Overconfidence is increased by market-wide uncertainty.[26] Even among executives, ambiguity in corporate accounting heralds the presence of behavioral biases such as loss aversion and overconfidence among management.

An interesting reversal of ambiguity aversion occurs when people feel the *need* to make more money than that offered in a certain outcome. In one gambling experiment, when participants' financial need was greater than the known option's expected average payout, subjects preferred the ambiguous (high volatility) option.[27] People are more willing to take a chance when other options won't give them the payoff they want. During the Internet bubble, as investors and portfolio managers scrambled to catch up with their perceptions of others' wealth, they may have felt a more acute need to take a chance for profit.

This need-based pursuit of ambiguity supports loss aversion and the disposition effect. When investors are painfully losing in an investment, they would rather take an unknown chance for a comeback in the stock than sell it for a guaranteed loss.

In other scenarios, psychologists have found that people tend to believe they can have what they want, regardless of evidence to the contrary. The intensity of one's desire for an outcome increases one's estimation of the likelihood he or she will actually get it.[28] Their wanting creates overconfidence in their skills, which translates into an expectation of success.

In another study, participants told to expect an outcome that conflicted with their desires gave no weight to the evidence. They remembered information that supported their ability to get what they wanted, rather than the explicit information telling them to expect otherwise.[29] If investors want to believe that a money-losing Internet stock is more valuable than one with earnings, then they will value it higher, regardless of the evidence. These studies demonstrate the "confirmation bias," in which information supporting one's desires is accepted, but evidence contradicting them is ignored.

NEUROSCIENCE OF AMBIGUITY, RISK, AND REWARD

> *"Markets are constantly in a state of uncertainty and flux and money is made by discounting the obvious and betting on the unexpected."*
> —George Soros

Caltech researchers designed a monetary experiment to identify the different brain regions directing *risky* decision making (where probabilities are known) and *uncertain* decision making (where information about probabilities and outcomes is absent). As seen above, in prior experiments on risky decision making, participants were more likely to take risk when the probabilities were known versus when the odds were ambiguous.[30]

The researchers, including economist Colin Camerer, found that higher levels of ambiguity led to increasing activation in the amygdala (fear and memory) and orbitofrontal cortex (emotion and reason integration) and decreasing activation in the nucleus accumbens (reward). That is, participants appeared to find ambiguity fearsome, and tried to integrate their consideration of unknown risks with their prior experiences in such situations. Ambiguity caused decreased activity in the nucleus accumbens, thus implying that ambiguity arouses disappointment. However, higher-expected-value decisions (without ambiguity), led to increasing activation in the nucleus accumbens.

When patients with lesions in the orbitofrontal cortex (the excessive risk takers famously identified by Damasio) were tested in the Caltech task, they were found to be insensitive to the level of risk and ambiguity in choices. That is, they made the same decisions regardless of whether the outcome probabilities were known or not. Thus, it appears that the orbitofrontal cortex governs the integration of emotion and reason—weighing information about actual probabilities and payoffs against one's feelings about risk. Impairment of the orbitofrontal cortex leads to difficulty integrating ambiguity aversion (fear) into decision making.[31]

THE POSSIBILITY THAT YOU ARE OVERWEIGHT

Investors are uniquely susceptible to distortions in probability assessment, especially when events are novel or rare. The market future is uncertain, and information is too often ambiguous. Emotions play a large role in biasing low probability assessments. The following is a list of conditions in which investors are vulnerable to overweighting low probabilities and becoming biased by the possibility effect:

- Vivid or easily imagined results.
- Minimal awareness about the event's likely outcomes.
- Minimal investor conditioning or experience with such events.
- Event is represented as a relatively novel/unique phenomenon.
- Desiring, wanting, or needing the outcome to occur.
- Feeling a personal or emotional stake in the outcome.
- Feeling excited or fearful about the event happening.
- Ambiguous information about the event.

While investors can try to be aware of the above conditions during their decision making, it is extremely difficult to do so. The list is long and complex, and some of the effects are subconscious and quite subtle. Nonetheless, I hope that this list will provoke some thought about how your own odds assessments might be impacted. The next sections address the problem of trust. What role does trust play in investors' interpretations of market information or interactions with clients?

THE TRUSTING BRAIN

When people hear ambiguous or uncertain information and must make a rapid decision, how do they assess if it is truthful? If they trust the *source*, then they are likely to take the information at face value.

A Securities and Exchange Commission (SEC) filing from a respected corporation is one of the most trustworthy types of corporate information, in part because a fraudulent SEC filing leads to prison time for executives. Both a history of honesty from the source and harsh consequences for misinformation are crucial support for the veracity of provided information.

Among the least believable sources of stock information are anonymous faxes, e-mails, cold calls, and Internet message boards. A promotional fax about a small gold-mining stock in Alberta is untrustworthy for obvious reasons. There are no consequences for misinformation, and one has no history of experience with the promoter.

Investment information is always somewhat suspect. Yet most investors believe dubious information if it appears under the banner of a trusted news source. Researchers in Muenster, Germany, found that subjects were more likely to believe an ambiguous headline if it was in the banner of a trusted brand-name magazine. Their trust activated the medial prefrontal cortex (MPFC).[32] The MPFC is activated by emotionally satisfying events and learning about rewards. It appears that trust feels good, and people trust a news source when it agrees with their underlying political beliefs and biases.

NEUROSCIENCE OF THE ULTIMATUM GAME

One of the simplest ways to elicit trusting (or distrustful) behavior in economic experiments is to use a paradigm called the ultimatum game. In each round of the ultimatum game, participants have the opportunity to send money provided by an experimenter to another participant. This money is tripled, and the receiving player can return all, some, or none of this money back to the player who sent the money to him. The "proposer" is given a sum of money, for example, $10. Then the proposer offers some percentage of that $10 to a "responder," say $5. The amount of money transferred to the responder is tripled by the experimenters, so it is now $15. The responder then has an opportunity to reciprocate the transfer by sending some of the $15 back to the proposer. Obviously, some proposers and responders never send money, some transfer a little, and some transfer the majority. There are tremendous individual differences in money transfers.

Money transfers are also affected by "trust signals," namely how much money one player sends to the other over each round.

In a study using the ultimatum game, some fascinating disparities among age groups and genders were noticed. In the experiment, people tended to preferentially trust others in their own age group. Young participants were significantly more trusting than older subjects, sending 24 percent more money to their partners than did older players. There was also a very strong gender effect in this study, where women were both more trusting of others and perceived to be more trustworthy than men.[33]

In a variation of the trust game called the "ultimatum game," proposers offer to split a sum of money with the responders. If the responders reject the proposal, then neither party receives money. In a fMRI study, responders with high activation in the insula when they contemplated unfair offers were more likely to reject them.[34] By refusing the unfair offer, responders were acting based on their emotions (disgust and pain) and forgoing guaranteed profits. In the markets, such a rejection of "unfair"events can be damaging. For example, after a company's negative earnings surprise, investors should suppress the urge to punish it (by selling stock) if their research shows that it continues to be fundamentally undervalued.

British fMRI researchers asked subjects to rate pictures of faces in terms of their "trustworthiness." Activity in the bilateral amygdala and right insula increased when faces judged to be untrustworthy were presented. An area of the temporal lobe was activated when trustworthy faces were viewed. The researchers noted that the temporal cortex activation implied a cognitive intention to trust, while mistrust was an automatic negative emotional reaction.[35]

If untrustworthy individuals have an "honest face," then they can avoid provoking immediately negative emotional assessments. Of course, intentional facial manipulation, such as former Enron CEO Ken Lay's generous smiles, can disarm the automatic negative amygdala and insula reactions that would have promoted avoidance. Additionally, now there is some indirect evidence that it is important for financial advisers to be both physically presentable and financially generous (e.g., fee discounts) with clients in order to encourage trust and prevent emotional misunderstandings.

THE TRUST HORMONE

Paul Zak, a professor at Claremont Graduate University in southern California, has taken a keen interest in the cultural role of trust in economic activity. Zak has run several studies examining the role of a hormone called oxytocin in facilitating trust. Zak first became interested in oxytocin when he read a *Science* magazine article describing the role of oxytocin in voles.

Voles are a genus of rodent living in North America. Prairie voles live on the Great Plains, while the mountain vole inhabits the Rocky Mountains. These two species are identical in all respects except sexual behavior. The mountain vole is very promiscuous, while the prairie vole selects one mate for life. When researchers examined the voles' hormone levels, they found that the prairie vole has very high oxytocin levels relative to its promiscuous mountain cousin.[36]

Oxytocin in humans facilitates bonding between mother and baby. Breast-feeding releases oxytocin in both the mother and infant. Additionally, orgasm increases a woman's oxytocin levels, perhaps allowing her to bond with her mate. Zak wondered whether oxytocin might affect trusting behavior during a "trust game" (the ultimatum game), so he set up a study to find out.

Zak found that responders who were given higher levels of money by the proposer had increased oxytocin following the transfer.[37] Additionally, responders who returned more money to the proposer were found to have higher levels of oxytocin prior to reciprocating. Zak believes it was the responders' *perception* of trusting behavior from the Proposer that raised their oxytocin levels. Simply receiving money without implied trust did not raise oxytocin levels.[38]

Zak, in collaboration with Swiss researchers, found that proposers given an oxytocin medication (via intranasal squirts) were more likely to transfer a larger amount of money to responders[39] at the beginning of the experiment. In fact, approximately 45 percent of the proposers given oxytocin transferred the entire initial sum, versus 20 percent of those given placebo.

Zak may have uncovered a biological mechanism (oxytocin level) for such investor biases as the endowment effect (loving a stock), the urge to reciprocate financial adviser fee discounts, confusion between loving a company and seeing its stock as a good investment, and the home bias.

IMPLICATIONS

Investors should calculate the expected value of every investment option before selecting the optimal choice. However, judgments of expected value are biased by risk perception. The fear of "riots" before the 2000 Mexican presidential election raised risk perceptions and sent the markets tumbling 20 percent.

Because the future is intrinsically uncertain and market dynamics change, the past is a poor guide to the future. When assessing ambiguous or uncertain information, investors overestimate the probability of danger. They often utilize the emotional defense mechanism of projection, which drives them to overestimate risk in ambiguous data due to their own fear.

Emotions such as fear also lead to the overestimation of the likelihood of low probability events that are vivid or emotionally weighted. Ego attachment to particular outcomes increases the severity of such biases. Self-awareness of risk-perception biases is challenging due to the thought distortions that arise from unconscious emotions. One will truly think that the danger exists and will search for confirming evidence to justify their fearful risk aversion.

Trust appears to be strongly related to perceptions of risk, and investors perceive less risk in situations where they trust both the information they receive and the source delivering it. In the case of unfamiliar stocks or markets, investors will usually be less trusting and will thus have greater risk perceptions. This may explain why most developed-world investors prefer local or national, rather than international, investments, even when greater returns are available overseas.

The hormone oxytocin promotes trust. Its levels rise when people are shown generosity, and it correlates with increased attachment, investment, and reciprocal behavior. On a broad national and cultural level, trust appears to correlate with market returns. Professor Paul Zak found that OECD countries with higher trust levels had higher stock market returns during his sample period (1990–2000).

CHAPTER 14

Framing Your Options

Seeing the World in Black and White

"Selling companies that are doing well and purchasing ones that are faring poorly is like watering the weeds and cutting the flowers."
—Peter Lynch, Fidelity Positions

J R. Simplot is an American eighth-grade dropout and a self-made multi-billionaire. He made his fortune through saavy investments in potato farming and french fry production. Currently, he owns the largest ranch in the United States, the ZX Ranch in southern Oregon. His ranch is larger than the state of Delaware. Despite his tremendous wealth, Simplot is a modest man. He describes his accumulation of wealth to Eric Schlosser in *Fast Food Nation*:

> *"Hell, fellow, I'm just an old farmer got some luck," Simplot said, when I asked about the keys to his success. "The only thing I did smart, and just remember this—ninety-nine percent of people would have sold out when they got their first twenty-five or thirty million. I didn't sell out. I just hung on."[1]*

While there is a select group of individuals who resist the urge, most investors sell their winning positions too soon, thus "cutting winners short," and missing out on greater long-term gains.

Researchers have found the "cutting winners short" bias in simple investment experiments. Professors Kuhnen and Knutson noticed that subjects in their Behavioral Investment Allocation Strategy (BIAS) task were more likely to switch to the "bond" in the next trial if they had previously won $10 from a stock. There was no rational reason for subjects to switch to a more conservative strategy after a gain. Kuhnen notes that "this behavior indicates that people wanted to 'conserve' their gains and it resembles loss aversion."[2]

According to some experts, selling winning positions too soon is a result of "seeking pride." Others believe that cutting winners short is driven by the fear that one might lose what one has recently earned ("I don't want to give it back"). As we'll see in this chapter, selling winners too soon is one side of the psychological bias called the *disposition effect*.[3]

THE DISPOSITION EFFECT

There is an old Wall Street adage: *"Let your winners ride, and cut your losers short."* This saying is a warning against the cognitive bias of "loss aversion." Loss aversion is characterized by a strong desire to avoid *realizing* losses. People are more sensitive to the possibility of losing money or objects than they are to the possibility of gaining the same objects or amount of money. Loss aversion is at the root of a bias called the disposition effect. Researchers use the name *disposition effect* to describe the application of loss aversion to investing. Investors who suffer from the disposition effect inappropriately cut their winners short and let their losers run.

Loss aversion is one tenet of the Nobel Prize winning theory of decision making called *prospect theory*. Propect theory is built on a foundation of simple psychological experiments that show how most people rely too heavily on frames, reference points, and anchors when making risky decisions. People perceive many financial decisions in terms of their frame—whether they are viewed as a potential loss or a potential gain. Reliance on frames and reference points causes systematic distortions in decision making. One tenet of prospect theory, loss aversion, explains that people typically overweight the pain of losses *twice* as much as the pleasure of gains when making decisions. Entire books have been written about prospect theory, and I cannot do it sufficient justice in these few pages. In this and the next chapter I will summarize the effects of framing and loss aversion on financial decisions, such as those of investors.

The concept of loss aversion is not easy to understand. In Chapter 9 you read a study from Greg Berns at Emory University indicating that "dread" spurs individuals to take their losses as soon as possible. The "dreaders" paid money so that they could experience a feared electric shock sooner. On the surface, this result appears to contradict the disposition effect, in which people essentially pay more to avoid taking losses. The fact is, in disposition effect experiments there is always a chance that the feared loss will not occur. When a loss is believed to be certain, as in the Emory study in Chapter 9, then people will actually pay more to "get it over with."

In the markets, because the future is uncertain, the gap between dread-relieving selling and loss-averse holding lies in one's beliefs about how the future is likely to play out. Namely, if people think they have a chance to make their loss back, then they will hold on. However, when strong emotions take hold, they overwhelm the prefrontal cortex and drive thinking. Strong fear, and the physiological effects of stress hormones, will predispose one to catastrophic thoughts of further declines and financial ruin. If an investor thinks their position is hopeless, or the stress of holding a losing position has grown too intense, then they will impulsively cave in to the sell urge. Panic selling occurs when further losses appear guaranteed or the tension of holding a loser has grown too high.

The disposition effect is particularly a problem for individuals who buy and sell investments based on price movements. When such investors are watching their profits and losses (P/L), and they are significantly profitable, they are more likely to see an uncertain future as dangerous to their wealth (potentially taking away their gains so far). When they are losing money in the investment, they perceive the future as a chance to make back their losses.

A FATHER-SON STOCK SALE

Many factors influence who is susceptible to the disposition effect. An acquaintance of mine has been an executive at Cisco Systems since the early 1990s. When he started his job, he recommeded to his father that he buy some Cisco stock. His father made the purchase, and by late 1999 his stock was worth $7 million. The son had exercised his stock options in 1999, and he too had multimillion dollars in Cisco stock. One day they had an important conversation.

The father said, "Son, I'm going to sell that Cisco stock. Seven million dollars in the bank will change my lifestyle forever."

The son said, "But Dad, if you hold on you'll make even more money."

"I've seen this happen before in Silicon Valley," his dad replied, "and I don't want to ride it down. With this money I can retire early and live the life I've always wanted. Thank you for the tip."

His son was puzzled and a little angry. He told his father, "You'll regret this decision. I know how great this company is."

Of course the rest is history. The father now lives a relaxed and comfortable lifestyle, while his son is still working at Cisco. The son is by no means financially uncomfortable, but he still regrets holding on to all of his Cisco shares through the burst of the bubble.

Through the lens of the disposition effect, one could say that the father cut his winner short, and he only looks smart in hindsight. Further, one could say that the son held on to a loser too long. Of course, hindsight is 20/20. In this case, how can one differentiate between biased and sensible decision making?

The father recognized that the technology stocks were in an unsustainable bubble. He had specific plans for the profits, and he had achieved his financial goals. He bought when Cisco stock was selling cheaply, and now it was outrageously expensive. Every rally was seen as "gravy" (an unexpected but welcome addition). He understood that when one's financial goal is achieved, and one does not expect significant further progress, it is time to change course.

His son, having less market experience, was unaware of the cyclical nature of booms and busts. He had no sense of fair value for Cisco stock. Based on his limited experience, he expected this bubble to make him ultra-rich if he only held on a little longer. For the son, every stock price rally was expected and declines were terrifying.

For both men, it was their perspective that determined how they felt about their wealth. For the father, once he surpassed his financial goals, and the stock began to look overvalued, he was looking to sell. The son expected gains into the foreseeable future, and he was dismayed by sideways or downward stock price action. When declines began, the son couldn't rationally factor the changing market conditions. The son was paralyzed by his inability to accept the decline when it began. Rather than selling out with an enormous profit, his shares lost 90 percent of their value, and he held on all the way to the bottom.

TEASING OUT THE PROBLEM

The following problems illustrate the psychological process of "aversion to a sure loss," which often occurs during risky decision making and underlies the disposition effect.

- **Problem 1:** Imagine that you face the following choice. You can accept a guaranteed $1,000 or take a risk. If you take the risk, the outcome will be determined by the toss of a fair coin. If heads comes up, you win $2,000. If tails comes up, you win $0. Would you accept the guaranteed $1,000 or take the risk?
- **Problem 2:** Imagine you face the following choice. You can pay $1,000 now and the gamble is over, or you can take a risk whose outcome will

be determined by the toss of a coin. If heads comes up, you lose $0. If tails comes up, you lose $2,000. Would you take the guaranteed $1,000 loss or take the risk?

Of course, how you choose doesn't really matter. Each option has the same expected value. Yet even so, most people feel inclined to take the guaranteed gain in Problem 1 and take the risk in Problem 2. In a similar decision situation, Nobel Prize winner Daniel Kahneman (working with Amos Tversky) found that 84 percent of subjects chose the sure gain in Problem 1, and 70 percent chose to take the risk in Problem 2.[4]

During my seminars, I've found that audiences consistently favor the guaranteed gain (78 percent) in Problem 1, while the majority takes the risk in Problem 2 (72 percent). As one professional trader pointed out, "I can feel the inclination to reverse my choice between Problem 1 and Problem 2, so I assume it must be a problem." He's right. What feeling inclines people to reverse such decisions?

In any decision that involves a risk of loss, there is fear. The brain is exquisitely more sensitive to losses than gains—losses are weighted twice as heavily as gains—and decisions that can be taken to avoid realizing losses are prioritized. When operating with an existing gain (in the "gain" frame), the fear is that one will lose paper profits. When operating under the shadow of an ongoing loss, there is a powerful avoidance mechanism, also driven by fear. In the short term, the most ego-gratifying action for a paper gain is to sell for a profit. Capturing the gain relieves the fear of "giving back" what one has already earned and sustains a feeling of self-satisfaction and pride. For a paper loss, the most ego-protective action is to hold on to the losing position, denying that it is a problem while hoping to "break-even." Therefore, how investors deal with risk depends on the decision "frame."

In academic parlance, most investors are "risk averse in the realm of gains" (so they cut winners short, preferring the certain gain), and they are "risk seeking in the realm of losses" (they prefer the gamble over the certain loss)). In the case of losses, the decision to hold on to a losing stock is inspired by the same bias that inclines people to prefer the gamble over the sure loss in Problem 2 above. The preference for the risky gamble is assumed to be "risk seeking" in the realm of losses, and it underlies investors' attempts to "dollar-cost average" into losers and hope for a "comeback." In each case, loss-averse investors are trapped in the "frame" of seeing risks to their wealth, which biases their objectivity. Remember, loss-aversion describes the psychological process that underlies the disposition effect (cutting winners short and holding losers too long).

Sometimes investors pump more and more resources into losing positions. For example, the "sunk cost" bias refers to the phenomenon of business investors believing, "Since I've already invested so much money in this project, I might as well continue funding it until it pays off." In reality, this thinking shows evidence of loss aversion. Many municipal governments demonstrate this type of flawed reasoning as more and more funds are poured into overbudget and poor-quality construction projects (e.g., Boston's "big dig" highway project). The sunk cost bias is a result of hoping a losing idea will make a comeback, and it irrationally works against the retooling of moribund schemes.

FRAMING RISK

When a decision is explained as a potential gain, then the brain's reward pursuit system is engaged. When the decision is made in relation to what one might lose, the loss avoidance system is activated. The differential activation of these two motivational systems depends on how one predominantly sees the decision—as a potential opportunity or a potential risk. The different presentations of a decision, in terms of either what one might lose or what one might gain, is called *framing*.

Dan Ariely, when teaching psychology at Harvard, informed two of his undergraduate classes that he planned on reading his original poetry to selected students. One class was asked if they would pay $5 to listen to 10 minutes of his poetry, and if not, they were asked to write down a monetary sum that would suffice. The other class was asked if they would take $5 to listen to 10 minutes of his poetry, and if not, they were asked to write down their price. All students either offered to pay (in the first class) or demanded to be paid (in the second class). No one in either class wrote down a price of opposite sign (pay/take) from that presented. The expectations of these students were anchored by the framing of the decision situation Ariely presented.[5]

Framing studies show that how an investment is offered—think "golden opportunity" versus "risky and speculative"—skews decision making. At its heart, framing is the psychological process underlying loss aversion. Investigators in London decided to look for the underlying neural process.

A FRAME IN THE MEMBRANE

Neuroscientists in London designed an experiment that used framing to elicit the neural process underlying loss aversion. In an fMRI study at University College London, Benedetto De Martino recruited 20 men and women to undergo three 17-minute brain scans. At the start of each trial,

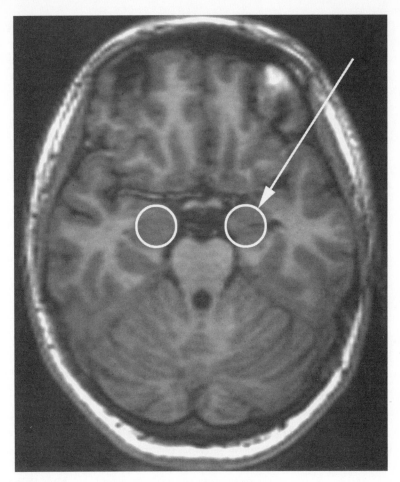

FIGURE 14.1 Transverse depiction of the amygdala.

the subjects were given English pounds worth about $95. They were then asked to make a choice between either a certain outcome (a gain or a loss) or taking a gamble. The gamble they could accept was a simple 50–50 bet in which they wagered a predefined amount of their money. The gamble's expected value was equivalent to that of the certain option, so there was no financial reason why subjects should show a preference for either the certain outcome or the gamble.[6]

When the choice was framed as a decision between "keeping" a certain amount of money or gambling, most participants chose to "keep" their money. For example, told they would "keep" 40 percent of the starting sum if they chose not to gamble (as in "Keep $38"), the volunteers typically

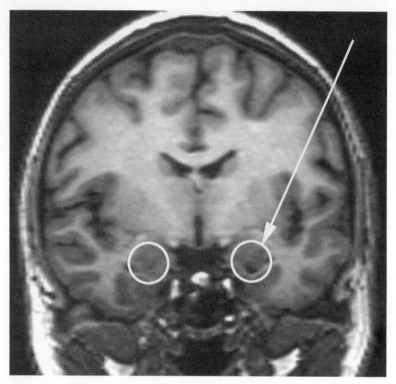

FIGURE 14.2 Coronal depiction of the amygdala.

played it safe, choosing to take the 50–50 gamble only 43 percent of the time. Told they would "lose" 60 percent of their initial pot if they didn't gamble, they took the risk 62 percent of the time, even though the gambles always had the same expected value as the certain option. Interestingly, DeMartino's results provide evidence that loss aversion is induced by the language used to frame a risky choice.

The subjects had the odds explained to them in detail before the experiment, and they knew that the probabilities in each situation were identical. Nonetheless, their decisions were altered by the language: "Keep $38" put them in a gain frame, and "Lose $38" induced a loss frame. When succumbing to loss aversion, the subjects' amygdalas (stimulated by danger) activated vigorously. When participants resisted the framing effect, the orbitofrontal cortex (involved in integrating emotion and reason) and the anterior cingulate cortex (responsible for sorting out internal conflicts) both activated. "We found everyone showed emotional biases, more or less; no one was totally free of them," De Martino said.[7] Four of the study participants acknowledged that they had been inconsistent in their decision making, choosing according to the frame rather than the odds, and in explanation they said, "I know, I just couldn't help myself," according to DeMartino.[8]

In lower animals, the amygdala prompts "fight-or-flight" behavior in response to an immediate threat. When the amygdala is activated, people will go to great lengths to avoid perceived threats to themselves or their resources (wealth). Figures 14.1 and 14.2 shows two views of the amygdala.

HOLDING LOSERS: "DOUBLE-OR-NOTHING!"

"Even being right 3 or 4 times out of 10 should yield a person a fortune if he has the sense to cut his losses quickly on the ventures where he has been wrong."
—Bernard Baruch, Financier

Loss aversion has been found in many professional groups: stock investors, real estate investors, and traders. As a group, no financial professionals are immune. In a year 2000 paper entitled "Do Professional Traders Exhibit Loss Realization Aversion?" Locke and Mann studied the trading patterns of Chicago Mercantile Exchange (CME) floor traders. They found that the most successful traders exhibit less loss aversion: "Relatively successful traders are less prone to sit on losing trades."[9]

In a 1998 study of individual investors, Odean found that retail traders hold their losers longer than their winners, leading to deteriorating profitability.[10] And in a 2005 study, researchers found that Chicago Board of Trade (CBOT) traders who had morning losses take 16 percent more risk in the afternoon, trading larger positions with decreasing profitability after lunch.[11] Taking more risk when down is considered of the same ilk as not selling a loser—in each case one should cut the loss short, not hold it or increase its size.

Not only are professional traders and individual investors suffering from the disposition effect, but mutual fund portfolio managers are as well.[12] In other studies, investors have been found to display loss aversion in assets as diverse as real estate,[13] company stock options,[14] and futures.[15]

When an investor monitors fundamental business values, then the price of stock is meaningful only as an indication of a market discount or overvaluation. Great long-term value investors such as Warren Buffett and David Dreman buy businesses that the market has priced far below fundamental value. After buying, they don't sell their shares until the business is no longer priced at a discount by the market.

DIFFERENCES IN AVERSION

The level of loss aversion is different from person to person, and within one person it changes over time depending on recent events. Earlier, I mentioned that, when given the chance to take a risky financial gamble, most people negatively value losses twice as intensely as they positively value gains. The ratio of loss aversion is (2:1). The ratio 2:1 means that the average "lambda" (the loss aversion coefficient) is 2 (actually, the average is around 2.5, depending on the situation). The lambda represents the amount by which the value of the avoidance of losses is overweighted (in expected utility) versus the pursuit of gains.

In constitutionally anxious people, the lambda is over 6. They are so afraid of losses that the majority of these "high-lambda" individuals will not take a gamble with even odds (a coin flip) unless the potential gain is more than *six times* as large as the potential loss.

Many great investors have low lambdas, just over one. They understand that a series of risks with favorable odds will lead to long-term returns. Pathological risk takers (such as problem gamblers) have lambdas less than one. They are willing to pay for the thrill of risk taking. Among those who have high lambdas, researchers have found that many do not learn from their mistakes—as if loss aversion is a stable personality trait (such as neuroticism).

There can be many rationalizations that investors cite to support holding their losers too long. There's something about losing—maybe it's the pain or the humiliation, the guilt or the shame—so that it's difficult to accept the loss. And the most dangerous aspect of this tendency is that most of us avoid admitting our losses even to ourselves.

One's level of loss aversion (and thus one's lambda) can change over time. After experiencing a recent loss, most people become *more* loss averse, as if the amygdala has become primed. Losses of any kind have this effect—the death of a loved one, illnesses, accidents, work-related losses, and trading losses all affect us similarly. Perhaps this is why faces with fearful expressions have a subliminal effect that reduces risk taking. Following losses people will become more loss averse, conservatively sticking with what they know to avoid further pain.

In a recent investigation of the disposition effect in market practitioners, Professors Martin Weber and Frank Welfens at the University of Mannheim, Germany, analyzed the purchase and sales transactions of 3,000 individual investors at a German online broker from January 1997 to April 2001. Weber found that most investors are affected by the disposition effect, but a considerable number (about one-third of the total) display a reversed disposition effect, selling their losers more quickly than their winners. In another interesting finding, the investors who sell their winners too soon are not the same investors who hold their losers too long.[16] Weber also found cutting winners short is localized to particular individuals, while holding losers too long is a trait that is common across most investors.[17]

Many studies have teased out the nuances of loss aversion within individuals and across groups. Some characteristics of investors predict a propensity to loss aversion. High-income investors and professionals (in any career) sell their losers more rapidly than lower-income and working-class investors. Investors following aggressive investment strategies sell their winners more quickly than others. Additionally, loss aversion decreases as experience increases. For example, investors who trade more frequently tend to let their winners run, and cut short their losers, more readily. The longer individual investors held a stock, the less likely they were to suffer from the disposition effect.[18]

LETTING WINNERS RIDE

Beware your rationalizations about selling a winning stock—chances are that you're unable to identify how your own reasoning is distorted. If you're guilty of the disposition effect, try the following techniques for minimizing the impact on your returns:

1. Document your plan for each investment in advance. Know when and under what circumstances you will sell a stock. Don't deviate from your plan. Keep the plan in your trading or tax records.

2. When you feel yourself becoming fearful about a winning position, especially one that has had a terrifying pullback, don't sell yet. Instead reevaluate your selling criteria. Did the position meet your profit target? Has something fundamental changed about the security that indicates you should sell now? If the price appreciation was rapid and psychology driven, then it may actually be a good time to get out, but you've got to consider such moves in your plan, in advance.

3. As with the biases above, cutting your winners short is the result of short-term emotional influences overriding your rational thinking. Notice your emotional state after a position appreciates much more than your expectations. Are you afraid of giving back your profits (and feeling regret)? Are you worried that you'll feel stupid if you don't sell? Do you want to take the money off the table to feel proud of yourself,

to show off to others, or to purchase something? There can be many explanations, depending on your life experiences and your recent financial progress.

4. Be prepared for your short-term winners to give back some of their gains. You may want to utilize profit caps (or trailing stops) to take advantage of rapid price spikes, but be sure to be systematic about it. Reversals are very common after a rapid, large price rise.

5. Don't check your prices frequently! This is especially true for long-term investors and nonprofessionals. If you are trading in positions of one year average duration, don't check the prices quotes daily. Checking too frequently leads to increased awareness of volatility, emotional reactivity, and a VERY high likelihood of overtrading. If you have an explicit plan in advance (see number 1 above), remember to follow it.

SUMMARY

Many great long-term investors develop their businesses for the long term. Small setbacks are seen as opportunities, not reasons to sell out. Yet that is an inclination that most investors feel. When times are good, and dark clouds appear on the horizon, many investors sell out early.

To prevent this inclination to "cut winners short," professional value investors buy stocks that are steeply discounted from the company's fundamental value. As a result, there is less short-term price risk. If the companies become overvalued relative to their fundamentals, then they are sold.

The framing effect is the tendency to view investments as either potential opportunities (gains) or potential risks (losses). Depending on which stance one takes, their choices are likely to be different. In general, most people fear losing. In the realm of gains, they prefer to lock in gains rather than risking a loss of their profits. In the realm of losses, they would rather gamble for the chance to lose nothing than accept a guaranteed loss. This aversion to losses is true even when the potential gain is twice as great as the potential loss. This ratio of 2:1 preference for risk is called the lamda. Many things change the value of lambda, including recent events (such as losses or gains), the framing of the decision problem, one's personality style, and one's experience with similar gambles.

Loss aversion is rooted in basic brain structures in the loss avoidance system and prefrontal cortex. The loss frame activates these structures and deviates decisions to become more self-protective. Interestingly, people who are swayed by their fear of losses are often unaware of their intrinsic decision bias.

A number of steps can be taken to lessen loss aversion. In particular, investment plans and goals help people stay on track. Every day updating your investment perspective to the morning's opening can reduce anchoring and reference point biases (such as feeling that one is "losing" or "winning" in a position). Keeping track of one's level of fear about an investment can be useful as well, especially if it is pushing one off plan. The next chapter will examine in detail the financially destructive but prevalent behavior of holding losers too long.

CHAPTER 15

Loss Aversion

Learning to Cut Losers Short

"You can't be afraid to take a loss. The people who are successful in this business are the people who are willing to lose money."

—Jack Schwager[1]

"I'm not better than the next trader, just quicker at admitting my mistakes and moving on to the next opportunity."

—George Soros

Some investors "fall in love" with a stock or a position. Maybe they love the stock because it has had a high return thus far, or they love the idea behind the company, or they work for the company and enjoy owning shares. In any case, when investors become attached to or overidentified with a stock, they lose the ability to think rationally when the time comes to sell. Like letting go of a favorite old car, or cleaning the "junk" out of the basement, selling a stock can feel painful and unnecessary, even though one wouldn't purchase so many shares *de novo*, given the chance. People's propensity to become emotionally attached to items they own, such as stocks, is called the *endowment effect*. The endowment effect is an easily measurable result of loss aversion.

Because investors have difficulty selling stocks that they already own, especially if they are losing, researchers surveyed stock investors about how much time they spend on buy versus sell decisions. Ninety percent of active individual investors reported spending more time on buy

203

decisions than sell decisions. However, less than 20 percent said that buy decisions were more difficult. Investors are spending less time making sell decisions, but more than 80 percent report that those decisions are more difficult.[2] What is so difficult about the sell decision? While buy decisions are typically based on a consideration of objective information, sell decisions are often emotionally weighted.

Recall that the endowment effect refers to the phenomenon where people overvalue items they own. In a classic demonstration of the endowment effect, I randomly gave pens to one-half of "behavioral finance" seminar participants. I asked the new pen owners to write down something they liked about the pens. The other half of the audience—the nonowners—were asked to write down objective qualities of the pens. As an aside, please note that researchers have found that when subjects write down admired qualities of an owned item the endowment effect is enhanced, while documenting objective qualities reduces the endowment effect.

The new owners then set a price at which they would sell their pens to the nonowners. The nonowners set a price at which they would buy the pen. The average bid from the nonowners was $1.50 while the average asking price from the owners was $5.50. The people who owned the pen valued it far more than the non-owners. The pen had actually cost $1.50. In general, investors value items they own more than nonowners do, and as a result, they are reluctant to part with them for what appears to be an excessively low price.

An interesting example of the endowment effect was noticed in online auctions. Researchers proposed that the highest bidders in an online eBay-style auction, realizing that they are the highest bidders, might start thinking more concretely about possessing the desired item. As a result, they could become partially attached to it—producing a bias they term a *quasi-endowment effect*. The researchers found what they had expected. Online auction participants whose bid is highest at some point during an auction more aggressively pursue the item if their high bid is bested by another's.[3] A similar effect may happen in stocks as investors "chase" the price higher after missing a fill on a limit order.

As seen in Professor Jennifer Lerner's studies in Chapter 6, one's emotional state modifies the strength of the endowment effect. For example, sadness prompts people to think about changing their circumstances. As a result, the endowment effect is eliminated in sad people, since they are now focusing on shifting their circumstances (selling what they own and buying items they do not).[4]

It's not only emotional states that alter the strength of the endowment effect. The intention to spend money on a purchase or, in the case of investors, to sell a stock in one's portfolio appears to reduce the endowment effect. Making up one's mind to let go of a stock discharges the mental constructs that supported ownership. When it comes time to sell, there are no emotional connections spurring second thoughts.

It doesn't make sense that the endowment effect would persist in professionals, due to the erosion in profitability it would cause. In structured experiments, professional baseball card traders showed a steady reduction (to extinction) of the endowment effect as they traded over many rounds.[5] However, it remains unclear whether the endowment effect is reduced through experience in stock market participants.

NEUROSCIENCE OF LOSS AVERSION

If loss aversion is so common, affecting almost two-thirds of investors, then it's reasonable to speculate that it may have a biological basis. Chapter 14 described an fMRI study in the United Kingdom that identified amygdala activation (fear) as one cause of the effect. Interestingly, loss aversion and the endowment effect are evident in the behavior of monkeys.

An enterprising economist, Keith Chen at Yale University, trained capuchin monkeys to use and value "currency" (small metal tokens). He observed the choice behavior of his monkeys during a number of different decisions, in which they chose among different quantities of one of their favorite foods—apple slices. Chen wondered whether biases such as loss aversion are the result of social or cultural learning, specific environmental experiences, or some fundamental neural process shared by all primates.[6]

The tufted capuchin is native to the South American tropics. Capuchins live in a male dominance hierarchy with a single alpha-male and several nondominant males and females living in small bands. Capuchins are "extractive foragers"—they prefer easy-to-eat fruit but when pressed are capable of pounding apart hard nuts, stripping tree bark, raiding beehives, and even killing small vertebrates.[7]

The capuchins were presented with choices between different quantities of apple slices. Some choices were framed as gains and others as losses. Chen found that the monkeys obeyed many of the axioms of prospect theory, for example. "Capuchins seem to weigh those losses more heavily than comparable gains, displaying not just reference-dependence but loss-aversion." Chen concludes that "our results may suggest that loss aversion is an innate and evolutionarily ancient feature of human preferences, a function of decision-making systems which evolved before the common ancestors of capuchins and humans diverged."

It's not just tropical monkeys that are susceptible to loss aversion. Human children, while unable to express gambles in terms of expected value, also demonstrate loss aversion, with no age-diminishing influence through college.[8]

THE EQUITY PREMIUM PUZZLE

The equity premium puzzle refers to the historically high returns of stocks relative to bonds. According to economists, the average annual real return (i.e., the inflation-adjusted return) on the U.S. stock market for the past 110 years has been about 7.9 percent. In the same period, the real return on a relatively riskless security was 1.0 percent. The difference between these two returns, 6.9 percentage points, is the equity premium.[9] Why U.S. bonds are so popular, even with a relatively low yield, is the puzzle. Individuals must perceive a significantly higher level of risk in stocks than has been shown historically for the puzzle to be reconciled with "rational" economic models.[10]

Investors are sensitive to volatility, and the more they check prices, the more risk they see in the stock market. When experimenters change the feedback frequency of price quotes, they find that individuals tend to invest more in equities when the performance of their prior decisions is assessed less frequently (i.e., when they see price quotes less often).[11]

Professors Shlomo Benartzi and Richard Thaler at the University of Chicago proposed that this feedback-induced conservatism was due to a process of "myopic loss aversion." As people receive more frequent feedback about price changes, they become short-sighted in their risk assessments. Given their more numerous sample periods, frequent price checkers have higher odds of seeing negative price changes, which they perceive as threatening (risky) to their wealth. Thaler argued that the size of the equity premium (6 percent) is consistent with investors evaluating their investments annually and weighing losses about twice as heavily as gains.[12]

Investors' myopic loss aversion is increased by exposure to both information quantity and frequency. Loss-averse clients may have compelled Israel's largest mutual fund manager, Bank Hapoalim, to change the frequency of its fund performance reports from every month to every three months, while noting that "investors should not be scared by the occasional drop in prices."[13]

In an experiment comparing university students and pit traders from the Chicago Board of Trade (CBOT), traders actually exhibited *more* myopic loss aversion than students.[14] Floor traders may have honed a skill for rapid risk/reward assessment, which encourages short-term evaluations and decisions—not necessarily compatible with choosing the best long-term option.

Along these lines, researchers have found that professional traders and investors are largely incapable of arbitraging psychological biases out of market prices. Price anomalies such as the equity premium puzzle have persisted despite the recognition of greater profits available to investors who understand them.

So what would a savvy investor do? They should put all their long-term savings in equities, none in bonds or cash. Unfortunately, this advice is easier said than done, which explains why the equity premium has persisted.

THE IMPLIED PUT OPTION

In early 2006, Brian Hunter, a 32-year-old physics and applied math graduate from Calgary, Canada, placed large bets on the convergence of long-dated natural gas contracts (such as the March and April 2007 expirations). As the prices of those and other contracts diverged in September 2006, and Hunter lost more and more money, he repeatedly increased his risk exposure. By September 2006, Hunter's firm, Amaranth Capital, had purportedly lost more than $6 billion (out of a total capital pool of $9 billion). The firm subsequently closed, liquidated its positions, and the remaining assets were returned to investors.[15]

In 2005, Hunter earned $75 million for his stellar trading performance, with a rally in natural gas prices due to Hurricane Katrina responsible for the bulk of those gains. While his lifetime trading gains had been spectacular, in 2006 investors in his firm lost 66 percent of their capital.

Hunter was exceedingly profitable for several years prior to the collapse of his fund, yet he may have grown overconfident in his ability to manage risk. He increased his risk exposure as his losses first swelled in May 2006. Fortunately, his gambit paid off during the summer of 2006. However, Hunter remained excessively exposed when markets again reversed in September 2006, and this time he didn't get bailed out. The same pattern of loss averse trading characterized John Meriwether, the founder of Long-Term Capital Management. In both cases, each trader increased risk exposure when losing (loss aversion). Because they couldn't accept the pain of the loss, they held on longer. Occasionally, loss averse investors even "double down" with more capital while insisting that their losing positions are rational.

Hedge fund traders who take excessive risk operate with an ethical dilemma in mind. They are working with an "implied put option," which means that they are extremely well compensated if they take large risks that payoff, but a catastrophic loss is unlikely to affect them beyond the current year (unless they invested in their own fund). The worst that can happen to them personally, especially in a hedge fund, is that they lose their job, their current income, and any forthcoming annual bonus. In the case of Hunter, he made $75 million in 2005, and beyond the one-third of his bonus that he had invested in Amaranth, he will emerge from the debacle with tens of millions in the bank from his trading in 2004 and 2005.[16] Not bad for someone who lost $6 billion in 2006.

One especially interesting aspect of Hunter's success and subsequent downfall is the respect and admiration afforded him by other traders. According to "former Deutsche Bank colleague Bruno Stanziale, 34, 'He has an understanding of the market that others do not.'" Another former colleague remarks that Hunter should get back into trading, "'Otherwise, it would be too much intellectual capital wasted to have him on the sidelines.'"[17] Similar praise was conferred on John Meriwether after the collapse of Long-Term Capital.

While there is no doubt that both Hunter and Meriwether are remarkable men, it is surprising that many traders miss the essential lesson of their downfalls. A few years of hefty profits and sagacious market insights do not immunize traders from the risk of total collapse. Risk management is key, yet it is often boring and restricts profitability. Firms that are trapped in a death spiral will often take far more risk to get out of their hole. Often, "doubling-down" works, and then an "addiction to risk" can become entrenched.

Interestingly, it is excessive risk taking when losing that also characterized the downfalls of "rogue trader" Nick Leeson at Barings Bank in Singapore (in 1994) and Toshihide Iguchi at Daiwa Bank in New York City (1995). Like Hunter, both Leeson and Iguchi had been considered "stars" of their firms and as such had been given less risk management oversight.

OVERCOMING LOSS AVERSION

> *"I was determined to win back the losses. And as the spring wore on, I traded harder and harder, risking more and more. I was well down, but increasingly sure that my doubling up and doubling up would pay off . . . I redoubled my exposure . . . it became an addiction."*
>
> —Nick Leeson[18]

It doesn't feel good to take losses, but it has to be done. Following are a number of tips for investors and traders who have noticed loss aversion in their transactions (avoiding selling losers, "doubling down," and "hoping for a comeback"). In truth, the result of doubling down may be a rebound in one's positions and greater overall profits. But, eventually, the rebound will not come, and one will lose everything.

Loss aversion usually dissipates with experience, and the following tips should help yours along into the dustbin of history. Many of the tips are repeated elsewhere in the book.

1. **When you reevaluate your investments holdings, consider preferentially selling some of the losers instead of the winners.** Ask yourself, "All things being equal, would I enter this position today?" If your answer is "no," then place it on your sell list.
2. **Be aware of rationalizations or excuses you make in order to hold a losing position longer.** Many traders who break their stop-loss rules report that they wanted to "see if it would come back a little before I sold it." Don't believe yourself—while you were waiting for that retracement, you were rationalizing your poor money management. You didn't want to take the pain. It takes a lot of courage to admit defeat. And you can't regroup for the next engagement until you've taken the pain.
3. **Beware of letting naked options expire worthless instead of selling them according to plan.** It is easy to let out-of-the-money options or long-dated "low-risk" arbitrage positions sit, hoping for a comeback, rather than selling them for a loss. On a similar note, when shorting stock, be sure to have a stringent (and realistic) sell criterion.
4. **Remember that you are more susceptible to loss aversion after recent or large losses of any nature.** Be aware of losses and disappointments in your life and how these may affect your investing.
5. **Humility is essential.** Developing a reputation as an excellent or insightful trader could make you cocky. When you are eventually wrong, you'll be less likely to admit it, for fear of damaging your reputation. Remember, the markets are always bigger than you.
6. **Be sure to set and follow stop-loss rules.** If you don't have a defined money management system, then be sure to put one in place. See number 1 above.

THE HOUSE MONEY EFFECT

Most investors are susceptible to investing errors related to loss aversion, such as holding losers too long. Not as many investors cut their winners short. In particular, a seemingly contradictory mistake has been noted by researchers. Professor and money manager Richard Thaler found that many of his experimental subjects took increased risk after wins, which he called the *house money effect*. The *house money* name is derived from an expression often heard at casinos, where gamblers who bet more after big wins are said to be playing "with the house's money." They have not yet internalized their ownership of the winnings yet, and thus they aren't as afraid of losing it.

This contrast between "cutting winners short" due to loss aversion and "letting winners ride" due to the house money effect is frankly confusing. The existence of these two seemingly contradictory biases can be attributed to the framing of prior gains. According to professor and behavioral finance expert Hersh Shefrin, "If a prior gain is followed by a gamble whose maximum loss is not larger in absolute value than the prior gain, then a person might act as if he or she is risk seeking in the domain of gains, in contrast to a situation where there was no prior gain but the underlying cash flows were the same, and the person was risk averse in the domain of gains."[19,20] If one is struggling to maintain a profitable trading account, then gains are quickly realized (cut short) in order to cement the account in positive territory. However, if an investor is flush with excess cash, then risks will not be as worrisome, and gains will be left to "ride."

Researchers have identified the house money effect among market makers on the Taiwan Futures Exchange. Every options transaction on the exchange between 2001 and 2004 was analyzed.[21] Market makers were found to take more risk in the afternoon after a successful morning of trading. Other studies with individual investors have often found the same effect; they increase subsequent trading intensity and take on greater risks after making profitable trades.[22] Among investors, the house money effect is often present among more successful individuals. That is, more successful investors are more likely to let their winners run. However, the effect does appear to decline with experience.

As noted in the quotation from Hersh Shefrin above, an investor's frame of reference regarding recent gains or losses often determines which type of bias they show. Investors may become excessively loss averse if they are worried about giving back profits, while they may become excessively risk seeking if they feel that they have "nothing to lose." In each case, feelings about potential gains and losses are driving risk-taking. In the examples of professional investors below, notice how each prevents himself from interpreting gains and losses in ways that provoke an emotional response.

LESSONS FROM THE POPE

Jim Leitner, manager of Falcon Management, a New Jersey–based hedge fund, is considered by some to be the "Pope" of global macro investing.

By his own estimate, he has taken $2 billion out of the markets for himself and his employers over the course of his career. Leitner is hardworking, humble, intellectually curious, and willing to sacrifice in the short-term in order to advance his experience or knowledge. Since founding Falcon Management in 1997, he earned approximately 30 percent annually. Author and hedge fund consultant Steven Drobny interviewed Leitner to discover some of his investing secrets.[23]

When asked how he can tell when prices are out of line, Leitner responds, "I don't have an innate skill. It comes from being extremely interested in markets and looking at everything all the time." Through his interest and experience, Leitner has developed a "mental database of where things should be."[24] In a sense, Leitner has honed his ability to assess expected value and notice deviations from it on his mental "radar screen."

As a result of his innate evaluation mechanism, which is driven by factual events and prices, not by overt feelings, Leitner describes his trading as being "absolutely unemotional." "Losses did not have an effect on me because I viewed them as purely probability-driven, which meant sometimes you came up with a loss. . . . To this day, my wife never knows if I've had a bad day or a good day in the markets."[25]

How does Leitner remain unaffected by his performance? His ego is uninvolved, because he remains unattached to outcomes. In addition to being unemotional: ". . . I'm really humble about my ignorance. I truly feel that I'm ignorant despite having made enormous amounts of money." Leitner is never trying to prove something with his ability to make money. He approaches investing as an intellectual game, one that he loves to play. Leitner describes his favorite trade as one in which he made one tick overnight on the Swiss franc by relying on his wits, ". . . My wife still remembers me jumping up and down in the middle of the night screaming 'I did it! I did it!' . . . It was the most phenomenal feeling of control and creativity all coming together."[26]

Leitner displays no hubris or overconfidence in his interview—only an intense curiosity about the markets, humility, and a willingness to constantly reexamine his assumptions. He does recount an episode when he forgot to be humble: "Finland devalued once when I was working for myself and I was caught long. I was partially asleep and a bit cocky because it had never happened to me before. The trading gods had to remind me to be humble."[27]

For the aspiring investor, Leitner recommends openness to the "entire spectrum of market experiences," avoiding becoming too much of an expert, and learning not to "buy into stories." To combat the "buying into stories bias," Leitner suggests, "We need to quantify things and understand why things are cheap or expensive by using some hard measure of what cheap or expensive means." Yet we shouldn't dismiss stories. "A story is still required since a story will appeal to other people and appeal is what drives markets."[28]

Leitner practices looking at both sides of an issue, essentially balancing his frame of reference. He is aware of the psychological confirmation bias that drives many investors to seek only information that supports their beliefs. "Very few people train themselves to look for disconfirming evidence.... What I try to do in my trades is look for disconfirming evidence. It's a very difficult practice, and I have to continually train myself to ask why I believe something is going to go down, not why it should go up."[29]

COMMENTS FROM SOROS, TUDOR, AND CRAMER: "BOOYAH!"

> *"I think I am the single most conservative trader on earth in the sense that I absolutely hate losing money."*
>
> —Paul Tudor Jones[30]

> *"Rule No.1: Never lose money. Rule No.2: Never forget rule No.1."*
>
> —Warren Buffett

If most investors are susceptible to loss aversion, then how can they get over it? According to a paper by Professors Seasholes and Feng at the University of California at Berkeley, investor sophistication (measured by trading characteristics such as portfolio diversity) and trading experience together eliminate loss aversion over time. Trading experience alone does not account for extinguished loss aversion—sophistication must also be present. One unusual finding of their paper was that sophistication and trading experience reduce the propensity to realize gains somewhat (by 37 percent) but not entirely.[31] Even professional investors, with extensive experience, may be playing scared—and cutting winners short.

George Soros announced the closure of his largest equity funds—Quantum and Quota—at the peak of the technology bubble. His portfolio manager, Stanley Druckenmiller, commented that stock markets in late April 2000 were, "now crazy insane, unbelievably dangerous."[32] Regarding their departure from the stock market, Soros commented, "Being the last in, we felt it incumbent to be the first out."[33] By being first out, Soros was displaying an eagerness to realize his losses and get out of a market that he no longer understood.

Paul Tudor Jones is one of the greatest traders in history. In Jack Schwager's book *Stock Market Wizards*, Jones comments on how his life and trading have changed since a large loss he suffered during one of his first years as a professional trader: "Now I spend my day trying to make myself as happy and relaxed as I can be. If I have positions going against me, I get right out; if they are going for me, I keep them."[34] Jones optimizes his mental state during the trading day by reducing emotional interference, and one way of doing that is by cutting losers quickly.

Jones tackles the framing bias that leads to loss aversion by daily updating his frame of reference: "Don't be too concerned about where you got in to a position. The only relevant question is whether you are bullish or bearish on the position that day. Always think of your entry point as last night's close."[35] Price changes are unimportant. Is there new information (besides price changes) that alters the fundamental outlook?

Jones offers suggestions on preventing trying to make back prior losses. "Don't average losers. Decrease trading volume when you're trading poorly. Increase volume when you're trading well." In order to preempt any urge to hold on too long when a position isn't moving, Tudor recommends, "Don't just use a price stop, use a time stop. If you think a market should break and it doesn't, get out even if you aren't losing any money."[36]

On March 11, 2000, days from the all-time high of the NASDAQ, James J. Cramer, former hedge fund manager, founder of TheStreet.com, and currently star of CNBC's *Mad Money*, rewrote his wife's 10 trading commandments. The first of those commandments urged disciplined selling of losers:

> ***Discipline is more important than conviction.*** *My wife's trading was all about fallibility. She knew that a lot of her ideas would be stinkers, even if she believed in them. So she had ironclad rules. Don't let emotions get in the way. Don't ride things down. Don't get smitten.*[37]

Discipline is all-encompassing—it stops every emotional bias in its tracks. In the above quoted article, Cramer went on to recommend that investors (in March 2000) take money out of the markets, explaining they would thank him later for that advice.

The professionals above use analytical detachment from profits and losses, engage in strictly disciplined selling of losers, and cultivate humility in order to prevent the emergence of emotional biases such as loss aversion. In the next chapter you'll see one effect of emotion on thinking—time discounting and the pursuit of immediate gratification.

CHAPTER 16

Time Discounting

Why We Eat Dessert First

"Our favorite holding period is forever."
—Warren Buffet in Letter to Berkshire Hathaway
Shareholders, 1988

How many people actually complete their New Year's resolutions? It shouldn't be difficult, but year after year, whether it is to maintain their ideal weight, save adequately for retirement, or otherwise accept short-term pain for a long-term benefit, very few people can stick to the plan. They simply cannot defer gratification. The difficulty people have in delaying pleasure is a result of time discounting.[1]

Time discounting describes the tendency to give in to immediate gratification urges—going for small short-term gains in the present while sacrificing larger future rewards as a consequence. What is fascinating about time discounting is that people intellectually *know* they will experience bad consequences from current misbehavior *later*, but at the moment of temptation their limbic gratification-seeking self overrides this warning while the prefrontal cortex looks on helplessly.

The normal brain's discounting function has been defined by a series of economics experiments. In the prototypical experiment, when asked if they would prefer $10 now to $11 in a week, most people choose the immediate $10. If asked whether they would prefer $10 a year from now or $11 a year and a week from now, most people choose the $11 in a year and a week. If they chose the $11 in a year and a week, and a year passed, and they were offered the opportunity to change their decision, a majority would now go for the $10 today. This pattern suggests that many people practice hyperbolic-like discounting, with a disproportionate

215

preference for immediate and imminent rewards.[2] In general, people are more impatient when making decisions about smaller shorter-term gains versus longer-term larger ones.

In general, the average person prefers $100 now to $140 delivered in one year, implying a "discount rate" for immediate rewards of 40 percent,[3] much higher than an average stock market return. The only rational reason they would want the $100 now is if they can expect to make a larger annual return than 40 percent with the money, which is very doubtful.

When the potential monetary rewards are displaced in time so that subjects are choosing between $100 in one year and a larger sum thereafter (e.g., two years), the "long-term discount rate" is typically measured to be around 4.3 percent,[4] which is slightly less than short-term interest rates would dictate.

The pursuit of immediate gains can lead investors to abandon stable long-term investment plans. Mutual fund purchases (when investors flock into last year's best performers), short-term trading decisions (especially in a long-term investor), and retirement savings decisions are all often biased by time discounting. Many investors pursuing short-term gains are more inclined to pay premiums over fair values. Those investors who get a "hot" stock tip may rush to buy, even borrowing on margin, to catch an anticipated share price jump. In the options market, short-term thinking (time discounting) leads to options premiums out of line with mathematical models.

Discounting also occurs for potential punishments, though this chapter is primarily about gains. Most people avoid small, immediate punishments if they can choose to wait for larger, later ones.[5] Procrastination (putting off unwanted duties until later) is an effect of such punishment discounting. In Chapter 9, we saw a counterpoint to procrastination in which "high dreaders" will accept a large electric shock immediately rather than wait (and suffer the anticipation) of a smaller one. The effect in which dread inspires higher cost avoidance is due to the immediacy of the punishments on offer. The experiments that test the "dread" effect don't require waits longer than five minutes. Even procrastinators will get down to work and accept the pain when the pressure grows too intense as their deadline nears.

Not everyone is subject to the same discounting tendencies. For the most part, people fall on a spectrum, from highly discounting (drug addicts) to gratification delaying (the most disciplined savers). Furthermore, certain conditions predispose people to become more or less discounting. Cues that a desired goal is near provoke discounting. Time pressure incites discounting. People who are self-controlled, such as those who are high in the personality trait of conscientiousness (self-disciplined, organized, and rule following), exhibit less discounting than those who are more impulsive. Among substance abusers, researchers have found that their personal discounting curves are correlated with both their degree of impulsiveness and their addiction severity.[6]

GET YOUR HAND OUT OF THE COOKIE JAR

When I was a psychiatry resident, we watched an educational film about self-control experiments with children. In the movie, four- and five-year-old children were brought into a room and seated at a desk. A cookie was placed on the desk, and the experimenter said something to the effect of, "This is your cookie. You can eat it whenever you want. I'm going to step out of the room for a few minutes. If you haven't eaten the cookie when I get back, then I'll give you a second cookie and you can eat both of them." The researcher would leave the room for a few minutes. The kids would sit at the desk and think about their predicament.

Some of the kids would immediately gobble up their cookie. When the researcher returned and didn't give them a second one, they complained, "That's not fair!" Some kids simply leaned back in their chairs and calmly waited, deferring their gratification until they could double up. Some kids wanted to wait, but, almost as if by no intention of their own, their hands would creep across the desk toward the cookie. One kid was really tormented—he ended up sitting on his hands, bouncing up and down, and practically squealing in agony until the researcher returned.

The study tracked these kids for 10 years. A child's ability to wait for the second cookie was a pretty accurate prediction of later academic success and SAT scores. Ten years later, parents of the two-cookie hold-outs rated their children as more attentive, better able to concentrate, more goal oriented, and more intelligent than the parents of the one-cookie gluttons. The two-cookie parents also viewed their children as more able to resist temptation, tolerate frustration, and cope with stress.

How the cookies were presented also affected performance. When the cookies were hidden from sight, children could wait longer. When they were asked to think about the taste of the cookie, the children waited less. If they were asked to think about objective aspects of the cookie—such as shape and color—the children were able to calm their desire and delay longer. The authors found that self-control, modulated by thinking, begins between ages 9 and 12, and they concluded that the ability to delay gratification is an important, and overlooked, type of intelligence.[7]

A follow-up study in 2006 reported that children who were able to turn their attention away from the cookie (implying better cognitive control over attention and focus) can better delay gratification. The ability of these children to intentionally shift their attention away from temptations may be the key to their success later in life. The researchers speculate that because attention relies on frontal cortex connections with the "striatum" (which contains the nucleus accumbens), the ability to defer gratification may be an "early marker of individual differences in the functional integrity of this circuitry [impulse inhibition circuits]."[8]

BRAIN BASIS OF DELAYED GRATIFICATION

Instant gratification is the preferred choice of the reward system, while exercising self-control and long-term planning is the function of the brain's prefrontal cortex. Samuel McClure, a neuroscientist at Princeton University, performed a brain-imaging experiment with volunteers engaged in a time discounting task. Subjects were given several decision pairs, between which they were asked to state their preference. For example, they could choose between either an Amazon.com gift certificate worth $20.28 today or one worth $23.32 in one month. In a longer-term example, they asked subjects to, for example, choose between $30 in two weeks and $40 in six weeks.

McClure found that time discounting results from the combined influence of two neural systems. Limbic regions drive choices in favor of immediately available rewards. The frontal and parietal cortices are recruited for all choices. These two systems are separately implicated in emotional and cognitive brain processes, and there appears to be a competition between the two systems during discounting-type decisions, with higher limbic activation indicating a greater likelihood that immediate gratification will be pursued.

In particular, McClure found that when experimental subjects choose larger delayed rewards, cortical areas such as the lateral and prefrontal cortex showed activity enhancement.[9] These brain regions are associated with higher-level cognitive functions including planning and numerical calculation. McClure's theory is supported by a finding that in prisoners the cortical regions activated by delayed gratification are thinned. This may explain why their decisions are more often short-sighted than others.[10] According to McClure, "Our results help to explain why many factors other than temporal proximity, such as the sight or smell or touch of a desired object, are associated with impulsive behavior."[11] If impatient behavior is driven by limbic activation, it follows that any factor that produces such activation may have effects similar to that of immediacy.[12] According to McClure, immediacy in time may be only one of many factors that, by producing limbic activation, engenders impatience[13] and impulsive action.

The implications of discounting extend far beyond financial decisions. "'This can explain why we engage in all manner of self-defeating behaviour,' Professor Laibson said. 'The emotion centre says stopping smoking today will be very painful, but agrees it would be OK in a week. A week later, it says, 'I know I agreed a week ago, but I still want to postpone it.'"[14]

The ability to exercise self-restraint is essential for accumulating capital—according to some studies, those who exercise more self-control are, on average, wealthier. Any positively arousing aspect of an investment, such as an association with opportunity, success, or imminent gain, may cause similar limbic activations to those found during time discounting. Emotion shifts decision making to limbic circuits and weakens one's ability to delay gratification. However, strong prefrontal cortex activity can inhibit the limbic urges to chase immediate gratification.

CHEMICAL IMPULSES

On the chemical level, opiate chemicals (such as morphine) induce time discounting, leading to greater impulsive choice. For example, heroin addicts temporally discount money more steeply when they are in a drug-craving state (immediately before receiving an opioid agonist, such as heroin) than when they are not in a drug-craving state (immediately after using heroin).[15] The addict's impatience for a "hit" also prompts greater impatience (discounting) in other areas of reward processing.

Medications that reduce the frequency of impulsive choices include opioid receptor blockers, which inhibit the release of dopamine in the reward pathways. Attenuated dopamine decreases the pleasure of immediate gratification. Successful treatment of impulse-control disorders such as pathological gambling and kleptomania (addiction to stealing) is seen with opiate receptor blockers such as naltrexone[16] and nalmefene.

MONKEY BUSINESS

Evolutionarily, discounting may make some sense for the survival of our species. Steep discounting may have been highly adaptive when most (if not all) valuable resources were perishable or were difficult to defend given the lack of defined or enforced property rights.[17] Supporting this theory is the finding that our primate cousins, both monkeys and apes, have great difficulty delaying gratification.

For example, in a type of experimental game called a reverse-contingency task, the experimenter delivers a large reward whenever the subject reaches for a smaller treat and delivers a small reward whenever the subject reaches for the larger treat. When playing this game, monkeys and apes do not learn to reach for the small reward (in order to get a larger meal). When the task is modified so that they are reaching towards a *symbol* of a smaller reward or larger reward, most primates catch on. It may be that the sight of the *actual* reward ignites their limbic circuits, undermining the inhibitory function of the prefrontal cortex.[18]

Professor Dan Ariely at Massachusetts Institute of Technology (MIT) designed a functional magnetic resonance imaging (fMRI) study in which subjects were asked to choose between receiving money in one month or viewing an alluring pornographic photograph immediately. Participants had to respond continuously, by pressing a button, in order to avoid seeing the photograph and receive the money. Ariely made the experiment challenging by scaling the payments for avoiding the photo. When he offered small rewards for bypassing a high-quality image, more people chose to view the photo than to receive the (small) payout. Ariely found that charging higher prices makes self-control easier. The brain regions that activated when subjects declined the pornography and chose the one month later payout were in the—you guessed it—prefrontal cortex (inhibition) and also in the parietal cortex (a brain area associated with calculation of expected returns).[19]

In the modern world, technologies such as the Internet, bank account fees, credit cards, and retirement savings plans have vastly increased the personal financial costs of time discounting and impulsiveness. The remarkable array of desirable and immediately available consumer products, coupled with clever advertising schemes that appeal to basic impulses and desires, may be important contributors to the persistent failure of people to save adequately for their own retirement.[20]

MAKING A KILLING IN THE OPTIONS PIT

In the markets, time discounting is most dramatic during investor panics. The immediate short-term gain being sought is relief from painful declining positions. According to Richard Friesen, a retired options specialist and former seat holder on the Pacific Stock Exchange, during periods of market volatility, emotional responses can become the major driver of risk perceptions and option values. At these times, investors may be more preoccupied with licking recent wounds than taking risk. As a result of the immediacy engendered by unforeseen crises, out-of-the-money options, particularly puts, gain large premiums. This would seem to be the best time for option writers and premium sellers to exploit investors' increased risk perceptions, but sometimes the market's fear is contagious.

Ideally professional options traders are conditioned to maintain equanimity during periods that others perceive as dangerous crises. They should be able to maintain a long-term perspective even when others see the world with steep, fear-induced, discounting curves. According to Friesen, during market crises "we couldn't sell option premium fast enough."

As Friesen tells it, in the midst of the October 1987 stock market crash, he and his options trading colleagues were stunned by the irrational option values. The trick was to avoid going into shock while the entire financial system appeared to be heading towards a cliff.

On that October Monday, the trading pits were eerily tense, loaded with bids to buy puts, but with none of the floor traders willing to step in and sell them. Friesen recalls that one of his colleagues walked forward into the inaction of the trading pit and offered to sell options for an enormous premium. Panicked investors and brokers under orders to forcibly liquidate bankrupt accounts snapped up his puts. His selling price guaranteed that he would make money unless the stock market dropped by another 50 percent. Soon his firm was doing the rational behavior of selling puts to emotional buyers. According to Friesen, "Trading at times like these is magic. You are standing on rational grounds and trading with a crowd in emotional panic. It is like an 'out of the body experience.' You know exactly what is going to happen, and can watch the prices collapse as trader after trader sees the truth you already knew."

IMPROVING SELF-CONTROL

> *"We don't get paid for activity, just for being right.*
> *As to how long we'll wait, we'll wait indefinitely."*
> —Warren Buffett at 1998 Berkshire Hathaway
> Annual Meeting

Researchers have found that the best way to enforce self-control and reduce procrastination is to have an external rule enforcer, such as a colleague or spouse, who can set meaningful punishments and rewards for adhering to the plan.[21]

Another behavioral strategy for reinforcing self-control is avoidance. If a dieter walks by a tempting donut shop every morning on the way to work, he might shift his path to avoid the donut shop, thus bypassing the cues that normally trigger irresistible cravings—the smells and sights of sweet, warm donuts. Similarly, if an investor finds that she tends to panic out of long-term positions when she checks quotes and sees the price declining, she can either avoid the information source or enter protective stops.

Professor Terry Burnham, co-author of *Mean Genes*, reports in the book that he enjoyed day trading so much in the late 1990s that it interfered with his social life. One year, he made a quarter billion dollars in transactions. He realized that he needed to use external measures to help him slow his trading, and he tried several techniques. He used a dial-up instead of a broadband connection to the Internet, he closed his discount brokerage account (requiring him to call a human broker to place trades), and he occasionally had friends hold on to his Internet cable during the evenings so he would not check the markets after hours. External behavioral enforcers, such as those used by Burnham, are some of the most effective self-control fail-safes.

Much of the art of self-control is cognitive—using different thoughts, feelings, and memories to convince oneself of the value of restraint—while other techniques are behavioral. For example, an ex-smoker may pine after "just one" cigarette but then call to mind the deceased grandfather whose emphysema devastated his vitality. The association of cigarettes with the suffering of a family member might evoke strong disgust and a reflexive urge to avoid smoking.

Practitioners of neurolinguistic programming, such as motivational speaker Anthony Robbins, locate the emotional origin of one's desire to continue a noxious habit. Then mental exercises are used to reverse one's emotional association from good to extremely negative. For example, if one is unable to follow a diet plan because of a propensity to sneak bites of dessert, then one should locate the fond memory or association driving the craving.

One may have childhood memories of being brought desserts by her grandmother when lying ill from the flu. To reverse this loving and positive association with dessert, one can call to mind all the negative and damaging aspects of desserts. Repeatedly *feel* the emotional intensity of the following images and associate them with desserts. For example, bring to mind that heart disease runs in the family, having killed one's uncle, and recall that dessert will cause that effect in other loved ones. Picture the bulging atherosclerotic plaques on their arteries (find photos on the Internet if you need a reference). Imagine how the sugar is accelerating your aging process and weakening your immune system, predisposing you to colds and chronic illness. These are only examples.

For yourself, consider a habit you'd like to break, find appropriate reversed associations, and *feel* them. Then repeatedly feel how toxic that habit is until the very thought of it makes you extremely uncomfortable.

For example, investors might want to break a habit of falling in love with stocks (the endowment effect). Such investors should take extra effort to find negative information or opinions about the company. When feeling amorous, they can consciously recall how badly they felt when other stocks they loved let them down (and damaged their bank account).

IN PRACTICE

According to the *Wall Street Journal,* the best biotech analyst of 2005 was Martin Auster, MD.[22] When I asked Auster what differentiated him from other analysts, he indicated that he takes a longer-term view of the stocks he covers. While most analysts look at upcoming clinical trials and products over the next 6 to 12 months, Auster looks ahead 12 to 18 months. This longer-term perspective ensures that he is well positioned when other analysts turn their attention to events he had already priced into his recommendations.

Investors can enhance self-control and combat time discounting by identifying where they are vulnerable. For most investors, discounting drives short-term thinking when they are feeling emotional (such as in volatile markets). For example, a professed "long-term" investor may inappropriately buy a stock due to excitement about an upcoming product release or earnings announcement.

There are many advantages to understanding time discounting that depend on one's specific needs. Professional analysts can benefit from looking out further than their competition. Options traders can take advantage of investors during panic, when they see only immediate danger and want immediate protection from further losses, at almost any price. Portfolio managers can remember to avoid being swayed by short-term earnings anomalies. Interestingly, investors occasionally engage in discounting collectively, leading to conformity in perceptions and herding behavior in the markets.

CHAPTER 17

Herding

Keeping up with the Joneses

"Never, ever listen to other opinions.
To succeed in the markets, it is essential to make
your own decisions. Numerous traders cited listen-
ing to others as their worst blunder. Walton and
Minervini lost their entire investment stake be-
cause of this misjudgement."

—Jack Schwager[1]

Never follow a stock tip. That's the received wisdom.
But what if it's a trusted friend with the advice, and she's an insider
of sorts, and she's extra-specially certain that this stock is about to
rocket?

I hadn't bought a stock on a "tip" for many moons. I'd been preaching
to others—"Don't buy stocks on tips!"—for years.

So I was a hardened cynic when my trusted friend from college (let's
call her "F") told me she had a great stock tip. F works at a hedge fund in
London. She's a biotech specialist of sorts, and she had the inside juice on
Neurocell (not a real name). Neurocell was a small pharmaceutical company seeking U.S. Food and Drug Administration (FDA) approval for a
revolutionary new treatment for Alzheimer's disease. Neurocell had approval for its medication in Europe, and it was awaiting FDA approval in
the United States.

Reported F, "They're gonna get FDA approval any day now—I've
talked to all the main investigators who studied their drug."

F told me she had cold-called neurologist and psychiatrist researchers
at 12 medical centers where the drug had been tested, and they had been
quick to praise the compound.

225

When I expressed some skepticism and concern that researchers don't see the long-term side effects data, and they had all been blinded to the real identity of the compound during those trials, she dismissed my concerns with a self-confident wave of her hand.

"I'd buy it for your children's college fund is what I'd do."

Wow! Now to me that seemed like a pretty heavy endorsement—I'd be negligent not to wager my children's college education on this one. I hadn't seen F get so excited about many things in the past. She was practically obsessed with this company and its product.

I knew that her fund has had great success over the years, with a greater than 20 percent average annual return since 1996. I'd previously met with the founder of the fund. "We don't buy anything unless we're sure it'll jump 30 percent over the next year," he'd said.

Neurocell was a guaranteed winner, a great company endorsed by a hedge fund with a fantastic track record. It looked like a 'strong buy' if I'd ever heard one. I briefly thought, "I shouldn't buy this stock based on a tip," but then the certainty of someone who had called 12 medical centers infected me.

I bought a few shares. And then I bought some more shares until I had accumulated, in hindsight, too many. The FDA approval letter was expected any day, and the excitement was building.

But then the FDA rejected Neurocell's application. Ouch.

The FDA's letter was pessimistic due to a higher rate of strokes in people who received the drug, but it still had a chance for approval. More data was needed from the company. The FDA rejection caused a 60 percent decline in Neurocell's stock price within the first week.

My doubts were festering. "Why did I buy this stupid stock?" I asked myself. "I don't know anything about cardiac catheterization, and now I've lost 60 percent!"

I soon realized I was in deeper trouble than I knew.

I heard from F a week after the FDA rejection letter. She sounded very upbeat. She said, "Gosh, work's been crazy. Neurocell is at such a discount, we're buying as much as we can get. We bought a ton the first day of the drop."

"Buying more?" I thought incredulously. Now I've done some quantitative research in my time, and the general price pattern after a surprisingly negative news shock is a brief dead-cat bounce, and then more selling. Why had she bought on the first day of the decline? Then I remembered the old saying from business lore, "If you don't know who the sucker is, then it's probably you." Oh. Double-ouch.

Of course, F didn't tell only me to bet the ranch on Neurocell. She had also endorsed the stock to many of her other friends and family.

Now F was in a bit of a pickle. She had many friends with money lost, and so she was compelled, via the sunk-cost bias (like the endowment effect), to continue cheerleading Neurocell. She had all this social pressure to deliver good news, and she was stuck in the frame of positive analysis. She couldn't be objective anymore.

If you've ever given a stock tip, you've probably regretted it. In general. by the time someone gets excited enough about a stock to recommend it to others, much of the good news has been priced in. It probably already appreciated in price, and chances are that other owners feel as enthusiastic as you—not usually a good sign. Plus, when you commit yourself to a stock by declaring it a sure winner to your social group, then for the sake of consistency, your mind will have trouble abandoning that belief.

I sold my Neurocell shares shortly thereafter. I hadn't had a plan in case of an FDA rejection letter. I had been too ill disciplined to make one. "When in doubt, get out," as the old Wall Street saying goes. If you let your guard down just a little, Mr. Market will always make you the sucker.

Following stock tips is one type of herding. In finance, *herding* refers to the collective and contagious influence of investment ideas. When the majority of investors are following a leader's advice, without doing the necessary due diligence themselves, they are herding.

HERDING

> *"Men, it has been well said, think in herds; it will be seen that they go mad in herds, while they only recover their senses slowly, and one by one."*
> —Charles MacKay[2]

Biologically speaking, *herding* refers to the tendency of some species of animals to seek safety in numbers. Herding occurs both when animals feel threatened and when they sense that one of their number has found an opportunity. Sometimes the entire flock startles abruptly into flight. Sometimes they rush simultaneously into the same green pastures.

Investors often confuse herding with other phenomena. Groupthink is the tendency for members of homogenous groups to come to the same (and often wrong) conclusion. "Mob" or "crowd" behavior refers to the contagious quality of sudden actions by someone in a crowd—usually toward panic or violence. Groupthink is a particular problem for investment committees, while an example of crowd behavior is a run on a bank, as in Moscow during the Russian debt default and ruble devaluation in 1998.

Is herding really such a bad thing? It can cost you money if your timing is poor, but if you're a first mover, it can make you rich. By the time you see the herd stampeding, you may be too late to get out of the way. However, if you identify a greener pasture, you can get there first. When the crowd follows, you will be well positioned.

Leadership is an essential feature of herding. Sheep follow the alpha male. Often, a sheepdog can direct an entire flock by identifying and cajoling the leader alone. This tendency to follow becomes more pronounced when fear (as of a predatory sheepdog) sets in.

In the markets, you can make money by watching the leaders. Where are they focusing their attention? What are they selling off? In publicly traded companies, the leaders are the executives, board members, and other insiders. Often when there is significant insider selling or a secondary offering, trouble follows. Of course, the insiders will never acknowledge the warning. As a savvy investor, it's your job to scrutinize, not follow, authority.

In 2000, I did some interesting work at a hedge fund in San Francisco. The partners were scouring the United States markets for inexpensive railroad and energy stocks. If you recommended railroad or coal stocks to your golf buddies in 2000, they would have thought you were crazy. Of course, in 2000, the herd was in Internet, technology, and biotech stocks, not in energy. But this fund was prescient. In 2002, the market's vanguard migrated into railroad and energy stocks. By 2006, such stocks were the darlings of the market. Many of the stocks of the hedge fund I worked for had appreciated tenfold.

It is relatively easy to see investors herding if one watches money flows and media attention. However, it is not easy to identify the next fresh pastures, and it is particularly difficult to prevent oneself from following the herd. Social and peer pressure can be intense.

Within a decision-making body, such as an investment committee or board of directors, herding is very difficult to prevent. Groupthink, deference to authority, and social pressure to agree cause herding among insiders. The presence of authoritative or charismatic leaders often unintentionally stifles dissent. It feels socially unacceptable to contradict a group leader, even when members are encouraged to do so. Identifying the process of herding, preventing it in oneself and one's groups, and taking advantage of it in the markets, is the theme of this chapter.

SOCIAL PROOF

> *"Let me tell you the story of the oil prospector who met St. Peter at the Pearly Gates. When told his occupation, St. Peter said, 'Oh, I'm really sorry. You seem to meet all the tests to get into heaven. But we've got a terrible problem. See that pen over there?*

> *That's where we keep the oil prospectors waiting to get into heaven. And it's filled—we haven't got room for even one more.' The oil prospector thought for a minute and said, 'Would you mind if I just said four words to those folks?' 'I can't see any harm in that,' said St. Pete. So the old-timer cupped his hands and yelled out, 'Oil discovered in hell!' Immediately, the oil prospectors wrenched the lock off the door of the pen and out they flew, flapping their wings as hard as they could for the lower regions. 'You know, that's a pretty good trick,' St. Pete said. 'Move in. The place is yours. You've got plenty of room.' The old fellow scratched his head and said, 'No. If you don't mind, I think I'll go along with the rest of 'em. There may be some truth to that rumor after all.'*
>
> —Warren Buffett retelling a favorite story of
> Ben Graham

Too often, we learn what to do in an uncertain situation from observing others. We wait for others to "confirm" the right course of action rather than assuming the responsibility to figure it out ourselves. Psychologist Robert Cialdini calls the search for confirmation "social proof."[3] Social proof provides a mental shortcut. Rather than having to think through each step of a problem, people can simply watch their comrades and follow their lead. Then they ride on their coattails.

In the markets, herd behavior usually ends in losses for the latecomers. Investors succumbing to social proof and herding have depended on others' critical decision making. When herd leaders are shown to be wrong, most mistaken investors then begin to lose faith and bail out. However, for many, strong emotional defense mechanisms kick in. They cannot accept that their beliefs and their leaders are wrong.

Such true believers were among the investors promoting Internet stocks both on the way up and on the way down in the early 2000s. They could not change their firm beliefs about the promise of Internet stocks. It wasn't until many of the stock analyst cheerleaders of the Internet bubble were indicted for crimes in 2002 that they finally lost the mass of their followings.

Strangely, even after the "new Internet economy" was shown to be a fantasy, many true believers continued to proselytize vigorously. Why would anyone continue to identify with a style of thinking that had been proven wrong, much less try to spread the word? It is too painful for these proselytizers to accept defeat, so in a move reminiscent of loss aversion, they hold on for any sign of hope, and even try to gather new converts.

In the minds of die-hard believers, the greater the number of people who believe their doctrine, the more likely they themselves are to be correct.

Sometimes investors will feel compelled to follow a price trend. This is a type of "herding-by-proxy." They know others are buying the stock, but they don't know who. When a stock is trending, people are prone to believe that the investors driving the price move know the future better than them. They then "chase" the trend higher. Some investors wait for such price "confirmation" (favorable trend) before entering an investment. An expected price movement "confirms" that one's opinions were correct, and it now feels safe to open a position.

If the market is declining sharply, and investors feel nervous, they will look at the actions of acknowledged leaders, to see how best to respond. Investors especially look to those they see as similar to themselves. If an investor identifies with members of his investing club more than Wall Street personalities, then he will likely take his cues from his colleagues during times of uncertainty, and especially from the acknowledged leaders of the club.

SOCIAL COMPARISON

> "After reading some part of the history of Alexander, Caesar sat a great while very thoughtful, and at last burst out into tears. His friends were surprised, and asked him the reason of it. "Do you think," said he, "I have not just cause to weep, when I consider that Alexander at my age had conquered so many nations, and I have all this time done nothing that is memorable?"
>
> —Plutarch in *Life of Caesar*

At that stage in his life—his mid-30s—Caesar was known as an accomplished lawyer, second only to Cicero, but also as a man too much in debt for his own good. All his military feats—and they were spectacular—came shortly after this expression of grief. In fact, after lamenting his inferior status to Alexander the Great, Caesar moved quickly to pay off his debts and conquer previously independent tribes of Spain.

Caesar was reacting to an unfavorable social comparison. He derived his goals and personal expectations from the life of Alexander the Great, and he calibrated his performance against that of his role model. After realizing that he had fallen behind Alexander's example, Caesar immediately set about to repair his creditworthiness and reestablish his military reputation.

Social comparison can explain one's level of satisfaction with their financial circumstances. Most people prefer being the "big fish in a small pond" when it comes to their wealth. In 1995, Harvard researchers asked subjects if they would prefer to live in a society where they had an income of $50,000 and the average person had an income of $25,000, or would they prefer to have an income of $100,000 in a community where the average person had an income of $200,000 (prices were specified as constant). Among the 159 students interviewed, 52 percent preferred the $50,000 income. Thirty-five percent of the 75 Harvard faculty and staff answered similarly. They chose to earn half as much money in absolute terms as long as they could make twice as much as the average in their community.[4]

Comparisons to peers not only drive goal pursuit, they also motivate us to overcome deep fears. Albert Bandura, a famous social science researcher, has shown that people can be cured of phobias simply by watching someone they identify with, who has a similar phobia, overcome it themselves. Adults with herpephobia (fear of snakes) can be cured of their fear by watching videos in which actors, pretending to be fearful of snakes, gradually overcome their phobia on screen. By the conclusion of the video, the actors have the snake draped over their shoulders.

Bandura did a study with nursery-school-age children who were terrified of dogs. The fearful children watched other children play with dogs for 20 minutes each day. After four days, 67 percent of the previously terrified children were willing to climb into a playpen with a dog and remain confined there, petting and scratching it, while everyone else left the room. The children recovered from their fear even more quickly when watching a video with a variety of children playing with dogs. Apparently, social proof works best when the proof is provided by lots of other people.[5]

Bandura's study may apply to the weakening of investors' risk aversion. Investors' fear of a risky market sector declines as they watch others buy into it. On my own, I never would have bought Neurocell stock. Hearing about my friend F and our other mutual friends buying shares of Neurocell lowered my risk perception. Without doing my own due diligence, I was convinced that Neurocell was a guaranteed winner based on watching other people. My usual cautionary red flags had been lowered by the siren song of guaranteed profits and shared experience.

ASCH AND CONFORMITY

In 1951, social psychologist Solomon Asch devised an experiment to examine the extent to which pressure from other people could affect one's perceptions. A participant was placed in a group of 8 to 10 other "participants" (actually confidants of the experimenter). The group was shown a

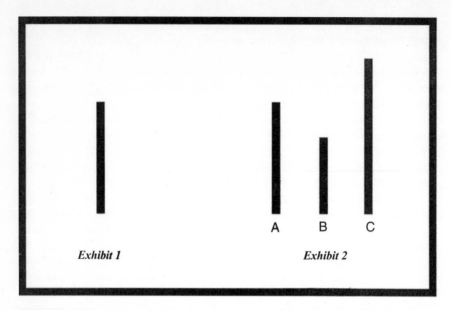

FIGURE 17.1 Experimental columns similar to those used by Solomon Asch.

picture like that in Figure 17.1 and told that the experimenter was studying visual perception. Each group member was then asked to state out loud which line in Exhibit 2 most closely resembled that in Exhibit 1. The actual experimental subject answered second to last.

The experimenter's confidants were instructed to report that lines C or B were most closely related to the line in Exhibit 1 on 12 of the 18 trials—a clearly false answer. Out of 50 subjects in this experiment, 37 conformed to the majority at least once, and the average subject conformed on 4 of the 12 trials. After further experiments, Asch concluded that people conform for two main reasons: because they want to be liked by the group and because they believe the group is better informed than they are.

INFORMATION CASCADES

Investors typically get their investment information from similar sources—data providers, Securities and Exchange Commission (SEC) filings, a company's customers and suppliers, corporate executives and employees, and the media. While investors have different ways of processing the information, there is a limited number of potential sources.

At times, the available information leads investors to similar conclusions. When these conclusions are acted on, they cause market price movements. Some investors take their directional cues only from the market price action, which they use as a proxy for the actions of better-informed investors. An informational cascade occurs when someone, having observed the actions of those preceding, mimics their behavior.

It's not only price action that can induce an informational cascade by communicating what others are thinking and feeling. Many investors inadvertently observe the verbal, body language, and emotional cues from their colleagues and media personalities. This nonverbal communication reflects "the pulse of the market."

The downside of such nonverbal communication is that people who interact with each other frequently tend to think and behave similarly.[6] They derive similar conclusions from new information, and they respond in kind. Studying the language and nonverbal cues of people within such a group can provide insight into their collective reasoning. As seen in Chapter 1, by understanding biased collective reasoning an outsider can gain the ability to identify market opportunities.

Stock message boards are a common gathering place for investors who wish to discuss a stock's future (and who want to debate each other's competence). Amidst the name-calling and raucous debate on stock message boards, researchers have found that useful information can be extracted from the language that participants use.

In a fascinating and technically demanding study, Professor Sanjiv Das at Santa Clara University and colleagues analyzed 103,000 stock message board postings from 12,000 unique users over a seven-month period. The researchers found that there is a positive correlation between the number of postings, stock trading volume, and subsequent stock price underperformance. More messages are written as stock prices decline, and the opinions of investors become more diverse (and presumably less bullish) as prices fall. Loss aversion is evident in posting discussions, with investors hoping for a price rebound. Overall message board sentiment is a reaction to prior trading volume and price action. According to Das, there was no predictive power to be gained by measuring sentiment.[7]

STANLEY MILGRAM AND THE SHOCKING TRUTH

Many investors do not realize the extent to which they are influenced by market experts and opinion leaders. One classic and disturbing study on the "authority effect" was carried out in the decades following World War

II. Stanley Milgram, a professor at Yale University, was planning to investigate the obedience of Germans to authority, with the goal of gaining insight into the rise of authoritarian Nazism.[8] He performed his pilot experiments at Yale, and he quickly realized that he didn't need to go overseas to find incredibly compliant subjects.

Milgram's experiments provide clear evidence that people are wired to follow authority, even in very sadistic ways. When experimental subjects arrived at Milgram's psychology lab, they were met by two people: a researcher wearing a lab coat and carrying a clipboard and another person, average in all respects, introduced as another volunteer. The other "volunteer" was actually an experimenter posing as a research subject.

The subjects were told that the experiment was a test of how punishment affects learning and memory. The experimenter posing as a volunteer was selected as the learner, while the real volunteer was assigned to be the teacher. Of course, the teacher believed that the learner was just another volunteer, but actually it was the teacher who was being studied in this experiment.

The learner attempted to memorize a list of word pairs. After memorization, the learner entered a lab room, where he could be viewed through a glass wall. The learner was strapped into a chair, and his skin was wired with false electrodes that appeared to deliver electric shocks. As the teacher read the first word of a word pair, the learner tried to remember and name the other half of the pair. If the learner recalled incorrectly, then the teacher was told to administer an electric shock.

For every wrong answer, the teacher announced the voltage of the shock to be delivered and then flipped a switch to administer it. After each shock, the voltage was increased by 15 volts for the next one. If the teacher asked about the severity of the electric shocks, the researcher responded that while painful, they caused "no permanent tissue damage." In general, the first part of the test proceeded normally. But as the voltage climbed, the learner began to complain.

The learner grunted in pain at 75-, 80-, and 105-volt shocks. At 120 volts, the learner yelled into a microphone connected to the teacher's control booth that the shocks are really starting to hurt. At 150 volts, the learner shouted in to the microphone, "That's all! Get me out of here! Get me out of here, please! Let me out!" The researcher continued to pose the next question for the teacher to ask the learner. Inevitably, the teacher continued. Between 200 and 300 volts, the learner writhed and shrieked when the shocks were administered. The learner kicked the wall, screamed, and pleaded to be released.

Remember, the learner is an actor and no real shock was being delivered, but the teacher didn't know this. Two-thirds of the volunteer teachers pulled every one of the shock switches and continued to engage the last switch at 450 volts until the researcher ended the experiment. None of the teachers stopped until 300 volts, at which point the learner was emitting, in Milgram's words, "definitely an agonized scream." Many of the teachers appeared anguished at this point, asking the researcher to please stop the experiment. The researcher simply droned on with the next question, and the teachers complied with the next level of shock. At 300 volts, the learner shouted that he would no longer provide answers to the memory test. That point was the first time that any of the teachers refused to go on.

Milgram and his colleagues were surprised by the results. Before the experiment they had asked students and colleagues to guess how many volunteer teachers would go up to 450 volts. Their answers fell in the 1 to 2 percent range. A separate group of 39 psychiatrists predicted that only 1 in 1,000 would be willing to continue to the end of the experiment.[9] Actually, two-thirds of the volunteers went to the maximum voltage. Apparently, people think they are much more independent of this effect than they actually are.

In a modification of the experiment, even when the learner exclaimed that he had "heart trouble" and the shocks were beginning to affect his heart, 65 percent of teachers proceeded to the maximum voltage. In yet another variation, two researchers were present. As the shock intensity increased, and the learner cried out for release, one researcher told the teacher to go on, and the other said to stop. Typically, the teachers scanned back and forth between researchers, looking and asking for some indication of who was the higher authority. When they couldn't figure out who was superior, the teachers stopped the experiment.

NICE CLOTHES, FAST CARS, AND FANCY TITLES

> *"Clothes make the man. Naked people have little or no influence on society."*
>
> —Mark Twain

When meeting someone for the first time, it is not uncommon to inquire about his or her line of work. Business cards list one's position in an organization. Short biographical sketches on company web sites refer to schools attended, degrees earned, jobs held, and articles or books published. A pedigree can establish one as an authority, while actual competence must be sorted out later.

More easily apparent at a distance than titles and pedigree, one's clothing also conveys authority. Researchers in Texas discovered that three and a half times as many people follow a jaywalker into traffic when he is dressed in a well-tailored suit as when wearing a work shirt and trousers.[10] Besides clothing, jewelry and cars are also visible signs of wealth.

In a San Francisco study, researchers driving either luxury cars or economy cars stopped in front of a green traffic light. Nearly all motorists behind the economy car sounded their horns, and two even rammed into its rear bumper. Fifty percent of the motorists waited patiently behind the luxury car, never beeping their horns, until it drove on.

Most of us don't believe we act with such deference to authority. *We* wouldn't wait behind a luxury car or blindly follow the recommendations of experts. The San Francisco researchers asked a class of students to estimate what they would do if stuck behind the luxury or economy car at a green light. Male students estimated that they would honk faster at the luxury car than at the economy car, believing they would do the opposite of what actually occurred.[11]

In the electric shock experiment, Milgram's colleagues greatly underestimated the percentage of people who would increase the voltage to the maximum. We don't think it could be us. Social psychologist Robert Cialdini describes obedience to authority as occurring beneath awareness, in a "*click, whirr*" reaction. Subconsciously, after receiving an instruction from an authority, we move from *thinking* about a situation to *reacting*. "Information from a recognized authority can provide us with a valuable shortcut for deciding how to act in a situation."[12]

Financial analysts are Wall Street's authorities on stocks and market sectors. Their opinions and recommendations lead to shifts of billions of dollars across securities. Given the results of Milgram's experiment, it is no surprise that investors herd into the stocks recommended by analysts. This is a problem when analysts are corrupt or unethical. In the late 1990s, when star Internet analysts Henry Blodgett, Mary Meeker, or Abby Joseph Cohen said "Buy," millions followed at their own peril.

THE NEUROSCIENCE OF COOPERATION

Serotonin appears to modulate the acquisition of socially cooperative behavior. The amino acid precursor of serotonin is tryptophan (Trp). Its role in the brain is described in Chapter 4. When tryptophan is removed from the diet, brain levels of serotonin are depleted. In a prisoner's dilemma game (a trust and cooperation game, defined in the glossary), Trp-depleted volunteers defected more and cooperated less on the first day after depletion, as if low serotonin levels increased self-interest and decreased cooperativeness.

On functional magnetic resonance imaging (fMRI) scanning during the prisoner's dilemma task, anterior cingulate gyrus and orbitofrontal cortex activation were decreased in Trp-depleted volunteers, implying that people with low serotonin require less social reinforcement and use less prefrontal cortex (impulse inhibiting) input when making sociofinancial decisions that affect other people.

In a modified version of Asch's experiment described above, neuroscientists found that individuals who go against peer pressure and give the correct answer have increased amygdala and caudate activation, which reflects the tremendous emotional strain undergone by nonconformists and the courage needed to disagree with obviously erroneous accepted opinion.[13]

ANALYSTS' ABUSE OF AUTHORITY

"When I was an analyst ... I placed too much stock in the opinions of those who seemed to know more than I did (my fault, not theirs). More unsettlingly, I saw others do the same with me."
—Henry Blodgett, former Wall Street analyst[14]

Security analysts work in a high pressure environment, often jockeying to develop cozy relationships with corporate management. The performance of their stock recommendations is monitored closely by rating agencies. It's no wonder that new analysts might feel pressured to "follow the leader" when a more successful analyst changes a stock recommendation.

Finance professor Ivo Welch found that analysts are significantly influenced by each other's opinions. A change in the buy or sell recommendation of an analyst influences the recommendations of the next two analysts who issue opinions.[15]

During the late 1990s, many Wall Street Internet stock analysts were paid high salaries and encouraged to tout stocks that they actually held in disdain. Analysts' employers, the major investment banks such as Merrill Lynch, Deutsche Bank, and Morgan Stanley, wanted the lucrative banking business of the companies whose shares their analysts were promoting. The banks demoted or fired analysts who put "sell" recommendations on the companies whose business they were wooing.

Morgan Stanley made millions in fees raising money for Priceline. One of Morgan's Internet analysts, Mary Meeker, recommended buying Priceline's stock at $134 a share. When it fell to $78, she repeated her buy recommendation, and she kept recommending Priceline as a buy as it fell to less than $3 per share.[16]

Merrill Lynch analyst Henry Blodgett (quoted above) covered the stock of Pets.com. Much of Pets.com's financing was raised by Merrill Lynch, who made millions. Blodgett placed a buy recommendation on Pets.com at $16 per share. When it fell to $7, Blodgett said "buy" again. Again a "buy" at $2, and again at $1.69. When it hit $1.43 a share, Blodgett downgraded the stock to "accumulate." Pets.com was ultimately delisted from the stock exchange. Investors may have lost a fortune, but in 2000 Blodgett and Meeker were paid about $15 million each.[17]

The Internet stock frenzy was enhanced by television business channels. CNBC, CNNfn, and other financial television channels needed guests for their programming segments. Some analysts appeared on CNBC's *Squawk Box*, hosted by Mark Haines. After a stock was recommended by a guest, Haines remembered, "I'd look down at the quote machine, and all of a sudden it had jumped 5 bucks or 10 bucks." Thousands, new to investing, were watching the show's guests with no idea that a conflict of interest might exist between the objectivity of their stock recommendations and their income. CNBC now requires its guests reveal conflicts of interest before they appear.[18]

Such conflicts were well known on Wall Street, and it is unfortunate that they were not somehow made clear to amateur Internet stock investors. Indignation arose in the political world to satisfy constituents who had lost millions of dollars following analysts' recommendations from 2000 through 2002. Are the losses the fault of the analysts who unethically (but not illegally) touted stocks that they privately despised, or can we blame the millions of investors who, driven by greed, piled into worthless stocks on the advice of a presumed expert?

THE HERDING HABIT

> *"It is difficult to get a man to understand something when his salary depends upon his not understanding it."*
>
> —Upton Sinclair

Mutual funds have also been found to exhibit herding behavior, especially growth and small-cap oriented funds. For funds, herding is not always irrational; in fact, herding is profitable for the vanguard of mutual funds. The stocks the herd buys tend to outperform those they sell by 4 percent over the subsequent six months.[19]

Herding by mutual funds is related to word-of-mouth communication between portfolio managers. In fact, portfolio managers in the same city demonstrate greater herding. In a study of 1,635 mutual funds headquartered in 15 large U.S. cities, funds located in the same city traded in concert more often and to a greater degree than funds located in different cities.[20]

Researchers looked at how analysts treat information that they believe is "private" to them. Their sample was comprised of 1.3 million forecasts by 5,306 analysts, relative to 3,195 firms, from 1985 to 2001. On average, analysts tended to overweight information that they believed to be private. Yet analysts tend to overweight their private information more when their forecast is more favorable than the consensus forecast but underweight their private information when their forecast is less favorable than the consensus. That is, most analysts interpret their private information as reflecting favorably on the companies they cover. The authors found that this misweighting is not due to an explicit cognitive bias, rather analysts misweight in order to draw more trading commissions to their firm.[21]

If you're an individual investor, learning about how your unconscious biases sabotage you might make you feel a little jaded. How can you possibly succeed under such adverse psychological circumstances? Some individual investors adopt a contrarian perspective on the markets.

LIVING THE CONTRARIAN LIFESTYLE

> *"The most important quality for an investor is temperament, not intellect. . . . You need a temperament that neither derives great pleasure from being with the crowd or against the crowd."*
>
> —Warren Buffett

Investors who consider themselves contrarians are generally "countertrend" specialists. There is no uniform personality style, though many contrarians are suspicious of popular investing techniques and the "in-crowd." I had a fascinating telephone conversation with one die-hard contrarian.

James had been a floor trader in London and emigrated to the United States to set up a hedge fund. He had done well for himself on the floor, and he had an excellent reputation as a trader. Unfortunately, he had little respect for his colleagues, explaining, "They just play 'follow the leader.' It's stupid, really, makes me sick."

He was having trouble marketing his hedge fund because he despised the people he was marketing to, "They don't know squat about the markets.

They just have some fancy degree and they knew the right people at some pension fund."

I mentioned that he seemed pretty hostile to his potential clientele.

James responded, "Look, I don't like morons!" He didn't lack opinions.

I asked, "How are you going to sell this fund?"

"I need to find people like me, who really understand what's going on in the markets."

I asked why that was hard. He told me, "I make my money off the idiots who follow the trends. I know when they are turning, and that's my talent. I NEVER trade with a trend! But most people are part of the trend—that's what makes the trend in the first place. None of the big investors or pension funds understand why I would go against what everyone else is doing. They look at me like I'm crazy."

"If you make them money, I don't see why they'd think you're crazy."

"It's my personality, okay? I won't do anything that other people do. I live a contrarian life. If I go to see a movie at a theater and there's a line for it, then I'll go to a different movie. I won't do anything that other people do. I married my wife because people didn't think I would."

He was contrarian to the core, and he had found a niche in the markets that fit his personality. And he was probably right—few investors successfully identify the top or bottom of a trend because they are caught up in the story and unable to think clearly or critically.

Value and countertrend investing strategies are more characteristic of contrarians. Contrarians have the innate advantage of being able to search for opportunities away from the crowd. They often seek for solid investments in overlooked sectors. Every sector rotates into and out of popularity, given time.

Contrarians are also inclined to short emerging trends, which can be very painful. If you're contrarian, be sure to identify clear signs of reversal or exhaustion before shorting a popular security or sector.

Contrarianism can be a destructive habit. Some investors who call themselves contrarians see only danger, thus missing out on long bull markets while fretting about an impending crash. There is a difference between excessive anxiety and healthy critical thinking, so be sure to understand where you fall between those two. Anxious people won't last long as contrarians.

ADVICE FOR HERD ANIMALS AND TREND FOLLOWERS

In the marketplace, individual investors who herd are more likely to follow stock tips, the recommendations of "gurus," and rumors, rather than making independently researched investment decisions. Most investors fit into this group.

If you like to be aware of crowds and trends, be sure to keep perspective on the rationale behind the crowd's behavior. If you are a trend follower, consider adopting a strategy (such as momentum or growth) that accounts for your social personality. Investing in the "hot" sector is okay as long as you are aware that trends change, and you have definite rules for when to close out your positions.

If you're social, use it to your advantage. Learn about the new trends and fads, and see if you can identify strategies to take advantage of these. Avoid listening to financial media outlets such as CNBC and popular magazines. Due to the authority effect, virtually everyone is susceptible to jumping on the latest investment bandwagon publicized in the media, and it is typically a very bumpy ride.

ADVICE FOR INVESTMENT COMMITTEES

Investment committee decisions are often constrained by the members' desire to conform. Standing out from the group, especially for new or young employees, can be quite embarrassing. Their fear of making a foolish comment often restricts their input.

Professor Hersh Shefrin described several techniques for debiasing imvestment committees in his 2006 book, *Behavioral Corporate Finance:*

1. Ask group members to refrain from stating personal preferences at the outset of the discussion.

2. Explicitly cultivate debate, disagreement, and the sharing of information.

3. Designate one member of the group to play devil's advocate for each major proposal.

4. Regularly invite outside experts to attend meetings, with the charge that they challenge the group not to behave like meek conformists . . . in the drive for consensus. . . .[22]

This chapter has examined the psychological origins of herding. Most investors inadvertently follow the advice of leaders, experts, and the well dressed. Herding is more likely when decisions are complex or the future appears especially uncertain. Contrarians actively use their outsider perspective to their advantage. Investment committee members are constrained by internal pressure to conform.

CHAPTER 18

Charting and Data Mining

Reading Tea Leaves

"If enough independent phenomena are studied and correlations sought, some will of course be found...It is only what statisticians call 'the fallacy of the enumeration of favorable circumstances.'"

—Carl Sagan[1]

H uman ingenuity has an amazing capability for finding predictive power in random stock data. Historically, forecasters looked for predictive power in nature, such as from the movements of the stars, bird migrations, and tides. Even today numerous "astrofinance" web sites offer newsletters prognosticating on the direction of the financial markets using astrology.

Throughout the twentieth century, a variety of stock market leading indicators achieved notoriety. In the 1920s, the "hemline" indicator was popular. The market was said to rise as the length of women's skirts retreated—this was thought due to liberal attitudes during economic booms. The Super Bowl indicator, so called because the market was said to rise in years that an NFL team won the Super Bowl, was 90 percent accurate in predicting the annual stock market direction from 1967 to 1997. However, both the Super Bowl and hemline indicators are random coincidences.

Quantitative tools for forecasting markets have an allure of certainty, which can be visualized graphically. The earliest technical tools for predicting markets included candlestick charting, practiced as early as the seventeenth century by Japanese rice merchants. In the early twentieth century, practitioners such as Charles Dow used price charts to predict markets. These graphical tools were incorporated into computers as processing power increased dramatically in the late twentieth century.

In the early 1980s, computerized trading was successfully employed to find simple predictive mathematical price relationships. In the late 1980s, artificial intelligence was celebrated as the future of decision making on Wall Street, but it didn't live up to its promise. Then in the early 1990s, chaos and complexity theory appeared to be innovative techniques for market predictions, but they too did not provide consistently market-beating models. In the mid-1990s, neural networks arose as popular statistical tools for finding predictive patterns in historical price data. All of the above statistical tools have some value, but none were as paradigm shifting as their true believers proclaimed.

As computing power increases, predictive correlations can be sought in previously inaccessible places. Data-mining techniques allow researchers to examine millions of data points for market predictive potential. Unfortunately, using computers for data analysis also creates thousands of new ways for self-deception.

ARTIFICIAL NEURAL NETWORKS

> "In this business if you're good, you're right six times out of ten. You're never going to be right nine times out of ten."
>
> —Peter Lynch

Computers now serve as the platform for virtually every form of stock analysis on Wall Street—quantitative analysis, technical analysis, and fundamental analysis, among others. Some practitioners believe computers now have the capacity to make better investment decisions than humans. That belief assumes human technology operators will not interject their own failings into their systems.

I have had painful personal experience with the failings of quantitative forecasting tools. In 1995 and 1996, I developed financial software using neural network and genetic learning algorithms to find patterns in market price data. The forecasting software I designed predicted the market with significant accuracy, which at first felt like an enormous victory. The software had 59 percent directional accuracy during its first six months of real-time trading use. Not bad.

But then the software's predictions started to decay. By 1996, one year after implementation, the accuracy had dropped to 53 percent (essentially random). As a result, I developed new forecasting software. The new software worked well for a few months, but then its accuracy also dropped. By 1997, the advantage in developing new quantitative software was negligible. Clearly, what had been a decent tool for pattern recognition in the early and mid-1990s had expired.

When investors find a mispricing, their buying and selling activity (arbitrage) pushes prices towards fair values, gradually reducing their advantage. When enough money starts exploiting mispricings in the markets, the edge will disappear completely. That's probably why my neural networks stopped predicting the market—too many people using similar tools identified the same profit opportunities. They exploited it until it vanished.

I share my story to illustrate a point. When we find patterns in data, chances are that someone else has stumbled upon exactly the same thing. And when enough money chases opportunities, they quickly disappear. I've had firsthand experience with such vanishing profits. The markets are constantly evolving, and patterns that can be quantified will eventually be discovered. However, the price patterns whose origin lies in the human brain are likely to be the most enduring.

DATA MINING AND SELF-DECEPTION

> *"People in both fields [baseball and trading] operate with beliefs and biases. To the extent you can eliminate both and replace them with data, you gain a clear advantage."*
> —John Henry, hedge fund manager and owner of
> the Boston Red Sox[2]

Searching for predictive patterns in financial data is called data mining. Data mining often leads to the discovery of random coincidences. "Numerologists" and careless statisticians can be easily fooled. Massive computing power has increased the problem of statistical coincidence. Enormous databases of government economic statistics, past financial prices, Internet musings, and corporate data can be scoured to find predictive relationships with the stock market.

David Leinweber holds a doctorate in mathematics from Harvard, and he has worked in trading technology for many large Wall Street firms, including First Quadrant and Codex. During the early 1990s, Leinweber noticed so many Wall Streeters using computers to find spurious correlations in data that he decided to make light of the many useless results coming forth. He wrote a paper entitled "Stupid Data-mining Tricks: Overfitting the S&P 500."[3]

Leinweber analyzed a database of the United Nation's commodity production figures. He was curious if he could find correlations among these statistics and the Standard and Poor's (S&P) 500. He found that butter production in Bangladesh had a 75 percent predictive power over the S&P 500 (in sample). When sheep production in New Zealand was factored into his model, accuracy jumped to over 90 percent. He did this analysis lightly—to illustrate how easy it is to find highly predictive relationships in random data.

Unfortunately, the financial media often promote spurious relationships in market data. On July 17, 2006, just after the 2006 Israeli invasion of Lebanon commenced, the Money and Investing section of the *Wall Street Journal*, in the headline article entitled "Keeping Cool Amid Global Strife," presented a table of the daily and one year U.S. stock market returns following five Mid-East wars since 1967.[4] Out of five previous wars, the one-week and one-year returns were positive for three. The *Journal* concludes, "Almost never has Middle East fighting done long-term damage to the U.S. stock market." While I support the *Journal*'s intent, the article fails to mention that a sample of five provides insufficient statistical power to draw such a conclusion.

Whether we're predicting the stock market with baseball scores, Bangladeshi butter production, neural networks, or even historical prices and charts, we have to be very careful to avoid statistical overfitting, undersampling, and self-deception.

FINDING PATTERNS IN THE NOISE

> *"Like astrology, graphology seems to rest on the notion of 'pareidolia': the human infusion of patterns or meaning on random audio or visual events."*
> —Steven Goldstein[5]

Pareidolia describes a psychological phenomenon involving a vague and random stimulus being mistakenly perceived as recognizable.[6] Common examples are often religious in nature. In 1978, some 8,000 people made pilgrimages to the home of a New Mexico woman who discovered a picture of Jesus in a burned tortilla. Similar misperceptions happen with celebrities, such as Elvis "sightings." In finance, pareidolia can creep into chart reading and technical analysis.

Academics who have studied chart patterns, specifically those based on technical analysis, have found limited (but significant) predictive value. For example, economists at the Federal Reserve created a mathematical algorithm for automatically detecting head-and-shoulders patterns in foreign exchange data. They found that for two of the six currencies in their sample, the yen and the Deutsche mark, trading strategies based on the head-and-shoulders pattern could lead to statistically significant profits.[7]

Professor Andrew Lo at the Massachusetts Institute of Technology (MIT) quantified the principles underlying eight technical price chart patterns. In introducing his research, Lo acknowledged that "it is difficult to dispute the potential value of price/volume charts when confronted with the visual evidence." Lo noted that, "Technical analysis has survived through the years, perhaps because its visual mode of analysis is more conducive to human cognition, and because pattern recognition is one of the few repetitive activities for which computers do not have an absolute advantage (yet)."[8]

Lo translated the visual cues that technical analysts seek to find in charts into mathematical algorithms. Chart patterns such as the head-and-shoulders and double-bottom patterns were tested for their predictive power. Stock prices from 1962 to 1996 were used in the analysis. The researchers found that some technical patterns appeared to provide "incremental information" during intraday price movement. While not affirming that technical analysis can be reliably used for profit, Lo and colleagues concluded, "It does raise the possibility that technical analysis can add value to the investment process."[9] Lo now is head of research at his own hedge fund (AlphaSimplex), which employs quantitative analytic techniques.

THE TREND AND MEAN-REVERSION BIASES IN CHART READING

> *"The greater the uncertainty, the more people are influenced by the market trends; and the greater the influence of trend following speculation, the more uncertain the situation becomes."*
>
> —George Soros

Many economists in academia have argued against the merits of charting techniques such as technical analysis. According to Andrew Lo, "One of the main obstacles is the highly subjective nature of technical analysis—the presence of geometric shapes in historical price charts is often in the eyes of the beholder."[10] In his book, *A Random Walk down Wall Street*, Burton Malkiel (1996) concludes that: "Under scientific scrutiny, chart-reading must share a pedestal with alchemy." See Figure 18.1 for an

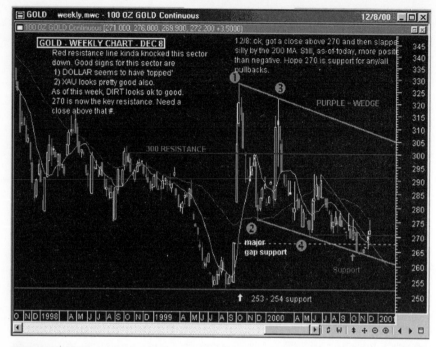

FIGURE 18.1 A chart of monthly gold prices in the late 1990s and early 2000s. Notice the support, resistance, and other metrics used by technical analysts' to gauge price trend.
Source: Securitytrader.com.

example of a chart that has been marked with the visual cues of the technical analyst.

Regardless of the academic skepticism, many individual investors use charts to aid their decision making. However, an excessive reliance on charts, in lieu of other information, can be detrimental to performance.

Psychologists have found that investors often preferentially buy stocks depending on how price information is displayed in a chart. Information such as the salient high and low, the most recent price trend, and the long-term average of the stock price influence investor judgments. When investors see a chart depicting a long-term upward price trend, they are more likely to want to buy stock, because they extrapolate that trend into the future. When they see a chart displaying a long-term downward trend, they prefer to sell.[11]

Stocks that are trading above or below their long-term average trend are thought likely to "mean revert." Mean reversion refers to the common belief that a stock price that has deviated away from its average price will eventually reverse course and return back to its average level. Mean reversion is a complicated way of saying, "What goes up must come down." In Figure 18.1, the "support" and "resistance" lines represent points at which the price is anticipated to mean revert, and if it does not, the price movement is called a "breakout."

Additionally, recent price trends, relative to the long term average, influence investor buy and sell preferences. In general, investors are more likely to forecast future positive returns if the recent price trend is up and to forecast future negative returns if the recent price trend is down.[12]

For example, in a study I perform during behavioral finance workshops, I ask participants which of the following hypothetical stocks they would rather buy and which they would rather sell. See Figures 18.2 and 18.3 for the charts I have used.

Each stock depicts a conflict between mean-reversion and the recent price trend. The majority of investors (60 percent on average) select to buy the stock depicted in Figure 18.2, while 40 percent select the stock depicted in Figure 18.3. Essentially, they are voting more strongly in favor of recent price trend as an influence on their decision making.

If the recent price up trend in Figure 18.2 was shorter and ended below the average trend, then it is likely that fewer investors would choose to buy the stock in Figure 18.2 due to both mean reversion and recent price-trend effects. In general, investors using charts weigh both the recent price trend and mean reversion in their assessments of future stock direction.

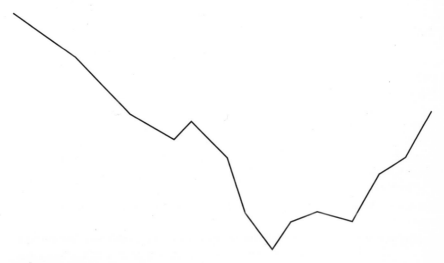

FIGURE 18.2 The recent up-trend.

FIGURE 18.3   The recent down-trend.

Whether investors believe in the continuation of a trend or mean re-version depends on the length of the price trend depicted. When a trend is shorter, people tend to follow the "hot hand" bias, believing that it will continue. When the trend is longer, investors are more likely to expect mean reversion.[13]

Professor Paul Slovic has remarked that in long term thinking and fore-casting, people generalize from available information. In short-term predic-tions they base their forecasts on details.[14] There is a systematic bias in information processing depending on the type of forecast (short or long-term) that one is making.

OVERRELIANCE ON CHARTS

When stock price charts depict a salient high or low, then the mean-reversion bias kicks in. German researchers Thomas Mussweiler and Karl Schneller set out to test the hypothesis that investors "anchor" their expec-tations to recent highs and lows in stock charts.[15] The researchers created 12-month stock price charts that either: (1) began in the midline, then rose to a peak as time passed, and then fell back to just above the midline (see Figure 18.4); or (2) began in the midline, dropped to a bottom as time pro-gressed, and then rose to just above the midline by the end of the period (see Figure 18.5). Overall, both charts showed a 20 percent return from the beginning to the end of the 12-month period depicted.

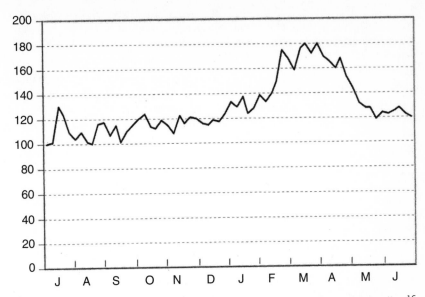

FIGURE 18.4 The high-point salience chart used by Mussweiler and Schneller.[16]
Source: Lawrence Erlbaum Associates.

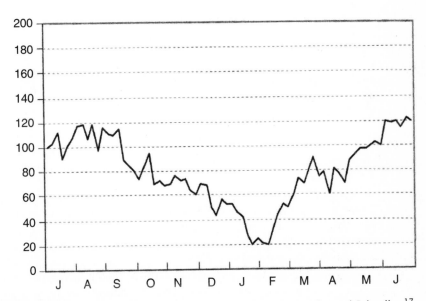

FIGURE 18.5 The low-point salience chart used by Mussweiler and Schneller.[17]
Source: Lawrence Erlbaum Associates.

The researchers then assembled groups of private and professional investors for their study. Participants were given a half page of text describing a hypothetical company, its fundamental economic statistics, and its price chart for the past year. The experimental subjects were asked to estimate the 12-month price target for the stock and then decide whether they would like to buy or sell the stock. Presentation of the charts was randomized to the textual information, because the researchers were interested to assess the effect of the charts alone. The textual information was the same for all the participants in the study—only the charts differed.

The authors explain their experimental design by referring to the "comparison effect." An investor who is confronted by a low on a stock chart will selectively look for negative information to explain that low, while an investor confronted with a high price peak will preferentially search for positive information to justify the higher price.

As the investigators expected, when subjects were asked to forecast the 12-month stock return, they predicted a higher price in one year if the chart showed a salient high versus a prominent low during the 12-month period. When a different group of investors was presented with the same experiment, and they were asked how much stock they would buy, they again chose to buy more (three times as much) of the stock with the price peak. When the experiment was reframed, and investors were asked how much stock they would sell, they chose to sell more (twice as much) of the stock with a salient low in its chart. Investors' expectations of future returns, buying choices, and selling plans were contingent on the chart patterns.

Importantly, when the researchers increased the amount of corporate information available to the subjects, the results became even more chart dependent. The investigators used the full textual information from a discount brokerage web site on a real Internet company—three and a half pages of statistical and company information. Subjects (including professional investors) bought almost twice as much of the stock with a salient high in its chart versus the salient low. Information overload drove investors to rely more heavily on the charts.

In a postexperiment survey, subjects mentioned more positive aspects of the stocks with salient high charts than those with the low price point. They justified their buy decision by citing more positive aspects of the textual information, even though they were clearly choosing based on the chart, not a consideration of the data, since all the textual information was randomized across subjects. The subjects' thinking changed depending on the appearance of the past price chart, but they were unaware of this profound effect.

THE GAMBLER'S FALLACY

The gambler's fallacy is a logical mistake in which independent past events are believed to influence future events. After a series of gambles with the same outcome, players often incorrectly believe that either (1) the past series will continue (the "hot-hand fallacy"), or (2) the past sequence will revert toward the mean. Regarding the first example, a continuation of a trend, a basketball player who has sunk several shots in a row is said to have a "hot hand." This player is incorrectly thought by fans to be more likely to make his next shot. In the second example, "mean reversion" thinking is the tendency of market strategists to forecast that the market will have opposite performance the following year as compared to the prior year. In fact, returns do not either trend or reverse from year to year, but a belief in these tendencies is common. Academics and professionals are more susceptible to mean reversion errors, while novices are more likely to project current trends into the future—"hot-hand" errors.

In both cases, investors are assuming that the markets have "memory" and are thus influenced by their past behavior. While that memory is influential to a small extent in the markets (as we'll see in the momentum and long-term reversals examples in Chapter 23), it does not explain future prices as much as investors think it does.

IRRATIONAL EXUBERANCE . . . CALLED TOO EARLY

On December 3, 1996, Yale Professors Robert Shiller and John Campbell spoke to the Federal Reserve Board and Chairman Alan Greenspan. They explained that historically, when the stock market price-to-earnings (P/E) ratio has been high, the return for holding stocks over the subsequent 10 years has tended to be low. Shiller asserted that markets were behaving irrationally at that moment in time.[18]

Shiller outlined his argument in detail in his synonymous book *Irrational Exuberance* published in early 2000.[19] Shiller noted, "The high recent valuations in the U.S. stock market come about for no good reasons. . . . The market is high because of the combined effect of indifferent thinking by millions of people, very few of whom feel the need to perform careful research on the long-term investment value of the aggregate stock market, and who are motivated substantially by their own emotions, random attentions, and perceptions of conventional wisdom."[20]

Alan Greenspan, chairman of the Fed, used the phrase "irrational exuberance" in a black-tie dinner speech on December 5, 1996, two days after his meeting with Shiller. Fourteen pages into his dinner speech, Greenspan asked a rhetorical question: "But how do we know when irrational exuberance has unduly escalated asset values, which then become subject to unexpected and prolonged contractions as they have in Japan over the past decade?" He then qualified his question, "We as central bankers need not be concerned if a collapsing financial asset bubble does not threaten to impair the real economy, its production, jobs and price stability."[21]

Greenspan's speech was televised live on C-SPAN. Shortly after he posed his question, the stock market in Tokyo declined sharply, closing down 3 percent. Hong Kong's Hang Seng index shed 3 percent. Then markets in Frankfurt and London fell 4 percent. The stock market in the United States fell 2 percent at the open of trading the following morning.[22] But after the sell-off, the markets quickly rebounded, and over the next three years world stock markets experienced the biggest financial bubble in history.

Shiller was correct to assert that P/E ratios predict 10-year returns based on historical data. However, the stock market's memory is not so simple. The historical mean for P/E is 14.2. For most of the time since 1872, average P/E ratios have moved in the range 8 to 20. In December 1996, the average P/E ratio stood at 28. As a result, Shiller and Campbell predicted that between 1997 and 2006, the stock market would lose about 40 percent of its real value, to an S&P 500 value of 450. In fact, by July 26, 2006, the S&P 500 was at 1273 with a P/E ratio of 17.5. What these professors did not foresee was the tremendous growth in corporate productivity and earnings facilitated by the adoption of information technology.

In 1996, *Barron's* asked strategists at major Wall Street investment banks their stock market outlooks for 1997. The Dow Jones Industrial Average (DJIA) had risen 33.5 percent in 1995 and 26 percent in 1996. Consistent with mean reversion, the seven strategists predicted, on average, a DJIA performance of –0.2 percent for 1997. The actual return of the DJIA in 1997 was 22.6 percent. When strategists were polled by *Barron's* after two down years in the markets, 2000 and 2001, they predicted large rises in the market over the subsequent year. For 2001 the strategists expected, on average, a return of 18.7 percent for the S&P 500. For 2002 the strategists predicted a 21 percent rise in the S&P 500. The S&P 500 actually declined 13 percent in 2001 and then again declined 23.4 percent in 2002.[23]

Mean-reverting predictions affect professionals and respected academics alike. But why not amateur investors? Why are they susceptible to the "hot-hand" bias, not mean reversion? In the case of amateur investors, their memory recall and experience is relatively short. These investors' attention is attracted to recent returns, which they then extrapolate into the future.

When one has a lot of information about past returns, as academics and professionals do, their attention is attracted to the remarkable highs (such as historically high P/E ratios) and the salient lows. They then begin their estimates of the future by anchoring their predictions from the salient high or low points, relative to the overall trend. If the market is currently at a relative high or low, then as can be seen in a review of history, it will probably mean revert. The problem with such thinking is that the future isn't always like the past, and salient highs and lows are only recognized as such in hindsight (they can extend much further before reverting).

Many professionals utilize strategies based on mean reversion. In order to cushion themselves from the effects of mistiming tops and bottoms, they trade small, they diversify, and they plan to hold for the long term. Jim Leitner says, "It's just a truism that, over time, mean reversion works. To take advantage of it, a one-year-plus time horizon is required at minimum, but a five-year-plus time horizon is ideal." Long-term time horizons work because many portfolio managers are under short-term performance pressures. "The large inefficiencies do not get arbitraged out because there's very little capital that actually gets allocated toward extracting value over multiple years." Opportunities for mean-reversion investing exist, but one must be very careful to properly manage risk when exploiting them.

THE SOOCHOW GAMBLING TASK

The gambler's fallacy (hot-hand effect) may be playing a role in an unusual pattern of money-losing behavior in gambling college students. Researchers at the Soochow and National Yang-Ming Universities of Taiwan found that gamblers choose a consistently losing strategy if it contains a series of several small wins and infrequent large losses. The researchers discovered this odd behavior using an experimental task called the Soochow Gambling Task (SGT),[24, 25] which is a variation of the Iowa Gambling Task used by Damasio (described in Chapter 2).

In the SGT subjects are told to make as much money as possible by selecting cards from one of four decks. The decks are labeled A, B, C, and D. Each card displays a monetary gain or loss. Decks A and B have expected values, for each five card flips, of −$250. Decks C and D have expected values of +$250 for each five cards. For each deck, the cards have very different payoffs. Deck A has four $200 wins for each $1,250 loss. Deck B has four $100 wins for each $650 loss. Deck C has four $200 losses for each $1,050 gain, and deck D has four $100 losses for each $650 gain.[26]

TABLE 18.1	The Outcome Odds and Frequencies for Each Card Deck in the Soochow Gambling Task. Notice the Expected Values at the Far Right Column

Soochow Gambling Task	Average Number of Gains per Five Cards	Size of Gains	Average Number of Losses per Five Cards	Size of Losses	Expected Value per Five Cards
Deck A	4	$200	1	−$1,250	−$250
Deck B	4	$100	1	−$650	−$250
Deck C	1	$1,250	4	−$200	+$250
Deck D	1	$650	4	−$100	+$250

Approximately 600 people have participated in the SGT studies so far. See Table 18.1 for details.

Unusually, most experimental participants prefer to select cards from the money-losing decks. Over 200 trials, more than 60 percent of the cards flipped were from decks A and B, losing money for most participants. Subjects had a financial incentive to make money in this game, but they consistently acted against their best interest, and they didn't learn to do better even over 200 trials (see Figure 18.6).

As a result of their consistently poor performance, researchers Ching-Hung Lin and Yao-Chu Chiu decided to alert subjects, after 100 card flips, to

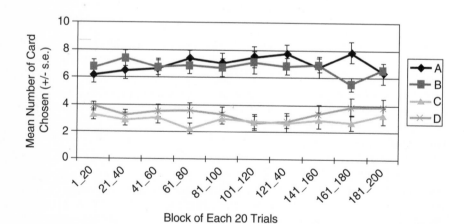

FIGURE 18.6 This is a plot of card deck choice frequency when individuals are not informed of the probabilities and payoff of each deck. Note that subjects do not learn to select the positive expected value decks.
Source: Courtesy of Ching-Hung Lin.

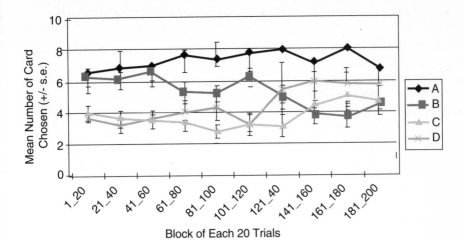

FIGURE 18.7 This plot of card deck choice frequency demonstrates how individuals continue to make negative expected value selections even after they are informed of the decks' expected values at flip 100.
Source: Courtesy of Ching-Hung Lin.

the actual payoffs and odds of each deck.[27] Yet even with this knowledge, the subjects continued to select almost half their cards from decks A and B. While participants stopped losing money once they knew the odds, they were still only breaking even.

Note in Figure 18.7 how the selection rates for decks A and B begin to converge with those of decks C and D after subjects are informed of the payoff probabilities on Trial 101 (See "101_120" on x-axis in Figure 18.7). By Trial 200, the subjects' choices were roughly equally distributed between decks A and B and decks C and D. According to researcher Ching-Hung Lin, "Almost everybody lost money in our experiment. We couldn't figure out how to help them under this uncertain situation."[28]

Why did the experimental subjects select from the lower paying decks? The series of wins was seductive. In decks A and B, the satisfaction of winning occurred four times, while the pain of the loss only happened once per five cards. A series of wins is, in a way, addictive. Gains feel so good that investors will risk large periodic losses as an accepted consequence of getting the good feelings from a series of small gains.

In a way, these results are similar to predictions of loss aversion. Investors would rather cut their winners short, ensuring a small gain, and hold their losers too long, experiencing occasional very large losses. If single losses are twice as painful as single gains are pleasurable, then four gains are twice as pleasurable as one loss is painful (size notwithstanding).

Professional investors do not experience the aversion to small losses that the SGT participants did. Many professional traders have poor win-loss ratios, numerically speaking. They may lose on 80 percent of their investments, but their 20 percent of winning positions are so lucrative that they more than make up for their small losses. Essentially, great investors are willing to draw from decks C and D consistently, accepting a string of small losses as the price of doing business while holding out for the big winners.

Excellent investors don't change their philosophy in response to a few losing investments. They know their edge in advance, and they understand that down periods are inevitable. Their high level of confidence in their judgment and methodology allows them to brush off small losses.

For many small investors who seek small gains, dividend payments provide a sense of security. Yet stocks paying high dividends may be a type of psychological trap for risk-averse investors. The quarterly dividends feel good even while the stock price stagnates. Studies have shown that high-dividend-paying stocks appreciate significantly less than lower-yield stocks.

THE LEARNED CAUDATE

The series of gains in the SGT trigger subjects' neural reward learning. Part of the brain, called the caudate nucleus (which arcs over the top of the nucleus accumbens), helps people learn to recognize the cues and patterns that predict financial rewards.

Researchers found that the caudate nucleus is more active as subjects begin playing a card game in which some cards (with a certain symbol) are predictive of potential losses and others of gains. As subjects learn which cards are predictive of gains and which of losses, the activity of the caudate decreases every time those cards appear, as if individuals are learning the financial outcomes represented by each card.[29]

In investors, caudate deactivation may occur as habits are formed. Investors learn which cues to pay attention to—such as certain aspects of earnings announcements or chart price patterns—in order to make better decisions. As they learn the connections, they become less vigilant and more vulnerable to surprise.

When investors' learned assumptions are unexpectedly violated, then following the initial surprise, they must reassess their environment. Such a scenario of learning, surprise, and relearning happens when investors become complacent about a company's consistently positive or negative earnings performance.

PATTERNS IN EARNINGS REPORTS

When companies report good (or bad) earnings for a prolonged period, investors begin to expect that the pattern will continue. When a company violates the "pattern" by either missing (or beating) expectations, there is a delayed reaction from the investing public. That is, the price reaction occurs over a longer time period than would be expected if all the good or bad news had been instantly incorporated into prices.

Researchers studied the reaction of stock prices to earnings surprises for listed U.S. companies over the period 1983–1999. The results suggested that investors show short-term underreaction to earnings announcements, incorporating the earnings news into the stock price with a delay. However, there is an overreaction during earnings surprises. That is, stock prices initially move too little in the direction of a positive or negative earnings announcement unless it is a highly unexpected earnings surprise.[30] It is possible that investors learn to associate earnings trends with a company and do not react adequately if they are in line with their forecasts, but surprises shock the caudate's habit-driven decision making offline and require a readjustment and relearning of reward cues. In the meantime, as investors readjust their expectations, they protectively overreact.

Some mutual funds take advantage of stock overreaction and underreaction around earnings announcements. Russ Fuller, president of Fuller and Thaler Asset Management in San Mateo, California, has commented that this is one of the strategies his firm exploited to achieve above-market returns. Several other "behavioral" funds have sprung up to capitalize on investors' apathy or collective surprise around earnings announcements.

FOOLED BY RANDOMNESS

In the stock market, there are more days of large negative price movements than would be expected in a "normal distribution" of returns. This is called the *fat tail* or leftward skew of return variability. Put simply, there are more big daily price drops in the stock market than would be expected by chance. Yet most investors tend to overlook the likelihood of a large daily price decline, especially if it has been a while since the last one.

As mentioned previously, put options are a type of insurance contract for investments. Put values increase when the market drops. But if the market does not drop, over time, puts lose their premium value. When puts are out-of-the-money, they will expire worthless if the market does not drop significantly before their expiration date.

When a large negative event has not happened recently in the markets, put premiums are relatively low. During and immediately after price shocks, put premiums are quite high. Low put premiums often reflect investors' poor long-term memories and their discounting of future risk.

In the SGT experiment described above, subjects were not adequately afraid of infrequent large losses, and they were enamored with small short-term gains. They essentially paid the experimenters so they would not have to experience frequent small losses, even with the possibility of occasional large gains.

To take advantage of investors' preference for small gains irregardless of occassional large disasters, Nassim Taleb argues for a style of investing called *catastrophe investing*. Taleb may invest in markets where returns have been good for some time. In such markets, investors are accustomed to small feel-good gains year after year, and the implied volatility of options in these markets has dropped (often to excessively low levels). Taleb may buy put options far out-of-the-money. Taleb's puts make money only if the market drops sharply within a given time period. Usually, he loses money on these puts.

Taleb describes his strategy as one relying on "black swans." Just because one has never seen a black swan does not prove that they do not exist. Taleb's strategies are constructed entirely on the premise that random and unexpected events do sweep the markets. "Taleb buys options because he is certain that, at root, he knows nothing, or, more precisely, that other people believe they know more than they do."[31]

Taleb has designed a strategy that can lose gradually for years. But over time, a large market event will earn him outsized long-run returns. In Malcolm Gladwell's *New Yorker* magazine article "Blowing Up," Taleb is quoted: "'We cannot blow up, we can only bleed to death,' Taleb says, and bleeding to death, absorbing the pain of steady losses, is precisely what human beings are hardwired to avoid." Taleb accepts fund investors who can think for the long term, potentially suffering year after year of small losses with the knowledge that one day, possibly several years hence, their patience will pay off handsomely. These investors are rare; their bias against losses is innate, which is why his strategies are likely to be lucrative for decades to come.

Taleb's strategies are not sexy. Perhaps they are cowardly. How could someone place himself in such a pessimistic position, gradually losing money while consistently betting on a large unexpected negative event that others were unprepared for? It goes against the risk-taking and heroism and optimism of the American business ethos. According to Gladwell, "That is the lesson of Taleb. . . . There is more courage and heroism in defying the human impulse, in taking the purposeful and painful steps to prepare for the unimaginable."[32]

CHAPTER 19

Attention and Memory

What's in a Name?

In 2003 I met a trader named Collin who was working at a proprietary trading firm. His specialty was scalping small dislocations in price, between markets, using high leverage. For example, he arbitraged small differentials in the bid and ask prices of American depositary receipts (ADRs) between London and New York or New York and Tokyo.

Collin's scalping opportunities often only lasted for seconds. He needed to enter nearly simultaneous buy and sell orders in order to capture a profit. If he was too slow, he lost transaction costs (and sometimes more). He once told me that he could spot an opportunity, enter orders, and complete the entire transaction within two seconds. In order to ply his trade, Collin had to be constantly vigilant to price data. If he looked away during the trading day, he could miss an opportunity.

The devotion of his attention to the markets was exhausting, but over time he adapted to the conditions and could watch prices for long periods. As Collin learned to focus his attention at work, he noticed deterioration in other areas. He had trouble listening to his girlfriend, he couldn't sit still to read, he was easily irritated, and he didn't feel comfortable when not engaged in high-intensity activities.

He enjoyed online poker when not trading, and he purchased three desktop computers for playing simultaneous late-night poker games. He justified this activity by citing the extra profits he earned (which were actually far below his trading income).

Toward the end of 2003, Collin's work was becoming more competitive due to computerized "robot traders." He needed better attention and faster reactions to exploit good opportunities. He tried chemical supplements to improve his attention and work performance. A low dose of the selective serotonin reuptake inhibitor (SSRI) fluoxetine (Prozac) improved his irritability, but not his distractibility.

He tried modafinil (Provigil) and noticed a striking improvement in his ability to focus. But then he started to abuse modafinil. He stayed up late playing online poker and then awakened every trading day at 5 A.M. (Pacific Time) to prepare for the New York market open. He took a modafinil tablet each weekday morning to maintain his alertness during the workday. Neurally speaking, the dopamine receptors in Collin's reward system were becoming desensitized, leading to a chronic experience of decreased pleasure, distractibility, and a drive to gamble and take risks (online poker) to stimulate adequate dopamine release. He began to need risk-induced dopamine release just to feel normal.

Collin's sleep deficit had its own dangers. In general, sleeping four to five hours per night for a week leads to cognitive impairment equivalent to that of a blood alcohol level of 0.1 percent (legally intoxicated). The same result occurs after not sleeping at all for one night. Delayed reaction time, poor problem solving, and impaired judgment are common the following day.

Collin's use of modafinil decreased his *desire* to sleep (which is the purported effect of the drug), but not his *need* to sleep. As a result, he accumulated a massive sleep deficit over months of four-hour-per-night sleep and daily modafinil use, which resulted in poor judgment in complex tasks (such as human relationships and planning for the future).

Eventually, his girlfriend left him, breaking their engagement and canceling her lease on the apartment. Collin kept up his unhealthy nocturnal poker games. Due to the sleep debt and relationship problems, his trading performance started to suffer. He forgot that his apartment's lease had been canceled, and he didn't prepare to move out on time.

He fell asleep one weekend, and he was unrousable when his landlord arrived to check on the apartment. He had accumulated a large sleep debt during the prior months, and now he was paying it back. Collin was passed out on the floor of his apartment in front of the television, and he didn't respond to his landlord's efforts to wake him. An ambulance was called, and Collin remained largely incoherent when the paramedics arrived. He spent the night in a hospital emergency room, snoozing on a gurney in the hall.

After this experience Collin realized his life had to drastically change. He quit trading, moved into a hotel, and planned a long vacation. He booked tickets for a year-long around-the-world trip.

When he returned to San Francisco a year and a half later, we went to dinner. He was a very different (and very happy) person. He told me he had attended a one-month silent mindfulness meditation retreat in India

(Vipassana), and he credited this experience with the transformation in his personality. He had also reconnected with family in Ireland, including cousins he had never met.

During the year that he was away, computerized trading robots had completely taken over his prior trading strategies. Automated software agents could screen far more market price information than a human could, not to mention the extreme speed with which they could enter orders (measured in milliseconds).

Collin found work as a institutional trader for a Bay Area hedge fund. He stopped practicing mindfulness mediation, and some of his inattentiveness reemerged. As Collin put it, "There's something about staring at that screen all day—it changes me." Collin's story illustrates the effects of trader attention burnout.

TERMINAL ILLNESS

Most trading desks are backed by a wall of liquid crystal display (LCD) monitors and television screens. Some of the traders intensely watching those monitors are unknowingly changing their neurochemistry. Studies of children and television watching indicate that increased daily television viewing time correlates with decreased attention span. American children aged one year old watch an average of 2.2 hours and children three years old watch 3.6 hours of daily television. For each hour above average that children watch TV at these ages, there is a 10 percent increase in the rate of diagnosed attention deficit–hyperactivity disorder (ADHD) when these children turn seven years old. This result is independent of the effects of home cognitive environment. In children, watching excessive TV reduces attention span. Is this true for traders? For some, yes, but definitely not for all.

If television is such an attention drain, what about computer monitors? Adolescents who spend more hours on their computers are more likely to be depressed. Since the bulk of the evidence for harmful attention and mood effects from television and computer use is found in the developing brain, a mature trader will have significantly less problems with prolonged market watching than an infant or adolescent. Yet in my clinical practice, I have occasionally seen traders who were burned out by their constant vigilance to news feeds.

Information overload occurs when people are faced with too much information to process. When overload occurs, most people prefer to withdraw and avoid making a decision until they better understand the situation. If they cannot delay the decision, then they rely on how their feelings and memories. As a result, when too much information is present, people are more vulnerable to biases. Novice investors who have not prioritized the information they use in decision making are susceptible to overload.

REPRESENTATIVE RETURNS

While watching information flow, many traders monitor the daily "most actives" list. Many inexperienced investors view recent returns as representative of what they can expect for future performance.

The bias associated with overweighting recent events in one's future forecasts is called the *representativeness* heuristic, and it is related to the "hot-hand" bias mentioned in Chapter 18. Fundamentally, the representativeness heuristic is a short-term memory bias in which simple, recent information cues are overweighted in decision making.

Professors Dhar and Kumar investigated stocks bought by more than 40,000 American households at a discount brokerage during a five-year period. On average, the stocks that investors bought had already increased by 0.6 percent during the week before the purchase. When Dhar and Kumar expanded their window of investigation, they found an increase of 1.2 percent, 2.2 percent, and 7.3 percent for the two-week, one-month, and three-month periods before the purchase, respectively. Individual investors were buying stocks that had recently outperformed.[1]

Academics are also affected by the representativeness bias in their stock market forecasts. Professor Ivo Welch elicited professors' estimates of the expected annual equity risk premium over the next 30 years via surveys. The equity risk premium is the annual percent return by which stocks are expected to outperform bonds. Recent market price trends strongly biased their 30-year estimates.

The first series of surveys were implemented during the bull market of 1997–1999.[2] Finance professors judged the expected annual equity risk premium over the next 30 years at an average of 7.2 percent.

Welch again surveyed the professors during the bear market of 2001.[3] If professors had previously estimated returns according to mean reversion, then one might expect respondents to estimate a higher equity risk premium after a market decline. In fact, in 2001 the average expectation for the annual 30-year equity risk premium was 5.5 percent, about 1.7 percent lower than the bull market estimate. This pattern of high estimates when things are good and low estimates when they are bad is consistent with the representativeness bias. That is, the professors derive their estimates not from an objective consideration of past decades, but rather from recent events in the markets.

In Welch's study of academics forecasting the equity premium, the subjects did not succumb to a "mean-reversion" bias. In Chapter 18, there is evidence that professionals and academics are more susceptible to mean-reversion biases in their forecasts, so there is an apparent contradiction. Perhaps academics exhibited representativeness because they were (1) not able to reference a historical price chart of the equity premium and (2) were making 30-year forecasts rather than annual predictions (as they were in the example in Chapter 18).

Because of the strong influence of the representativeness heuristic in investor purchase decisions, securities authorities have ruled that the disclaimer "past performance does not guarantee future returns" must be attached to all mutual fund advertising. In effect, government regulators are warning investors away from biased decision making.

FOND MEMORIES

In general, people preferentially remember events that have a strong emotional association (either good or bad). As a result, they overweight the significance of these events when referencing the past to make forecasts about the future. If an investor has a strongly negative or positive experience in the markets, then that single experience is likely to be overweighted when the investor is making future plans.

For people who lost all their savings in the stock markets of 1929 and 1930, if they never reentered the markets, they would always think of the stock market as a very dangerous place to invest. Those who did muster the courage to reenter would better remember their large gains in the 1940s and 1950s, since those memories would be more recent and overweighted versus one's fading recall of the 1929 crash.

Using Professor Knutson's monetary incentive delay (MID) task, in which scaled monetary rewards and losses are delivered to experimental subjects during functional magnetic resonance imaging (fMRI) scanning, Stanford postgraduate researcher Alison Adcock tested the strength of reward memory formation. Pictures of neutral scenes and objects that followed a high-value reward cue (the possibility to earn $5) were more clearly remembered three weeks after the experiment. When subjects recalled these pictures, the nucleus accumbens and the hippocampus (an explicit memory region) were much more activated when viewing the images that accompanied the high value reward cue. According to Adcock and Knutson, the findings are consistent with the hypothesis that reward motivation promotes memory formation via dopamine release in the hippocampus prior to learning.

Interestingly, the researchers found individual differences in memory encoding, where individuals who showed greater anticipatory reward system activation also demonstrated superior memory. The more excited one is about a potential reward (nucleus accumbens activation), the more they remember the context and environment where the reward cue occurred (hippocampal activation).[4] Investors who see sexy models and fast sports cars in stock promotions are more likely to remember the name of the stock. When recalling the stock, they are more likely to feel positively about it, and thus more likely to take a chance and buy it.

Memories ensconced in the hippocampus appear to bias one's thoughts about the future. It turns out that the hippocampus is accessed when people make forward-looking estimates or projections.[5] That finding may imply that people are unable to disregard their memories during considerations of the future. In fact, they use their memories to construct possible scenarios that are used in planning, which may explain (1) why investors are susceptible to the representativeness (recency) bias, and (2) why investors tend to be miscalibrated (overconfident) when estimating future outcomes. Professionals cannot escape the tyranny of their own memories without practice and training. Financial markets have no memory, and investors stuck in past mental models will be less adaptable to changing market conditions.

BEATING THE HINDSIGHT BIAS

One of the most pernicious memory biases is called the *hindsight bias.* The hindsight bias refers to the fact that most people think they "knew it all along." After an event occurs, they think that they had predicted it would happen in advance, when in fact they did not. The danger of the hindsight bias is that it prevents people from learning from their mistakes. Unless they documented their forecasts in advance, they have no objective evidence that they did not expect the event to happen.

Professor Paul Slovic found that the best mechanism for fighting the hindsight bias was to encourage people to explicitly think about the "counterfactuals." That is, after an event happened, experimental subjects were encouraged to consider how other possible outcomes might have occurred. What conditions could have contributed to different results? Considering such a question, subjects became less anchored to the actual outcome (which dominated their recollection), and became more open to other possible lines of reasoning in advance of the event.

In experiments, Slovic found that the hindsight bias was still present when this technique was followed, but it was much reduced.[6] Slovic's result supports the value of journaling. For example, while an investor may claim to have known that the U.S. dollar would peak in 2002, if they had been recording their thoughts and observations in a journal, they could confirm their memories. They could reexamine the risks and opportunities they had identified in macroeconomic and currency systems. Were they as certain about the dollar's decline as they remember being? Importantly, reviewing a journal can help one identify the risks that were overlooked and the opportunities that were discounted (which memory alone cannot recall). Such a review of one's thought process, being sure to identify counterfactual evidence, improves future reasoning.

The next two sections will move away from memory biases and address attention biases. Specifically, they discuss how people focus, what interrupts their concentration, and the neuroscience behind paying attention.

ATTENTION DEFICIT

The process of paying attention should be distinguished from arousal. Vigilance, wakefulness, arousal, and alertness are not types of attention. Focus and concentration are. Drinking 10 double-shot lattes will increase one's vigilance (and bladder tension), but will decrease one's ability to concentrate.

Some people are very good at maintaining focus, while others struggle with constant distractibility. Some people are unable to function in a normal workplace or relationships due to constant distractibility and inattention. They may be suffering from attention deficit–hyperactivity disorder (ADHD). ADHD is a well-studied illness with neural origins and medication treatments (described in the following section).

Excellent concentration is often found among meditation masters. Meditators who exercise their "attention muscles" regularly during long sitting sessions have improved abilities to focus, attend, and concentrate. Many long-time meditators can demonstrate fascinating benefits of such attentiveness, occasionally using mental concentration to self-regulate physiological processes (such as heart rate, blood pressure, and skin temperature). Furthermore, there is fMRI evidence that experienced meditators can inhibit limbic impulses, such as the startle response and fear, better than nonmeditators. There is evidence that meditators' superior powers of concentration originate in the prefrontal cortex. Researchers have found much greater prefrontal cortex electrical activations on electroencephalography in trained meditators. The prefrontal cortex is not the only brain region involved in attention.

The reward system will try to shift one's focus toward anything new or unusual for further investigation. Neuroimaging research demonstrates that the reward system is activated by novelty,[7] and it is a driver of curiosity and discovery. In order to maintain attention on one task, people need to inhibit the frequent novelty-seeking impulses arising from their reward system.

The reward system's novelty-seeking and attention-shifting urges are prioritized and managed by the prefrontal cortex. It considers the various signals from the reward system and then decides whether to continue with the current task or to shift attention. Sometimes the prefrontal cortex is thinned, and it loses the strength to enforce discipline on the reward system. Chronic drug addicts, older adults (over 80 years old), and prisoners have all been found to have thinner prefrontal cortices than healthy middle-aged adults. These populations have difficulty maintaining focus on one task for prolonged periods, and they all struggle to resist potentially rewarding temptations (drugs, investment scams, and crime, respectively).

Poor prefrontal cortex function, and the inattention that results, can be managed with exercises (such as meditation or yoga) or medications. Researchers found that a regular yoga practice, in which the attention is continuously maintained on either a repeated mantra (phrase) or the sensation of breathing, can reduce the signs and symptoms of ADHD in children. The medications that are capable of managing ADHD can shed light on the chemical origins of the disorder.

KEEP YOUR EYE ON THE PILLS

The medications that are most successful in improving attention in sufferers of ADHD are amphetamines and their chemical derivatives. Amphetamines are stimulant medications that block the neuronal reuptake of norepinephrine and dopamine, increasing their concentrations in the synaptic cleft. In the 1950s and 1960s amphetamines were prescribed as pick-me-up pills, because for most people they provide alertness as well as attention. In the United States they are now under stricter government control. Commerical medications used to treat ADHD include methylphenidate (Ritalin), Adderall, Concerta, and others.

Neuroimaging researchers have found that ADHD sufferers have decreased activation in the anterior cingulate cortex (ACC) versus normals. This difference may represent a lack of conflict resolution in ADHD brains, where incoming stimuli are usually prioritized through ACC processing.[8] Anatomically, the ACC is a region of the prefrontal cortex.

Professor Knutson administered intravenous amphetamines to subjects before they played his monetary incentive delay (MID) task in a fMRI scanner. Subjects who received amphetamines had decreased peak activity but longer time of activation in the nucleus accumbens (NAcc) when anticipating financial gains. This activation pattern may be a result of improved modulation of attention—decreased sudden reactivity to any particular reward stimulus.[9]

Knutson also discovered that children with ADHD have decreased activation of the reward system, and specifically the NAcc, when anticipating rewards.[10] This hypoactivation may represent the neural basis of difficulty maintaining goal orientation, impaired memory and learning, and susceptibility to depression among ADHD patients.

Consider Collin's story, which opened this chapter. For day traders, if intense market monitoring desensitizes dopamine circuits, then this may explain Collin's gradual decline in relationship skills and pleasure. During the trading day he learned to take his prefrontal cortex off-line so he could quickly find and attend to potential trades. Every potential opportunity caused a surge of dopamine. Eventually, the downstream neurons would downregulate their dopamine receptors after several days of continual stimulation. Such desensitization can be recovered by training. Collin's silent one-month mindfulness retreat may have reequilibrated his reward system and reinforced his use of the prefrontal cortex.

WHAT'S IN A NAME?

While the stock exchange's "most actives" list is one way that stocks are brought to investors' attention, their names can also be a useful marketing "hook." Studies have shown that investors more often put their money in equities with catchy (easily remembered) or seductive (exciting) names. At the core of this naming bias is the usual neural culprit—the reward system.

Researchers found that for 296 mutual funds over the period 1994–2001, name changes associated with currently "hot" investment styles prompted increased net fund inflows of 27 percent for the year following the name change. This effect occurred regardless of whether the name change was only symbolic and without any underlying change in investment style or strategy.

On average, investors who moved into renamed mutual funds lost money. According to the study authors, it appeared that the name changes were timed to trick investors into expecting better future performance than was actually delivered.[11]

Companies can change their stock tickers to be more compelling, such as Harley Davidson changing from HDI to HOG. Interestingly, such symbol-changing stocks have increased returns, versus the overall market, following the change. Examples of evocative stock symbols include LUV for Southwest Airlines, Sotheby's (BID), and Advanced Medical Optics (EYE). From 1984 through 2004, stocks with clever symbols appreciated 23.6 percent compounded annually, compared with 12.3 percent for all stocks on the New York Stock Exchange and NASDAQ.[12] According to researchers, "One possible explanation for the results is that people prefer to work with information they can easily process."[13]

Further evidence for the "irrational" value of names came from a study by Princeton psychologists. They found that a basket of companies with pronounceable stock symbols gained 11.2 percent more in the first day of trading after their initial public offerings (IPOs) than other stocks.[14] "These results imply that simple, cognitive approaches to modeling human behavior sometimes outperform more typical, complex alternatives."[15] Catchy stock symbols and pronounceable names are more mentally accessible as investment decisions are formulated. They provide an easy processing shortcut, are often titillating (rewarding), and are thus more attention-getting and easily available for recall.[16]

It's not only mutual fund names and clever stock symbols that draw investors. Concepts such as *new economy* reflected perceptions of a fundamental transformation in business, suggesting that the old risks of investing no longer applied. Internet and technology stock investors were often seduced by the novelty and limitless potential of the "new economy."

At the turn of the millennium, newly opening export markets, such as those of the former Soviet Block, China, and India, provided billions of new consumers to whom American companies could peddle their wares. One of these opening markets—China—and a world-changing technology—the Internet—provided the context for one of the most overhyped stocks in history, solely based on its name.

CHINA PROSPERITY INTERNET HOLDINGS

As foreign firms set up shop in China in the 1990's, considerable euphoria accompanied their efforts. China was portrayed as an untapped market of 1.3 billion consumers, ripe for the first movers. Stock investors were keen to find companies that were well-positioned in this market. The stock of one company, China Prosperity Internet Holdings, experienced an investor frenzy in late 1999 based solely on the expectations attached to the company's name.

In November 1999, I was surfing stock message boards where Chinese stocks were discussed. At that time I was using stock trading strategies of my own design, based on the psychology of stock message board conversations. On the morning of November 16, 1999, I noticed a message about a stock called China Prosperity Internet Holdings (CPIH) on one of the boards I was following.

A message board poster claimed that CPIH was going to be the next big thing. "Catchy name," I thought, and I decided to check it out. Oddly, I thought, I couldn't find any substantive information on the company fundamentals through an Internet search, Yahoo! Finance, the SEC, or the Bulletin Board Stock Exchange web site.

I looked at the stock price chart. Over the past three months, few shares of the stock had traded at all, and it had remained priced at $0.25. So far that day, November 16, 1999, the stock had jumped from $0.25 to $1.00. Five hours remained in the trading day. The stock rose rapidly as I watched, and by the market close CPIH was over $14 per share. The next day, the stock continued its ascent. It opened around $20 and then was mentioned on CNBC. Within an hour it had hit $82, the day's high. It closed that day, November 17, 1999, at $32 per share. In the following days, the price gradually declined. Trading dried up in early 2000, and the stock was subsequently delisted.

Investors who dug deep enough could have found news regarding CPIH. It turned out that the directors of CPIH were under indictment for fraud by the Hong Kong securities authorities. Apparently, they had lied about a merger between their company and a Bermuda-based company. Somehow, they managed to get a U.S. market listing on the bulletin board exchange in the spring of 1999, prior to the announcement of their indictment. So it appeared that this company was simply an apparition—a fraud—whose price had been drifting along sideways pending an indictment.

If CPIH wasn't a real company, how could it rise 32,000 percent in two days and be mentioned on CNBC? There was no positive information about the company except its name, and anonymous tips on message boards didn't initially tout the stock, but rather suggested "check it out."

Because there was no other information besides a price chart and bulletin board speculation, much of CPIH's move was probably due to its name. Day traders loved the idea of stocks with enormous potential markets, in this case "China" and the Internet. On a more subtle level, investors usually want some confidence in their stock purchases. "Prosperity" is a reassuring word. "Holdings" implied that the company wasn't some one-hit wonder, and that it may have a complex corporate structure (hence the lack of concrete financials) and perhaps (considered by an excitement-stoked imagination) sizable assets or mutiple revenue streams. All-in-all,

CPIH had an essentially perfect name for elevating expectations and inducing a short-term investor buying frenzy.

CPIH's ascent to $14 was due to the viral spread of message board endorsements. On the second day of trading, CPIH got an extra boost after being mentioned on CNBC. Even without substantive fundamental information, investors bought CPIH simply because they had heard about it, its name was evocative, and its price was rising. With so many sources available to research, and so little time to peruse, how do investors find quality stocks to buy?

"ALL THAT GLITTERS"

Individual investors often research those stocks that catch their attention. Yet attention is a limited resource. Since many investors observe the same sources of financial information (such as CNBC or Bloomberg), there are often herds of buyers chasing the latest stocks in the news. Stocks in the news, such as those mentioned by Maria Bartiromo on the *Midday Call* on CNBC, experience almost five-fold increases in volume in the minutes following the mention.[17] It's not only Bartiromo's show that stokes investor buying.

Finance professor Terrance Odean found that, over a large sample of brokerage accounts, individual investors are net buyers of attention-grabbing stocks (e.g., stocks in the news, stocks experiencing high abnormal trading volume, and stocks with extreme one-day returns). Odean analyzed data at two brokerage firms and discovered that stocks bought by individual investors on "high-attention days" (when they are in the news) tended to subsequently underperform stocks sold by those investors. A larger proportion of investors buy individual stocks after news announcements than at other times. "When calculated by number for the large discount brokerage, buy-sell imbalance is 2.70 percent for stocks out of the news and 9.35 percent for those stocks in the news. At the large retail brokerage, buy-sell imbalance is −1.84 percent for stocks out of the news and 16.17 percent for those in the news."[18]

No matter what the news, investors tend to buy stocks that are in the public eye. Individual investors buy following many attention-getting events: high volume days, extremely negative and extremely positive one-day returns, news releases. Investors even buy following earnings surprises, regardless of whether they are negative or positive.[19]

While amateurs often fall into the attention-based buying trap, the same cannot be said for professional investors. Odean found that institutional investors (especially value-strategy investors—presumably more savvy than individual investors) did not exhibit attention-based buying. Other researchers have observed professional investors taking advantage of amateurs who chase big winners.

Professor Mark Seasholes and colleagues demonstrated that, on the Shanghai Stock Exchange, individual investors are net buyers the day after a stock hits an upper price limit. A larger percentage of purchases is made by first-time buyers on these days than on other days. The effect of individual investor buying is transitory, with reversion to prelimit-day levels within 10 trading days. According to Seasholes, a small group of professional investors profit at the expense of individual investors by anticipating this temporary bump in share price and demand.[20]

On the New York Stock Exchange, researchers found a similar pattern to that in China.[21] The next day gap up, following a large one-day gain, is often called "overreaction." The morning gap up is called "overreaction" because the price tends to decline from the open throughout the remainder of the trading day. This overreaction pattern has been found to be stronger following bad news (negative open with daytime rally) than good.[22] Other researchers have found this pattern in Tokyo for the most actively traded stocks.[23] It appears that investors buy into the price momentum in a frenzy and then sell out the next day after the price momentum stalls.

Is there money to be made by fading (trading against) other investors' attention-based enthusiasm? Professor Seasholes discovered such a short-term trading strategy. Using a dataset of over 21 million matched transactions on the Shanghai Stock Exchange, Seasholes found that traders who buy nearly limit-up stocks at the market close and sell them at the next day's open make an average of 1.16 percent per day per trade (on the opening gap).[24] Seasholes speculates that the opening gap may occur due to the influence of evening Chinese television business news programs. Individual investors who watch those programs then herd into the top performing stocks in the morning.

Traders pay attention to the market's big movers. When amateur investors buy or sell the "most actives" or large price movers, they are chasing those stocks (buying after a run-up or selling during a downturn). Unfortunately, such a momentum strategy is unprofitable. Only professionals who have learned how to manage momentum-driven enthusiasm can profit from such an attention-based strategy.

CHAPTER 20

Age, Sex, and Culture

Risk Taking around the World

Jim is an entrepreneurial financial planner I met at a seminar. He occasionally felt frustrated with his clients, and he wanted to discuss some of his client difficulties with me. In particular, he had been flummoxed by recent events with a client named Sharon. Sharon fell into responsibility of a large sum of money through her husband, Tom, who had recently and suddenly died. Tom had worked for International Paper (IP), and he had a sizable amount of IP stock in their retirement fund. In fact, he had never owned any other stocks—his only equity holding was IP, and it contributed over 70 percent of the value of all of Sharon and Tom's assets.

Sharon and Tom had never discussed buying stocks or bonds. She had no interest in investing. She approached Jim in order to get her finances in order before retirement.

Over their first few meetings, Jim discussed the concept of financial risk diversification and its foundation in mathematical principles. He explained that Sharon could greatly reduce her financial risk and probably make better returns over time if she was willing to sell some of the IP stock. He offered a number of suggestions including the addition of bonds and mutual funds to her portfolio, and this would require paring back the number of IP shares held.

Sharon politely declined his offers to sell some of the IP stock. After several meetings, and feeling that he wasn't properly communicating the facts of her financial risk to her, Jim more insistently pushed the idea of diversification. He felt that it was his job to protect her from unexpected market risk, and she wasn't letting him do his job if she so stubbornly

275

resisted selling some IP shares. Jim pushed Sharon to let him diversify her portfolio more aggressively at each meeting.

Six months after they had entered an adviser-client relationship, Sharon told Jim, "Please stop."

Jim responded, "I don't understand."

"Stop telling me to diversify."

"Okay, I'll stop if you'll just explain why."

Sharon replied impatiently, "Look, I've been telling you for months, I can't sell that stock."

"Why not?'

"Because it's Tom's!"

"*Tom's* stock!?!?"

Sharon didn't respond. She looked away, and Jim saw that she was upset. He realized he had said something wrong, but he still didn't quite understand the problem. Sharon was attached to IP because she associated it with her husband.

Investors often become emotionally attached to stocks for different reasons, such as special memories or a feeling of gratitude for its previous financial rewards.

In general, women are more susceptible to attachment and biases of emotion and memory than men, and these biases affect how women deal with stocks. In the following section, I outline some of the research that demonstrates men and women's different propensities for emotion-based investing. Later in the chapter, the discussion turns to the effects of aging on investment decision making and notable differences between Eastern and Western stock investors.

EMOTIONAL MEMORIES

Though it may sound stereotypical, in numerous psychology and neuroimaging studies, women demonstrate better memories of emotional events then men. In one experiment, subjects either viewed negatively arousing pictures (such as pictures of surgical operations) or neutral pictures (such as a door). Three weeks after the experiment, negatively emotional pictures were remembered better by the female participants than the male. During recall, women had brain activations characterized by negative emotional experience (the left amygdala), while men used a more fact-based memory structure (the right amygdala). In general, women appear to have enhanced memory (over men) when emotion is associated with an event.[1]

Some interesting hypotheses can be drawn for investors. Women who have lost money in the markets are more likely to retain negative memories of investing, and as a result, they are more likely to keep their money on the sidelines after a bear market. Men are more resilient following negative emotional experiences, and are thus more likely to "get back on the bull" even after a painful correction. This can be unfortunate for men who don't know what they're doing—difficulty learning from painful investing mistakes is probably a key contributor to overtrading among men.

Since people differ in their levels of "masculinity" and "femininity," some researchers asked subjects their masculinity/femininity ratings and then tested their memory function. People who rated themselves highly on femininity had strong emotional memory formation, while self rated masculine respondents exhibited enhanced factual recall.[2] In general, men (and masculine women) process investment information more according to its factual basis (such as the raw numbers), while women (and feminine men) may be more attuned to emotional aspects of an investment (such as its degree of social responsibility).

THE FEMALE BRAIN: ESTROGEN, EMOTION, AND COOPERATION

Women's superior emotional memories are enhanced by the effects of the hormones estrogen and progesterone. These hormones alter emotional experience and behavior, most notably when estrogen is *low* just prior to menstruation, which is associated with the irritability of premenstrual syndrome. During pregnancy, estrogen remains at relatively *high* levels, and many women report feeling especially joyful during the second and third trimesters of pregnancy due to the saturation of their brain's estrogen receptors.

Studies of rats in estrus (low estrogen) find that these rats have a poorer ability to withstand cognitive stress. Researchers hypothesize that this cognitive stress reactivity is related to supportive effects of estrogen on the prefrontal cortex, and this support is withdrawn when estrogen levels are low.[3,4] It seems to follow that female investors, especially those with significant premenstrual dysphoria (bad mood before menstruation), may be better off avoiding stress-inducing investment decisions when their estrogen is low. Low estrogen women are more sensitive to potential risks, and their reactivity to negative events is likely to be enhanced.

One tool that economists use to measure people's tendency to cooperate versus cheat is a game called the prisoner's dilemma (described in the glossary). Using functional magnetic resonance imaging (fMRI), researchers have found that during a prisoner's dilemma game, women showed greater reward system activation on fMRI when engaging in cooperative behavior than in deceptive behavior.[5] Other studies have shown that men are more likely to experience reward system activation when taking revenge.[6] These findings may underlie the tendency for women to value cooperation over conflict, even when deceived, while men are more openly aggressive when believing that another has cheated them.

I often receive questions from participants in investment committees about how roles and relationships can be facilitated. There are interesting implications of gender research to such groups. In investment committees, men may be more driven to settle political scores or engage in one-upmanship than cooperate in choosing optimal stock investments. Conversely, men's aggressive drives may lead them to stand against an erroneous crowd decision, while some women may be more likely to agree with the group majority in order to preserve social harmony. Men are less likely to communicate about conflict before they act, while women tend to use language to understand and defuse interpersonal crises. However, it should be noted that one's degree of of masculinity or femininity is probably more influential over investment committee behavior than one's gender.

FINANCIAL PLANNING FOR DIVORCEES

Mark is a financial planner who shared with me a story of gender-related misunderstanding. Mark had left his job at a nationally known investment advisory to start his own firm, and he asked his existing clients to follow him into his private practice.

Mark said that among his advisory clients, it was the middle-aged female divorcees who were reluctant to follow him to his new firm. He had explained the financial and personal benefits of the new arrangement with them, and he had encouraged them to think about the costs and benefits of the transition before making a decision. "Couldn't they understand the benefits—lower fees and personalized services?" he asked me. Mark had repeatedly discussed the "facts"—data about potential fee savings and higher returns—with his reluctant clients. He was mystified that they were still uncertain.

Mark was trapped in an empathy gap. He did not understand how his clients were feeling, so he could not address their needs. Women are less convinced of an investment's benefits by numerical analyses (factual information) than by their trust and confidence in the planner (emotional rapport). Furthermore, for Mark's divorced clients, watching him leave his established firm to strike out on his own may have provoked a vaguely familiar and painful memory of when their own long-term relationship ended. Additionally, Mark may not have understood that women are more risk averse than men, and a transition to a new office felt like more risk than they were willing to take.

I discussed these issues with Mark, and he seemed a bit baffled. He had trouble believing that some women would be driven by subtle feelings and memories instead of the data. For Mark, his clients' feelings seemed irrelevant, and potentially threatening. If he acknowledged their importance, he might realize that an enormous domain of human experience had previously been hidden to him.

MALE OVERCONFIDENCE

While women are more often risk averse, men (especially young men) are overconfident in their ability to handle risk. Professors Odean and Barber analyzed the trading records of 35,000 households from a large discount brokerage firm from February 1991 through January 1997. "Consistent with the predictions of the overconfidence models, we document that men trade 45 percent more than women and earn annual risk-adjusted net returns that are 1.4 percent less than those earned by women."[7] Being single increases the risk of overconfident trading: "These differences are more pronounced between single men and single women; single men trade 67 percent more than single women and earn annual risk-adjusted net returns that are 2.3 percent less than those earned by single women."[8]

In general, young men are more risk seeking in their investments, trading stocks more and taking greater overall financial risks than younger women.[9] Biologically, such risk taking may result from the fact that young men have a relatively desensitized reward system dopamine circuit compared to later in life—just like pathological gamblers and people induced into a sad state, they seek risk taking and novelty to stimulate their dopamine tone. It's not only dopamine that drives male risk-taking. Their bodies are hormonally primed to take risks during their youth.[10]

Evolutionary biologists hypothesize that young single men are driven to try to capture more social and financial gains while young, thus taking more risk in pursuit of their goals. When older, men spend more time consolidating and leveraging their existing assets than seeking high-risk new opportunities.

AGE

There is a plethora of data emerging about the ways in which our brains change with age. Those changes can be either helpful or hurtful to one's finances. Most people age gracefully, working around age-induced limitations and focusing more adroitly on their strengths. Older adults are also favored by two healthy personality trends.

As people age, they tend to become both less neurotic and more conscientious. In Chapter 12, neurotic investors reported making more investment mistakes than emotionally stable investors. On average, older adults report strikingly decreased levels of neuroticism (increased emotional stability) as compared to the young. Further, older adults tend to be more conscientious (more self-disciplined and organized) than younger adults.

A brain imaging study showed that the process by which older adults become more emotionally stable is credited not to a loss of limbic system vitality, but to increased strength in the prefrontal cortex, which inhibits unruly limbic impulses.[11] Emotional stability improves linearly over seven decades of the human life span. Technically speaking, improved emotional stability and impulse control (conscientiousness) is due to a shift toward greater medial prefrontal control over negative emotional input.[12]

Younger people have greater nucleus accumbens activation than older adults on fMRI studies of financial reward anticipation.[13] Older investors are more likely to take their time researching and forming strategy before buying into a stock. And older adults take fewer financial risks overall, especially after retirement.[14]

In general, as people age from childhood to adulthood, they process less information more qualitatively. The same information processing pattern is seen as people increase in their level of expertise.[15] Mental shortcuts provide for increased cognitive efficiency and thus faster processing of decision situations that have previously been experienced.

As older adults reach their seventies, the strength of the connection between their prefrontal cortex and the limbic system weakens. If the connection is significantly impaired, and their prefrontal cortex cannot inhibit excited impulses or integrate risk-related information, then they may be more easily coerced into fraudulent investment "opportunities."

In general, older people are more risk averse than younger participants during experimental gambles. Older adults (over 70) are more easily confused by complex financial decisions. Because of this easy confusion, which may be a result of cognitive slowing, they often avoid dealing with investments, instead deferring decisions to younger family members or entirely refusing to make decisions. Younger people are more likely to make financial mistakes due to excessive risk taking.[16]

THE SEATTLE LONGITUDINAL STUDY OF ADULT DEVELOPMENT

Since 1903, psychologists, schoolteachers, and other researchers have been administering standardized psychological tests to cohorts of

TABLE 20.1 Cognitive Skills and the Age of Initial Decline

Skill	Definition	Age at Which Gradual Decline Begins
Verbal Ability (Comprehension)	The ability to understand ideas expressed in words.	81, but today's youth have decreased skill compared with prior generations
Spatial Orientation	The ability to visualize and mentally manipulate spatial configurations in two or three dimensions, to maintain orientation with respect to spatial objects, and to perceive relationships among objects in space.	67
Inductive Reasoning	The ability to recognize and understand novel concepts or relationships; it involves the solution of logical problems—to foresee and plan.	67
Numeric Ability	The ability to understand numerical relationships, to work with figures, and to solve simple quantitative problems rapidly and accurately.	60, but today's youth have decreased skill compared with prior generations
Perceptual Speed	The ability to find figures, make comparisons, and carry out other simple tasks involving visual perception with speed and accuracy.	60
Verbal Memory	The ability that involves memorization and recall of meaningful language units primarily measured by memorizing lists.	67

thousands of individuals in Seattle, Washington. The goal of the research is to keep track of cognitive performance of individuals as they age. The researchers give a battery of tests to their subjects, and they retest each individual every seven years over their life span. The tests assess verbal skills, spatial skills, reasoning ability, numeric ability, and other characteristics of cognitive functioning. See Table 20.1 for a complete list and definitions of skills assessed.[17]

The researchers looked at how individual scores changed over time—over the lifespan. Do people lose certain abilities, gain some skills, or a mix of the two? Next, the authors examined how individuals born in one decade compared to individuals of the same age studied in subsequent decades. Do people born 50 years ago have the same talents and skills as modern adults?

When groups from 1903 and every seven years thereafter are followed over time, the earliest observed cognitive decline occurs for perceptual speed and numeric facility beginning at age 60. Inductive reasoning, spatial orientation, and verbal memory begin to decline by age 67. Verbal ability remains robust until age 81.[18] In general, the declines are relatively minor until age 80, when they all begin a more precipitous drop.

In an alternative analysis of the data, different generations are compared to each other when they are at similar ages. For example, the cognitive skills of 20-year-olds in 1903 could be compared to those of 20-year-olds in 2005. When such a comparison is made, there is generally a superiority of skills evident in the more recent generations, except in the areas of verbal and numeric ability, which are inferior to those of their grandparents' generation.

It's also known that genetic factors contribute to decreasing cognitive abilities over the lifespan. In particular, the apolipoprotein E (ApoE) gene is a risk factor for Alzheimer's disease, a form of dementia. In the Seattle study, a significantly greater rate of cognitive decline over the seven-year intervals was noted in individuals with one or two copies of the ApoE gene (e4/2 and e4/4 allele pairings).[19]

There are small decrements in declarative memory that accompany normal aging. These may be represented by an inability to recall people or events that have recently occurred. These decrements are related to small age-related impairments in the function of the hippocampus, a brain region that encodes recently experienced events, conversations, and daily interactions. People with the ApoE4 allele have more pronounced deficits in the hippocampus due to a build-up of proteins (transcribed by the gene) that interferes with neural transmission during aging. Fortunately, one's memory for facts and figures remains relatively intact until later in normal aging.

Another prominent change in the brain with aging is thinning of the prefrontal cortex. A decreasing ability to multi-task, perform mental calculations, and rapidly shift attention are caused by this thinning.

The preceding changes may explain, in part, the tendency for older people to be vulnerable to financial fraud. If their numeric ability falters while their verbal ability remains intact, they may not understand the fundamental risks of an investment prospect yet show no outward signs of incompetence. Up to one-half of all elder abuse cases in the United States involve financial fraud, accounting for over 500,000 victims.[20] Also, due to their slower processing speed, they may simply accept a financial adviser's "word for it" rather than taking the time and effort to do their own due diligence.

What causes these age-related deficits? Given the strong results from a skill-training protocol, it appears that much of the decline can be attributed to a lack of use: "Use it or lose it." Increasing prefrontal usage may improve the ability to learn and plan, thus minimizing age-related cognitive losses.[21]

In the 1970s, the Seattle researchers began a training program, to see if they could sustainably improve the skills of the test subjects and forestall or prevent decline. They found that when a simple training program is administered to older individuals in order to delay or reverse the decline in skills, the trained subjects show a sustained improvement in their skills over time. Those who do not receive the training have a precipitous drop in their abilities.[22]

The bad news about brain aging is that the prefrontal cortex and the hippocampus (factual memory center) do lose some of their strength. The good news is that there are now books and software products that promote specific exercises to strengthen these areas of the brain in the aged. A San Francsico company, Posit Science, sells software products that it reports can train the brain to lose the cognitive equivalent of one decade of aging. But before you run out and buy software or puzzle books for your aging brain, a simpler answer is close at hand—novelty. Engaging in unique challenges and new activities can strengthen the brain just as well as specific exercises. The brain is like a muscle, and you can either exercise specific areas using software or books, or you can challenge the whole thing to explore and solve on a larger scale (or do both).

There are some benefits to aging as well. Older adults are more emotionally stable, conscientious, and able to recognize patterns in relationships and life events. They can make more rapid routine decisions because they have entrenched "heuristics" (short-cuts) for thinking about familiar circumstances. Older adults also maintain their accumulated expert knowledge well. As long as adults remain curious and interested in the world and their workplace, and they are physically healthy, they should be able to maintain employment at least until the mid-80s. It may be the case that too many are retiring early because they think they should, not because they have lost any particular expertise.

CULTURE (EAST AND WEST)

The first time I visited China, in 1992, communism was still very much in evidence and the Shanghai and Shenzhen stock exchanges had been in existence for less than two years. State-run department stores were the source of most retail goods. State employees seemed laconic, condescending, and occasionally hostile. The stock exchanges were new and small, with most shares only nominally traded.

When I again visited China in 2001 and 2004, China and its capital markets had undergone a revolution. Elaborate stock brokerage houses were situated on large thoroughfares throughout major cities. Day traders and retirees flocked to trading houses, where they sat in customized trading stations and intently watched computer monitors and the "big boards" in the stadium-sized brokerage foyers.

When a country of 1.3 billion people undergoes an economic renaissance over only twenty years, there are bound to be extraordinary periods of investor and stock market behavior. Unfortunately, there is a very limited amount of cultural comparative literature relevant to finance. Most of the research into cultural investment attitudes compares Western (American or European) to Eastern (Chinese, Japanese, or Taiwanese) investors. There has been little research done on South Asian, Middle-Eastern, Latin American, or African investors.

While you saw earlier in this chapter that there are significant biological differences between male and female and older and younger investors, there are few significant cultural differences in investment behavior between Easterners and Westerners that cannot be explained by differing levels of economic development or financial education. Yet cross-cultural investment research does yield some interesting findings.

CHINESE RISK TAKERS

Many studies of financial risk taking and perception find that Easterners are more risk tolerant than Westerners. Professor Elke Weber found such a result when comparing risk attitudes and behavior of Chinese to American investors. Dr. Weber attributes Chinese risk taking to larger social structures, which insulate members against catastrophic losses.[23] Other researchers speculate that a lack of knowledge about the relationship between risk and return among the current generation of Chinese investors may alter risk taking attitudes,[24] and there is one study with evidence to that effect among horse bettors.[25]

When examining the process of decision making, as inferred from Chinese and American novels, Professor Weber found that Chinese decision-making patterns are more focused on relational considerations and role-based logic. Analytic modes of processing, in which decisions are based on a cost-benefit consideration of best outcomes, was more typical of American novels.[26] Perhaps worryingly, Chinese corporate boards may be more deferential to leaders' opinions and less influenced by cost-benefit analyses.

The above findings indicate that while Chinese take more financial risk, they are less attuned to probabilistic outcomes and are more aware of the social networks that provide support for risk taking (in case of failure). Because Chinese investors have a form of extended social (family) insurance, they can be less concerned with the probability of large losses. As a result, they will engage in more rational risk-taking behavior than risk-averse Americans.

BIASES AMONG CHINESE STOCK TRADERS

Individual Chinese investors demonstrate similar behavioral biases to Western investors. Chinese and American researchers examined the trading records of 46,969 individual investor accounts from five cities in the People's Republic of China from May 20, 1998, to September 30, 2002. The authors found evidence for overconfidence (overtrading and buying based on too little information), the disposition effect (holding losers too long and cutting winners short), and representativeness (chasing) among Chinese investors. Even experienced Chinese investors showed significant evidence of such behavioral biases.[27]

Chinese investors held past losers too long and sold past winners too soon. After one year, the stocks they sold outperformed the stocks they bought by 2.5 percent. This was a return that is negative, but slightly better, than that found by Odean in his study of over 60,000 American brokerage accounts.

Chinese investors also "chased" past winners. The average returns of stocks four months before their purchase was over 17 percent (a 32 percent excess return). The past one-year return of these stocks was 2.9 percent, implying that investors focus on the most recent short-term performance of the stocks purchased. In this case, Chinese investors are focused on the short term, chasing fast moving stocks upwards, even more than investors in other regions.

Because of their insufficient diversification and frequent trading, the authors labeled the studied Chinese investors as "overconfident." However, it should be noted that more frequent trading actually led to higher returns (on the order of 0.5 percent per month) during the study period than for less frequent traders.[28]

More evidence of the disposition effect was gathered in a survey of investors by the Shenzhen Stock Exchange in 2002—54.1 percent of individual investors reported that they would sell their stocks if prices rose by 10 percent. When asked what they would do if they suffered a loss, only 27 percent of the investors reported that they would close their positions.

In Taiwan, market makers on the TAIEX index options exchange were found to take above-average risks in afternoon trading after morning gains. In fact, the proportion of market makers with morning gains influences liquidity and volatility in afternoon trading.[29] This evidence of the house money effect is stronger for the TAIEX traders than among professional traders in Chicago, where researchers also found that more successful traders took greater afternoon risk after morning gains. With experience, however, the extent of increased afternoon risk taking after morning wins appears to decrease.[30]

Using past price patterns as a proxy, evidence for herding has been found in Chinese equities—more strongly in the more illiquid B-share markets.[31] Among Chinese investors, trading can be a virtual team sport. Researchers found that investors who work near each other are more likely to buy the same stocks (usually locally headquarted), probably due to "word-of-mouth" effects. These investors are also more likely to sell stock in the same companies (typically nonlocal).[32] The same type of clustering has even been found among American mutual fund portfolio managers who work at different funds but live in the same city. Such idea-contagion is true internationally, but exaggerated in China due to the "team-sport" configuration of stock trading houses.

In summary, women and men have different trading patterns. Women better retain emotional memories and are more risk averse, while men take excessive financial risks and have lower long-term returns. Investment risk taking varies over the life cycle, which may be a result of changes in cognition as age progresses and risks are more difficult to understand. Chinese stock traders take more risk than their Western counterparts, but also are susceptible to many of the same behavioral biases, such as overconfidence and the disposition effect. Representativeness (chasing) is more common among Chinese risk takers.

PART IV

In Practice

CHAPTER 21

Emotion Management

A Balancing Act

"Always acknowledge a fault. This will throw those in authority off their guard and give you an opportunity to commit more."

—Mark Twain

George Soros, Warren Buffett, Paul Tudor Jones—these men seem like investing naturals. Do they have an innate talent? Undoubtedly. What psychological characteristics make them great? Certain traits, such as adaptability, confidence, optimism, and emotional stability, lead to outstanding performance. But, in general, it is a congruence of characteristics, not any one individual trait, that leads to true excellence.

To achieve greatness in investing, education is the first step. You've got to know what you're doing in the markets. What is your strategy? Why is it superior? How will you manage volatility?

The next step is a self-evaluation. Identify your strengths and weaknesses and inventory your resources. What is your psychological Achilles' heel, and how will you protect it? Where do you draw your social support and your business network? Do you have a safety net, a fall-back plan? It's not simple to do a full self-assessment, in part because of the numerous self-deceptions and biases that everyone is subject to.

Biases can seriously impair financial performance. They prompt portfolio managers and individual investors to overtrade, feel excessively optimistic, and hold losers too long. Financial analysts are particularly susceptible to social biases such as herding. Professional traders take too much risk after recent losses. Such biased behavior is rooted in the brain's hard-wired cognitive and emotional systems. As a result of their deep subconscious origins, such biases are challenging to identify in oneself, much less to correct.

Small positive changes in psychological well-being, mental training, and physical health improve the probability of successful decision making. A slightly increased probability of success, over years of decision making, leads to better long-term outcomes.

This chapter is about the simple steps you can take to optimize your mind for reducing biases and improving investment decision making. It reviews fundamental concepts in psychology, offers brief lessons on emotional adaptability and coping skills, and outlines steps necessary to developing self-discipline. This chapter should help you start the journey, and maybe provide some help along the way, but it will not fundamentally change *who* you are. In the end, it's what you make of this information that counts. As motivational philosopher Jim Rohn puts it, "No one can do your push-ups for you."

DO IT FOR LOVE, NOT MONEY

I've heard some investors describe their goals as earning "obscene" amounts of money or accumulating "generational" wealth. However, the pursuit of profit for its own sake can quickly go awry. Such motivations involve the ego in decision making and increase emotional reactivity to outcomes. Furthermore, pursuing wealth as a goal is a symptom of decreased personal well-being and low self-esteem.

Individuals who identify "aspirations for financial success" as an important personal value have lower levels of "psychological vitality" and "self-actualization" and more physical complaints than others. People who endorse aspirations for self-acceptance, affiliation, community feeling, and physical health have superior well-being and less distress overall.[1] It may seem paradoxical, but pursuing profit as one's primary goal can be a sign of emotional ill health.

Of course, it is only natural that people in the financial industry are interested in making money. However, when money becomes the goal, rather than a by-product of enjoyable work, then emotional stability is apt to suffer.

The best investors, bankers, and businesspeople do their jobs well not for the financial rewards, but because they love them. Management guru Peter Drucker left investment banking because he wasn't passionate about it: "I was doing very well as a young investment banker in London in the mid-1930s, and the work clearly fit my strengths. Yet I did not see myself making a contribution as an asset manager. People, I realized, were what

I valued, and I saw no point in being the richest man in the cemetery. I had no money and no job prospects. Despite the continuing Depression, I quit—and it was the right thing to do."[2] The world is a better place because Drucker followed his career passion.

A focus on monetary outcomes also biases investing decisions. Some trading books and articles recommend a "Zen" (nonattachment) approach to short-term profits and losses.[3,4] Ego attachment to gains and losses induces greater emotional reactivity due to the comparison of short-term progress against expectations and goals. Detachment from outcomes and focus on the investment decision process improves emotional stability during volatility and yields greater long-term returns as strategy is gradually honed.

MONEY CHANGES YOU

Researchers have found that thinking about money unconsciously influences behavior, and the effects are not subtle. In a series of experiments, seeing a money cue (such as a wall poster depicting cash or unscrambling a sentence with a financial subject) changed how people solved problems and related to others. Money cues increased subjects' self-sufficiency and generated the desire to be free of dependency and dependents.

The subjects who were primed by money cues waited longer to ask the experimenter for help during a challenging task (314 seconds versus 173 seconds), spent half as much time assisting a confused peer (67 seconds versus 148 seconds), and donated half as much money ($0.77 versus $1.34) to the "University Student Fund" drop-box when they left the experiment room. In further experiments subjects primed with money preferred to play alone, work alone, and put more physical distance between themselves and a new acquaintance (118 cm versus 80 cm).[5] Overall, money-primed subjects became more self-sufficient, less generous, and more detached from others. Such effects of "money consciousness" are generated beneath awareness, and as seen above, they have a profound effect on social interaction and behavior.

EMOTIONAL DEFENSES

The brain doesn't like the discomfort of negative emotions, and it has devised strategies to avoid dealing with such feelings as anxiety, disappointment, and anger. Emotional defense mechanisms including denial, repression, and rationalization attempt to keep the discomfort unconscious. Negative emotions often linger underneath awareness, subtly influencing judgment and behavior. Insight is difficult and can be painful. The real reason people don't learn from their mistakes (or by observing the mistakes of others) is that they refuse to, and are often unable to, acknowledge those mistakes in the first place. Accepting responsibility for error is simply too painful for most people. As a result, it is extremely difficult to gain awareness of unconscious negative emotions.

Earlier in the book, I described experiments in which participants' emotions were manipulated beneath their awareness, and their judgments and behaviors changed as a result. The subjects themselves reported *feeling* the same both before and after the subliminal emotion induction. Unconscious emotions affect people *beneath* their awareness, yet they have profound effects on how people make decisions. In order to address and manage unconscious emotions, it's useful to understand how they arise. Much of unconscious emotional experience is fueled by internal predispositions, while other aspects of emotional life are learned over time or experienced in reaction to events.

There are techniques available for using the conscious mind *offensively* against emotional biases—exposing emotional undercurrents and using them to one's advantage. These techniques fall under the rubric of psychotherapy and self-help and are discussed in the following chapter.

THE PURSUIT OF HAPPINESS

Some people chronically wear "rose-colored glasses." Their positive sense of well-being is, to a large extent, inherited. In general, an individual's average level of well-being correlates with that of his or her parents. The heritability of happiness may be as high as 80 percent,[6] though 50 percent is a more widely accepted number.[7] It appears that everyone has a baseline level of happiness, which is determined primarily by genetics. While there may be significant variation in levels of happiness in the short term, the long-term average will be around a partially inherited baseline.

Beyond inheritance, one's learned coping strategies for success, failure, ease, and adversity contribute to one's level of well-being. There are also short-term emotional influences from unconscious emotions, such as those generated by the brain's comparator in response to short-term events, such as an unexpected financial windfall. But short-term emotions don't last long.

Perhaps surprisingly, people become emotionally acclimated to their new state of affairs after major life events, returning to their chronic baseline. For example, individuals who receive a financial windfall will initially be happier, but over a year their life satisfaction level returns to near its baseline state, which is called "hedonic adaptation" in the psychology literature.[8] Happiness researchers have shown that recent lottery winners were not happier than nonwinners,[9] and recent victims of paralysis were only slightly less happy than others after one year had passed.[10] People readily adjust to the facts of their new situation, and they reset their expectations accordingly.

The goal of psychotherapy is to increase a client's psychological adaptability by increasing their awareness of the connections between thoughts, feelings, and subsequent decisions. One study showed that talking about and analyzing the worst experience of one's life for 15 minutes per day for three days increased life satisfaction and physical and mental well-being when measured four weeks later. The same researchers found that simply thinking about the same bad experience, without analyzing, speaking, or writing about it, did not improve well-being.[11]

Because people are typically unconscious of their underlying feelings, both Western psychotherapy and Eastern contemplative techniques provide tools for gaining awareness of and working through feelings. These tools are not simple or easy to use. In fact, they involve serious time and energy commitments. And if you engage in one of these paths, you've got to ask yourself if you're ready to dedicate the time and effort required to find a therapist or meditation technique that fits your needs.

NEUROPLASTICITY

Where we can see the error of our ways, focus our corrective efforts, and practice with discipline, our brains will slowly rewire. Some hardwired biases can be mitigated via a process of neuronal resculpting called *neuroplasticity*. Neuroplasticity refers to neurons' tendency to change their structure and function in order to adapt to the demands of new environments. For a pianist, the neurons coordinating and controlling rapid finger movements will be more extensively networked and that area of the brain is physically larger than in the brain of a nonpianist. Such extensive neural networking occurs over time, due to practice and concentrated use. People who do not practice the piano will not have extensive networking of these neurons.

Similarly, if one is practicing techniques for enhancing emotional intelligence, then it's likely that the one's ability to attend, maintain self-awareness, and exercise impulse control will be strengthened. Tibetan Buddhist monks spend many hours daily meditating. In one unpublished study, brain monitoring (fMRI) of Buddhist meditators who had practiced greater than 10,000 hours of compassion meditation were compared with those from a group of novice meditators. At baseline, the monks' brains showed greater activation in brain areas related to positive feelings (left prefrontal cortex) and less activation in areas associated with negative emotions such as anxiety and anger (right prefrontal cortex) than did the novice meditators.[12]

In a study using electroencephalography (EEG) to monitor brain waves in the cortex, researchers found that Buddhist meditators have very high levels of gamma-wave synchrony (relative to novices) when meditating. It appeared that through meditation practice, the monks had learned to focus and synchronize their brain activity, resulting in enhanced attention and improved mood. "Our study is consistent with the idea that attention and affective processes, which gamma-band EEG synchronization may reflect, are flexible skills that can be trained."[13] According to a *Wall Street Journal* commentary, "That opens up the tantalizing possibility that the brain, like the rest of the body, can be altered intentionally. Just as aerobics sculpt the muscles, so mental training sculpts the gray matter in ways scientists are only beginning to fathom."[14]

The chief lesson of neuroplasticity is that with guided training, frequent practice, and self-discipline, the structure and function of the brain can be altered. Mental and emotional exercise is like athletic exercise. When directed effort is applied, the body and mind can be trained to facilitate achievement. Mental "athletes" don't show their genius outwardly, until they are making decisions. Their prowess can be observed in their responses to new information, how they handle price volatility, losses, and gains, and in their analytic techniques and intuitive judgment.

CHEMICAL STABILIZERS

Dietary chemicals, medications, and illicit drugs have numerous effects on financial judgment (as reviewed in Chapter 4). Dietary substances, such as the fats consumed, caffeine intake, and alcohol consumption can change decision making profoundly, yet few investors consider these substances as problematic. Probably the reason chemicals and diet are largely ignored by traders and investors is that the effects are subtle. Additionally, substances such as caffeine can be beneficial for some individual investors while impairing the cognitive flexibility of others.

While dietary changes can lead to more flexible and adaptive decision making, there is no medication that does the same in all market conditions. For those with existing medical and psychiatric conditions, some medications appear to improve financial judgment and behavior. Some investors using beta-blocker medications for high blood pressure or performance anxiety have later found them useful for assessing investments. Beta blockers can allow a measure of detachment from the worries of the crowd. Selective serotonin reuptake inhibitors (SSRIs) have been used by CEOs for reducing their anxiety in leadership roles. One trader I described took lithium for bipolar disorder and self-modified his dose in response to his need for a few days of quick thinking, late-night working, and creativity. Personally, I don't endorse medications for improving investment decision making.

Illicit substances that some investors use to self-medicate, such as alcohol, cocaine, and amphetamines, often result in worse long-term outcomes. Traders who decompress after a day's work with a glass of beer are chemically dampening their anxiety and hypervigilance from a day on the job. Unfortunately, the alcohol disrupts their rapid eye movement (REM) sleep, leading to easy cognitive fatigue and slightly impaired judgment the following day. Traders who use stimulants (such as cocaine or amphetamines) at work are enhancing their dopamine function and increasing their confidence, but they may be dosing incorrectly and are at risk of addiction and permanent adverse events.

One professional poker player gamely reported that taking prescription amphetamines (Adderall) had helped him earn millions of dollars by increasing his alertness after long hours of play, relative to other players. Increased alertness is useful in cognitively exhausting games such as poker or chess, especially if one's opponents are unmedicated, but benefits for investors are unlikely.

SELF-DISCIPLINE

> *"Self-discipline is the single most important success factor. Without it, nothing else matters."*
> —Howard Fleischman, PhD, performance
> psychologist

Self-discipline is a personality trait that varies across individuals. Importantly, one's degree of self-discipline correlates with wealth level. In general, pursuing immediate gratification erodes prosperity. Self-discipline is a prerequisite to performing any of the self-help exercises in this book. Before embarking on a path of personal change, be sure you have the inner motivation to begin, the personal curiosity to explore, and the discipline to stay with the work when it becomes challenging. If you falter, then begin again.

Investing "rules" are useless for people who don't first have discipline. In fact, without discipline, one should stay away from any type of active, strategy-driven investing. So how can those who are undisciplined become more organized?

The essence of self-discipline is emotion management, which is different from emotional control. Management focuses on awareness and redirection rather than confrontation and repression of emotion. The internal tension resulting from the confrontation with and repression of undesired feelings strains cognitive resources. At the turn of the nineteenth century, Sigmund Freud even theorized that the repression of emotions was the root cause of mental illness. Redirecting strong emotions towards productive outlets is important for maintaining personal happiness and harmonious relations with others.

Self-discipline does not refer to a rigid adherence to an investment strategy, but rather to a focused and organized mind-set about examining investments. Many investors have inadequate experience and education with the markets to understand proper boundaries and the role of flexibility.

Traders such as "Stock Market Wizard" Mark D. Cook have learned to use emotional awareness and self-discipline to their advantage. Cook is considered one of the most successful short-term traders in history. Cook remarks, "Whenever I am most fearful of the market, that emotion helps me decide to go long and buy.... Whenever my fears become overwhelming, my discipline tells me to buy and discipline must win out or you are doomed to failure."[15] It is not only important to identify one's emotional impulses, but Cook actually uses those impulses as contradictory trading signals. He summons enough courage to do the opposite of his strong emotional drives.

Techniques for enhancing one's level of investing self-discipline are outlined in Table 21.1.

With a balance of self-discipline and cognitive flexibility, rules can be applied to enhance performance without inducing excessive rigidity. Short-term investors and traders will especially benefit from the following ideas, but analysts and portfolio managers can use them as well.

1. **Start every day fresh.** Options specialist Richard Friesen, no matter what his recent performance had been, reminded himself daily that risks were lurking in the markets by thinking: "There's a bullet coming toward my head today, and I've got to figure out where it's coming from and how to stop it." This mantra brought down overconfidence, instilled humility, and encouraged preparedness.

2. **Invest an amount of money that's comfortable.** If you are fearful or excited about the money you have on the line or what you stand to gain

TABLE 21.1 Identifying the Emotional Precipitants of Lapses in Self-Discipline

Self-Discipline	Questions to Diagnose Lapses
Self-Awareness	What feelings compel you to break your personal rules? Is this a pattern for you? What are your reasons or rationalizations?
Perspective	What do you stand to lose by exercising self-discipline?
Courage	What has prevented you from creating a strategy or disciplined mindset? What are the tough issues you'd prefer not to address?
Structure	Can you design a program of analysis that fits well into your strengths but does not overlook other key factors?

from a trade, then your judgment will be useless, and you're not going to think clearly. Don't invest more than you can tolerate losing. When emotions become overwhelming, "throw a maiden in the volcano."

3. **Plan and anticipate, don't react**. Market Wizard Linda Bradford Raschke counsels, "Know what you are going to do *before* the market opens."[16] Mark Cook remarks, "Planning is the objective part of trading. Start with the worst case scenario and work from there.... Once you are in a trade, emotions take over, so the plan must be in place before the activity takes place."[17]

CREATING A DECISION JOURNAL

Some researchers believe that traders can learn to behave more rationally by recognizing and learning from their past mistakes. Journaling is the most commonly prescribed method. Documenting both the assumptions that drive decisions and the resulting consequences of those decisions provides valuable insight into patterns of strength and weakness in judgment.

A psychological decision journal should follow a format approximately like that in Table 21.2. The format should be modified to fit your specific decision process. As trading psychologist Brett Steenbarger points out, keeping a decision journal is an important part of a trader's daily training and practice. While athletes exercise their bodies and hone their physical techniques, investors need to be aware of defects and advantages in their mental game.[18] While the journaling process may seem excessively cumbersome and time consuming, consider that physical athletes must spend hundreds of hours in practice and training for each hour of actual competition. If you have difficulty following such a template, then simplify it until acceptable.

TABLE 21.2	Questions that May Help in the Development of a Psychological Decision Journal (should be supplemented by a quantitative journal)

Psychological Decision Journal: Ask Yourself These Questions and Document Your Responses.

Predecision	What are my qualitative reasons for investing in this security? Prioritize and list them in order of importance.
	How am I feeling about this investment?
	What is my level of confidence in this decision?
	What is my advantage?
	Why have others not identified this opportunity?
	What objective changes in conditions will change my decision?
	What are my specific sell criteria?
Postdecision, Pre-outcome	Am I doubting or feeling anything about my decision?
Postoutcome	Was it an accurate decision?
	Were there any flaws in the judgment or decision-making process?
	Can I find any patterns that this decision shared with my previous decisions?
	Did I deviate from my investment philosophy?
	What were the most successful aspects of this decision?

After monitoring dozens of decisions, it is helpful to review the data you gathered. Look for patterns in your feelings and decisions. Because feelings distort how we evaluate information and assess consequences, observe whether your feelings had anything to do with your judgments.

This psychological decision journal template should be used as a complement to a standard spreadsheet format with quantifiable statistics such as style of trading (swing trade, day trade, long-term position investment), stop boundaries (both time and price), and objectives (price, news, time, or fundamental value). Important data to measure include your expected risk/reward probabilities (based on historical analysis), expected and actual profit/loss per trade, number of long and short transactions, number of winning and losing trades, time spent holding losing trades versus winners, and the profitability of strategies in different market environments.[19]

Biases can be detected not only in your responses on the psychological decision template, but also in the statistical data. For example, by comparing the duration of winning and losing positions, one can find evidence of loss aversion (holding losers longer than winners). Having more winning trades during bullish or bearish markets may indicate that one's strategy or decision process is biased towards periods of favorable sentiment. Whatever the bias, it will remain problematic until it is dragged out into the light of day.

The next chapter discusses more involved strategies for psychological management when dealing with losses, fear, or stress.

CHAPTER 22

Change
Techniques

Going Deep

"*[Profitability] comes when the investor realizes that investment success does not come from external control, but from internal control.*"
—Van K. Tharp

This chapter deals with techniques for minimizing excessive risk perception, stress, and anxiety. An entire chapter is needed about these emotions because they are the chief result of activation in the brain's loss avoidance system and probably the leading cause of investing errors. These emotions drive such individual and collective investor mistakes as the disposition effect, the equity premium puzzle, overestimation of low probability risks, and market panics. Collectively, emotions generated by the loss avoidance system affect perception and pricing of securities, leading to some of the best opportunities for courageous investors (as explained in the next chapter).

Theoretically, it should be relatively straightforward to minimize these emotions. Unfortunately, pain and potential loss activate automatic neural processes. They function beneath conscious awareness, and it is very difficult to avoid their influence. Research cited in this book documents that even professional traders and investors are susceptible to loss aversion and the disposition effect (holding losers too long). It appears that experience, even with frequent performance feedback and financial incentives, is inadequate to entirely eliminate biases originating in the brain's loss avoidance system.

In fact, biases such as loss aversion are exacerbated by market losses. For example, in Professor Baba Shiv's $20 coin-flipping experiment with brain-damaged and normal subjects (see Chapter 15), the normals' performance actually deteriorated over the course of the experiment. Participants became more irrational, abstaining from the gamble more frequently and making less money over time.

Loss avoidance mistakes are very costly in terms of lost returns, so how can they be reduced? A number of investment advisers have approached me with a question: how can they sell risky products to their clients when they know that their clients will be angry and bail out after one quarter of underperformance? It is difficult for them to watch their clients' wealth stagnate in cash accounts, but they know that their clients might be too nervous if they own more stocks.

Education and experience should be the best techniques for reducing these investors' biases. Education is useful, but it is also intellectual, and doesn't connect with their anxiety during a down quarter. Deeper psychological techniques, which are outlined briefly in this chapter, are likely to be helpful for excessively risk-averse investors and clients.

DEALING WITH FEARFUL AND OVERCONFIDENT CLIENTS

For investment advisers who have had no training in working with anxious clients, the experience can be aggravating. During market downturns is when the truly anxious and risk averse clients become apparent. Some advisers have mentioned to me that they cannot believe their clients' responses on risk tolerance questionnaires. Many clients think they can handle volatility, but when it happens, they become panicked. Advisers have jokingly mentioned that the frequency of worried client telephone calls to their offices is a contrarian market indicator.

So what can advisers do to calm their stressed-out clients? There are many techniques, such as full accommodation with their wish to sell, requesting to sell a small part of their position to relieve the pressure ("throwing a maiden in the volcano"), or a conversation which attempts to calm their loss avoidance system and help them retain a long-term focus. I've prepared a script that financial advisers can use with worried clients during volatility (see Table 22.1). I use the acronym "IDEAS" so that the script can be easily remembered. The same script can be modified to help manage client overconfidence, as seen in the secondary examples in the table.

If you are an investment adviser, you will want to alter the dialogue to your needs, but the gist of the table should apply to most emotion-loaded

TABLE 22.1	Script that Can Be Used with Fearful or Overconfident Financial Planning Clients (IDEAS)	

Ideas	Steps to Take	Example Questions for Fearful (F) and Overconfident Clients (O)
I	Inquire how they are doing.	(F): "How are you doing with the market action lately?" (O): "Have you been following any particular stocks lately?"
D	Describe what you heard them say. (Called *mirroring* or *reflecting*.)	(F): "Okay, so you're uncomfortable with the volatility." (O): "Okay, so you're excited by the prospects of Nanotech stocks."
E	Empathize with their feelings.	(F): "Naturally it's difficult for you to watch your savings fluctuate. Maybe we should sell a small part of your holdings to take the pressure off." (O): "Naturally, it's fun to research new and interesting companies."
A	Add another perspective. Also called *reframing*.	(F): "One of the greatest investors in history said: 'Buy when there is blood on the streets.' The best opportunities are during fearful periods." (O): "How could we satisfy your interest in volatile start-up stocks without risking your retirement savings?"
S	Suggest solutions.	(F): "If I remember correctly, you mentioned that you have a 10-year investment horizon. Try to avoid watching the market news or checking prices. The quarterly and yearly market action isn't important in the long-term." (O): "Why don't you use a trading account with money you can afford to lose. Why don't we set one up with 5 percent of your savings?"

interactions. The IDEAS script should help facilitate communication, and it assumes that you have an established relationship and you have already developed a financial plan and educated your clients about long-term risk and reward.

The IDEAS script cannot change deep psychological issues. Cognitive techniques for reframing anxious thoughts and attenuating the stress response are outlined in the following paragraphs. Additionally, anxiety and stress management techniques related to breath-work, meditation, and lifestyle are discussed.

COGNITIVE-BEHAVIORAL THERAPY AND STRESS MANAGEMENT

Much of the remainder of this chapter is devoted to cognitive-behavioral psychotherapy and stress management techniques. Cognitive-behavioral therapy (CBT) is a popular and effective form of psychotherapy used for everything from getting high-performers out of a slump to clinical treatment of anxiety and depression. CBT therapists help clients develop concrete coping skills and strategies. They use such techniques as: (1) challenging self-defeating beliefs, (2) teaching positive self-talk skills, (3) replacing negative thoughts, (4) desensitization or conditioning, (5) education about symptoms, and (6) teaching coping skills such as relaxation breathing.

CBT therapists have discovered that one's thoughts and feelings during stress are often repeating patterns. If the stressful pattern can be mentally broken, then the stress response is halted. Individuals should learn what their maladaptive, stress-inducing thoughts are. You can use the following exercises for assistance. Challenge your negative thoughts and consciously replace them with more adaptive scripts. If you do conscious thought replacement exercises daily, and keep track of the changes you notice in your daily life, you're likely to discover subtle improvements. In time, you will notice decreased reactivity to chronically stressful events, people, and circumstances.

Ask yourself these questions to disrupt negative patterns of thinking:

- Is there an alternate explanation?
- What is the evidence that this thought is true?
- What will be the effect of continuing to think this way?
- What is the best outcome, worst outcome, and most realistic outcome?
- What is the likelihood that this will happen?[1]

Record your responses to stressful events in a table like Table 22.2 in order to develop clearer comprehension of how they affect you.

The core skills learned in stress management programs are self-observation, cognitive restructuring (as noted above), relaxation training, time management, and problem solving. Self-observation is often practiced using a daily diary or journal (such as in Table 22.2). In the journal, people write down stressful moments of their day in the first column. In the next column, they write down antecedents to the stressful event. In the third column, they document their behavioral reaction, and in the fourth column, they describe the consequences of their behavior. Investors using this strategy can gain awareness of their automatic behavioral

TABLE 22.2 Journal Format for Recording Stress-Related Events

Antecedents (the Stressful Event and Preceding Triggers)	Stress Rating (from 0 to 100)	Behavioral Responses	Consequences (Outcome)	Rational Response (Reframing Options)
Example: A major financial loss.	80	Thoughts: "My quarter is ruined. I'm going to lose my best clients. Maybe I'm dong this all wrong." Feelings: Frustrated, angry, upset. Physiological response: Distractible, tension headache, craving alcohol and sweets, clenching teeth, stomach churning, tight chest. Behaviors: Started shouting at an analyst employee for a minor infraction, frequently looking away when in conversation, driving recklessly.	As soon as I realized I was off my plan, I immediately closed out the position. I'll have to work with the loss from here, but at least it's not bleeding anymore. Since closing the position, I've been able to generate a plan for the future. I'm nicer to my family and friends now.	Rational thought: "My quarter is what it is. I have strong relationships with my clients, and they trust me. This is the first time anything like this has happened. The markets are inherently uncertain, and I followed the best decision process I am aware of.

patterns, learn to identify the precursors (eventually, they may see repeating patterns), and reduce stress-related biases. Consciously addressing the triggers, reactions, and consequences encourages interruption and eventual prevention of the response pattern.

The most convenient stress-reduction techniques are simple alterations of daily patterns: idle conversation with supportive friends, exercise, prayer, and meditation. Some activities, such as religious service or yoga practice, combine two or more of the above.

YOGA, MEDITATION, AND LIFESTYLE

Study after study shows the benefits of exercise, especially cardiovascular exercise, for the average person. Exercise improves mood and focus and decreases stress. Social or team sports can be excellent sources of stress relief, especially those involving positive interactions with cohesive teammates.

Individual exercises such as yoga hone breathing and meditation skills while toning the musculature. Research indicates that yoga reduces the signs and symptoms of anxiety,[2] depression,[3] attention deficit–hyperactivity disorder (ADHD),[4] addiction,[5] and obsessive-compulsive disorder (OCD).[6] Additionally, emotional stability and patience increase during a regular yoga practice. Some studies have found improved cognitive function for research subjects randomized to learn and practice yoga versus those assigned to learn and practice swimming or dancing.

Studies have shown that meditation practice leads to improved emotional health. Meditation is an ancient technique practiced for spiritual, mental, and physical growth. There are several styles of meditation. Mindfulness meditation is one technique for learning to consciously and systematically work with one's own stress, pain, illness, and the challenges and demands of everyday life.[7] Mindfulness meditation has been shown to increase life satisfaction and bolster the immune system (increasing the antibody response to cold viruses).[8] On a psychological level, different styles of meditation have been shown to improve mood,[9] decrease anxiety,[10] lengthen attention span,[11] and enhance feelings of connectedness, gratitude, and compassion.[12] For example, "concentration" meditation cultivates the ability to direct attention. If one is practicing sustained attention on a daily basis, then the neurons that support concentration and impulse control will be strengthened.

Exercise and diet are the cornerstones of every doctor's recommendations for optimal health. Eating whole grains, lots of vegetables, and cold-water fish (and other high-omega-3 foods) all have benefits. Exercise can be anything from strolling to mountain climbing. The general idea with exercise is that you are gradually increasing (or maintaining) the limits of your endurance—exercise should be somewhat challenging, but not painful. Cardiovascular exercise is particularly beneficial for longevity. Exercise releases growth factors, both in the tissues and also in the brain, which enhances new neuronal growth and repair. Along those lines, a varying routine of exercise, in a playful or challenging context such as competitive sports, is especially healthy for the brain.

One of the most taken-for-granted factors in emotional well-being is social connection. Positive social interactions, including in one's work environment, are essential to long-term well-being. Many women know this fact intuitively, but for men, social connections can be easily put aside while work responsibilities dominate. Intimate friendships (in which outside problems can be vented) and family support significantly promote health.

SIMPLE STRESS REDUCTION

The stress and anxiety management techniques listed above require self-discipline and a commitment to practice; however, there are some immediate stress-reduction techniques that can be used anytime, anywhere. The easiest and most immediate technique for relaxation is deep breathing. The first time I was wired to psychophysiology equipment used to measure arousal in facial muscle tone and skin conductance, I thought I was relaxed. Then I was instructed to take a deep breath, and I was amazed at the underlying tension that was release from my body. I had been completely unaware of it. Try the following technique. On your inhale, silently count "one one-thousand (1-1,000), 2-1,000, 3-1,000," as you smoothly and evenly draw in the breath. Then pause for one beat. On your exhale, silently count-down "3-1,000, 2-1,000, 1-1,000" as you slowly and evenly let your breath out. After a one-count pause, repeat the cycle. You can do this breath-work for 5 to 20 minutes and experience significant stress relief.

Another way to reduce stress is to put your current troubles into a long-term, big-picture perspective. For example, imagine yourself on a mountaintop. See the view out over the plains and mountains beyond, or the ocean stretching into the horizon. Alternatively, imagine yourself looking up at the stars at night while hearing the crackle of a campfire. Slowly feel yourself expanding into the space all around you.

Another technique for reducing physical tension involves, paradoxically, contracting the tense muscles intentionally and holding the tension tightly for several seconds, and then relaxing. For whole body relaxation, progressively tense and release the muscles in your body from lower to upper. For example, tighten your feet, hold the tension for a breath, and then slowly relax the muscles. Then tighten your calves, hold the tension for a breath, and then release. Move upward, breath by breath, contracting and releasing your thighs, buttocks, abdomen, hands, arms, chest, shoulders, neck, face, and scalp. When finished sit silently, eyes closed, breathing slowly and evenly, for three to five minutes.

There is a large variety of tension reduction techniques that can be used to clear the mind and improve judgment when under stress. Aromatherapy scents such as lavender and jasmine improve alertness and relax the mind. Incense and soft music have been shown to reduce stress.

Walks in nature and warm baths are helpful for some people. Exercise, play, and dance are other methods of stress relief. Long-term changes in lifestyle, such as exercise, mediation, religious practice, and social affiliation, provide the best long-term relief. See below for a full list of anxiety-reduction techniques. Short-term tools such as muscle relaxation, deep breathing, and the long-term perspective are useful in a pinch. Anxiety and stress management techniques (both immediate and long-term) include:

- Breathing exercises
- Relaxation techniques
- Proper sleep
- Regular, vigorous exercise
- Laughing
- Meditation
- Time management
- Faith in one's meaning and purpose
- Reduction in caffeine and sugar intake
- Reduction in alcohol and marijuana consumption
- Psychotherapy, such as cognitive-behavioral therapy
- Herbal remedies such as chamomile tea and lavender aromatherapy
- For clinical anxiety disorders, medications such as selective serotonin reuptake inhibitors (SSRIs), benzodiazepines, and beta blockers are used

GETTING OUT OF A SLUMP

Many investors, at one time or another, find themselves making consistently bad decisions. Often, a losing streak is simply bad luck, but many investors believe it reflects problems with their strategy or personality. That's one reason why back-testing one's strategy (with the appropriate caveats) is so important—it supports confidence in your strategy during a series of draw-downs. As slumps weaken one's decision making, they may fuel a vicious cycle. In order to get through a slump, try the following cognitive techniques (many were adapted from trading coach Doug Hirschhorn and Shane Murphy's excellent book, *The Trading Athlete*[13]):

1. Recognize that slumps happen to everyone.
2. A slump is a statistical reality—go over your historical data and determine the length and breadth of the worst draw-downs over that time period. Chances are you aren't doing any worse now than you would have during some historical periods.

3. Remember that slumps are temporary. Slumps always reverse, though they may need some time. For example, value investors had trouble sticking to their strategies during the Internet bubble, when they severely underperformed the markets for approximately three years. Those who persisted were rewarded handsomely during 2000 and 2001.

4. Don't fight the slump. Cultivate patience and use this opportunity to do more fundamental research.

5. View the slump as a time to rest and regenerate. When the markets turn in your favor, be sure to reemerge even stronger.

6. Imagine that the slump is a much-needed vacation. This reframing technique will help you take advantage of the slump more constructively.

7. Remember: it's not about you. The markets aren't personal.

8. While slumps are inevitable, how you interpret it is within your control. If you wallow in self-pity, then it's hard to get anything constructive done. If you see a setback as a way to learn and improve your performance, then you'll emerge even stronger.[14]

9. If you continue to own declining positions that are further depressing you, then think to yourself, given the current fundamentals and technicals, "Would I buy this position today?" If not, then you shouldn't be owning it.

After a large loss, it is important to stay involved in investing, even in a very small way, to work through one's experiences. The memory of a traumatic event in the markets will linger as long as one stays uninvolved. There is a saying in psychotherapy that every session with the therapist begins at the same subconscious point where the last one left off. The same could be said of one's dealings with the markets. Psychologically, you will begin reinvesting in the state of mind induced by your last experience in the markets. It is very helpful to stay in the game and keep learning so that personal doubts don't overwhelm one's ability to grow and maintain perspective.

TRADING COACHES

Trading coaches are useful for traders who have an established edge, but who need some help refining their talent. Most investors and analysts need honest feedback about where they might be deceiving themselves. It is one thing to get price feedback from the markets, which may or may not be random noise. It is another thing to get an expert interpretation of one's decision process. If we truly want to optimize our financial decisions, then we've got to control what we can and ignore the noise. Trading coaches help filter the noise from what's really important.

Investment coaches share many "tricks of the trade" with athletic coaches. While athletes excel at physical activity, investors must excel in mental decision making. The primary functions of investor coaching are to: (1) facilitate goal setting, (2) establish a structure for practice and training, (3) review performance, (4) refresh passion for the decision process (not outcomes), (5) support self-confidence (especially during downturns), and (6) provide positive support and motivation.[15] All of these functions of coaching improve athletic performance, and from my experience with clients, they also enhance investment decision making.

Flavia Cymbalista

Some trading coaches work directly with traders' decision-related emotions in order to help them improve performance. Raised in Brazil and trained as a PhD economist in Germany, Flavia Cymbalista recognized a gaping hole in traditional economic theory regarding how people make decisions under uncertainty. She wondered, with uncertainty endemic to economic decisions, how could economics and market behavior possibly be rational?

She studied psychology in a postdoctoral fellowship at the University of California at Berkeley, and her interest in the philsophical/psychotherapy technique "focusing" led her to develop a methodology called MarketFocusing. MarketFocusing combines gut feeling and logic to improve decision making in markets. For several years, she has been helping traders improve their performance by accessing their bodily knowledge and increasing its reliability. In other words, she teaches traders how to develop their biological software.[16]

Cymbalista wrote a series of four articles for the magazine *Stocks, Futures, and Options* with the collaboration of George Soros. Cymbalista explained that Soros integrates subtle feelings and an analytical decision process to achieve his final market decisions. Soros provides evidence that some experts are utilizing intuitive decision-making processes in situations of uncertainty. In the case of Soros, self-awareness of his physical reactions may have contributed greatly to his success.

Denise Shull

Denise Shull is a neuropsychologist, student of modern psychoanalysis, and a long-time trader. She works with individuals and groups of traders to improve their performance. According to Shull, "I am having better results than I imagined with getting ... traders to think/talk/feel their feelings." Shull encourages traders to frame feelings as if they are objects, asking questions about feelings not in a personal way (which might arouse emotional defenses), but in an object-oriented format. She also finds that many traders are afflicted by repetitive mistakes, as if they are compelled to repeat an emotionally salient event from earlier in their lives.

Shull remarks that many traders are resistant to keeping journals. "As for journaling, that is the amazing part—how few traders actually keep one and how much resistance there is to doing it. I have gotten some clients to just speak into a tape recorder. The other tool I use—and love—is Microsoft One Note."[17] Shull emphasizes that any tool for keeping track of trader experiences is important. Self-analyzing what went wrong in one's investment decision making, in a curious nonjudgmental way, tends to improve subsequent performance.

MODELING OTHERS

When you feel an internal resistance to change, one solution is role-playing. Trading coach Van K. Tharp advises some investors to model other people, such as great investors. Imagine what state of mind such a super investor would need to be in to deal your current situation. Role-play that you are that super investor. Tharp's advice to model the state or person you want to be is borne out by studies into the origins of happiness.

One's well-being can be improved by imagining oneself as the person one would like to be. In a four-week study, researchers asked participants to regularly practice two mental exercises—counting one's blessings ("gratitude") and visualizing their "best possible selves." These practices boosted positive emotion, and continued to do so if practice was continued.[18] Of the two exercises, visualizing one's best possible self is the most beneficial for raising and maintaining positive mood.[19] As Tharp suggests, investors can extend this idea beyond happiness, to investing or any endeavor in which one would like to model excellence.

GROWING HAPPIER

Most people want to be happier. Yet few people understand how happiness is cultivated. The factors that predispose one to happiness are both innate (genetic) and learned. The best predictors of happiness are: (1) an optimistic personality style, with traits such as high extraversion and low neuroticism; (2) healthy social relationships (satisfaction with friendships and absence of loneliness); (3) a sense of purpose in life; and (4) overall life satisfaction.[20] Some of these factors are fixed, and some merit intervention.

In general, a person's happiness level is governed by three major factors, only one of which is predetermined. Those three factors include one's genetically determined set point, life circumstances, and happiness-related activities and practices.[21] In order to increase one's happiness level, activities that bring joy are the most straightforward to implement. Hobbies, religion, recreation, learning, and volunteering are some of the activities that promote happiness. Each person has to find a few that resonate. Sometimes a simple change in life circumstances, such as a move in residence or job, can be very beneficial for well-being (especially if there is some noxious element in one's current situation).

Positive psychologists emphasize that people can learn to feel happier by using a number of mental exercises. For example, people can schedule more positive experiences in their day. They can take time to appreciate and notice beauty. After losses, people are taught to focus on their strengths and coping skills rather than reviewing what went wrong over and over.

Many therapists advise clients to create a gratitude list in which they write-down everything they are grateful for. Every morning they add one or a few items to the list. Many long-term gratitude list makers have thousands of items in their lists, and they feel happier thinking about their good fortune when they (literally) count their blessings.

NEUROFEEDBACK

After I give talks about neurofinance, I'm invariably asked if I can give someone (usually the questioner) a brain scan to improve their investing. Through 2006 I had to answer, "I don't know, the technology just isn't available yet." However, exciting recent advances in functional magnetic resonance imaging (fMRI) technology, especially "real-time" fMRI, suggest that the days of investor scanning are almost here. But before we use real-time fMRI to improve trading talent, there are a few obstacles to surmount.

The MRI scanner is sensitive. The one-ton, $2 million MRI magnet requires its own ferrous-metal-free room, often at a major medical or research center. When scanning at Stanford, the scan itself may require one and a half hours, but the preparation time will be at least one additional hour, and the travel time is also significant—not to mention the cost of magnet time: $500 per hour. Subjects cannot be using psychoactive medications (even ibuprofen). Additionally, up to one-third of subjects move their heads too much, ruining the data. As a result of these barriers, it has been difficult to find Bay Area investors willing to commute to our facility.

Now that researchers have identified four areas of the brain that predict different biases in financial decision making, the NAcc, MPFC, anterior insula, and amygdala, we can compare new subjects to averages. Unfortunately, different individuals show strikingly different activations in these areas during experiments. On any given trial, it's often not easy to see the exact locations of activations—the fMRI images themselves appear noisy and imprecise for each trial. It is only the grouping and averaging of the results that produces the clean images seen in this book.

One breakthrough in fMRI that has brought routine investor scanning closer to reality is real-time fMRI (rtfMRI). rtfMRI allows users to visualize their own brain activity *as it occurs*. By watching how their own thoughts and feelings affect brain activations, they can learn to consciously change how they feel and think in response to certain events and before important decisions. rtfMRI is like biofeedback techniques, where users are trained to increase their skin temperature or reduce their heart rate by consciously altering their thoughts and feelings. But rtfMRI is more fundamental and more precise. People can actually learn to change how they think and feel using rtfMRI.

Christopher deCharms is a former Stanford fMRI researcher and now CEO of Omneuron, a venture-funded Menlo Park, California–based company. Omneuron is developing clinical applications for rtfMRI. The Omneuron researchers wondered whether people could learn to dial up or down activity in a particular brain region in order to produce a therapeutic effect.

In a 2005 study, deCharms reported that participants could control the amount of pain they felt from a heated metal cube by modulating activations in their rostral anterior cingulate cortex (rACC). The rACC is a brain region thought involved in pain perception and regulation. "When subjects deliberately induced increases or decreases in rACC fMRI activation, there was a corresponding change in the perception of pain caused by an applied noxious thermal stimulus."[22]

Chronic pain patients who underwent rtfMRI training reported decreases in their ongoing level of pain after training. "These findings show that individuals can gain voluntary control over activation in a specific brain region given appropriate training, that voluntary control over activation in rACC leads to control over pain perception, and that these effects were powerful enough to impact severe, chronic clinical pain."[23]

Neurofeedback techniques will initially be developed for the therapy of pain, anxiety, and other mood disorders. These disorders are clearly linked to dysfunctional neural regulation. Strategic business and investment decisions are complex, and optimization is still several years away as a rtfMRI technique. It is likely that psychological biases such as overconfidence (seen in the NAcc), risk aversion (arising from the anterior insula), loss aversion, herding, and attention and memory biases can be reduced through real-time "neurofeedback techniques." This technology holds great promise for investor performance enhancement, but it will be some time before we have reliable results across individuals given the logistical challenges outlined above.

In essence, neurofeedback techniques promise to be a sophisticated type of performance-enhancement. Neurofeedback gives users a framework and structure for the exercise of psychological tools, and it demonstrates the immediate results in a real-time brain image.

While there are likely to be therapeutic benefits for investors using neurofeedback in the future, there is no need to wait to begin positive change in your investing, or in your life. The other techniques mentioned in this chapter, such as yoga and meditation, have been in use for thousands of years, and classes are widely available. Additionally, CBT, coaching, journaling, social support, stress management, and healthy lifestyle choices (such as regular sleep and avoiding nighttime alcohol) are straightforward and accessible. Cultivating gratitude, visualizing your best possible self, and looking for the positive in your day will improve your sense of well-being. Incorporating any of these changes into your life will be an adjustment, but there will be positive outcomes for your stock portfolio and beyond.

MAINTAIN "LEARNING GOALS"

Stanford University psychologist Carol Dweck has spent decades studying the role of mental attitude in success. She realized that while it is important to success to have an optimistic mental attitude, it is more helpful to be interested and curious in personal growth and learning. What motivates people to be curious and open?

Dweck examined the effects of fixed external versus dynamic internal goals on performance. She used EEG to monitor cortical electrical activity in one group of students who had primarily performance goals (and fixed beliefs of achievement) and those who had predominantly learning goals. Previously Dweck had found that performance-oriented students were less able to learn from their mistakes and performed more poorly on challenging tasks. On EEG exam, they showed more attention to negative feedback and reduced time remembering and learning from such feedback.[24] Dweck's evidence suggests that one who tries to achieve a goal (such as financial gain or high investment returns) will experience worse outcomes than one who pays attention to learning and growing into the process of successful investing.

Dweck performed a study at the Life Sciences Secondary School in East Harlem. Most of the students at Life Sciences are low achieving. Dweck divided eighth graders into two groups and entered each group into an eight-session workshop. One group was taught study skills, and the second was taught both study skills and a module about how intelligence is not innate. The second group saw slides of the brain and learned about how the brain grows new neurons when challenged.

The results for the students in the second group were surprising. Their study habits and grades improved, and their math scores ended their long decline. "The only difference between the control group and the test group was two lessons, a total of 50 minutes spent teaching not math but a single idea: that the brain is a muscle. Giving it a harder workout makes you smarter. That alone improved their math scores."[25]

Optimal goals should remain internal and in progress. Knowing that one can improve leads to higher achievement. A focus on achievements themselves leads to lower returns. It's a sort of positive placebo effect. If one understands that it takes time, and they have hope that their performance can improve, then by exercising that bulky mental muscle, greater success will come. The beauty of the brain is its ability to learn and adapt and grow in response to any challenge. Only through humility, courage, curiousity, and exertion can unconscious biases be managed and mad markets channeled into money flow.

CHAPTER 23

Behavioral Finance Investing

Playing the Players

"The principles of successful stock speculation are based on the supposition that people will continue in the future to make the mistakes that they have made in the past."

—Thomas F. Woodlock[1]

The majority of this book is concerned with brain processes that bias *individual* investment behavior. However, when individuals' biases align, a diversity breakdown occurs, and market prices can suddenly become predictable. This chapter describes market patterns generated by collectively biased investors.

My interest in this area arose while working as a quantitative analyst. From 1995 to 1997 I designed neural network-based stock prediction software. My software had a slight advantage over random prediction, but it rapidly lost its advantage over time. Because quantitative prediction systems are easily replicable by others, leading to decreased profitability over time, I decided to model investor behavior. I assumed that mathematical arbitrage would have difficulty eliminating powerful, biologically driven, market price patterns.

As I researched behavioral finance, it became apparent that one can improve investment profitability using psychology-informed strategies. Fortunately, these strategies are quantifiable, so they can be tested and statistically confirmed. In my research I found that most outperforming behavioral strategies are long term and occasionally suffer large drawdowns. Their outperformance is not enormous, but in a world where

317

most fund managers underperform the markets year after year, behavioral considerations provide a crucial key to beating one's benchmark.

None of the strategies described here are "bullet-proof," and since they are all publicly known, there is a good chance that they will gradually disappear from the markets over time (perhaps not for a long time). In fact, many of the investing strategies that were originally considered "behavioral," such as value and momentum investing, are now part of mainstream finance. First, this chapter examines how one pro, Jim Leitner, uses other investors' biased risk perceptions to his advantage. Later in this chapter, we'll examine the outperformance of the value versus glamour effect, momentum investing, and other psychology-based investment opportunities.

HARVESTING RISK PREMIA

Fear can best be translated into financial language as "risk perceptions." When risk perceptions are high, so is the *risk premium*. Risk perceptions often deviate from actual risk due to the biases described earlier in this book: emotion (fear leads to overestimation of low probability catastrophes), time discounting (seeing an immediate danger), herding (investors observe each other for cues), uncertainty and mistrust (the veracity of government-published statistics is ambiguous), and loss framing (default is seen as a risk, not an opportunity). Over time, strategies that arbitrage risk perceptions can do very well.

Falcon Management principal Jim Leitner, profiled in Chapter 15, noted that in currencies, differences in risk perception are often reflected in interest rate yields. Currencies that are at risk of devaluation typically have higher-yielding bonds. Investors perceive risk of devaluation if they believe that the government may: (1) default on debt payments (bond yields); (2) significantly increase its money supply, which sparks inflation; or (3) devalue its currency via other means, such as deficit spending. Bond interest rates will rise for debt denominated in currencies that have a high perceived risk of devaluation. The risk premium is a dynamic function of investors' fear and myopia.

The Brazilian government was believed to be on the verge of defaulting on its debt, denominated in the Brazilian real, in 2002. In the years following its narrow avoidance of default, investors continued to perceive a high risk of devaluation in the Brazilian real due to representativeness. Brazilian bonds commanded relatively high interest rates, which were necessary in order to attract investors.

However, risk perception does not always reflect the actual risk. Investors who bet that interest rates would drop in a country perceived as financially unstable, such as Brazil, and rise in a financially stable country such as the United States, could have profited as the interest rates partially moved toward convergence over the subsequent years.

Leitner himself carries such trades, exploiting the differences in risk premia between high-yielding and low-yielding currencies. These trades must be held for years: "At times it doesn't work, but over many, many years it does." Leitner is taking advantage of other investors' biased risk perceptions.

Option premiums contain an estimate of future price volatility—in short, a measure of investors' risk perceptions. Leitner has found that investors' fear of potential losses leads to option mispricing: "Short-dated volatility is too high because of an insurance premium component in short-dated options." That is, investors become excessively worried about the short-term price performance of their investments, and thus they are willing to pay too much for the portfolio "insurance" provided by options. Another investor who profits from this effect, Richard Friesen, was profiled in Chapter 17.

A technique for taking advantage of both investors' overconfidence (specifically, miscalibration) and fearful myopia involves Leitner's observation that "longer-dated options are priced expensively versus future daily volatility, but cheaply versus the drift in the future spot price."[2] Most people cannot accurately estimate their confidence interval of future market price trends. As noted in Chapter 8, only 39 percent of CFOs correctly estimated the one-year stock market close in their 80 percent confidence interval. Investors are afraid of short-term volatility in their holdings, thus bidding prices for option insurance too high. But, over the long term, they are unable to foresee the likelihood that the option price will trend to another level based on their intrinsic miscalibration. That is, when looking out longer term, investors are overconfident in their ability to estimate future price ranges. When buying options for the short term, they are excessively myopic and fearful.

RISK PREMIA AND EXPECTATIONS

The 2001 book *Expectations Investing* by Michael Mauboussin and Bernard Rappaport, delineates a strategy for taking advantage of myopia in investors' expectations. The authors argue that the disparity between long-term corporate cash flow trends and investors' short-term cash flow expectations, as reflected in current share price, can be exploited as a source of alpha. The authors assert that in order to generate a positive alpha, one must develop superior forecasts of changes in others' expectations.

The Economist magazine alluded to the importance of expectations in driving prices while Brazil threatened debt default in the summer of 2002. Brazil was faced with increasing interest rates due to a contagion of risk perception after a meltdown in the finances of its neighbor, Argentina. Though Brazil was financially stable at current interest rates, a significant rise in rates and drop in the value of its currency, the real, would have created conditions in which Brazil was unable to meet debt payment obligations. Understanding this risk, speculators and risk-averse investors began to sell bonds. Their selling pressure gradually pushed interest rates higher. Interest rates were on the verge of surpassing Brazil's ability to pay, and the risk of a debt default suddenly became real.

Whether Brazil would default hinged on the confidence of bond investors. If the mass of investors expected default, then their bond selling would drive interest rates so high that the government would have been unable to pay its interest obligations. If investors regained confidence in the Brazilian government's ability to pay, then rates would drop, and default would be averted. Default hinged on the risk perceptions, and expectations, of market participants. *The Economist* magazine described the conundrum in terms of complexity theory and expectations:

> *More recently, a theory of "multiple equilibria" has gained support, in which there is more than one probable outcome, with market expectations usually the deciding factor. Brazil's total public debt, or its foreign debt, both public and private, could either be sustainable or could become unmanageably large, depending on what the markets henceforth expect.*[3]

Brazil ultimately did not default on its debt obligations. Soothing words from the world's deep-pocketed bankers rapidly restored confidence and diminished risk perceptions.

In other cases, investors' risk perceptions are too sanguine, even when risks are communicated clearly in official company reports. In a fascinating study, Professor Li Feng at the University of Michigan counted the frequencies of the words *risk, risks, risky, uncertainty, uncertain,* and *uncertainties* in 10-K Securities and Exchange Commission (SEC) filings for over 34,000 firm-years of annual corporate reports. He found that companies with large increases in risk-related word frequency *underperformed* companies with slight increases by a magnitude of 10 percent annually. Feng concludes, "I find that a stronger emphasis on risk in the annual report is associated with lower future earnings. The risk sentiment of annual reports can also predict future returns."[4] It appears, in this context, that even when companies explicitly remark upon their stock risk, investors underreact. Perhaps investors are focusing on the wrong information when developing expectations.

VALUE VERSUS GLAMOUR

One of the first identified market anomalies is the long-term outperformance of "cheap" value stocks relative to more expensive "glamour" stocks. Because of their lengthy use and outperformance, value strategies have been incorporated into modern financial education. Warren Buffett is one notable value-investing practitioner. Value stocks' shares sell inexpensively relative to the actual, underlying worth of their physical assets (such as buildings, factories, equiptment, patents, brand, or market penetration), their projected earnings growth, or their cash flow potential. Three widely used financial ratios for measuring a stock's value are: (1) the price-to-book ratio, (2) the price-to-earnings ratio, and (3) the price-to-cash flow ratio.

The price-to-book ratio measures the ratio of current share price to asset value. When the ratio is low, then a stock is relatively inexpensive, and when it is below 1, then a stock is selling for *less* than the value of all its assets. The price to earnings (P/E) ratio is another measure of value. When a company's current earnings are high relative to the share price, then the P/E ratio is low and the stock is relatively cheap. Subpar pricing happens for some companies, particularly if earnings expectations are low or its business is out of favor.

Value-investing strategies were described in the early twentieth century by Benjamin Graham, and in the latter half they were promoted by David Dreman. Researchers who investigated value strategies found that they outperformed significantly. In 1992, Professors Fama and French analyzed returns of U.S. stocks from 1963 to 1990.[5] They divided stocks into 10 tiers based on their price-to-book ratio. The average return of those stocks with the lowest price-to-book ratio ("value" stocks) was 1.53 percent per month higher than the average return on the highest price-to-book ratio tier ("glamour" stocks). When they analyzed stocks by P/E ratio, they found a 0.68 percent per month outperformance by the lowest P/E stocks (value) versus the highest P/E stocks (glamour). Value outperformance has been found in stock markets around the world.[6]

Using Factset software, in February 2005 I performed an analysis of value stocks that had both low price-to-book and low P/E ratios. I rank ordered all United States stocks over $250 million in market capitalization according to each ratio independently. Then I summed their two independent rankings and reranked them. The subsequent ranked list was divided into hundredths. Each year for the prior 15 years (1990–2004) the list was reordered on January 1 and then run forward one year. The average returns of each hundredth over the past 15 years are displayed in Figure 23.1. You can see that the annual returns of the top hundredths of inexpensive value stocks (far left) was almost twice as high as the top hundredths of "glamour" stocks (far right). The bar to the furthest right is the performance of delisted stocks.

MOMENTUM, SIZE, AND THE OPTIMAL PORTFOLIO

While value stocks tend to do well over the long term, finding the best short-term winners requires a different skill set. Researchers found that stocks whose prices rose over the prior six months tended to continue outperforming the market over the next two years. Momentum strategies exploit the "price momentum" that carries rising stocks even higher.

Professors Jegadeesh and Titman identified the momentum anomaly by ranking stocks into 10 tiers according to their past performance.[6] All U.S. stocks with available data were grouped into prior six month returns over the period 1963 to 1989. The researchers then computed the average returns of each tier over the next six months. The biggest prior winners outperformed the biggest prior losers by an average of 10 percent on an annual basis. In a later study, researchers demonstrated that the winners outperform the losers up to three years into the future.[7]

Other modifications of the momentum strategy have been examined. Professors Lee and Swaminathan report on a volume and momentum investment strategy in their 1999 paper "Price Momentum and Trading Volume."[8]

Their results depict the returns for three momentum strategies that consider prior trading volume. The early-stage momentum strategy buys low volume winners and sells high volume losers. The late-stage momentum strategy buys high-volume winners and sells low-volume losers. All strategies outperform for one year. The early-stage momentum strategy significantly outperforms the late strategy and the market for four years (35 percent outperformance). The late strategy begins to underperform the market after one year. The lesson is that low-volume winners are most likely to continue performing well. High-volume losers are likely to continue downward.

In the short term, unsupported momentum reverses rapidly. When prices jump without being correlated with a news event, then they tend to reverse direction over the following month.[9] In the case of unfounded price rises, there is no price momentum.

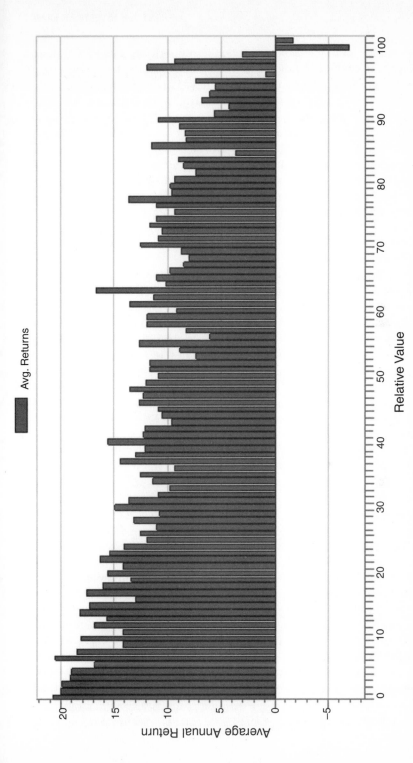

FIGURE 23.1 The average annual returns of U.S. stocks ranked according to their relative value (leftmost is deep value, rightmost is most expensive). Bars represent hundredths, ranked according to summed price-to-book and P/E ranks. Covers the period 1990 through 2004. The leftmost hundredths are deep value, while the rightmost are "glamour" stocks.

Momentum strategies can theoretically outperform, but they require higher turnover (shorter holding periods) and thus higher transaction costs. Furthermore, momentum strategies have been faltering in 2006. One large Wall Street bank closed its momentum trading desks in mid-2006 as a result of poor performance.

In an interesting reversal of the momentum effect over longer time periods, three- to five-year stock underperformers will, on average, reverse trend over the subsequent three to five years. Professor Richard Thaler measured the returns of all stocks traded on the New York Stock Exchange (NYSE) every three years from 1926 to 1982.[10] A "winner" portfolio of the 35 stocks with the best performance and a "loser" portfolio of the 35 worst-performing stocks was formed. Over the following three years, the average annual return of the loser portfolio was about 8 percent per year greater than the winner portfolio.

On a different note, small stocks tend to do better than large ones over time. Stock returns every year from 1963 to 1990 were examined for returns relative to the market capitalization of the companies. Stocks on the NYSE, American Exchange (Amex), and the NASDAQ were grouped into deciles according to their size. The average return of the smallest stock decile was 0.74 percent per month greater than the average return of the highest decile. The difference in risk is not enough to explain the difference in returns.

So how can all of these market anomalies be combined into a market-beating portfolio? Emory University professors Shanken and Kothari attempted to find the optimum asset allocation to take advantage of combined small stock, value, and momentum anomalies.[11] The authors sampled stocks from 1963 to 2000. They allowed for the possibility that the positive alphas of their three anomaly portfolios might not be as large in the future as they had appeared to be in the past. They found that even if portfolio alphas were expected to be just a quarter of the size they were in the past, an optimal portfolio would invest more than half in value stocks and about one-third in momentum stocks. This strategy increased the annual expected return by about 0.6 percent, relative to the market index, holding risk constant. With alphas half of the historical level, the authors found that the increase in expected return is more substantial, almost 2 percent.

As we saw in Chapter 1, active investment management is a losing proposition for the vast majority of investors, both individual and professional. As a result, academics recommend that individuals buy index funds and avoid checking their prices for 10 years (for long-term investors). Index funds have low expenses, and they are likely to outperform bonds significantly over the long term (taking advantage of the equity premium puzzle). Risk management is easier with index funds than with a portfolio of individual stocks. Different types of index funds—sector, international, currencies, and commodities—can be balanced to create diversified portfolios with lower overall risk profiles. Buying and holding index funds for the long term is the highest-returning investment plan for most investors. However, if one checks their prices repeatedly, they will see more downside risk and will thus be more likely to sell.

"BUY ON THE RUMOR AND SELL ON THE NEWS"

The "Buy on the rumor and sell on the news" (BRSN) price pattern describes a phenomenon in which a stock price rises in anticipation of a positive event, and then falls immediately after the event happens. It appears to be caused by several biases. Many traders buy shares in *anticipation* of a positive event, such as a "better-than-expected" earnings report, a hyped product release, or good economic news. It is said that traders are "buying on the rumor" because the good event has not yet occurred. When the expected event does occur, prices often fall, which is the opposite of what was expected.

Investors' positive expectations for an anticipated event trigger the nucleus accumbens (NAcc). The NAcc drives excessive risk-taking. As the event approaches in time, investors' expectations for "better-than-expected" news increase due to the NAcc-induced effects of excitement, time discounting, and the exaggeration of expectations by desire. As a side effect of such overoptimism, the probability that investors will be disappointed also increases. One study that examined the BRSN effect during the Internet bubble found it to be strikingly consistent.

Professor Brett Trueman and colleagues at the University of California at Berkeley identified the BRSN pattern around the earnings announcements of Internet stocks. They analyzed a large sample of earnings announcements for 393 Internet firms over 1,875 firm-quarters between January 1998 and August 2000. They found that purchasing an Internet stock five days prior to its earnings announcement and then selling that stock at the open on the day immediately following the earnings release yielded an average market adjusted return of 4.9 percent. Shorting the same stock at the open the day after its earnings release yielded an average market-adjusted return of 6.4 percent when the short was covered at the market close five days later.[12] The optimism that was brewing around Internet stocks transformed into excitement around their earnings reports.

As with most diversity breakdowns in the markets, an exclusive focus on sentiment or behavioral indicators is inadequate for designing a market-beating strategy. Multiple conditions facilitate the "buy on the rumor and sell on the news" pattern in prices. Specific psychological and neuroscientific factors all amplify the emergence of this pattern in a stock, including:

- Significantly limited or ambiguous accounting information available.
- Excess liquidity available to traders.
- High vividness or imaginability of the concept (even a vivid name helps).
- A virtually "unlimited" potential market to drive revenues.
- Groupthink and herding (for example, unconfirmed rumors and media mentions).
- Preexisting optimism about the company or market sector
- Large potential magnitude of potential payoff.
- Perceived certainty of payoff.
- Recent trending price movement.
- Event is approaching in time.
- A high level of impulsivity in traders chasing the potential gain.[13]

Each of these factors can be reversed so that traders can take advantage of the pattern in a "Sell on the rumor, buy on the news" scenario, but the dynamics of such a strategy differs from BRSN.[14]

LIMITS TO ARBITRAGE

"Limits to arbitrage" prevent behavioral price distortions from being traded for profit. Patterns are easy to find in the markets, but finding patterns that can profitably be exploited after transaction costs and structural barriers (such as short-sale constraints) are accounted for, is much more difficult.

The limits to arbitrage fall into three distinct categories: short-sale constraints, size constraints, and transaction costs. Some preconditions prevent the shorting of securities on certain markets, such as the over-the-counter (OTC) bulletin boards or some foreign markets. In some markets, only market makers can short. In others, regulations prevent any shorting. Many brokerages will not allow shorting of securities priced below a certain dollar amount, particularly for smaller clients. Additionally, it is often the case that a broker cannot borrow the security for shorting.

Size constraints are represented by the inability to enter a substantial arbitrage position without moving the market into closing that arbitrage opportunity. In the worst-case scenario, unraveling large arbitrage positions pushes prices back into the former pricing inefficiency. Such a case was seen as Long-Term Capital Management considered exiting its positions.

Transaction costs are one of the most overlooked aspects of investment. Transaction costs are typically assumed to include commissions and slippage in securities and up-front and redemption fees in mutual funds. Transaction costs in large-cap stocks can consume about 0.1 percent of capital for each purchase or sale of shares. Small and micro-cap stocks have much steeper transaction costs, sometimes up to 10 percent when the bid-ask spread is wide. Futures often have the smallest transaction costs—less than 0.05 percent. Active investors can lose a large portion of their profits through transaction costs.

One example of an obvious arbitrage opportunity that could not be executed involved the initial public offering (IPO) of Palm Inc. from 3Com Inc. In March 2000, 3Com Inc. sold 5 percent of its wholly owned subsidary Palm Inc. in an IPO, retaining ownership of the remaining 95 percent. After the IPO, a shareholder of 3Com indirectly owned 1.5 shares of Palm (with full spin-off planned in nine months). At the end of the first IPO trading day, Palm shares closed at $95, thus valuing 3Com at more than $142. But 3Com was actually trading at $81, implying a market valuation of 3Com's significant businesses outside of Palm at *negative* $60 per share. Arbitrage seemed like a no-brainer, as the prices would likely converge within nine months, but it was virtually impossible to execute due to short-sale constraints (limited shares available to borrow). What should have been certain profits, gained through arbitrage, were unavailable to many attentive traders.

BEHAVIORAL FINANCE FUND PERFORMANCE

Behavioral finance represents the application of principles of investor psychology to investing. Flagship funds using behavioral finance-based investment strategies have outperformed their benchmarks significantly over time. One notable fund group is Fuller and Thaler Asset Management. They have achieved an average alpha of almost 4 percent on their funds since inception. However, a recent flood of money into behavioral strategies may have eliminated some of the advantages that Fuller and Thaler's strategies held.

LGT Capital Management of Lichtenstein utilizes principles of behavioral finance, in combination with technical and fundamental market valuation approaches, to design portfolios. Some LGT strategies take advantage of "asymmetric risk perception as well as the various investment horizons of investors."[15] According to an LGT brochure, "the financial markets deal not in realities, but in expectations, or more precisely *changes in expectations*."[16] LGT's funds have consistently delivered lower volatility than the markets and higher returns since inception. Their flagship fund is up 65 percent since opening on December 31, 1998, while the Morgan Stanley Global Index is up 43 percent.

Dimensional Fund Advisers manages $69 billion and was founded by two students of Professors Fama and French at the University of Chicago Business School. Fama and French were two of the most adamant proponents of the efficient markets hypothesis in the latter half of the twentieth century. However, Professor French currently posts excellent examples of market-beating portfolios on his web site,[17] and both men are on the advisory board of Dimensional. Dimensional follows three principles in stock selection. They allocate more assets to equities over fixed income (taking advantage of the equity risk premium. They invest more in small company stocks due to their higher long-term returns. And they allocate more resources to lower-priced value stocks, which have higher expected returns than higher-priced growth stocks.[18]

Other notable behavioral finance-oriented fund groups with significant track records include funds managed by David Dremen and LSV Asset Management (LSV was founded by some of the pioneers in behavioral finance). In the past few years, many large banks and fund management organizations have been jumping on the behavioral finance bandwagon, including Morgan Stanley and J. P. Morgan.

BEHAVIORAL INVESTMENT PRODUCTS

Individual investors can benefit from investment programs that accommodate their emotional biases. Currently, few Americans save enough for retirement, often due to a combination of several biases: time discounting (procrastinating the pain of saving), inertia (indecision and doing nothing), fear of market risk (avoiding investing in the equity markets), and overconfidence (believing one can save more later).

Professors Shlomo Benartzi and Richard Thaler designed a retirement program to improve savings rates, which they called the SMarT plan. "Our goal was to design a program to help those employees who would like to save more, but lack the willpower to act on this desire." The program has been a tremendous success in increasing retirement savings rates, with the average saving rates for SMarT program participants increasing from 3.5 percent to 13.6 percent over the course of 40 months.[19]

The SMarT plan is implemented as follows. First, employees are approached about increasing their contribution rates approximately three months before their scheduled pay increase. Second, once they join, their contribution to the plan is increased beginning with the first paycheck after

a raise. Third, their contribution rate continues to increase on each scheduled raise until the contribution rate reaches a preset maximum. Fourth,
the employee can opt out of the plan at any time.

In order to encourage employees to sign up for the SMarT plan, the researchers postponed the pain of the savings until later. Additionally, they
allocated a higher percentage of employees' future raises to go toward
their savings, so short-term pain was minimized. Furthermore, the design-
ers take advantage of automaticity, which ensures that individuals do not
need to take action in order to save. U.S. government legislation passed
in 2006 requires the implementation of "opt-out" retirement programs. In
opt-out programs, employees are automatically placed into a retirement
savings scheme, with a percentage of income regularly deducted toward
retirement savings. They will remain enrolled every year unless they take
action to be removed. Every year they are automatically reenrolled. Such
automaticity challenges individual inertia.

Besides the SMarT plan, there are numerous other attempts to include
behavioral finance principles in the design of financial products. "Goal-
based investing" harnesses the psychological bias of mental accounting by
placing one's savings in multiple targeted portfolios. The goal of this approach is to simplify the investing process and render it more understand-
able.

"Life cycle" asset allocation strategies increase the distribution of investments to fixed-income (bonds) from riskier equities as one ages. This
is an automatic change based on one's age at enrollment, and it accommo-
dates the natural increase in risk aversion beyond retirement.

FINAL NOTES

This book has covered a lot of ground, not all of it elegantly or concisely.
While the field of behavioral finance is now getting its "legs," neurofinance
is still in its infancy. However, the tools offered by neurofinance, such as
neurofeedback, brain-oriented coaching and training paradigms, and financial personality typing, are coming along quickly. The main factor impeding
progress is the lack of trained talent to both perform research and apply it
to investing. Another impediment is the lack of portable, comfortable, and
convenient neuroscience technologies.

Is "neurofinance" shaping up to be another fad—here today, gone tomorrow? I don't think so. Neurofinance has not yet been significantly
exploited by investors, both on a personal level and in the design of
portfolios and trading strategies. Neurofinance has a fundamental power,
based on the inner processing of millions of interacting brains, and rooted

in psychological laws. As the decades pass, technology becomes more developed, and acceptance increases, neurofinance will make large-scale contributions to the investing process. However, neurofinance is currently in its infancy.

It is my hope that individual investors can apply some of the insights and knowledge in this book to their daily investing. While emotions, motivations, cognitive biases, and emotional defenses are all subconscious, learning about them brings them closer to the surface. With awareness and discipline, action can be taken to correct one's vulnerabilities and enhance one's strengths. People have been struggling with unconscious biases for millennia. Training regimens, such as those provided by meditation and yoga, have been developed and honed over generations.

Suggestions for self-help are distributed throughout this book, but one caveat is that without an external coach or guide, the use of these techniques can be easily disregarded (another emotional defense!).

If you choose to embark on a journey of inner work, remember that the outer rewards (profits) are only a side benefit. A happy and rewarding life is the ultimate achievement.

Thank you for taking the time to read this book. Please feel free to communicate questions and comments to the author. May you be prosperous and well.

Notes

Introduction

1. Lewis, M. 1990. *Liar's Poker* New York: Penguin, p. 15.
2. Loewenstein, R. 2000. *When Genius Failed: The Rise and Fall of Long Term Capital Management.* New York: Random House.
3. MacKay, C. 1841. *Extraordinary Popular Delusions & the Madness of Crowds.* Crown Publishing: London. www.historyhouse.com/book.asp?isbn=051788433X.
4. Powers, R. 2005. *Mark Twain: A Life.* New York: Free Press, p. xi.
5. Twain, Mark. 1872. *Roughing It,* Chapter 26. Free Public Domain Books from the Classic Literature Library. http://mark-twain.classic-literature.co.uk/roughing-it/.
6. Ibid.
7. Ibid., Chapter 58.
8. Ibid.
9. Statman, M. 2003. "A Century of Investors." *Financial Analysts Journal* 59(3) (May/June).

Chapter 1: Markets on the Mind

1. Johnson, R. L. 1998. "Day Trading: An Analysis of Public Day Trading at a Retail Day Trading Firm." www.nasaa.org/searchable_files/1405/Day_Trading_Analysis.pdf.
2. Frew, A. 1999. "States Spearhead the Crackdown on Day Trading, but Is It Warranted?" Money.CNN.com. September 1. http://money.cnn.com/1999/09/01/investing/daytrade_regulators/.
3. Karmin, C., and M. Sesit. 2005. "Currency Markets Draw Speculation, Fraud Day Traders Find New Outlet in Foreign-Exchange Wagers; 'A Lot of George Soros Wannabes.'" *Wall Street Journal,* July 26.
4. Barber, B. M., Yi-Tsung Lee, Yu-Jane Liu, and Terrance Odean. 2005. "Who Loses from Trade? Evidence from Taiwan." AFA 2006 Boston Meetings Paper. http://ssrn.com/abstract=529062.

5. Odean, T., and B. Barber. 2000. "Trading Is Hazardous to Your Wealth: The Common Stock Investment Performance of Individual Investors." *Journal of Finance* 55(2): 773–806.

6. Odean, T. 1998. "Are Investors Reluctant to Realize Their Losses?" *Journal of Finance* 53: 1775–1798.

7. Odean, T., and B. Barber. 2000. "You Are What You Trade," *Bloomberg Personal Finance*, May.

8. Odean, T. 1999. "Do Investors Trade Too Much?" *American Economic Review*, December: 1279–1298.

9. Bogle, J. C. 2005. "The Mutual Fund Industry Sixty Years Later: For Better or Worse?" *Financial Analysts Journal* 61(1) (January/February): 15–24.

10. Dalbar Press Release. 2003. DALBAR's 2003 update to the Quantitative Analysis of Investor Behavior (QAIB) www.dalbarinc.com/content/printerfriendly.asp?page=2003071601.

11. Wermers, R. 2000. "Mutual Fund Performance: An Empirical Decomposition into Stock-Picking Talent, Style, Transactions Costs, and Expenses." *Journal of Finance* 55(4) (August).

12. Carhart, M. 1997. "On Persistence in Mutual Fund Performance." *Journal of Finance* 52: 57–82.

13. Wermer, et al., 2006. "Can Mutual Fund Stars Really Pick Stocks? New Evidence from a Bootstrap Analysis." SSRN working paper.

14. Mizrach, B., and S. Weerts. 2004. "Experts Online: An Analysis of Trading Activity in a Public Internet Chat Room." Departmental Working Papers 200412, Rutgers University, Department of Economics.

15. Georgette, J. 2002. "Putting Away the Darts after 14 Years: The *Wall Street Journal*'s Dartboard Ends Its Run." *Wall Street Journal*, April 18.

16. Michaely, R., and K. Womack. 2005. "Market Efficiency and Biases." In Richard Thaler (ed.), *Advances in Behavioral Finance*, vol. II. New York: Russell Sage Foundation.

17. Barber, B., and D. Loeffler. 1993. "The 'Dartboard' Column: Second-Hand Information and Price Pressure." *Journal of Financial and Quantitative Analysis* 28: 273–284.

18. Barber, B., R. Lehavy, M. Nichols, and B. Trueman. 2001. "Can Investors Profit from the Prophets? Security Analyst Recommendations and Stock Returns." *Journal of Finance*, 61, no. 2: 531–563.

19. Fuller, R. 1998. "Behavioral Finance and the Sources of Alpha." *Journal of Pension Plan Investing* 2(3) (Winter).

20. Ibid.

21. An average alpha computed from "returns since inception" versus the benchmarks. Taken from 2Q 2006 report. www.fullerthaler.com/QuarterlyReview/newsltr2006Q2.pdf.

22. Mauboussin, M. 2006. *More Than You Know*. New York: Columbia University Press.
23. Ibid., p. 83.
24. Hirshleifer, D., and T. Shumway. 2003. "Good Day Sunshine: Stock Returns and the Weather." *Journal of Finance* 58(3) (June): 1009–1032.
25. Kamstra, M., L. Kramer, and M. Levi. 2003. "Winter Blues: A SAD Stock Market Cycle." *American Economic Review* 93(1) (March): 324–343.
26. Limpaphayom, P., P. Locke, and P. Sarajoti. 2005. "Gone with the Wind: Chicago Weather and Futures Trading." 2005 FMA Annual Meeting conference paper. www.fma.org/Chicago/Papers/gloom_doom_weather_futures_trading.pdf.
27. Krivelyova, A., and C. Robotti. 2003. "Playing the Field: Geomagnetic Storms and the Stock Market." Working paper, Federal Reserve Bank of Atlanta.
28. Yuan, K. Z., L. Zheng, and Q. Zhu. 2001. "Are Investors Moonstruck? Lunar Phases and Stock Returns." September 5. http://ssrn.com/abstract=283156 or http://dx.doi.org/10.2139/ssrn.283156" \t "_blank.
29. Clarke, R., and M. Statman. 1998. "Bullish or Bearish?" *Financial Analysts Journal*, May/June.
30. Fisher, K., and M. Statman. 2000. "Investor Sentiment and Stock Returns." *Financial Analysts Journal*, March/April.
31. Ibid.
32. Ibid.
33. Fisher, K., and M. Statman. 2004. "Sentiment, Value, and Market-Timing." *Journal of Investing*, Fall: 10–21.

Chapter 2: Brain Basics

1. Goleman, D. 1995. *Emotional Intelligence: Why It Can Matter More than IQ*. New York: Bantam.
2. Damasio, A. 1999. *The Feeling of What Happens: Body and Emotion in the Making of Consciouness*. New York, Harcourt Brace & Company.
3. Beer, J. S., R. T. Knight, and M. D'Esposito. 2006. "Controlling the Integration of Emotion and Cognition: The role of Frontal Cortex in Distinguishing Helpful from Hurtful Emotional Information." *Psychological Science* 17 (May): 448–453.
4. Bechara, A., A. R. Damasio, H. Damasio, and S. W. Anderson. 1994. "Insensitivity to Future Consequences Following Damage to Human Prefrontal Cortex." *Cognition* 50: 7–15.

5. Bechara, A., H. Damasio, D. Tranel, and A. R. Damasio. 2005. "The Iowa Gambling Task and the Somatic Marker Hypothesis: Some Questions and Answers." *Trends in Cognitive Sciences* 9(4) (April).

6. Bechara, A., H. Damasio, D. Tranel, and A. R. Damasio. 1997. "Deciding Advantageously before Knowing the Advantageous Strategy." *Science* 275: 1293–1295.

7. MacLean, P. D. 1990. *The Triune Brain in Evolution: Role in Paleo-cerebral Functions*. New York: Plenum Press.

8. Prabhakaran, V., B. Rypma, and J. D. Gabrieli. 2001. "Neural Substrates of Mathematical Reasoning: A Functional Magnetic Resonance Imaging Study of Neocortical Activation during Performance of the Necessary Arithmetic Operations Test." *Neuropsychology* 15(1) (January): 115–127.

9. Davidson, R. J., D. C. Jackson, and N. H. Kalin NH. 2000. "Emotion, Plasticity, Context, and Regulation: Perspectives from Affective Neuroscience." *Psychological Bulletin* 126: 890.

10. Spencer, H. 1880. *Principles of Psychology*. New York: Appleton Press.

11. Heath, R. G. 1964. "Pleasure Response of Human Subjects to Direct Stimulation of the Brain: Physiologic and Psychodynamic Considerations." In R. G. Heath (ed.), *The Role of Pleasure in Human Behavior*. New York: Hoeber, pp. 219–243.

12. O'Doherty, J., R. Deichmann, H. D. Critchley, and R. J. Dolan. 2003. "Temporal Difference Models and Reward-Related Learning in the Human Brain." *Neuron* 38: 329–337.

13. Karama, S., A. R. Lecours, J. M. Leroux, et al. 2002. "Areas of Brain Activation in Males and Females during Viewing of Erotic Film Excerpts." *Human Brain Mapping* 16(1): 1–13.

14. Rilling, J., D. Gutman, T. Zeh, et al. 2002. "A Neural Basis for Social Cooperation." *Neuron* 35(2): 395.

15. Erk, S., M. Spitzer, A. P. Wunderlich, et al. 2002. "Cultural Objects Modulate Reward Circuitry." *Neuroreport* 13(18): 499–503.

16. Mobbs, D., M. D. Greicius, E. Abdel-Azim, et al. 2003. "Humor Modulates the Mesolimbic Reward Centers." *Neuron* 40(5): 1041–1048.

17. de Quervain, D. J., U. Fischbacher, V. Treyer, et al. 1994. "The Neural Basis of Altruistic Punishment." *Science* 305(5688): 1254.

18. "Lessons from the Brain-Damaged Investor." *Wall Street Journal*, July 21, 2005.

19. Chang, H. K. 2005. "Emotions Can Negatively Impact Investment Decisions" (September). Stanford GSB. www.gsb.stanford.edu/news/research/finance_shiv_invesmtdecisions.shtml.

Chapter 3: Origins of Mind

1. Schultz, W., P. Dayan, P., and P. R. Montague. 1997. "A Neural Substrate of Prediction and Reward." *Science* 275: 1593–1599.
2. Suri, R. E., and W. Schultz. 2001. "Temporal Difference Model Reproduces Anticipatory Neural Activity." *Neural Computation* 13: 841–862.
3. See note 1.
4. Medvec, V. H., S. F. Madey, and T. Gilovich. 1995. "When Less Is More: Counterfactual Thinking and Satisfaction among Olympic Medalists." *Journal of Personality and Social Psychology* 69(4) (October): 603–610.
5. Kirsch, I., and G. Sapirstein. 1998. "Listening to Prozac but Hearing Placebo: A Meta-Analysis of Antidepressant Medication." *Prevention & Treatment* 1 (June).
6. Talbot, M. 2000. "The Placebo Prescription." New York Times, January 9.
7. BBC. 1987. "Shares Plunge after Wall Street Crash." October 19. http://news.bbc.co.uk/onthisday/hi/dates/stories/october/19/newsid_3959000/3959713.stm.
8. Ibid.
9. Kunda, Z. 1990. "The Case for Motivated Reasoning." *Psychological Bulletin* 108(3) (November): 480–498.
10. Ditto, P. H., G. D. Munro, A. M. Apanovitch, et al. 2003. "Spontaneous Skepticism: The Interplay of Motivation and Expectation in Responses to Favorable and Unfavorable Medical Diagnoses." *Personality and Social Psychology Bulletin* 29(9): 1120–1132.
11. Westen, D., P. Blagov, K. Harenski, C. Kilts, and S. Hamann. 2006. "An fMRI Study of Motivated Reasoning: Partisan Political Reasoning in the U.S. Presidential Election." Working paper. October 1. http://www.uky.edu/AS/PoliSci/Peffley/pdf/Westen%20The%20neural%20basis%20of%20motivated%20reasoning.pdf.
12. Ibid.
13. Ibid.
14. Dawson, E., T. Gilovich, and D. Regan. 2002. "Motivated Reasoning and Performance on the Wason Selection Task." *Personality Social Psychology Bulletin* 28: 1379–1387.

Chapter 4: Neurochemistry

1. Foer, J. 2005. "The Adderall Me: My Romance with ADHD Meds." Updated Tuesday, May 10, 2005, at 7:26 A.M. ET. Slate.com. www.slate.com/id/2118315/.

2. Aghajanian, G., and E. Sanders-Bush. 2006. "Serotonin." *Neuropsychopharmacology: The Fifth Generation Process*. www.acnp.org/Docs/G5/CH2_15–34.pdf.

3. Grace, A. 2006. "Dopamine." *Neuropsychopharmacology: The Fifth Generation Process*. www.acnp.org/G4/GN401000014/CH014.html.

4. "The Top 300 Prescriptions for 2005 by Number of US Prescriptions Dispensed" 2006. RxList: The Internet Drug Index. www.rxlist.com/top200.htm

5. Reif, A., and K. P. Lesch. "Toward a Molecular Architecture of Personality." *Behavioral Brain Research*, 2003.

6. Canli, T., K. Omura, B. W. Haas, et al. 2005. "Beyond Affect: A Role for Genetic Variation of the Serotonin Transporter in Neural Activation during a Cognitive Attention Task." *Proceedings of the National Academy of Science*. 102(34) (August 23): 12224–12229 (Epub August 10, 2005).

7. Herrmann, M. J., T. Huter, F. Muller, et al. 2006. "Additive Effects of Serotonin Transporter and Tryptophan Hydroxylase-2 Gene Variation on Emotional Processing." *Cerebral Cortex* June 26 (Epub ahead of print).

8. Rogers, R. D., M. Lancaster, J. Wakeley, and Z. Bhagwagar. 2004. "Effects of Beta-Adrenoceptor Blockade on Components of Human Decision-Making." *Psychopharmacology* (Berlin), 172(2) (March): 157–164.

9. Lovallo, W.R., M. al' Absi, K. Blick, T.L. Whitsett, and M.F. Wilson. 1996. Stress-like adrenocorticotropin responses to caffeine in young healthy men. *Pharmacology Biochemistry & Behavior*, 55, 365–36.

10. Kuriyama, S., T. Shimazu, K. Ohmori, N. Kikuchi, et al. 2006. "Green Tea Consumption and Mortality Due to Cardiovascular Disease, Cancer, and All Causes in Japan." *Journal of the American Medical Association* (September 13): 1255–1265.

11. Gesch, C. B., S. M. Hammond, S. E. Hampson, et al. 2002. "Influence of Supplementary Vitamins, Minerals and Essential Fatty Acids on the Antisocial Behaviour of Young Adult Prisoners: Randomised, Placebo-Controlled Trial." *British Journal of Psychiatry*, 181 (July): 22–28.

12. Bernhardt, S. L. 2005. "Bipolar Disorder: Tempering the Mania of Manic Depression." www.have-a-heart.com/bipolar-depression.html.

13. Fieve, R. 1978. *Moodswing: The Third Revolution in Psychiatry*. New York: Bantam Books.

14. American Psychiatric Association. 2000. *Diagnostic and Statistical Manual of Mental Disorders*, 4th ed., Text Revision (DSM-IV-TR). 2000. Washington, D.C.: American Psychiatric Association.

15. Kim, S. W., J. E. Grant, D. E. Adson, and Y. C. Shin. 2001. "Double-Blind Naltrexone and Placebo Comparison Study in the Treatment of Pathological Gambling." *Biological Psychiatry* 49(11) (June 1): 914–921.

16. Di Chiara, G., and A. Imperato. 1988. "Opposite Effects of Mu and Kappa Opiate Agonists on Dopamine Release in the Nucleus Accumbens and in the Dorsal Caudate of Freely Moving Rats." *Journal of Pharmacology and Experimental Therapeutics* 244: 1067–1080.

17. Jayaram-Lindstrom, N., P. Wennberg, Y. L. Hurd, J. Franck. 2004. *Journal of Clinical Psychopharmacolology.* 24(6) (December): 665–669.

18. Bullock K and L. Koran. 2003. "Psychopharmacology of compulsive buying." *Drugs of Today (Barcelona)* 39(9) (September): 695–700.

19. Saxena S, Maidment KM. 2004. "Treatment of compulsive hoarding." *Journal of Clinical Psychology* 60(11) (November): 1143–1154.

20. Jacobs, A. 2005. "The Adderall Advantage." *New York Times*, July 31. www.nytimes.com/2005/07/31/education/edlife/jacobs31.html?ex=1160280000&en=7662c0a7d4339c43&ei=5070.

21. Phillips, P. 2005. "The 2005 World Series of Poker: How I Blew $350,000. Plus: My Chemical Weapon, Modafinil." Slate.com. July 7.

22. Nesse, R. 2000. "Is the Market on Prozac?" *The Third Culture*, February 28, 2000.

23. Kramer, P. D. 1993. *Listening to Prozac: A Psychiatrist Explores Antidepressant Drugs and the Remaking of the Self.* New York: Viking.

24. Knutson, B.,O. M. Wolkowitz, S. W. Cole, et al. 1998. "Selective Alteration of Personality and Social Behavior by Serotonergic Intervention." *American Journal of Psychiatry* 155: 373–379.

25. Del-Ben, C. M., Deakin, J. F., McKie, S., et al. 2005. "The Effect of Citalopram Pretreatment on Neuronal Responses to Neuropsychological Tasks in Normal Volunteers: An fMRI Study." *Neuropsychopharmacology*, April 13.

26. Lane, S. D., Cherek, D. R., Tcheremissine, O. V., et al. 2005. "Acute Marijuana Effects on Human Risk Taking." *Neuropsychopharmacology* 30(4) (April): 800–809.

27. Lane, S. D., Cherek, D. R., Pietras, C. J., and Tcheremissine, O. V. 2004. "Alcohol Effects on Human Risk Taking." *Psychopharmacology* (Berlin) 172(1) (February): 68–77.

28. Rogers, R. D., Lancaster, M., Wakeley, J., and Bhagwagar, Z. 2004. "Effects of Beta-Adrenoceptor Blockade on Components of Human Decision-Making." *Psychopharmacology* (Berlin), 172(2) (March): 157–164.

29. Deakin, J. B., Aitken, M. R., Dowson, J. H., et al. 2004. "Diazepam Produces Disinhibitory Cognitive Effects in Male Volunteers." *Psychopharmacology* (Berlin). 173(1–2) (April): 88–97.
30. Lane, S. D., Tcheremissine, O. V., Lieving, L. M., et al. 2005. "Acute Effects of Alprazolam on Risky Decision Making in Humans." *Psychopharmacology* (Berlin), April 14.
31. Morgan, D., K. Grant, H. Gage, et al. 2002. "Social Dominance in Monkeys: Dopamine D2 Receptors and Cocaine Self-Administration," *Nature Neuroscience* 5: 169–174.
32. Ibid.

Chapter 5: Intuition

1. Browning, E. S. 2006. "Keeping Cool amid Global Strife." *Wall Street Journal*, July 17.
2. Cohen, J. 2005. "The Vulcanization of the Human Brain: A Neural Perspective on Interactions between Cognition and Emotion." *Journal of Economic Perspectives* 19: 3–24.
3. Norretranders, T. 1998. *The User Illusion: Cutting Consciousness Down to Size*. New York: Penguin Viking.
4. Kaufman, M. 2002. *Soros: The Life and Times of a Messianic Billionaire*. New York: Vintage, p. 140.
5. Cymbalista, F., and D. MacRae. 2004. "George Soros: How He Knows What He Knows, Part 1: The Belief in Fallibility." *Stocks, Futures, and Options*, March 8.
6. Hirshhorn, D. 2007. Personal comunication, February 16.
7. Lefevre, E. 1923. *Reminiscences of a Stock Operator*. American Research Council.
8. Peters, E., I. M. Lipkus, and M. A. Diefenbach. "The Functions of Affect in Health Communications and in the Construction of Health Preferences." *Journal of Communication* 56: S140–S162.
9. Ibid.
10. Peters, E., and D. Västfjäll. 2005. "Affective Processes in the Decision Making by Older Adults." *Papers from the Workshop on Decision Making Needs of Older Adults*. Working Paper. //www7.nationalacademies.org/csbd/peters_paper.pdf#search=%22fear%20induction%20loss%20aversion%20curve%22.
11. Goleman, D. 1998. *Working with Emotional Intelligence*. London: Bloomsbury, p. 317.
12. Ibid., p. 319.
13. Loewenstein, G., and J. S. Lerner. 2003. "The Role of Affect in Decision Making." *Handbook of Affective Science*, ed. R. Davidson,

H. Goldsmith, and K. Scherer. Oxford: Oxford University Press, pp. 619–642.

14. Ibid.

15. Winkielman, P., K.C. Berridge, and J.L. Wilbarger. 2005. "Unconscious affective reactions to masked happy versus angry faces influence consumption behavior and judgments of value." *Personality and Social Psychology Bulletin* 1: 121–135.

16. Trujillo, J., B. Knutson, M. P. Paulus, P. Winkielman. 2006. "Taking Gambles at Face Value: Effects of Emotional Expressions on Risky Decisions." Working paper. http://www.gsb.stanford.edu/FACSEMINARS/events/marketing/pdfs%202006/2006_04-19_Winkielman_paper2.pdf.

Chapter 6: Money Emotions

1. Niedenthal, P., J. Halberstadt, and A. Innes-Ker. 1999. "Emotional Response Categorization." *Psychological Review* 106(22): 337–361.

2. Niedenthal, P. M., and S. Kitayama (eds.). 1994. *The Heart's Eye: Emotional Influences in Perception and Attention.* New York: Academic Press.

3. Lerner, J. S. and Keltner, D. (2000). "Beyond Valence: Toward a Model of Emotion-Specific Influences on Judgment and Choice." *Cognition and Emotion 14*: 473–493

4. Loewenstein, G., and J. S. Lerner. 2003. "The Role of Affect in Decision Making." In Davidson, R., H. Goldsmith, and K. Scherer (eds.), *Handbook of Affective Science.* Oxford: Oxford University Press, pp. 619–642.

5. Fredrickson, B. L. 2001. "The Role of Positive Emotions in Positive Psychology: The Broaden-and-Build Theory of Positive Emotions." *American Psychologist* 56: 218–226.

6. Lyubomirsky, S., K. M. Sheldon, and D. Schkade. 2005. "The Benefits of Frequent Positive Affect." *Psychological Bulletin* 131: 803–855.

7. Abbe, A., C. Tkach, and S. Lyubomirsky. 2003. "The Art of Living by Dispositionally Happy People." *Journal of Happiness Studies* 4: 385–404.

8. Bodenhausen, G. V., G. P. Kramer, and K. Süsser. 1994. "Happiness and Stereotypic Thinking in Social Judgment." *Journal of Personality and Social Psychology* 66: 621–632.

9. Isen, A. M., and B. Means. 1983. "The Influence of Positive Affect on Decision-Making Strategy." *Social Cognition* 2: 18–31.

10. Forgas, J. P. 1991. "Affect and Social Judgments: An Introductory Review." *Emotion and Social Judgments,* ed. J. P. Forgas. Oxford: Pergamon Press, pp. 3–29.

11. Ibid.

12. Isen, A. M., T. E. Nygren, and F. G. Ashby. 1988. "Influence of Positive Affect on the Subjective Utility of Gains and Losses: It Is Just Not Worth the Risk." *Journal of Personality and Social Psychology* 55(5) (November): 710–717.
13. Isen, A. 1999. "Positive Affect." *Handbook of Cognition and Emotion*, ed. T. Dalgleish and M. Power. Chichester, England: John Wiley & Sons.
14. Lyubomirsky, S., and S. Nolen-Hoeksema. 1995. "Effects of Self-Focused Rumination on Negative Thinking and Interpersonal Problem-Solving." *Journal of Personality and Social Psychology* 69: 176–190.
15. Mellers, B. A., A. Schwartz, and I. Ritov. 1999. "Emotion-Based Choice." *Journal of Experimental Psychology* 128: 332–345.
16. Fogel, S. O., and T. Berry. 2006. "The Disposition Effect and Individual Investor Decisions: The Roles of Regret and Counterfactual Alternatives." *Journal of Behavioral Finance* 7(2): 107–116.
17. Ibid.
18. Hurley, D. 2005. "Divorce Rate: It's Not as High as You Think." *The New York Times*, April 19.
19. Lerner, J. S., D. A. Small, and G. Loewenstein. 2004. "Heart Strings and Purse Strings: Carry-over Effects of Emotions on Economic Transactions." *Psychological Science* 15: 337–341.
20. Ibid.
21. Lerner, J. S., and D. Keltner. 2001"Fear, Anger, and Risk." *Journal of Personality and Social Psychology* 81: 146–159.
22. See note 19.
23. Bodenhausen, D., L. Sheppard, and G. Kramer. 1994. "Negative Affect and Social Judgment: The Differential Impact of Anger and Sadness." *European Journal of Social Psychology* 24(1): 45–62.
24. See note 19.
25. Sieff, E. M., R. M. Dawes, and G. Loewenstein. 1999. "Anticipated versus Actual Responses to HIV Test Results." *American Journal of Psychology* 112(2): 297–311.
26. Read, D., and G. Loewenstein. 1999. "Enduring Pain for Money: Decisions Based on the Perception and Memory of Pain." *Journal of Behavioral Decision Making* 12(1): 1–17.
27. Dunning, D., L. Van Boven, and G. Loewenstein. 2001. "Egocentric Empathy Gaps in Social Interaction and Exchange." In Lawler, E., M. Macey, S. Thye, and H. Walker (eds.), *Advances in Group Processes*, vol. 18. New York: Elsevier Limited, pp. 65–97.
28. Gilbert, D. T., E. C. Pinel, T. D. Wilson, and S. J. Blumberg. 1998. "Immune Neglect: A Source of Durability Bias in Affective Forecasting." *Journal of Personality and Social Psychology* 75(3): 617–638.

29. Mellers, B. A., A. Schwartz, K. Ho, and I. Ritov. 1997. "Decision Affect Theory: Emotional Reactions to the Outcomes of Risky Options." *Psychological Science* 8: 423–429.
30. See note 4.
31. Wilson, T. D., T. Wheatley, J. M. Meyers, et al.. 2000. "A Source of Durability Bias in Affective Forecasting." *Journal of Personality and Social Psychology* 78(5) (May): 821–836.
32. Gross, J. J., and R. W. Levenson. 1993. "Emotional Suppression: Physiology, Self-Report, and Expressive Behavior." *Journal of Personality and Social Psychology* 64: 970–986.
33. Keltner, D., K. D. Locke, and P. C. Audrain. 1993. "The Influence of Attributions on the Relevance of Negative Feelings to Personal Satisfaction." *Personality and Social Psychology Bulletin* 19: 21–29.
34. Gasper, K., and G, L. Clore. 1998. "The Persistent Use of Negative Affect by Anxious Individuals to Estimate Risk." *Journal of Personality and Social Psychology* 74: 1350–1363.
35. Lerner, J., and P. E. Tetlock. 1999. "Accounting for the Effects of Accountability." *Psychological Bulletin* 125: 255–275.

Chapter 7: Joy, Hope, and Greed

1. Securities and Exchange Commission 2000. "SEC Brings Fraud Charges in Internet Manipulation Scheme: Settlement Calls for Return of $285,000 in Illegal Gains." Case 2000-135. Washington, D.C., September 20, 2000. Securities and Exchange Commission Press Release. www.sec.gov/news/press/2000-135.txt.
2. Lewis, M. 2001. "Jonathan Lebed: Stock Manipulator, S.E.C. Nemesis—and 15." *New York Times Magazine*, February 25.
3. "Pump and Dump." 2000. *60 Minutes*. CBS News: New York, October 19.
4. Berg, S. Z. 2000. "Fraudulent Stock Schemes Still Vexing Investors, SEC." *TheStreet.com: Personal Finance: Investing*. TheStreet.com. December 16.
5. Elsbach, K. D., and Barr, P. S. 1999. "The Effects of Mood on Individuals' Use of Structured Decision Protocols." *Organizational Science* 181: 185–194.
6. Office of the New York State Attorney General Eliot Spitzer. 1999. "From Wall Street to Web Street: A Report on the Problems and Promise of the On-line Brokerage Industry." Prepared by Investor Protection Internet Bureau and Securities Bureau, 1189 PLI/Corp 355, 395 (1999). www.oag.state.ny.us/investors/1999_on-line_brokers/brokers.html.

7. Kahn, J. 1999. "On-line Brokerages Use Advertising in a Battle for New Customers." *New York Times*, October 4. www.nytimes.com/library/tech/99/10/biztech/articles/04trad.html.

8. Nofsinger, J. R. 2001. *Investment Madness: How Psychology Affects Your Investing ... and What to Do about It.* Upper Saddle River, N.J.: Prentice Hall, p. 129.

9. Levitt, A. 1999. "Plain Talk About On-line Investing." Speech at the National Press Club (May 4); see also Report of NASDR Concerning the Advertisement of On-line Brokerages (September 21, 1999).

10. See note 6.

11. SEC Office of Compliance Inspections and Examinations. 2001. "Examinations of Broker-Dealers Offering On-line Trading: Summary of Findings and Recommendations" 1 (January 26). www.sec.gov/news/studies/online.htm.

12. Cassidy, J. 2002. "The Greed Cycle: How the Financial System Encouraged Corporations to Go Crazy." *The New Yorker*, September 23.

13. Krugman, P. 2002. "Greed Is Bad." *New York Times*, June 4.

14. Kuhnen, C., and B. Knutson. 2005. "The Neural Basis of Financial Risk-Taking." *Neuron*, 47(5) (September 1).

15. Knutson, B., S. Rick, G. E. Wimmer, et al. 2007. "Neural Predictors of Purchases." *Neuron* 4;53(1): 147–156.

16. Heath, R. G. 1964. "Pleasure Response of Human Subjects to Direct Stimulation of the Brain: Physiologic and Psychodynamic Considerations." In Heath, R. G. (ed.), *The Role of Pleasure in Human Behavior* New York: Hoeber, pp. 219–243.

17. Knutson, B., G. W. Fong, S. M. Bennett, et al. 2003. "A Region of Mesial Prefrontal Cortex Tracks Monetarily Rewarding Outcomes: Characterization with Rapid Event-Related fMRI." *NeuroImage* 18: 263–272.

18. Knutson, B., C. S. Adams, G. W. Fong, and D. Hommer. 2001. "Anticipation of Monetary Reward Selectively Recruits Nucleus Accumbens." *Journal of Neuroscience* 21: RC159.

Chapter 8: Overconfidence and Hubris

1. Samuelson, P. 2002. "Is There Life after Nobel Coronation?" *Nobel Web.* http://nobelprize.org/economics/articles/samuelson/index.html.

2. Byrne, J. A., W. C. Symonds, and J. E. Siler. 1991. "CEO Disease." *Business Week*, April 1: 52–60.

3. Lenzner, R. 1998. "John Meriwether, Former Salomon Brothers Trader, Uses Leverage." Investing: Archimedes on Wall Street. *Forbes*, October 19.

4. Dreman D. 1977. *Psychology and the Stock Market: Investment Strategy Beyond Random Walk.* New York: AMACOM, p. 78.

5. Biais, B., D. Hilton, K. Mazurier, and S. Pouget. 2002. "Psychological Disposition and Trading Behavior." Unpublished manuscript.

6. O'Creevy, F, M. N. Nicholson, E. Soane, and P. Willman. 1998. "Individual and Contextual Influences on the Market Behavior of Finance Professionals." Unpublished manuscript.

7. Svenson, O. 1981. "Are We All less Risky and More Skillful than Our Fellow Drivers?" *Acta Psychologica* 47: 143–148.

8. Fischoff, B. 1977. "Perceived Informativeness of Facts." *Journal of Experimental Psychology: Human Perception and Performance* 3(2): 349–358.

9. Graham, J.R. and Harvey, C.R. 2005. "Expectations, Optimism, and Overconfidence." (April 12). Working Paper. http://icf.som.yale.edu/pdf/seminars04-05/Harvey.pdf.

10. Langer, E. J., and J. Roth. 1975. "Heads I Win, Tails It's Chance: The Illusion of Control as a Function of the Sequence of Outcomes in a Purely Chance Task." *Journal of Personality and Social Psychology* 32: 951–955.

11. Ibid.

12. Ibid.

13. Fischhoff, B., P. Slovic, and S. Lichtenstein. 1982. "Lay Foibles and Expert Fables in Judgments about Risk." *The American Statistician* 36(3): 240–255.

14. Hastorf, A. H., D. J. Schneider, and J. Polefka. 1970. *Person Perception.* Reading, Mass.: Addison-Wesley.

15. Cooper, A., C. Woo, and W. Dunkelberg. 1988. "Entrepreneurs' Perceived Chances for Success." *Journal of Business Venturing* 3: 97–108.

16. Stael von Holstein, C-A. 1972. "Probabilistic forecasting: An Experiment Related to the Stock Market." *Organizational Behavior and Human Performance* 8: 139–158.

17. Russo, J. E., and P. J. Schoemaker. 1992. "Managing Overconfidence." *Sloan Management Review* 33(2): 7–17.

18. Dittrich, D., V. Alexis, W. Guth, and B. Maciejovsky. 2005. "Overconfidence in Investment Decisions: An Experimental Approach." *European Journal of Finance* 11(6) (December): 471–491.

19. Kahneman, D., and M. W. Riepe. 1998. "Aspects of Investor Psychology." *Journal of Portfolio Management* 24(4) (Summer): 52–65.

20. See note 15.

21. Langer, E. 1975. "The Illusion of Control." *Journal of Personality and Social Psychology* 32: 311–328.

22. Presson, P., and Benassi, V. 1996. "Illusion of Control: A Meta-Analytic Review." *Journal of Social Behavior and Personality* 3: 493–510.

23. McClure, S. M., M. S. Gilzenrat, and J. D. Cohen. 2004. "An Exploration-Exploitation Model Based on Norepinephrine and Dopamine Activity." *Advances in Neural Information Processing Systems* 18.
24. Ibid.
25. Drobny, S. 2006. *Inside the House of Money*. Hoboken, N.J.: John Wiley & Sons, p. 72.
26. Ibid., pp. 76–77.
27. Ibid.
28. Ibid.
29. Ibid., p. 78.
30. Schwager, J. 2002. *Stock Market Wizards: Interviews with America's Top Stock Traders*. New York: John Wiley & Sons.
31. Schwager, J. 1992. *The New Market Wizards*. New York: HarperBusiness, pp. 467–468.
32. Oberlechner, T. 2004. *Psychology of the Foreign Exchange Market*. Chichester, England: John Wiley & Sons.
33. Kahn, H., and C. L. Cooper. 1996. "How Foreign Exchange Dealers in the City of London Cope with Occupational Stress." *International Journal of Stress Management* 3: 137–145.
34. Bloomfield, R., R. Libby, and M. M. Nelson. 1999. "Confidence and the Welfare of Less-Informed Investors." *Accounting, Organizations and Society* 24: 623–647.
35. Zacharakis, A. L., and D. A. Shepherd. 2001. "The Nature of Information and Venture Capitalists' Overconfidence. *Journal of Business Venturing* 16(4): 311–332.
36. Dittrich, D., V. Alexis, W. Guth, and B. Maciejovsky. "Overconfidence in Investment Decisions: An Experimental Approach." *European Journal of Finance* 11(6) (December): 471–491.

Chapter 9: Anxiety, Fear, and Nervousness

1. Cramer, J. 2000. "The Game of Calls and Strikes." *TheStreet.com*, March 17.
2. Roth, W. T., G. Breivik, P. E. Jorgensen, and S. Hofmann. 1996. "Activation in Novice and Expert Parachutists while Jumping." *Psychophysiology* 33: 63–72.
3. Monat, A. 1976. "Temporal Uncertainty, Anticipation Time, and Cognitive Coping under Threat." *Journal of Human Stress* 2: 32–43.
4. Van Boven, L., G. Loewenstein, D. Dunning, and N. Welch. 2005. "The Illusion of Courage: Underestimating the Impact of Fear of Embarrassment on the Self." Unpublished manuscript. Described in: Van Boven, L., and G. Loewenstein. 2005. "Cross-Situational Projection." In Alicke,

M., J. Krueger, and D. Dunning (eds.), *The Self in Social Judgment*. New York: Psychology Press, pp. 43–64.

5. "Abreast of the Market: Industrials Break 7600 and 7700; Polo Ralph Lauren IPO Surges." 1997. *Wall Street Journal*, June 13.

6. Berns, G. S., J. Chappelow, M. Cekic, et al. 2006. "Neurobiological Substrates of Dread." *Science*, 312(5774) (May 5): 704–706.

7. Miller, L., K. Taber, G. Gabbard, and R. Hurley. 2005. "Neural Underpinnings of Fear and Its Modulation: Implications for Anxiety Disorders." *Journal of Neuropsychiatry and Clinical Neuroscience* 17:1 (February): 1–6.

8. Khan, A., R. L. Kolts, M. H. Rapaport, et al. 2005. "Magnitude of Placebo Response and Drug-Placebo Differences across Psychiatric Disorders." *Psychological Medicine* 35(5) (May): 743–749.

9. Wager, T. D., J. K. Rilling, E. E. Smith, et al. 2004. "Placebo-Induced Changes in fMRI in the Anticipation and Experience of Pain." *Science* 303: 1162–1167.

10. Cohen, J. D. 2005. "The Vulcanization of the Human Brain: A Neural Perspective on Interactions between Cognition and Emotion." *Journal of Economic Perspectives* 19: 3–24.

11. Van Boven, L., and G. Loewenstein. 2003. "Social Projection of Transient Drive States." *Personality and Social Psychology Bulletin* 29: 1159–1168. Described in: Van Boven and Loewenstein, 2005.

Chapter 10: Stress and Burnout

1. Drobny, S. 2006. *Inside the House of Money*. Hoboken, N.J.: John Wiley & Sons.

2. Browning, E. S. 2006. "As Stocks Near a High, Pressure Builds for a Professional Investor." *Wall Street Journal*, September 29.

3. Ibid.

4. Sarafino, E. P. 1998. *Health Psychology: Biopsychosocial Interactions*, 3rd ed. New York: John Wiley & Sons.

5. Cramer, J. 2000. "Cramer Rewrites 'The Trading Goddess' 10 Commandments." *The Street.com*, March 11.

6. Ariely, D. 2006. "Large Stakes, Big Mistakes." Presentation to the Stanford Institute of Theoretical Economics, Psychology and Economics Session. (August 7, 2006.)

7. Ibid.

8. Ibid.

9. Sapolsky, Robert M. 2004. *Why Zebras Don't Get Ulcers*. New York: Henry Holt and Company, p. 264.

10. Schmid, R. E. 2004. "Researchers: Stress Causes Forgetfulness." *Associated Press*. October 28, 9:04 P.M. ET.
11. See note 4.
12. Glaser, R., J. Rice, J. Sheridan, et al. 1987. "Stress-Related Immune Suppression: Health Implications." *Brain Behaviour and Immunity* 1: 7–20.
13. Shelton, S. E., J. D. Berard, and N. H. Kalin. 1997. "Aggression, fear and cortisol in young rhesus monkeys." *Psychoneuroendocrinology* 22: Supplement 2, S198. Presented at the International Society of Psychoneuroendocrinology 28th Annual Meeting, San Francisco, California, July.
14. Birnbaum, S. G., P. X. Yuan, M. Wang, et al. 2004. "Protein Kinase C Overactivity Impairs Prefrontal Cortical Regulation of Working Memory." *Science* 306(5697) (October 29): 882–884.
15. See note 5.
16. Lo, A., and D. Repin. 2002. "The Psychophysiology of Real-Time Financial Risk Processing." *Journal of Cognitive Neuroscience* 14: 323–339.
17. Seligman, M., and S. Maier. 1967. "Failure to Escape Traumatic Shock." *Journal of Experimental Psychology* 74: 1–9.

Chapter 11: Love of Risk

1. Bennett, W. J. 1996. *The Book of Virtues*. New York: Simon & Schuster.
2. Kumar, A. 2006. "Who Gambles in the Stock Market?" (July 11). AFA 2006 Boston Meetings Paper Available at SSRN: http://ssrn.com/abstract=686022.
3. American Psychiatric Association. 1994. *Diagnostic and Statistical Manual of Mental Disorders*, 4th ed. Washington, D.C.: American Psychiatric Association.
4. Franzen, H. 2001. "Gambling—Like Food and Drugs—Produces Feelings of Reward in the Brain." *Scientific American* Online, May 24. www.sciam.com/article.cfm?articleID=0004400A-E6F5–1C5E-B882809EC588ED9F.
5. Goudriaan, A. E., J. Oosterlaan, E. de Beurs, and W. van den Brink. 2006. "Psychophysiological Determinants and Concomitants of Deficient Decision Making in Pathological Gamblers." *Drug and Alcohol Dependence*, March 28.
6. Reuter, J., T. Raedler, M. Rose, et al. 2005. "Pathological Gambling Is Linked to Reduced Activation of the Mesolimbic Reward System." *Nature Neuroscience* 8(2) (February): 147–148 (Epub January 9, 2005).
7. Dodd, M. L., K. J. Klos, J. H. Bower, et al. 2005. "Pathological Gambling Caused by Drugs Used to Treat Parkinson Disease." *Archives of Neurology* 62(9) (September): 1377–1381 (Epub July 11, 2005).

8. Goudriaan, A. E., J. Oosterlaan, E. de Beurs, and W. van den Brink. 2006. "Neurocognitive Functions in Pathological Gambling: A Comparison with Alcohol Dependence, Tourette Syndrome and Normal Controls." *Addiction* 101(4) (April): 534–547.

9. Northoff, G., S. Grimm, H. Boeker, et al. 2005. "Affective Judgment and Beneficial Decision Making: Ventromedial Prefrontal Activity Correlates with Performance in the Iowa Gambling Task." *Human Brain Mapping*, December 21.

10. Potenza, M. N., H. C. Leung, H. P. Blumberg, et al. 2003. "An fMRI Stroop Task Study of Ventromedial Prefrontal Cortical Function in Pathological Gamblers." *American Journal of Psychiatry* 160(11) (November): 1990–1994.

11. Green, J. 2003. "The Bookie of Virtue." *Washington Monthly* (June). www.washingtonmonthly.com/features/2003/0306.green.html.

12. Ibid.

13. See note 1.

14. Williams, R. J., and D. Connolly. 2006. "Does Learning about the Mathematics of Gambling Change Gambling Behavior?" *Psychology of Addictive Behaviors* 20(1) (March): 62–68.

15. Floyd, K., J. P. Whelan, and A. W. Meyers. 2006. "Use of Warning Messages to Modify Gambling Beliefs and Behavior in a Laboratory Investigation." *Psychology of Addictive Behaviors* 20(1) (March): 69–74.

16. Kim, S. W., J. E. Grant, D. E. Adson, and Y. C. Shin. 2001. "Double-blind naltrexone and placebo comparison study in the treatment of pathological gambling." *Biological Psychiatry* 49(11) (June 1): 914–921.

17. Grant, J. E., M. N. Potenza, E. Hollander, et al. 2006. "Multicenter Investigation of the Opioid Antagonist Nalmefene in the Treatment of Pathological Gambling." *American Journal of Psychiatry* 163(2) (February): 303–312.

18. Di Chiara, G., and A. Imperato. 1988. "Opposite Effects of Mu and Kappa Opiate Agonists on Dopamine Release in the Nucleus Accumbens and in the Dorsal Caudate of Freely Moving Rats." *Journal of Pharmacology and Experimental Therapeutics* 244: 1067–1080.

19. Jayaram-Lindstrom, N., P. Wennberg, Y. L. Hurd, and J. Franck. 2004. "Effects of Naltrexone on the Subjective Response to Amphetamine in Healthy Volunteers." *Journal of Clinical Psychopharmacology* 24(6) (December): 665–669.

20. Dannon, P.N., K. Lowengrub, E. Musin E, et al. 2005. "Sustained-Release Bupropion versus Naltrexone in the Treatment of Pathological Gambling: A Preliminary Blind-Rater Study." *Journal of Clinical Psychopharmacology* 25(6) (December): 593–596.

Chapter 12: Personality Factors

1. Mauboussin, M. 2006. *More Than You Know: Finding Financial Wisdom in Unconventional Places.* Chichester, England: Columbia University Press.
2. Hagstrom, R. 1999. *The Warren Buffett Portfolio.*Hoboken, N. J.: John Wiley & Sons.
3. Schwager, J. 2002. *Stock Market Wizards.* New York: HarperBusiness.
4. Dictionary.com. 2006. "Personality." *Dictionary.com.* http://dictionary. reference.com/search?q=personality.
5. McCrae, R. R., and P. T. Costa, Jr. 1996. "Toward a New Generation of Personality Theories: Theoretical Contexts for the Five-Factor Model." In J. S. Wiggins (ed.), *The Five-Factor Model of Personality: Theoretical perspectives* New York: Guilford, pp. 51–87.
6. Caspi, A. 2000. "The Child Is Father of the Man: Personality Continuities from Childhood to Adulthood." *Journal of Personality and Social Psychology* 78: 158–172.
7. See note 5.
8. Goldberg compiled these 300 questions into a new personality assessment tool, which he called the IPIP-NEO. John A. Johnson, a professor at Penn State University, posted Goldberg's phrases online in 1996. As of 2005, at least 175,000 people had answered the test items online. The five clusters remained consistent in others' research as well Costa, P. T., Jr., and McCrae, R. R. 1992. "Normal Personality Assessment in Clinical Practice: The NEO Personality Inventory." *Psychological Assessment* 4: 5–13.
9. Cohen, M. X., J. Young, J. M. Baek, et al. 2005. "Individual Differences in Extraversion and Dopamine Genetics Predict Neural Reward Responses."*Cognitive Brain Research* 25(3) (December): 851–861 (Epub November 11, 2005).
10. Paulus, M. P., C. Rogalsky, A. Simmons, et al. 2003. "Increased Activation in the Right Insula during Risk-Taking Decision Making Is Related to Harm Avoidance and Neuroticism." *Neuroimage* 19(4) (August): 1439–1448.
11. See note 5.
12. Fox, N. A., H. A. Henderson, K. H. Rubin, et al. 2001. "Continuity and Discontinuity of Behavioral Inhibition and Exuberance: Psychophysiological and Behavioral Influences across the First Four Years of Life." *Child Development* 72:1, 1–21.
13. Arnold, P. D., G. Zai, and M. A. Richter. 2004. "Genetics of Anxiety Disorders." *Current Psychiatry Reports* 6(4) (August): 243–254. Review.
14. Sen, S., M. Burmeister, and D. Ghosh. 2004. "Meta-analysis of the Association between a Serotonin Transporter Promoter Polymorphism

(5-HTTLPR) and Anxiety-Related Personality Traits." *American Journal of Medical Genetics. Part B, Neuropsychiatric Genetics.* 127(1) (May 15): 85–89.

15. Zuckerman, M. 1974. "The Sensation-Seeking Motive." In Maher, B. (ed.), *Progress in Experimental Personality Research,* vol. 7. New York: Academic Press, pp 79–148.

16. Zuckerman, M., and D. M. Kuhlman. 2000. "Personality and Risk-Taking: Common Biosocial Factors." *Journal of Personality* 68: 999–1029.

17. Grinblatt, M., M. Keloharju. 2006. "Sensation Seeking, Overconfidence, and Trading Activity" (September 14). Working Paper. http://icf.som.yale.edu/pdf/seminar06–07/Grinblatt.pdf.

18. Cloninger, C. R., R. Adolfsson, and N. M. Svrakic. 1996. "Mapping Genes for Human Personality." *Nature Genetics* 12(1) (January): 3–4.

19. Golimbet, V. E., M. V. Alfimova, I. K. Gritsenko, and R. P. Ebshtein. 2006. "[Dopamine System Genes and Personality Traits of Extraversion and Novelty Seeking]." Zhurnal vyssheĭ nervnoĭ deiatelnosti imeni I P Pavlova. 56(4) (July-August): 457–463. [Article in Russian].

20. Glassman, J.K. 2007. "Become a Better Investor." *Kiplinger's Personal Finance* magazine. (January). http://www.kiplinger.com/magazine/archives/2007/01/glassman.html.

21. Durand, R. B., R. Newby, and J. Sanghani. 2006. "An Intimate Portrait of the Individual Investor" (March). Available at SSRN: http://ssrn.com/abstract=887441.

22. O'Creevy, F., M. N. Nicholson, E. Soane, and P. Willman. 2004. *Traders: Risks, Decisions, and Management in Financial Markets.* Oxford: Oxford University Press.

23. Steenbarger, B. 2003. *The Psychology of Trading.* Hoboken, N.J.: John Wiley & Sons.

24. Hirschhorn, D. 2007. Personal email communication. (February 16).

25. Lo, A., and D. Repin. 2005. "Fear and Greed in Financial Markets: A Clinical Study of Day-Traders." Presentation to the annual conference of the American Economics Association, Philadelphia, January.

26. Oberlechner, T. 2004. "Perceptions of Successful Traders by Foreign Exchange Professionals." *Journal of Behavioral Finance* 5(1): 23–31.

27. Biais, B., D. Hilton, K. Mazurier, and S. Pouget. 2000. "Psychological Traits and Trading Strategies." Unpublished manuscript.

28. Goleman, D. 1998. *Working with Emotional Intelligence.* London: Bloomsbury.

29. Schwager, J. 2003. *Stock Market Wizards: Interviews with America's Top Traders.* New York: HarperBusiness.

30. Soros, G. 1995. *Soros on Soros*: John Wiley & Sons.

31. See note 1.

32. Cymbalista, F. 2003. "George Soros: How He Knows What He Knows: Part 1: The Belief in Fallibility." *Stocks, Futures, and Options* 2(7) (July).
33. Soros, G. 2000. *Open Society: Reforming Global Capitalism.* New York: PublicAffairs.

Chapter 13: Making Decisions

1. Mauboussin, M. 2006. *More Than You Know: Finding Financial Wisdom in Unconventional Places.* Chichester, England: Columbia University Press, p. 26.
2. Loewenstein, C. K., G. F. Loewenstein, E. U. Weber, and N. Welch. 2001. "Risk as Feelings." *Psychological Bulletin* 2: 267–286.
3. See note 1.
4. Miller, E. K., and J. D. Cohen. 2001. "An Integrative Theory of Prefrontal Cortex Function." *Annual Review of Neuroscience* 24: 167–202.
5. Breiter, H., I. Aharon, D. Kahneman, A. Dale, and P. Shizgal. 2001. "Functional Imaging of Neural Responses to Expectancy and Experience of Monetary Gains and Losses." *Neuron* 30: 619–639.
6. Knutson, B., G. W. Fong, C. S. Adams, and D. Hommer. 2001. "Dissociation of Reward Anticipation versus Outcome with Event-Related fMRI." *NeuroReport* 12: 3683–3687.
7. Knutson, B., C. S. Adams, G. W. Fong, and D. Hommer. 2001. "Anticipation of Monetary Reward Selectively Recruits Nucleus Accumbens." *Journal of Neuroscience* 21: RC159.
8. Knutson, B., G. W. Fong, S. M. Bennett, et al. 2003. "A Region of Mesial Prefrontal Cortex Tracks Monetarily Rewarding Outcomes: Characterization with Rapid Event-Related fMRI." *NeuroImage* 18: 263–272.
9. Ackert, L. F., N. Charupat, R. Deaves, and B. Kluger. 2006. "The Origins of Bubbles in Laboratory Asset Markets" (May). FRB of Atlanta Working Paper No. 2006–6 Available at SSRN: http://ssrn.com/abstract=903159.
10. Slovic, P., M. Finucane, E. Peters, and D. G. MacGregor. 2002. "The Affect Heuristic." In Gilovich, T., D. Griffin, and D. Kahneman (eds.), *Intuitive Judgment: Heuristics and Biases.* New York: Cambridge University Press, pp. 397–420.
11. Fox, C., and A. Tversky. 2000. "A Belief-Based Account of Decision under Uncertainty." In Kahneman, D., and A. Tversky (eds.), *Choices, Values, and Frames.* New York: Cambridge University Press and Russell Sage Foundation, pp. 118–142.
12. Prelec, D. 1998. "The Probability Weighting Function." *Econometrica* 60: 497–528.

13. Hausch, D. B., V. Lo, and W. T. Ziemba (eds.). 1994. *The Efficiency of Racetrack Betting Markets*. San Diego: Academic Press.
14. See note 2.
15. Hsee, C. K., and Y. Rottenstreich. 2001. "Money, Kisses, and Electric Shocks: On the Affective Psychology of Risk." *Psychological Science* 12: 185–190.
16. Wright, W., and G. H. Bower. 1992. "Mood Effects on Subjective Probability Assessment." *Organizational Behavior and Human Decision Processes*. 52(2): 276–291.
17. Loewenstein, G., and J. S. Lerner. 2003. "The Role of Affect in Decision Making." *Handbook of Affective Science*, ed. R. Davidson, H. Goldsmith, and K. Scherer. Oxford: Oxford University Press, pp. 619–642.
18. See note 1.
19. See note 2.
20. Ellsberg, D. 1961. "Risk, Ambiguity, and the Savage Axioms." *Quarterly Journal of Economics* 75: 643–669.
21. Kumar, A. 2006. "Valuation Uncertainty and Behavioral Biases," May 31. Available at SSRN: http://ssrn.com/abstract=903820.
22. Bartov, E., P. S. Mohanram, and C. Seethamraju. 2001. "Valuation of Internet Stocks—an IPO Perspective" (April). Available at SSRN: http://ssrn.com/abstract=267928 or DOI: 10.2139/ssrn.267928.
23. Baker, M. and J. Wurgler. 2006. "Investor Sentiment and the Cross-Section of Stock Returns." *The Journal of Finance* 61 (4): 1645–1680.
24. MacGregor, D. G., P. Slovic, D. Dremen, and M. Berry. 2000. "Imagery, Affect, and Financial Judgment." *Journal of Psychology and Financial Markets* 1: 104–110.
25. Francis, J., R. LaFond, P. M. Olsson, and K. Schipper. 2003. "Accounting Anomalies and Information Uncertainty" (February). AFA 2004 San Diego Meetings; EFA 2003 Annual Conference Paper No. 199. Available at SSRN: http://ssrn.com/abstract=414141 or DOI: 10.2139/ssrn.414141.
26. See note 21.
27. Rode, C., L. Cosmides, W. Hell, and J. Tooby. 1999. "When and Why Do People Avoid Unknown Probabilities in Decisions under Uncertainty? Testing Some Predictions from Optimal Foraging Theory." *Cognition* 72(3) (October 26): 269–304.
28. See Note 17.
29. McDonald, H. E., and E. R. Hirt. 1997. "When Expectancy Meets Desire: Motivational Effects in Reconstructive Memory." *Journal of Personality and Social Psychology* 72: 5–23.
30. Camerer, C., and M. Weber M. 1992. "Recent Developments in Modelling Preferences: Uncertainty and Ambiguity." *Journal of Risk and Uncertainty* 5: 325–370.

31. Hsu, M., M. Bhatt, R. Adolphs, et al. 2005. "Neural Systems Responding to Degrees of Uncertainty in Human Decision-Making." *Science* 310(5754) (December 9): 1680–1683.

32. Deppe, M., W. Schwindt, J. Kramer, et al. 2005. "Evidence for a Neural Correlate of a Framing Effect: Bias-Specific Activity in the Ventromedial Prefrontal Cortex during Credibility Judgments." *Brain Research Bulletin* 67(5) (November 15): 413–421 (Epub July 25, 2005).

33. Holm, H., and P. Nystedt. 2005. "Intra Generational Trust: A Semi Experimental Study of Trust Among Different Generations." *Journal of Economic Behavior and Organization* 58: 403–419.

34. Sanfey, A. G., J. K. Rilling, J. A. Aronson, et al.2003. "The Neural Basis of Economic Decision-Making in the Ultimatum Game." *Science* 300(5626) (June 13): 1755–1758.

35. Winston, J. S., B. A. Strange, J. O'Doherty, and R. J. Dolan. 2002. "Automatic and Intentional Brain Responses during Evaluation of Trustworthiness of Faces." *Nature Neuroscience* 5(3) (March): 192–193, 277–283.

36. Insel, T. R., Shapiro, L. E. 1992. "Oxytocin receptor distribution reflects social organization in monogamous and polygamous voles." *Proceedings of the National Academy of Sciences.* 89(13) (July 1): 5981–5985.

37. Zak, P. J., R. Kurzban, and W. T. Matzner. 2004. "The Neurobiology of Trust." *Annals of the New York Academy of Sciences* 1032 (December): 224–227.

38. Zak, P. J., R. Kurzban, and W. T. Matzner. 2005. "Oxytocin Is Associated with Human Trustworthiness." *Hormones and Behavior* 48: 522–527.

39. Kosfeld, M., M. Heinrichs, P. J. Zak, et al. 2005. "Oxytocin Increases Trust in Humans." *Nature* 435 (June 2): 673–676.

Chapter 14: Framing Your Options

1. Shlosser, Eric. 2001. *Fast Food Nation.* New York: Houghton-Mifflin.

2. Personal communication with Camelia Kuhnen, September 30, 2006.

3. Shefrin, H. M., and M. Statman. 1985. "The Disposition to Sell Winners Too Early and Ride Losers Too Long: Theory and Evidence." *Journal of Finance* 40, 777–792.

4. Kahneman, D., and A. Tversky. 1979. "Prospect Theory: An Analysis of Decision under Risk." *Econometrica* 47: 263–291.

5. Ariely, D. 2002. University of California at Berkeley, Psychology and Economics Spring Seminar.

6. De Martino, B., D. Kumaran, B. Seymour, and R. J. Dolan. 2006. "Biases, and Rational Decision-Making in the Human Brain." *Science* 313(5787) (August 4): 684–687.

7. Vergano, D. 2006. "Study: Ask with Care: Emotion Rules the Brain's Decisions." *USA Today*, August 7. pp. D4.
8. Ibid.
9. Locke, P. R., and S. C. Mann. 2000. "Do Professional Traders Exhibit Loss Realization Aversion?" (November). Available at SSRN: http://ssrn.com/abstract=251942 or DOI: 10.2139/ssrn.251942.
10. Odean, T. 1998. "Are Investors Reluctant to Realize Their Losses?" *Journal of Finance* 53(5) (October): 1775–1798.
11. Coval, J. D., T. Shumway. 2005. "Do Behavioral Biases Affect Prices?" *Journal of Finance*. 60(1) (February).
12. Brown, S., D. R. Gallagher, O. W. Steenbeck, and P. L. Swan. 2004. "Double or Nothing: Patterns of Equity Fund Holdings and Transactions." Working paper, New York University. Current Draft: May 1, 2005.
13. Genesove, D., and C. Mayer. 2001. "Loss Aversion and Seller Behavior: Evidence from the Housing Market," MIT Press, *Quarterly Journal of Economics*, 116(4) (November): 1233–1260.
14. Heath, C., S. Huddart, and M. Lang. 1999. "Psychological Factors and Stock Option Exercise." MIT Press, *Quarterly Journal of Economics* 114(2) (May): 601–627.
15. See note 7.
16. Weber, M., and F. Welfens. 2006. "An Individual Level Analysis of the Disposition Effect: Empirical and Experimental Evidence" (May). Available at SSRN: http://ssrn.com/abstract=889303.
17. Ibid.
18. Ibid.

Chapter 15: Loss Aversion

1. Schwager, J. 2002. "Wizard Lesson #14." *Stock Market Wizards: Interviews with America's Top Stock Traders*. New York: John Wiley & Sons.
2. Fogel, S. O., and T. Berry. 2006. "The Disposition Effect and Individual Investor Decisions: The Roles of Regret and Counterfactual Alternatives" *Journal of Behavioral Finance* 7(2): 107–116.
3. Heyman, J. E., Y. Orhun, and D. Ariely. 2004. "Auction Fever: The Effect of Opponents and Quasi-endowment on Product Valuations." *Journal of Interactive Marketing* 18(4): 7–21.
4. Novemsky, N., and D. Kahneman. 2005. "How Do Intentions Affect Loss Aversion?" *Journal of Marketing Research* 42 (May): 139–140.
5. List, J. A. 2003. "Does Market Experience Eliminate Market Anomalies?" *Quarterly Journal of Economics* 118(1): 41–71.

6. Chen, K., V. Lakshminarayanan, and L. Santos. 2006. "How Basic Are Behavioral Biases? Evidence from Capuchin Monkey Trading Behavior." *Journal of Political Economy,* June 2006.

7. Ibid.

8. Harbaugh, W. T., K. Krause, and L. Vesterlund. 2002. "Prospect Theory in Choice and Pricing Tasks," University of Oregon Economics Department Working Papers 2002–02, University of Oregon Economics Department, revised December 17, 2003.

9. Gneezy, U. 1997. "An experiment on Risk Taking and Evaluation Periods." *Quarterly Journal of Economics* 112: 631–645.

10. Shiv, B., G. Loewenstein, A. Bechara, et al. 2005. "Investment Behavior and the Negative Side of Emotion." *Psychological Science* 16(6).

11. Mehra, R. 2003. "The Equity Premium: Why Is It a Puzzle?" *Financial Analysts Journal,* January/February: 54–69.

12. Mehra, R., and E. C. Prescott. 1985. "The Equity Premium: A Puzzle." *Journal of Monetary Economics* 15(2) (March): 145–161.

13. Haigh, M., and J. List. 2005. "Do Professional Traders Exhibit Myopic Loss Aversion? An Experimental Analysis." *Journal of Finance* 60(1) (February): 523.

14. Benartzi, S., and R. Thaler. 1995. "Myopic Loss Aversion and the Equity Premium Puzzle," MIT Press, *Quarterly Journal of Economics,* 110(1) (February): 73–92.

15. Burton K. and J. Strasburg. 2006. "Amaranth's $6.6 Billion Slide Began With Trader's Bid to Quit." (December 6). Downloaded from: http://www.bloomberg.com/apps/news?pid=newsarchive&sid=aRJS5 7CQQbeE.

16. Ibid.

17. Ibid.

18. Leeson, N. 1996. *Rogue Trader.* New York: Little, Brown.

19. Thaler, R., and E. Johnson. 1990. "Gambling with the House Money and Trying to Break Even: The Effects of Prior Outcomes on Risky Choice." *Management Science* 36(6) (June): 643–660.

20. Personal e-mail communication with Hersh Shefrin, September 21, 2006. Shefrin commented: "The key driver of the shift in risk attitude is that the person segregates the two gains, the prior gain and the gain from the gamble. That kick from savoring the gains separately provides a psychological impetus to taking the gamble, given the cushion provided by the prior gain."

21. Liu, Y-J., C-L. Tsai, M-C. Wang, and N. Zhu. 2006. "House Money Effect: Evidence from Market Makers at Taiwan Futures Exchange" (April). http://faculty.gsm.ucdavis.edu/~nzhu/papers/housemoney.pdf.

22. Nicolosi, G., P. Liang, and N. Zhu. 2003. "Do Individual Investors Learn from Their Trading Experience?" Yale ICF Working paper No. 03–32.

23. Drobny, S. 2006. *Inside the House of Money*. Hoboken, N.J.: John Wiley & Sons.
24. Ibid., p. 40.
25. Ibid., p. 42.
26. Ibid., p. 47.
27. Ibid., p. 48.
28. Ibid., p. 43.
29. Ibid., pp. 50–51.
30. Jones, P. T. 1989. In Schwager, J. *Market Wizards: Interviews with Top Traders*. New York: Institute of Finance.
31. Seasholes, M. S., and L. Feng. 2005. "Do Investor Sophistication and Trading Experience Eliminate Behavioral Biases in Financial Markets?" June 6. Available at SSRN: http://ssrn.com/abstract=694769.
32. "The Taming of the Shrewd." *The Economist*, May 6, 2000.
33. Ibid.
34. Schwager, J. 1989. *Market Wizards: Interviews with Top Traders*. New York: Institute of Finance, p. 126.
35. Ibid., p. 127.
36. Szala, G., and J. Reerink. 1994. "Tip-offs from Top Traders." *Futures*, July.
37. Cramer, J. C. 2000. "Cramer Rewrites 'The Trading Goddess' 10 Commandments.' The Street.com, March 11.

Chapter 16: Time Discounting

1. Loewenstein, G., and J. S. Lerner. 2003. "The role of affect in decision making." In Davidson, R., H. Goldsmith, and K. Scherer (eds.), *Handbook of Affective Science*. Oxford: Oxford University Press, pp. 619–642.
2. Gray, J. R. 1999. "A Bias toward Short-Term Thinking in Threat-Related Negative Emotional States." *Personality and Social Psychology Bulletin* 25: 65–75.
3. Mitchell, J. M., H. Fields, M. D'Esposito, and C. Boettiger. 2005. "Impulsive Responding in Alcoholics: Neurobiological, Behavioral, and Environmental Relations to Drinking." *Alcoholism: Clinical & Experimental Research* 29(12) (December): 2158–2169.
4. Cohen, J. D. 2005. "The Vulcanization of the Human Brain: A Neural Perspective on Interactions between Cognition and Emotion." *Journal of Economic Perspectives* 19: 3–24.
5. Laibson, D., A. Repetto, and J. Tobacman. 2005. "Estimating Discount Functions with Consumption Choices over the Lifecycle." Working paper. Harvard University, August 11.
6. Ibid.

7. Mischel, W., Y. Shoda, M. I. Rodriguez. 1989. "Delay of Gratification in Children." *Science* 244(4907) (May 26): 933–938.

8. Eigsti, I. M., V. Zayas, W. Mischel, et al. 2006. "Predicting Cognitive Control from Preschool to Late Adolescence and Young Adulthood." *Psychological Science* 17(6) (June): 478–484.

9. McClure, S. M., D. I. Laibson, G. Loewenstein, and J. D. Cohen. 2004. "Separate Neural Systems Value Immediate and Delayed Monetary Rewards." *Science* 304: 503–507.

10. Yang, Y., A. Raine, T. Lencz, et al. 2005. "Volume Reduction in Prefrontal Gray Matter in Unsuccessful Criminal Psychopaths." *Biological Psychiatry* 57(10) (May 15): 1103–1108.

11. See note 9.

12. Loewenstein, G. 1996. "Out of Control: Visceral Influences on Behavior." *Organizational Behavior and Human Decision Processes* 65: 272–292.

13. See note 9.

14. Henderson, M. 2006. "Why Say No to Free Money? It's Neuro-economics, Stupid." *The Times*, London: October 7.

15. Giordano, L. A, W. K. Bickel, G. Loewenstein, et al. 2002. "Mild Opioid Deprivation Increases the Degree that Opioid-Dependent Outpatients Discount Delayed Heroin and Money." *Psychopharmacology* (Berlin) 163: 174.

16. Grant, J. E. "Outcome Study of Kleptomania Patients Treated with Naltrexone: A Chart Review." *Clinical Neuropharmacology* 28(1) (January–February): 11–14.

17. See note 4.

18. Chen, K., V. Lakshminarayanan, and L. Santos. 2006. "How Basic Are Behavioral Biases? Evidence from Capuchin Monkey Trading Behavior." *Journal of Political Economy*, June.

19. Ariely, D., J. Cohen, K. Ericson, et al. 2006. "Implementing Self-Control." Poster presentation at the Society for Neuroeconomics 2006 annual meeting. Park City, Utah.

20. See note 4.

21. Ariely, D., and K. Wertenbroch. 2002. "Procrastination, Deadlines, and Performance: Self-Control by Precommitment." *Psychological Science* 13(3): 219–224.

22. "Industry by Industry: The Stars, Their Stocks, and Their Latest Picks." *Wall Street Journal*, May 22, 2006, p. R3.

Chapter 17: Herding

1. Schwager, J. 2002. "Wizard Lesson #29." *Stock Market Wizards: Interviews with America's Top Stock Traders.* New York: John Wiley & Sons.

2. MacKay, C. 2003. *Extraordinary Popular Delusions and the Madness of Crowds.* Harriman House: Hampshire, U.K.
3. Cialdini, R. 1993. *Influence: The Psychology of Persuasion.* New York: Quill-William Morrow, p. 116.
4. Ibid., p. 128.
5. Solnick, S. J., and D. Hemenway D. 1998. "Is More Always Better? A survey on positional concerns." *Journal of Economic Behavior and Organization* 37(3): 373–383. The authors surveyed 155 students and 79 staff and faculty at Harvard's School of Public Health in 1995 to determine how important were positional concerns.
6. Cialdini, p. 118.
7. Warneryd, K-E. 2001. *Stock Market Psychology.* Northhampton, Mass.: Edward Elgar Publishing, p. 220.
8. Das, S., A. Martinez-Jerez, and P. Tufano. 2005. "'e' Information: A Clinical Study of Investor Discussion and Sentiment." *Financial Management* 34(3): 103–137.
9. Milgram S. 1974. *Obedience to Authority.* New York: Harper & Row.
10. Cialdini, p. 211.
11. Lefkowitz, M., R. Blake, and J. Mouton. 1955. "Status Factors in Pedestrian Violation of Traffic Signals." *Journal of Abnormal and Social Psychology* 51: 704–706.
12. Doob, A., and A. Gross. 1968. "Status of Frustrator as an Inhibitor of Horn-Honking Responses." *Journal of Social Psychology* 76: 213–218.
13. Cialdini, p. 218.
14. Berns, G. S., J. Chappelow, C. F. Zink, et al. 2005. "Neurobiological Correlates of Social Conformity and Independence during Mental Rotation." *Biological Psychiatry* 58(3) (August 1): 245–253.
15. Blodget, H. 2004. "Wall Street Self-Defense. Born Suckers: The Greatest Wall Street Danger of All: You." Slate.com, December 14.
16. Welch, I. 2000. "Herding among Security Analysts." *Journal of Financial Economics* 58(3) (December): 369–396.
17. "Wall Street Prophets." 2001. *60 Minutes II.* CBS, January 30.
18. Ibid.
19. Ibid.
20. Wermers, R. 1999. "Mutual Find Herding and the Impact on Stock Prices." *Journal of Finance* 54(2) (April): 581–622.
21. Hong, H., J. Kubik, and J. Stein. 2005. "Thy Neighbor's Portfolio: Word of Mouth Effects in the Holdings and Trades of Money Managers." *Journal of Finance.* 60(6): 2810–2824.
22. Chen, Q., and W. Jiang. 2006. "Analysts; Weighting of Private and Public Information." *Review of Financial Studies* 19(1): 319–355.
23. Shefrin, H. 2006. Behavioral Corporate Finance: Decisions that Create Value." McGraw-Hill Irwin: New York, p. 154.

Chapter 18: Charting and Data Mining

1. Sagan, C. 1983. *Broca's Brain.* New York: Ballantine Books.
2. Lewis, M. 2003. *Moneyball.* New York: W. W. Norton.
3. Leinweber, D. 1997. "Stupid Data Mining Tricks: Over-fitting the S&P 500." First Quadrant Monograph.
4. "Keeping Cool Amid Global Strife." *Wall Street Journal,* Money and Investing, July 17, 2006, p. C1.
5. Goldstein, S. 1994. "Watch What You're Thinking!" *Skeptical Inquirer,* June 22.
6. Ibid.
7. Osler, C., and K. Chang. 1995. "Head and Shoulders: Not Just a Flaky Pattern." Federal Reserve Bank of New York. Staff Report No. 4.
8. Lo, A., H. Mamaysky, and J. Wang. 2000. "Foundations of Technical Analysis: Computational Algorithms, Statistical Inference, and Empirical Implementation." *Journal of Finance* 55: 1705–1765.
9. Ibid.
10. Ibid., p. 11.
11. DeBondt, W. 1993. "Betting on Trends: Intuitive Forecasts of Financial Risk and Return." *International Journal of Forecasting* 9(3) (November): 355–371.
12. Schachter, S., R. Ouellette, B. Whittle, and W. Gerin. "Effects of Trend and of Profit or Loss on the Tendency to Sell Stock." *Basic and Applied Social Psychology* 8: 259–271.
13. Johnson, J., G. Tellis, D. Macinnis. 2005. "Winners. Losers, and Biased Trades" *Journal of Consumer Research,* v32, September, pp324–329.
14. Trope, Y., and Liberman, N. 2003. "Temporal Construal." *Psychological Review.* 110(3): 403–421.
15. Mussweiler, T., and K. Schneller. 2003. "What Goes up Must Come Down"—How Charts Influence Decisions to Buy and Sell Stocks." *Journal of Behavioral Finance* 4,(3): 121–130.
16. Ibid.
17. Ibid.
18. Downloaded on October 1, 2006, from: www.irrationalexuberance. com/definition.htm.
19. Shiller, R. J. 2000. *Irrational Exuberance.* Princeton, N.J.: Princeton University Press.
20. Mankiw, N. G. 2000. "First Principles: How Irrational Is Our Exuberance?" *Fortune,* April 17.
21. Greenspan, A. 1996. "The Challenge of Central Banking in a Democratic Society." Speech presented to the Annual Dinner and Francis Boyer Lecture of The American Enterprise Institute for Public Policy Research, Washington, D.C., December 5. www.federalreserve.gov/ BOARDDOCS/SPEECHES/19961205.htm.

22. See note 18.
23. Data obtained from Hersh Shefrin PowerPoint presentation to the 2005 T. Rowe Price Investment Symposium.
24. Chiu, Y-C., C-H. Lin, J-T. Huang, et al. 2005. "Immediate Gain Is Long-Term Loss: Are There Foresighted Decision Makers in Iowa Gambling Task?" Paper presented at the Society for Neuroeconomics 3rd Annual Meeting, Kiawah Island, South Carolina, September 15–18.
25. Chiu Y-C, C-H. Lin, S. Lin, and J-T. Huang. 2006. "Reexamining the Effect of Long-Term Outcome and Gain-Loss Frequency: From Uncertainty to Certainty." Paper presented at the Society for Neuroeconomics 4th Annual Meeting, Park City, Utah.
26. See note 24.
27. See note 25.
28. Personal communication with Ching-Hung Lin at the 4th Annual Meeting of Society of Neuroeconomics, Park City, Utah.
29. Delgado, M. R., M. M. Miller, S. Inati, and E. A. Phelps. 2005. "An fMRI Study of Reward-Related Probability Learning." *NeuroImage*, 24(3): 862–873.
30. Kaestner, M. 2006. "Investors Misreaction to Unexpected Earnings: Evidence of Simultaneous Overreaction and Underreaction" *ICFAI Journal of Behavioral Finance* 3(1) (March). Available at SSRN: http://ssrn.com/abstract=877246.
31. Gladwell, M. 2002. "Blowing Up." *The New Yorker*, April 22–29, 2002. www.gladwell.com/2002/2002_04_29_a_blowingup.htm.
32. Ibid.

Chapter 19: Attention and Memory

1. Kumar, A., and R. Dhar. 2001. "A Non-Random Walk Down the Main Street: Impact of Price Trends on Trading Decisions of Individual Investors." Yale School of Management Working Papers ysm208, Yale School of Management.
2. Welch, I. 2000. "Views of Financial Economists on the Equity Premium and Other Issues." *Journal of Business* 73(4) (October): 501–537.
3. Welch I. 2001. "The Equity Premium Consensus Forecast Revisited" (September). Cowles Foundation Discussion Paper No. 1325. Available at SSRN: http://ssrn.com/abstract=285169.
4. Adcock, R. A., A. Thangavel, S. Whitfield-Gabrieli, et al. 2006. "Reward-Motivated Learning: Mesolimbic Activation Precedes Memory Formation." *Neuron* 50: 507–517.
5. Hassabis, D., D. Kumaran, S. D. Vann, and E. A. Maguire. 2007. "Patients with hippocampal amnesia cannot imagine new experiences." *Proceedings of the National Academy of Sciences* 104: 1726–1731.

6. Slovic, P., and B. Fischhoff. 1977. "On the Psychology of Experimental Surprises." *Journal of Experimental Psychology: Human Performance and Perception*. 3: 544–551.

7. Knutson, B., and J. C. Cooper. 2006. "The Lure of the Unknown." *Neuron* 51: 280–282.

8. Schweitzer, J. B., D. O. Lee, R. B. Hanford, et al. 2004. "Effect of Methylphenidate on Executive Functioning in Adults with Attention-Deficit/Hyperactivity Disorder: Normalization of Behavior but Not Related Brain Activity." *Biological Psychiatry* 56(8) (October 15): 597–606.

9. Knutson, B., J. M. Bjork, G. W. Fong, et al. 2004. "Amphetamine Modulates Human Incentive Processing." *Neuron* 43: 261–269.

10. Scheres, A., M. P. Milham, B. Knutson, and F. X. Castellanos. 2007. "Ventral Striatal Hyporesponsiveness during Reward Prediction in Attention-Deficit/Hyperactivity Disorder." *Biological Psychiatry*. (March 1) 61(5):720–724.

11. 11. Cooper, M., H. Gulen, and P. R. Rau. 2005. "Changing Names with Style: Mutual Find Name Changes and Their Effects on Fund Flows." *Journal of Finance* 60(6) (December): 2825–2858.

12. Head, A., G. Smith, and J. Wilson. 2006. "Would a Stock by Any Other Ticker Smell as Sweet?" Working paper. www.economics.pomona.edu/GarySmith/Econ190/tickers.pdf#search=%22Would%20a%20Stock%20By%20Any%20Other%20Ticker%20Smell%20as%20Sweet%3F%22.

13. Valentino, J. 2006. "Does Stock by Any Other Name Smell as Sweet?" *Wall Street Journal*, September 28, p. C1.

14. Alter, A. A., and D. M. Oppenheimer DM. 2006. "Predicting Short-Term Stock Fluctuations by Using Processing Fluency." *Proceedings of the National Academy of Sciences* 103: 9369–9372 (published online before print June 5 2006, 10.1073/pnas.0601071103).

15. Ibid.

16. See note 12.

17. Busse, J., and T. Green. 2002. "Market Efficiency in Real Time." *Journal of Financial Economics* 65: 415–437.

18. Barber, B. M., and T. Odean. 2005. "All that Glitters: The Effect of Attention and News on the Buying Behavior of Individual and Institutional Investors" (March 2006). EFA 2005 Moscow Meetings Paper. Available at SSRN: http://ssrn.com/abstract=460660.

19. Hirshleifer, D., J. N. Myers, L. A. Myers, and S. H. Teoh. 2004. "Do Individual Investors Drive Post-Earnings Announcement Drift? Direct Evidence from Personal Trades." Working paper, EconWPA.

20. Seasholes, M., and G. Wu. 2006. "Predictable Behavior, Profits, and Attention." Working paper. http://faculty.haas.berkeley.edu/mss/

21. Amihud, Y., and H. Mendelson. 1987. "Trading Mechanisms and Stock Returns: Empirical Investigation." *Journal of Finance* 42(3): 533–553.

22. Atkins, A., and E. Dyl. 1990. "Price Reversals, Bid-Ask Spreads, and Market Efficiency." *Journal of Financial and Quantitative Analysis* 25: 535–547.
23. George, T. J., and C. Y. Hwang. 1995. "Transitory Price Changes and Price-Limit Rules: Evidence from the Tokyo Stock Exchange." *Journal of Financial and Quantitative Analysis* 30: 313–327.
24. See note 20.

Chapter 20: Age, Sex, and Culture

1. Canli, T., J. E. Desmond, Z. Zhao, and J. Gabrieli. 2002. "Sex Differences in the Neural Encoding of Emotional Experiences." Proceedings of the National Academy of Sciences 99(16): 10789–10794.
2. Hamann, S., and T. Canli. 2004. "Individual Differences in Emotion Processing." *Current Opinion in Neurobiology* 14: 233–238.
3. Shansky, R. M., K. Rubinow, A. Brennan, and A. F. Arnsten. 2006. "The Effects of Sex and Hormonal Status on Restraint-Stress-Induced Working Memory Impairment." *Behavior and Brain Function* 7(2) (March): 8.
4. Amin, Z., C. N. Epperson, R. T. Constable, and T. Canli. 2006. "Effects of Estrogen Variation on Neural Correlates of Emotional Response Inhibition." *Neuroimage*, April 25 (Epub ahead of print).
5. Rilling, J., D. Gutman, T. Zeh, et al. 2002. "A Neural Basis for Social Cooperation." *Neuron* 35: 395–405.
6. de Quervain, D. S., U. Fischbacher, V. Treyer, et al. 2004. "The neural basis of altruistic punishment." Science. 305(5688) (August 27): 1254–1258.
7. Odean, T., and B. Barber. 2001. "Boys Will Be Boys: Gender, Overconfidence, and Common Stock Investment." *Quarterly Journal of Economics* 116(1) (February): 261–292.
8. Ibid.
9. Nicholson, N., M. Fenton-O'Creevy, E. Soane, and P. Willman. 2006. "Risk Propensity and Personality." http://facultyresearch.london.edu/docs/risk.ps.pdf.
10. Miller, E. K. 2000. "The Prefrontal Cortex and Cognitive Control." *Nature: Review of Neuroscience* 1: 59–65.
11. Williams, L. M., K. J. Brown, D. Palmer, et al. 2006. "The Mellow Years?: Neural Basis of Improving Emotional Stability over Age." *Journal of Neuroscience* 26(24) (June 14): 6422–6430.
12. Hedden, T., and J. D. Gabrieli. 2005. "Healthy and Pathological Processes in Adult Development: New Evidence from Neuroimaging of the Aging Brain." *Current Opinion in Neurology* 18(6) (December): 740–747.

13. Marschner, A., T. Mell, I. Wartenburger, et al. 2005. "Reward-Based Decision-Making and Aging." *Brain Research Bulletin* 67(5) (November 15): 382–390 (Epub July 11, 2005).

14. See note 8.

15. Reyna, V. R. 2004. "How People Make Decisions that Involve Risk: A Dual-Processes Approach." *Current Directions in Psychological Science* 13: 60–66.

16. Kuhnen, C., and B. Knutson. 2006. Presentation by Camelia Kuhnen to the Stanford Institute of Theoretical Economics (SITE) conference. August 14, Stanford University.

17. Schaie, K. W. 2005. "What Can We Learn From Longitudinal Studies of Adult Development?" *Research in Human Development* 2(3): pp. 133–158.

18. Schaie, K. W. 2005. *Developmental Influences on Adult Intelligence: The Seattle Longitudinal Study.* New York: Oxford University Press, p. 127.

19. Ibid.

20. Tueth, M. J. 2000. "Exposing Financial Exploitation of Impaired Elderly Persons." *American Journal of Geriatric Psychiatry* 8 (May): 104–111.

21. Weber, E. U., C. K. Hsee, and J. Sokolowska. 1998. "What Folklore Tells Us about Risk and Risk Taking: Cross-Cultural Comparisons of American, German, and Chinese Proverbs." *Organizational Behavior and Human Decision Processes* 75(2) (August): 170–186.

22. Fan, J. X., and J. J. Xiao. 2003. "Cross-Cultural Differences in Risk Tolerance: A Comparison between Chinese and Americans." *Consumer Interest Annual* 49. The proceedings of the 49th annual conference. April 2–5, 2003 (Atlanta, GA).

23. See note 12.

24. See note 18.

25. Lau, L-Y., and R. Ranyard. 2005. "Chinese and English Probabilistic Thinking and Risk Taking in Gambling." *Journal of Cross-Cultural Psychology* 36: 621–627.

26. Weber, E., D. Ames, and A-R. Blais. 2005. "'How Do I Choose Thee? Let Me Count the Ways: A Textual Analysis of Similarities and Differences in Modes of Decision Making in the USA and China." *Management and Organization Review* 1(1) (March): 87–118.

27. Chen, G. M., K. A. Kim, J. R. Nofsinger, and O. M. Rui. 2005. "Behavior and Performance of Emerging Market Investors: Evidence from China." (Version: October 2005). Unpublished Washington State University working paper. www.darden.virginia.edu/batten/emipm/PDFs/EmergMarkConf_Chinese_Behavior.pdf.

28. Ibid.

29. Liu, Y-J., C-L. Tsai, M-C. Wang, and N. Zhu. 2006. "House Money Effect: Evidence from Market Makers at Taiwan Futures Exchange" (April). http://faculty.gsm.ucdavis.edu/~nzhu/papers/housemoney.pdf.

30. Locke, P. R., and S. C. Mann. 2004. "Prior Outcomes and Risky Choices by Professional Traders." Working paper. http://home.gwu.edu/~plocke/prioroutcomes.pdf.

31. Chen, G., O. Rui, and Y. Xu. 2006. "When Will Investors Herd?: Evidence from the Chinese Stock Markets." Working paper, School of Management, The University of Texas at Dallas, November 2003. http://ccfr.org.cn/cicf2005/paper/20050113024448.pdf.

32. Ng, L., and F. Wu. 2006. "Peer Effects in Investor Trading Decisions: Evidence from a Natural Experiment." Working paper. https://wpweb2.tepper.cmu.edu/wfa/wfasecure/upload/2006_5.768332E+07_PeerEffects_WFA05.pdf.

Chapter 21: Emotion Management

1. Kasser, T., and R. M. Ryan.1996 "Further Examining the American Dream: Differential Correlates of Intrinsic and Extrinsic Goals." *Personality and Social Psychology Bulletin* 22(3): 280–287.

2. Farrell, P. "Bobby Badfingers' Big Secret about Retiring!" Marketwatch.com. Last update: 5:36 P.M. ET, August 2, 2006. www.marketwatch.com/News/Story/Story.aspx?guid=%7B6A52568C-C650-4AFA-B654-407520B4EA6D%7D&siteid=mktw.

3. McCall, R. D. 1997. *Way of Warrior Trader: The Financial Risk-Taker's Guide to Samurai Courage, Confidence and Discipline.* New York: McGraw-Hill.

4. Ritholtz, B. 2005. "Apprenticed Investor: The Zen of Trading." RealMoney.com. Published online June 1, 2005, 11:37 A.M. EDT. www.thestreet.com/comment/barryritholtz/10226021.html.

5. Vohs, K. D., N. L. Mead, and M. R. Goode. 2006. "The Psychological Consequences of Money." *Science* 314(5802) (November 17): 1154–1156.

6. Lykken, D., and A. Tellegen. 1996. "Happiness Is a Stochastic Phenomenon." *Psychological Science* 7(3): 186–189.

7. Diener, E., E. Suh, R. Lucas, and H. Smith. 1999. "Subjective Well-Being: Three Decades of Progress." *Psychological Bulletin* 125(22): 276–302.

8. Frederick, S., and G. Loewenstein. 1999. "Hedonic Adaptation." *Well-Being: The Foundations of Hedonic Psychology.* Russell Sage Foundation Press: New York City.

9. Brickman, P., D. Coates, and R. Janoff-Bulman. 1978. "Lottery Winners and Accident Victims: Is Happiness Relative?" *Journal of Personality and Social Psychology* 36: 917–927.

10. Dijkers, M. 1997. "Quality of Life after Spinal Cord Injury: A Meta Analysis of the Effects of Disablement Components." *Nature* 35(12): 829–840.
11. Lyubomirksy, S., L. Sousa, and R. Dickerhoof. 2006. The Costs and Benefits of Writing, Talking, and Thinking about Life's Triumphs and Defeats. *Journal of Personality and Social Psychology* 90: 692–708.
12. Begley, S. 2004. "Scans of Monks' Brains Show Meditation Alters Structure, Functioning." *Wall Street Journal: Science Journal*, November 5.
13. Lutz, A., L. Greischar, N. Rawlings, et al. 2004. *Proceedings of the National Academy of Sciences* 101(46) (November 16): 16369–16373.
14. See note 15.
15. Cook, M. 2006. 'What Makes a Trader Successful." Handout at the Technical Securities Analysts of San Francsico Annual Conference.
16. Raschke, L. B. 1999. "Swing Trading: Rules and Philosophy." Downloaded on October 9, 1999, from: www.mrci.com/lbr/swgrules/index.cfm.
17. See note 18.
18. Steenbarger, B. 2005. "Trading Journals that Work." BrettSteenbarger.com, July 30. Downloaded on October 1, 2006, from: www.brettsteenbarger.com/articles.htm.
19. Steenbarger B. 2005. "When Trading Journals Don't Work." Trade2Win.com. August 18. Downloaded on October 1, 2006, from: www.trade2win.com/knowledge/articles/general%20articles/when-trading-journals-dont-work.

Chapter 22: Change Techniques

1. Beck, J. S. 1995. *Cognitive Therapy: Basics and Beyond.* New York: Guilford Press.
2. Shannahoff-Khalsa, D. S. 2004. "An Introduction to Kundalini Yoga Meditation Techniques that Are Specific for the Treatment of Psychiatric Disorders." *Journal of Alternative and Complementary Medicine* 10(1) (February): 91–101.
3. Woolery, A., H. Myers, B. Sternlieb, and L. Zeltzer. 2004. "A Yoga Intervention for Young Adults with Elevated Symptoms of Depression." *Alternative Therapies in Health and Medicine* 10(2) (March-April): 60–63.
4. Jensen, P. S., and D. T. Kenny. 2004. "The Effects of Yoga on the Attention and Behavior of Boys with Attention-Deficit/Hyperactivity Disorder (ADHD)." *Journal of Attention Disorders* 7(4) (May): 205–216.
5. Sharma, K., and V. Shukla. 1988. "Rehabilitation of Drug-Addicted Persons: The Experience of the Nav-Chetna Center in India." *Bulletin on Narcotics* 40(1): 43–49.

6. See note 3.
7. Center for Mindfulness in Medicine, Health Care, and Society (CFM). 2006. "Mindfulness-Based Stress Reduction Program Brochure." www.umassmed.edu/cfm/srp/.
8. Davidson, R. J., J. Kabat-Zinn, J. Schumacher, et al. 2003. *"Psychosomatic Medicine* 65: 564–570.
9. Speca, M., L. Carlson, E. Goodey, and M. Angen. 2000. "A Randomized, Wait-List Controlled Clinical Trial: The Effect of a Mindfulness Meditation-Based Stress Reduction Program on Mood and Symptoms of Stress in Cancer Outpatients." *Psychosomatic Medicine* 62: 613–622.
10. Schwartz, G. E., R. J. Davidson, and D. J. Goleman. 1978. "Patterning of Cognitive and Somatic Processes in the Self-Regulation of Anxiety: Effects of Meditation versus Exercise." *Psychosomatic Medicine* 40: 321–328.
11. Arnold, L. E. 2001. "Alternative Treatments for Adults with Attention-Deficit Hyperactivity Disorder (ADHD)." *Annals of the New York Academy of Sciences* 931 (June): 310–341.
12. Kristeller, J., and T. Johnson. 2003. "Cultivating Loving-Kindness: A Two-Stage Model for the Effects of Meditation on Compassion, Altruism and Spirituality. Portions presented at the conference: Works of Love: Scientific and Religious Perspectives on Altruism." Villanova University, Villanova, Pennsylvania, June 3.
13. Murphy, S., and D. Hirschhorn. 2001. *The Trading Athlete: Winning the Mental Game of Online Trading.* New York: John Wiley & Sons, p. 52.
14. Ibid.
15. Steenbarger, B. 2005. "How Experts Make Decisions Under Uncertainty —Part II." BrettSteenbarger.com, July 30. www.brettsteenbarger.com/articles.htm
16. Cymbalista, F., and D. MacRae. 2004. "George Soros: How He Knows What He Knows: Part 1: The Belief in Fallibility." *Stocks, Futures, and Options*, March 8.
17. Personal e-mail correspondence, May 2006.
18. Lyubomirsky, S., K. M. Sheldon, and D. Schkade. 2005. "Pursuing Happiness: The Architecture of Sustainable Change." *Review of General Psychology* 9: 111–131.
19. Sheldon, K., and S. Lyubomirsky. 2006. "How to Increase and Sustain Positive Emotion: The Effects of Expressing Gratitude and Visualizing Best Possible Selves." *Journal of Positive Psychology* 1: 73–82.
20. Lyubomirsky, S., C. Tkach, and M. R. DiMatteo. 2006. "What Are the Differences between Happiness and Self-Esteem? *Social Indicators Research* (September) v78, n3, 363–404.

21. See note 19.
22. deCharms, R., F. Maeda, G. Glover, et al. 2005. "Control over Brain Activation and Pain Learned by Using Real-Time Functional MRI." *Proceedings of the National Academy of Sciences* 102(51) (December 20): 18626–18631.
23. Ibid.
24. Mangels, J. A., B. Butterfield, J. Lamb, C. Good, and C. S. Dweck. 2006. "Why do beliefs about intelligence influence learning success? A social cognitive neuroscience model." *Social Cognitive and Affective Neuroscience*. 1(2): 75–86.
25. Bronson, P. 2007. "How Not to Talk to Your Kids: The Inverse Power of Praise." *New York Magazine*, February 19.

Chapter 23: Behavioral Finance Investing

1. Lefevre, E. 1923. *Reminiscences of a Stock Operator.* American Research Council.
2. Drobny, S. 2006. *Inside the House of Money.* Hoboken, N. J.: John Wiley & Sons.
3. "Brazil and the IMF: A Matter of Faith." *The Economist*, August 15, 2002.
4. Li, F., 2006. "Do Stock Market Investors Understand the Risk Sentiment of Corporate Annual Reports?" April 21. Available at SSRN: http://ssrn.com/abstract=898181.
5. Fama, E., and K. French. 1992. "The Cross-Section of Expected Stock Returns," *Journal of Finance* 47(2): 427–465.
6. Dimson, E., S. Nagel, and G. Quigley. 2003. "Capturing the Value Premium in the UK 1955–2001." *Financial Analysts Journal* 59: 35–45.
7. Jegadeesh, N., and S. Titman. 1993. "Returns to Buying Winners and Selling Losers: Implications for Stock Market Efficiency." *Journal of Finance* 48(1): 65–91.
8. Watkins, B. 2004. "Riding the Wave of Sentiment: An Analysis of Return Consistency as a Predictor of Future Returns." *Journal of Behavioral Finance*, April.
9. Lee, C., and B. Swaminathan. 2000. "Price Momentum and Trading Volume." *Journal of Finance* 55(5) (October): 2017.
10. Chan, W. 2002. "Stock Price Reaction to News and No-News. Drift and Reversal after Headlines." Cambridge: MIT Sloan School of Management, working paper. Downloaded on September 1, 2006, from: http://jfe.rochester.edu/02207.pdf.
11. DeBondt, W., and R. Thaler. 1985. "Does the Stock Market Overreact?" *Journal of Finance* 40: 793–805.

12. Kothari, S. P., and J. Shanken. 2002. "Anomalies and Efficient Portfolio Formation," The Research Foundation of AIMR Publications.
13. Trueman, B., F. M. H. Wong, and X-J. Zhang. 2003. "Anomalous Stock Returns around Internet Firms' Earnings Announcements." *Journal of Accounting and Economics* 34(1) (January): 249–271(23).
14. Peterson, R. 2002. "'Buy on the Rumor:' Anticipatory Affect and Investor Behavior." *Journal of Psychology and Financial Markets* 3(4), 218–226.
15. Peterson R. 2005. "Buy on the Rumor and Sell on the News." In Ong, M. (ed.), *Risk Management*. New York: Academic Press: pp. 677–698.
16. "LGT Investment Products—Active Management and Innovative Investment Philosophies." Downloaded on October 1, 2006, from: www.lgt-capital-management.com/cm/en/anlagefonds/.
17. "Investorama 2006." Downloaded on December 1, 2006, from: www.lgt-capital-management.com/cm/en/downloads/dok_marktinformationen/Investorama_1206_en.pdf.
18. http://mba.tuck.dartmouth.edu/pages/faculty/ken.french/data_library.html.
19. "Dimensions." Downloaded on October 1, 2006, from: www.dfaus.com/philosophy/dimensions/.
20. Thaler, R., and S. Benartzi. 2004. "Save More Tomorrow: Using Behavioral Economics to Increase Employee Saving." *Journal of Political Economy* 112: S164–S187.

Glossary

Affect. Feeling or emotion, especially as manifested by facial expression or body language. Affect can refer to the entire range of emotion-related mental experience. Attitudes, preferences, emotions, feelings, and moods are all affective processes.

Agreeableness. Agreeableness reflects individual differences in concern with cooperation and social harmony. Agreeable individuals value getting along with others.

Ambiguity. The existence of several possible meanings or implications, including conflicting attitudes or feelings.

Amphetamines. Amphetamines are stimulant medications that block the neuronal reuptake of norepinephrine and dopamine, increasing concentrations of these neurotransmitters in the synaptic cleft. Derivatives of amphetamine include commerical medications used to treat attention-deficit hyperacticity disorder (ADHD) such as methylphenidate (Ritalin, Concerta) amphetamine-dextroamphetamine (Adderall), and others. Methampetamines (d-amphetamine) are an easily manufactured and neurotoxic form of amphetamines used recreationally for intoxication—leading to overconfidence, euphoria, sexual arousal, improved stamina, and vigilance. In the 1950s and 1960s amphetamine medications were prescribed as "pick-me-up" pills, but they are now FDA schedule II (prescribed only with special prescription pads and government clearance).

Amygdala. A limbic system structure with a key role in aggression and fear, as well as emotional memory.

Analyst (financial). Professional who studies companies, analyzes financial statements, interviews corporate executives, and attends investment presentations to write reports recommending either purchasing, selling, or holding various stocks. Also called securities analyst or investment analyst.

Anterior cingulate cortex (ACC). Cortex along the medial fissure. The ACC is vital to cognitive functions, such as reward anticipation, decision making, empathy, and emotion. Neuroscientists indicate the dorsal anterior cingulate cortex is primarily related to rational cognition while the ventral is more related to emotional cognition.

Anterior insula. Cortex tissue located within the depths of the lateral fissure beneath the frontal, temporal, and parietal folds. It overlies the putamen.

Anticipation. Foreknowledge, intuition, and presentiment. Anticipation is a state of expectancy in which a known outcome is understood to be forthcoming.

Anxiety (worry/concern/dread). Anticipation of negative events, creating feelings of unease and discomfort. Leads to activation of the sympathetic nervous system and release of stress hormones such as cortisol and neurotransmitters such as norepinephrine.

Arbitrage. The purchase of securities on one market for immediate resale on another market in order to profit from a price discrepancy.

Arousal. Physiological activation, often characterized by somatic signs including sweating, tremulousness, hypervigilance, pupil dilation, and excitability.

Attention deficit–hyperactivity disorder (ADHD). Cognitive control, defined as the ability to suppress inappropriate thoughts and actions, is compromised in ADHD.

Authority. An expert whose views are taken as definitive.

Belief. Any thoughts held as logically true.

Benzodiazepines. Compounds that reduce anxiety. Synthetic versions include Valium, Xanax, Ativan, and Klonopin. They appear to act on the brain's gamma-aminobutyric acid (GABA) receptors.

"Big Five." The "Big Five" personality traits comprise the classification of a person's personality into the categories of neuroticism, extraversion, agreeableness, conscientiousness, and openness to experience. The Big Five are five broad factors or dimensions of personality traits discovered through empirical research. The Big Five are a descriptive model of personality, not a theory.

Book value. The monetary amount by which an asset is valued in business records, a figure not necessarily identical to the amount the asset could bring on the open market.

Bubble. An economic bubble occurs when speculation in a commodity causes the price to increase, thus producing more speculation. The price of the good then reaches absurd levels and the bubble is usually followed by a sudden drop in prices, known as a crash.

Buffett, Warren. Born August 30, 1930; a wealthy American investor and businessman. As of publication, he was the second wealthiest person in the world, worth over $45 billion.

Clemens, Samuel. Pen name "Mark Twain"; an American writer and humorist.

Comparator. The brain circuits used to compare expectations of goal progress versus reality. Feelings arise as a result of the comparison.

Confidence. Assurance, freedom from doubt, belief in one's abilities.

Conscientiousness. Describes one's tendency to plan and organize toward achieving goals, to follow rules while pursuing those goals, and to control impulses along the way.

Cramer, James. Journalist, successful retired hedge fund manager, founder of TheStreet.com, and currently star of CNBC's television show *Mad Money*.

Crash (market). A sudden large decline of business or the prices of stocks (especially one that causes additional failures).

Day trading. Buying and selling the same stock on the same day.

Decision making. The cognitive process of selecting a course of action from among multiple alternatives.

Defense mechanism (a.k.a. emotional defense mechanism). Automatic psychological process that protects the individual against anxiety and from awareness of internal or external stressors or dangers. Defense mechanisms mediate the individual's reaction to emotional conflicts and to external stressors. Some defense mechanisms (e.g., projection, splitting, and acting out) are almost invariably maladaptive.

Discounting (time). The preference for smaller immediate rewards over larger, later rewards.

Dopamine. A neurotransmitter essential to the normal functioning of the anticipation and receipt of pleasure, learning, sequential thought, and motor control.

Dorsolateral prefrontal cortex. Considered important for higher human brain functions such as working memory and conscious control of behavior. It is the last brain region to complete myelination, and it has been found to still be organizing into the third decade of life.

Emotion. In psychology and common use, emotion is the language of a person's mental state of being, normally based in or tied to the person's internal (physical) and external (social) sensory feeling. Feelings such as happiness, sadness, anger, elation, irritation, and joy are emotions.

Epinephrine (adrenaline). Both a neurotransmitter throughout the brain and a hormone released from the adrenal gland during stress, as a result of activation of the sympathetic nervous system.

Equity risk premium. The equity risk premium is the amount by which stocks are expected to outperform bonds.

Equity premium puzzle. The phenomenon that observed returns on stocks over the past century are higher, by approximately 6 percent, than returns on government bonds. Economists expect arbitrage opportunities would reduce the difference in returns on these two investment opportunities to reflect the risk premium investors demand to invest in relatively more risky stocks.

Excitement. Exhilaration; the feeling of lively and cheerful joy.

Expected value. In probability (and especially gambling), the expected value (or expectation) of a random variable is the sum of the probability of each possible outcome of the experiment multiplied by its payoff ("value"). Thus, it represents the average amount one "expects" to win per bet if bets with identical odds are repeated many times.

Extraversion. Characterized by a desire to socialize, gregariousness, and a tendency to optimism.

Fear. Defined as an unpleasant, often strong emotion caused by anticipation or awareness of danger.

Feelings. Conscious experiences that help in the identification of emotions. When one feels afraid, one can identify the emotion of fear. Not all feelings are emotions, but all (conscious) emotional experiences are feelings.

Frontal cortex. The portion of the brain involved with reasoning, planning, abstract thought and other complex cognitive functions in addition to motor function.

Functional magnetic resonance imaging (fMRI). Allows researchers to measure changes in brain activity over short time intervals (two seconds) in small regions of the brain (two cubic millimeters). Changes in brain activity are indicated by alterations in regional metabolism, tissue oxygen usage, and blood flow (blood-oxygen level dependent signal—BOLD).

Fundamental analysis. The use of corporate statistics—including management efficacy, earnings, asset value, and debt—to forecast future stock returns.

Futures contract. A derivvative that gives the owner the right to purchase a commodity or equity at a future date at a predetermined price.

Goal. The purpose toward which an endeavor is directed; an objective.

Greed. Excessive desire to acquire or possess more (especially more material wealth) than one needs.

Glucocorticoids. A class of steroid homones secreted during stress. They include cortisol (a stress hormone).

Herding. When many investors make the same choice based on the observations of others, independent of their own knowledge.

Hippocampus. A brain region within the limbic system that plays a central role in learning and memory.

Hope. The general feeling that some desire will be fulfilled.

Hormones. Chemical messengers dispersed by the blood that act on target organs. Main organs involved in hormone production are the pituitary, pancreas, ovary, testes, thyroid, and adrenal. Hormones have an effect on physiological functioning and psychological behavior.

Hubris. The lack of preparedness and attentiveness to risks that follows success in a venture. Hubris often precedes losses.

Hypothalamic-pituitary-adrenal (HPA) axis. A major part of the neuroendocrine system that controls reactions to stress. It is the mechanism for a set of interactions among glands, hormones and parts of the midbrain that mediate a general adaptation syndrome.

Illusion of control. The belief that one can influence a chance outcome. Occurs when lots of choices are available, you have early success at the task (as in the coin-flipping example above), the task you are undertaking is familiar to you, the amount of information available is high, and you have personal involvement.

Implied volatility. In options contracts, a figure derived from the market price of an option. Implied volatility can be thought of as a measure of the risk of an instrument or portfolio right now, as opposed to in some period in the past (historic volatility).

Impulse-control (impulsivity). The ability to manage one's urges, caprices, and sudden desires.

Investor. One who owns shares of a company or asset, typically with the expectation that the profits of the business or the value of the asset will increase over time.

Investment. The use of money for the purpose of making more money, to gain income or increase capital, or both, usually through the purchase of a security or asset.

Jones, Paul Tudor. Born in 1954 in Memphis, Tennessee; a well-known commodity trader. Having made $500 million in 2005, he is worth an estimated $2.5 billion, and was ranked by *Forbes* in September 2006 as the 117th richest person in the world.

Judgment. The cognitive process of reaching a decision or drawing conclusions.

Kahneman, Daniel. Born 1934 in Tel Aviv, Israel; a key pioneer and theorist of behavioral finance, which integrates economics and cognitive science to explain seemingly irrational risk management behavior in humans.

Knutson, Brian. Associate professor of psychology at Stanford University and director of the SPAN lab. His long-term research goal is to understand the neurochemical and neuroanatomical mechanisms responsible for emotional experience.

Kuhnen, Camelia. An assistant professor at the Kellogg School of Management at Northwestern University. Formerly a PhD student in finance at Stanford University and designer of neuroimaging experiments and the Behavioral Investment Allocation Strategy (BIAS) task.

Limbic system. A deep, evolutionarily older system of brain circuits and structures involved in emotion. Major subsections include the reward system (nucleus accumbens), the loss avoidance system (amygdala), hormonal control (the hypothalamus), and memory centers (the hippocampus).

Long-Term Capital Management (LTCM). Founded in 1994, this hedge fund boasted two Nobel Prize winners and several of Salomon Brothers top traders as principals. The fund's launch was the largest in history up to that time: $1.25 billion. While LTCM's fees were above the industry average (taking 25 percent of net returns), the profits over the fund's first four years were large, seeming to justify the high fees. By April 1998, $1 invested in the fund at its inception in 1994 was worth $2.85 (after fees). Due to highly leveraged and erroneous bets against volatility, the fund collapsed spectacularly in late 1998, endangering the global financial system. A bailout was organized by the New York Federal Reserve.

Loss aversion. In prospect theory, loss aversion refers to the tendency for people to strongly prefer avoiding losses than acquiring gains. Some studies suggest that losses are as much as twice as psychologically powerful as gains. Loss aversion was first theorized by Amos Tversky and Daniel Kahneman (winner of the 2002 Nobel Prize in economics).

Loss avoidance system. A fundamental motivation system in the brain, geared towards the avoidance of harm and potential danger. Consists of several subcortical structures related to negative emotion processing and response, including the amygdala, hippocampus, hypothalamus. Cortical structures include the insula and the anterior cingulate gyrus.

Lynch, Peter. Born January 19, 1944; a successful Wall Street investor, and arguably one of the best stock-pickers in the world. He is currently a president at Fidelity Investments.

Medial prefrontal cortex (MPFC). The gray matter on the medial aspect of the frontal lobes. Thought to be functionally related to liking, trust, and preference.

Meriwether, John. Born August 10, 1947, in Chicago, Illinois; an American financial executive on Wall Street seen as a pioneer of fixed income arbitrage. Meriwether worked as a bond trader at Salomon Brothers where he became the head of the domestic fixed income arbitrage group in the early 1980s and the vice-chairman of the company in 1988. The Long-Term Capital Management hedge fund, founded in 1994 in Greenwich, Connecticut, and notoriously collapsed in 1998, was his brainchild.

Momentum investing. A style of investing in which equities that have recently appreciated in price are purchased, with the presumption that they will continue to outperform over time. Academic research has identified the "momentum effect" in stocks that appreciate over the prior 6 months. These stocks are likely to have market-beating returns over the subsequent 6 to 18 months.

Motivated reasoning. Thinking biased to produce preferred conclusions. That is, we think about a problem in such a way as to logically lead to the conclusions we wanted to arrive at in the first place.

Neuroeconomics. A field of study examining the brain bases of economic decision making.

Neurofinance. The study and application of neuroscience to investment activity.

Neuroplasticity. The general notion that aspects of brain function change over time. In general, increased use of some neural pathways leads to strengthening of their connections. Decreased use leads to weakening of connectivity.

Neuroticism. Characterized by stress sensitivity and more frequent experiences of negative emotions than others.

Neurotransmitter. Chemical messengers released from axon terminals as a result of an electrical impulse. These chemicals travel across the synapse and bind to specific receptors on the postsynaptic side, thus changing the electrical excitation and protein expression of the second neuron. Excitatory neurotransmitters increase the likelihood that the next neuron will have an action potential, whereas inhibitory neurotransmitters decrease the likelihood.

Norepinephine (a.k.a. noradrenaline). A neurotransmitter whose functions include release from the ends of the final neurons in the sympathetic nervous system, as well as a role in depression (with, most likely, a depletion occurring).

Nucleus accumbens (NAcc). A nucleus forming the floor of the caudal part of the anterior prolongation of the lateral ventricle of the brain. Activated by anticipation of reward and reward pursuit and produces positive affect when activated.

Openness (personality). Openness to new experiences describes a dimension of personality that distinguishes imaginative, creative people from down-to-earth, conventional people.

Opiate. A type of depressant drug that diminishes pain and central nervous system activity. Prescription opiates include morphine, meperidine (Demerol), methadone, codeine, and various opioid drugs for coughing and pain. Illicit opioids include heroin.

Option. A contract whereby the contract buyer has a right to exercise a feature of the contract (the option) on or before a future date (the exercise date). The writer (seller) has the obligation to honor the specified feature of the contract. Since the option gives the buyer a right and the seller an obligation, the buyer has received something of value. The amount the buyer pays the seller for the option is called the option premium.

Orbital frontal cortex (OFC). The region of association cortex of the human brain involved in cognitive processes such as decision making. This region is named based on its location within the frontal lobes, resting above the orbits of the eyes.

Overconfidence. There are several varieties: one type of overconfidence is the "better than average" effect. Researchers who ask subjects to rate their abilities, such as skill in driving, athletic ability, or running a business, find that most people consider themselves better than average. Some individuals were found to overestimate the precision of their knowledge (miscalibration). Others are overconfident in their belief in control over random, independent events—called the "illusion of control."

Panic. A sudden terror that dominates thinking and often affects groups of people. An overwhelming feeling of fear and anxiety.

Parietal lobe. One of the four major regions of the cortex. This area deals with reception of sensory information from the body's opposite side. It also plays a part in reading, writing, language, and calculation.

Personality. The complex of all the attributes—behavioral, temperamental, emotional and mental—that characterize a unique individual.

Positron emission tomography (PET). A brain imaging technique that maps active brain areas via an injection of 2-deoxyglucose, which emits positrons when taken up by actively metabolizing cells.

Predict. The act of foretelling on the basis of observation, experience, or scientific reason.

Prefrontal cortex. A recently evolved region of the brain that plays a central role in executive cognitive function, decision making, gratification postponement, attention-shifting, and regulation (often inhibition) of limbic system impulses.

Price-to-earnings (P/E) ratio. The price-to-earnings ratio measures the ratio of a company's stock price to its earnings.

Prisoner's dilemma. A classic game theory scenario. The setup is along the following lines: Two inmates have made an escape attempt from prison, which was unsuccessful. On being separately questioned by the warden, the inmates must decide whether to "defect" (a.k.a. rat out, snitch) their confederate or "cooperate" and not give the warden any incriminating information. Highest payments go to those who defect when their confederate cooperates. Medium payment if both cooperate. Least payoff if one cooperates while the confederate defects.

Psychophysiology. The branch of psychology that is concerned with the physiological bases of psychological processes. Investigatory methods include measurements of galvanic skin response (GSR), muscle tone, and vital signs such as heart rate, blood pressure, and respiratory rate.

Reward system. The neural circuitry directing desire and motivation. Extends from dopamine nuclei in the ventral tegmental area through the nucleus accumbens (NAcc) to the medial prefrontal cortex (MPFC).

Rumor. A piece of unverified information of uncertain origin usually spread by word of mouth. Unverified information received from another; hearsay. Information, often of uncertain origin and veracity, spread throughout a subpopulation.

Security. An equity, derivative, or commodity share or contract.

Self-attribution bias. The tendency to attribute good outcomes to personal skill and bad outcomes to chance.

Self-control. The trait of resolutely managing one's own impulses, urges, and behavior to to follow a predefined plan or intention.

Self-regulation. Regulation of oneself automatically, via an intentional exertion of the will to achieve a goal.

Selective serotonin reuptake inhibitors (SSRIs). Drugs such as Prozac that block the removal of serotonin from the synapse. Since the introduction of Prozac, other SSRI medications developed include Paxil, Zoloft, Celexa, and Lexapro. SSRI medicines were found to decrease the severity of the symptoms of several disorders: depression, anxiety, obsessive-compulsive, post-traumatic stress, and premenstrual dysphoric disorders, to name a few. Insofar as they lessen the symptoms of depression and anxiety, this implies that these disorders involve a deficiency of serotonin.

Serotonin. A neurotransmitter. When either the concentration of brain serotonin or the one's sensitivity to brain serotonin change, one's behavior will change. In the 1970s, researchers discovered that people who committed violent suicide had lower levels of brain serotonin than people who died by other means. Serotonin levels have since been linked to mood disorders such as depression and anxiety and obsessive-compulsive disorder.

Somatic. Pertaining to the body.

Soros, George. Born August 12, 1930, in Budapest, Hungary, as Soros György; an American businessman. He is famous as a currency speculator and a philanthropist. Currently, he is the chairman of Soros Fund Management and the Open Society Institute and is also former member of the board of directors of the Council on Foreign Relations.

Stock market. A general term used to refer to the organized trading of securities through various physical exchanges, electronic platforms, and through the over-the-counter market. A "stock exchange" is a specific form of a stock market, a physical location where stocks and bonds are bought and sold, such as the New York Stock Exchange, NASDAQ or American Stock Exchange.

Stress. A state of mental or emotional strain or suspense.

Sympathetic nervous system. The half of the autonomic (automatic) nervous system associated with arousal and emergency physiological responses.

Synapse. The gap between two neurons, across which neurotransmission occurs.

Technical analysis. Also known as "charting"; utilizes quantitative and visual interpretations of financial data to generate forecasts.

Trader. Individuals who buy and sell for their own accounts for short-term profit. Also, an employee of a broker/dealer or financial institution who specializes in handling purchases and sales of securities for the firm and/or its clients

Trust. The trait of believing in the honesty and reliability of others

Ultimatum game. An experimental economics game in which two parties interact anonymously and only once, so reciprocation is not an issue. The first player proposes how to divide a sum of money with the second party. If the second player rejects this division, neither gets anything. If the second accepts, the first gets their demand and the second gets the rest.

Uncertainty. The state of being unsettled or in doubt. Conditions where outcomes and preexisting information are unknown. A mathematical state of 50 percent probability of a given outcome.

Valence (emotional). A bipolar conception of feeling, in which they lie on a spectrum from positive to negative.

Value (stocks). Stocks whose shares are priced cheaply relative to the value of their underlying assets or earnings potential. Three widely used financial ratios used to measure value (though there are many others) are: (1) the price-to-book ratio, (2) the price-to-earnings ratio, and (3) the price-to-cash flow ratio.

Zak, Paul. Founding director, Center for Neuroeconomics Studies at Claremont Graduate University. His current research focuses on how social cognition produces cooperation or conflict, decision making under uncertainty, the neural foundation of human capital, and the effect of institutional design on economic development. His previous research into the biology of trust is cited in this book.

Index